Economics of Visual Art

How can arts managers, artists, and art market observers approach the study of economics? Accompanied by hand-drawn illustrations, wide-ranging case studies, and expansive discussion resources, this interdisciplinary microeconomics primer engages with complex – and, at turns, political – questions of value and resourcefulness with the artist or manager as the decision-maker and the gallery, museum or studio as "the firm". Whitaker arms the reader with analytic and creative tools that can be used in service to economic sustainability for artists and organizations. By exploring the complexities of economics in application to art, design and creative industries, this book offers ways to approach the larger world as an art project.

AMY WHITAKER is an assistant professor in Visual Arts Administration at New York University and author of award-winning books *Museum Legs* and *Art Thinking*.

Economics of Visual Art

Market Practice and Market Resistance

AMY WHITAKER

New York University

CAMBRIDGE UNIVERSITY PRESS

CAMBRIDGE
UNIVERSITY PRESS

University Printing House, Cambridge CB2 8BS, United Kingdom

One Liberty Plaza, 20th Floor, New York, NY 10006, USA

477 Williamstown Road, Port Melbourne, VIC 3207, Australia

314–321, 3rd Floor, Plot 3, Splendor Forum, Jasola District Centre,
New Delhi – 110025, India

103 Penang Road, #05–06/07, Visioncrest Commercial, Singapore 238467

Cambridge University Press is part of the University of Cambridge.

It furthers the University's mission by disseminating knowledge in the pursuit of
education, learning, and research at the highest international levels of excellence.

www.cambridge.org
Information on this title: www.cambridge.org/9781108483421
DOI: 10.1017/9781108649919

First published 2021

Printed in the United Kingdom by TJ Books Limited, Padstow Cornwall

A catalogue record for this publication is available from the British Library.

Library of Congress Cataloging-in-Publication Data
Names: Whitaker, Amy, author.
Title: Economics of visual art : market practice and market resistance / Amy
Whitaker.
Description: Cambridge ; New York : Cambridge University Press, 2021. | Includes
bibliographical references and index.
Identifiers: LCCN 2021000987 (print) | LCCN 2021000988 (ebook) | ISBN
9781108483421 (hardback) | ISBN 9781108649919 (ebook)
Subjects: LCSH: Art – Economic aspects.
Classification: LCC N8600 .W48 2021 (print) | LCC N8600 (ebook) |
DDC 338.4/77–dc23
LC record available at https://lccn.loc.gov/2021000987
LC ebook record available at https://lccn.loc.gov/2021000988

ISBN 978-1-108-48342-1 Hardback
ISBN 978-1-108-70497-7 Paperback

for Michael J. Lewis and Eva Grudin

Human life is messy, never to be grasped in its full complexity or shaped according to plan .... Thus, the very real success of economists in establishing their professional dominion ... throws them into the rough and tumble of democratic politics and into a hazardous intimacy with economic, political, and administrative power.

Marion Fourcade, Étienne Ollion, and Yann Algan[1]

Art is the highest form of hope.

Gerhard Richter[2]

Contents

Figures

Tables

Preface

A Letter to the Reader

FIGURE A Eliza Squibb, *Supply and Demand Quilt Square*, 2011.
Courtesy of the artist.

Dear Reader:

No matter the reason you picked up this book – whether it was
assigned or freely chosen – I hope you feel warmly invited to pull up a
chair to the economics of art, to form your own opinion, and to build
your own tools. Although originally written for students in arts
administration, this book is also for working artists, practicing
managers, and anyone else who is trying to hold space for what the

economics of art represents: the ability to embrace risk, failure, willful inefficiency, beauty, and unquantifiable human work within a world structured as a market economy.

Holding both an MBA and an MFA – in that order – I began teaching business to fellow painters while studying at the Slade School of Fine Art almost twenty years ago. Prior to these studies, I worked in art museums. In 2010, the California College of the Arts asked me to teach economics in their design strategy MBA. I have taught economics and business strategy since.

The picture above depicts an artwork by Eliza Squibb, a student I taught at the Rhode Island School of Design in January 2011. For the final project – in an experimental class in economics as a studio-art practice – Eliza made *Supply and Demand Quilt Squares*. Trained as a textiles artist, Eliza stitched into patchwork form and crocheted a series of mesmerizingly dry economics charts we had found online. When she presented the work, she announced that she had already documented the piece and was giving the quilt squares away to the class. Everyone leaned into the pile of what looked like potholders and took one.

Eliza's project encapsulates the spirit of this book: understanding economics well enough to use it where it is helpful and to disregard it where other values – generosity, art, justice, community – are more important. Although economics is usually presented as a study of scarcity, utility, and profit, it is also, from first principles, a study of resourcefulness, value, and ownership. As with Eliza, to give something away, you must own it first.

It is the aim of this book to impart the tools of economics, so that we can, both collectively and individually, address the precariousness of artistic endeavor – as artist, manager, or organization – with a degree of honesty, curiosity, transparency, and strategy about money. I believe in markets the way that Winston Churchill believed in democracy, as the worst form there is except all the others.[3] Markets are powerful but also highly imperfect, demanding of vigilance, knowledge, and even creativity. In this book, the design principle of markets is not toward profit or price but toward value, in both economic and noneconomic senses. Designing toward value requires risk and vulnerability toward what is not yet known. Economic structures can be especially challenged to support that work. Markets were built to produce and trade known objects efficiently, but they can, with resourcefulness, sustain creative practice.

Most questions in the economics of art are political. They are political in the personal sense of your own beliefs about how insulated artistic practice should be from markets. They are also political in the larger sense of income inequality, histories of colonialism, cross-cultural understandings of property, and the socioeconomics of diversity, equity, and inclusion in the arts.

The language of economics is also political.[4] For economists, the term "market" describes the transfer of ownership or other rights to a good or service, usually in exchange for money.[5] One senior figure in the arts told me I should use "communities of support" instead of "markets" in the pages of this book. It is easy for language to lose people in both directions: to lose artists who see economic language as an admission of capitalistic intent, or to lose economists who are understandably committed to their discipline's defined terms and structures of thought. The spirit of this book is that the real words matter and that mastering economic language is necessary, whether to inhabit markets sustainably or to amass the wherewithal to reimagine and rebuild these systems with care, out of their own parts.

At the risk of sounding normative, the political ethos of this book is one of engagement: that within bounds of justice and human dignity, it does not matter as much *what* you think as it matters *that* you think, that it is more ethical to engage than to retreat into hopes for an ideal world, and that we would all be served by being able to learn – and sometimes fail – in public and with each other. The questions of the arts as a field – and the current questions facing the larger world – are big and complex enough that they take all of us and probably ask everything that we have.

Whatever your view of markets at the outset – whether you have been burned by them or conscientiously object to their present forms – I thank you for your patience and curiosity toward the subject, your good faith, and your time. I hope this book repays the effort – that it surpasses the cost–benefit analysis of economics and that, like art, it offers something broader than a purely transactional way of knowing.

Amy Whitaker, New York, 2021

Acknowledgments

My sincere thanks to the many people who contributed to this book. I am grateful to my editor Phil Good for giving me a chance to write this book and for his guidance throughout and to Erika Walsh for her excellent editorial shepherding of this project. I thank the reviewers, including Victor Ginsburgh, and also Toby Ginsberg and the rest of the team at Cambridge and in production, including Jessica Norman, Abigail Fiddes, Nick Massarelli, Kate Mertes, Jayavel Radhakrishnan, and Anny Mortada.

Many people contributed leads and stories or generously shared their own. These people include: Veronica Roberts, Nina Katchadourian, Lenka Clayton, Eliza Squibb, Anastasia Loginova, Michelle Millar Fisher, Jessica Glaser, Peter Bahr, Tamara Venit-Shelton, Nevenka Šivavec, Megan Chiemezie, Elisabeth Sunday, Damien Davis, Abdiel Lopez, Christopher McKeogh, Priya Parker, Christina Ferando, Heather Nolin, Michelle Yun, Cheryl Finley, Anne Bracegirdle, Corinna Till, Alexandra Tommasini, Adam Glick, Jongho Lee, Dexter Wimberly, Jonathan T. D. Neil, Scott and Marcia Stornetta, Stuart Haber, Sean Moss-Pultz, Agnes Yen, Casey Alt, Michael Nguyen, Mark Waugh, Darby English, Toby Kamps, Rory Riggs, Sunny Bates, Ruby Lerner, Patricia Phillips, Michael Danoff, Michael Mandiberg, William Powhida, Paddy Johnson, Sean Green, Nanne Dekking, Vanessa Hogarty, GiannaLia Cogliandro Beyens, Chaédria LaBouvier, Joy Bloser, Gina Wells, Bilha Bryant, Penny Catterall, Alexi Whitaker, Stewart Campbell, Sophia Belsheim, Matej Tomažin, Andrew Weiner, Angela Green, Theano Siaraferas, Clive Coward, Lisa Cole, Fala Al Urfali, Noah Phillips, Lizzie Conrad, Taylor Curry, Melanie Kimmelman, Maya Addady, Zoe Goetzmann, Jingru Li, Cheng Zhong, April Zhu, Young Zhou, Geena Brown, Lees Romano, Lauren Halilej, Constanza Valenzuela, Jane Sullivan,

Ricky Manne, Diane Ragsdale, Peter Murphy, Audrey Thier, Fiona Rose Greenland, Jennifer Rubenstein, Victoria Alexander, Gerald Lidstone, Sandra Lang, Rich Maloney, Carlo Lamagna, Erin Sircy, Emily Rubin, Pia Wilson, Heather Bhandari, Caroline Woolard, Pablo Helguera, Hannah Grannemann, Esther Robinson, Kay Takeda, Christa Blatchford, Yayoi Shionoiri, Scott Briscoe, Lena Walker, Gail Andrews, and Angie Kim. I especially thank Alex Beard, Nicholas Serota, and Dennis Stevenson for generously sharing their experiences of the founding days of Tate Modern and for reviewing the draft chapter. I also thank Sandy Nairne, who also helpfully reviewed pages, and Anna Jobson from whom I learned greatly in their own work on Tate Modern and in the arts more broadly.

Numerous academic colleagues and others generously shared time and expertise in reading chapters in their area, including: Susan Douglas, Doug Noonan, Michael Rushton, Sandy Lee, Emily Lanza, Lauren van Haaften-Schick, Steve Schindler, Nick Pozek, Mukti Khaire, Joanne Gentile, Valentina Castellani, Wendy Woon, Melissa Rachleff, Paola Antonelli, John Corso-Esquivel, Jeff Whitaker, Scott Montgomery, Susan de Menil, Anne Collins Goodyear, Warren Woodfin, and Anne Young. Barbara Strongin generously shared her auction expertise. I also thank Will Davies, Sahil Dutta, Nick Taylor, Filip Vermeylen, Will Goetzmann, Roman Kräussl, Renée Adams, Patton Hindle, Don Thompson, Finn Brunton, David Yermack, Bruce Altshuler, Jane Anderson, Māui Hudson, and Hans Ulrich Obrist. I am grateful to scholars or reporters whose work I rely on, including Caroline Donnellan, Alison Gerber, Jennifer Lena, Peter Watson, Christopher Mason, and Olav Velthuis. I also thank Helen Hofling for her general editorial read, as well as a few readers, friends, and colleagues who wished to remain anonymous.

This book received support from the New York University Center for the Humanities. I especially thank Molly Rogers, Gwynneth Malin, Denelia Valentin, Ken Castronuovo, Vonetta Moses, Jacob Mandel, Julia Olson, Jamie Sterns, Meghan Wilcox, Charlton McIlwain, Vincent Guilamo-Ramos, Deborah Borisoff, and

Marilyn Moffat. I wrote part of this book while a on an NYU Global Research Initiative Fellowship in London, and I thank the program, my fellow researchers, and Chloe Spinks, Ruth Tucker, Catherine Robson, and Jair Kessler. I am grateful to Adam Brandenburger for inviting me to NYU Shanghai as part of my research and to him and his colleagues Lulu Guo, Michelle Ji, Yanyue Yuan, and others. I thank my lovely colleagues in the Department of Art and Art Professions, many of whom are listed above, and also Gerry Pryor, Marlene McCarty, Jesse Bransford, RoseLee Goldberg, Linda Sormin, Kevin McCoy, and Nancy Deihl. Libraries are one of the very best parts of universities, and I thank the research librarians Giana Ricci and the late Tom McNulty, and also Karla Williams and Darwyn Morren, as well as archivists at other research institutions, especially Simon Frost at the Marshall Library, Cambridge University, and Marisa Bourgoin at the Archives of American Art, Washington, DC.

One of the first readers of the book was Kellie Riggs, my teaching assistant for Visual Arts Markets and a writing teacher herself. I thank her for excellent comments, and I also thank all of the students in that class who read the chapters in formation.

I also thank my own teachers and mentors in this field. These people include: John Maeda, who invited me to teach at RISD; Susan Worthman and Nathan Shedroff, who invited me to teach at California College of the Arts, and my other MBA colleagues including Will Hutchinson, Dan Sevall, and Tim Smith, among others; Allan Chochinov and other colleagues at the School of Visual Arts; Meghan Busse, my economics teacher in business school who took time to share her views of the core questions of economics as a discipline when I first started teaching; Sharon Oster and Fiona Scott Morton, for whom I worked as research assistant and case-writer, respectively; the late Paul MacAvoy who hired me as an Olin Fellow in Economics; Gary Jacobsohn, Sam Crane, Mark Reinhardt, and Ted Marmor in political science and Ed Epping, Mike Glier, Amy Podmore, and others in art; James Forcier, who shared 200 pages of his own lecture notes when I started teaching economics; Eva Grudin and

Mike Lewis, who sponsored the first course I ever taught, a Williams College Winter Study class which was cross-listed in art and economics; and the countless other artists, designers, managers, and fellow teachers I have gotten to work with and whose wise ethos informs and hopefully lifts this book.

A personal thanks to Beverly Chapin, Louise Mai Newberry, Lisa Kicielinski, Louise Cecil, Beverly Layton, Melinda Hayes, Sabrina Moyle, Julian Abdey, Matt Alsdorf, Mo Mullen, Martha O'Neill, Allison Fones, Charlotte Colvin, Yoko Mikata, Karen Lewis, Pat Winters-Liotta, Alison Rector, Ethan and Sally Kline, Michael Joseph Gross, Steve Roberts, Katy Kline, Bill Ryan, Rosie and Dick Gutman, Paul Gutman, Olivia and Sam Gutman, Jack Whitaker, and many others, especially Ulla Pitha, who gave me a monumental gift of space in which to write; and to my siblings Jeff and Stacey and especially our mother Elaine, who read the first half of this book in draft form with a Taking Care of Business pencil from Elvis Presley's Graceland, lending her retired English professor's precision and her generalist's curiosity to the subject matter. If you get bored or fight the text, she is with you. And if you don't, you have her to thank.

Introduction

It will not do to read only from economics to art. We must be able to read from art to economics as well.

Leigh Claire La Berge[1]

In the 1984 film *The Karate Kid*, Ralph Macchio's character, Daniel, becomes the target of bullies and is determined to fight back.[2] His neighbor, Mr. Miyagi, offers to teach Daniel to fight. When an eager Daniel arrives for his first lesson, he is given the seemingly menial task of polishing vintage cars. Mr. Miyagi's car-washing instructions are highly specific. Daniel must apply wax to the cars in one circular stroke and then take it off in another: "Wax on. Wax off." Exhausted from hours of repetitive motion, Daniel loses his temper. Only then does Mr. Miyagi reveal that the car-polishing moves mimic the fundamentals of karate.

Economics has an analogous relationship to art. The concepts can seem dry and abstract at first, requiring the same kind of repetitive faith in tedium as there is in time spent waxing on and waxing off. Once learned, those fundamentals can inform anything from the sustainable livelihood of artists to a top-of-the-market auction result. Yet those fundamentals of economics rarely apply in the arts without adaptation. The purpose of this book is to introduce these principles so that you can apply or reinvent them on your own terms and within your own beliefs about how art and markets do and do not – or should and should not – intersect.

Economics shares with art a starting point of *making* things, of dealing with materials and process, and of having to invest resources early, at the risk of failure and before value is known.

This idea of investing resources before value is known – of inventing point B, not just going from point A to point B – presents a unique challenge to economics itself, expanding the discipline from description of efficient manufacture to support of open-ended discovery.[3] This book aims to honor the dignity of artistic labor and find ways to support it.

This book focuses on microeconomics – the study of individuals and firms – rather than macroeconomics – the study of whole economies. Where macroeconomics takes the view, as if from an airplane window, of an entire country's productivity or employment or currency relative to other nations, microeconomics takes the viewpoint of the manager as decision-maker and the firm – in this case the gallery, museum, or studio – as the core economic entity.[4]

The artist is most like the maker, the manager, the decision-maker, or the strategist around whom traditional microeconomics is built. This perspective of the maker invites the reader to be the main character in the story – to learn the concepts in this book and how to apply them (and occasionally whether to ignore them). When visual art defies the economic rules it also depends on, the economics of art becomes a potential area of artistic practice unto itself.

I do not believe, as some pure economists do, that everything tracks back to the mechanical logic taught in traditional microeconomics classes. I do not believe that economic systems are explained by a motivation toward maximum profit, nor that individuals' choices are explained by maximum utility. People are generally far more complex and interesting. The black-box idea of "demand" – the economist's tool for describing audiences or purchasers – seems inadequate to express the honest, poetic, human decisions people make, especially in relation to something as subjective and with as many layers of value as art. However, I do believe that economics offers an important algebra underneath markets. It gives us tools to understand and to build the ways in which anything gets made and championed.

THE ARTISTIC FOUNDATIONS OF ECONOMIC THOUGHT

The sleek mechanics of economic theory belie the creative roots of the discipline. Some of the founding scholars had a direct relationship to painting, drawing, or collecting art, while others worked through ideas from scratch, in the manner of an art project. In 1776, Adam Smith published *The Wealth of Nations,* describing the "invisible hand" of markets and the benefits of the division of labor. Smith was not perceived as an economist out of modern central casting. In an essay called "Adam Smith as a Person," Walter Bagehot, the longtime editor of *The Economist,* described Smith as "one of the most unbusinesslike of mankind."[5] Smith's earlier work, the 1759 book *The Theory of Moral Sentiments,* had not been about economics at all but about the importance of sympathy – fellow feeling for others – as part of the fabric of society.[6]

Several of the nineteenth- and twentieth-century developers of economic thought also drew and painted or otherwise had connections to the arts. Alfred Marshall, who authored the 1890 book *Principles of Economics,* and Stanley Jevons, who was among the pioneers of the concept of marginal utility, were teachers at Cambridge University. They both worked out ideas by drawing. Marshall drew near-calligraphic diagrams of markets (Figure B) as intersections of buyers ("demand") and sellers ("supply"). Marshall also taught with gigantic diagrams of world commodity prices (Figure C), a crafting project so elaborate that it calls forth a deep need for a tome on the early history of magic markers. Jevons made delicate watercolors charting the change in price of beef or cotton over time and mapping histories of innovation (Figure D). Presumably these drawings or watercolors were not made under the economic assumptions of efficiency or marginal utility that these authors themselves championed. The drawings are a reminder that even economics as a discipline was once created from scratch – the same way that artworks are.

Another Cambridge economist, the macroeconomist John Maynard Keynes, also had strong connections to the arts. Keynes

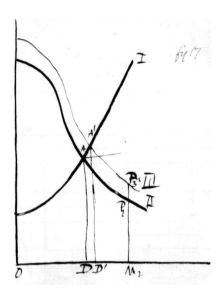

FIGURE B Alfred Marshall, drawing of supply and demand. Marshall Library, Cambridge University. Reproduced with the kind permission of the Marshall Librarian.

was a member of the Bloomsbury Group. He collected art both for himself and on behalf of the British Treasury.[7] Keynes's early work shares the artistic, trial-and-error character of Jevons or Marshall, which is a polite way of saying that when Keynes submitted what would go on to become the backbone of many existing geopolitical systems as a dissertation at King's College Cambridge, his professors initially failed him.[8] Like many now-famous artists, Keynes was underestimated at the outset.[9]

THE TENSION BETWEEN ART AND ECONOMICS

Both economics and art have grown as insular fields, making their intersections complicated and occasionally tense.[10] If art and economics were siblings, they would have a complex power dynamic in which economics felt that everything was neutral and art felt constantly encroached upon and misunderstood. This dynamic is not abstract but at the heart of the fundamental question of this book: Can economics fully describe the value of art, and if not, can economics still be used to build important structures of sustainability for the arts?

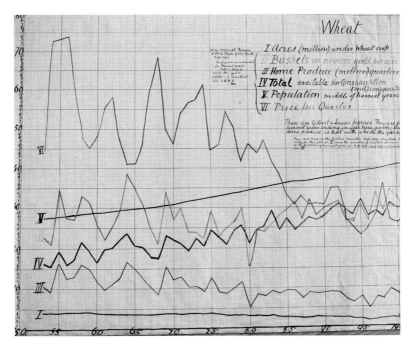

FIGURE C Alfred Marshall, teaching aids. Marshall Library, Cambridge University. Reproduced with the kind permission of the Marshall Librarian.

The artist and writer Andrea Fraser explores this tension in her 2018 essay "Toward a Reflexive Resistance." In the wake of the 2016 US presidential election, Fraser found herself agreeing with some, but not all, of the sentiments within a political petition she was asked to sign. She agreed with the calls to make resistance a priority but found herself unable to promise categorically that she would "reject calls to compromise, to understand, or to collaborate."[11] In reflecting on why that was, Fraser invokes theories formed by the French sociologist Pierre Bourdieu. Bourdieu analyzed the class politics and cultural consumption of the French public, a topic to which he turned after spending his early academic career studying Algerian peasant communities as a self-described "blissful structuralist."[12]

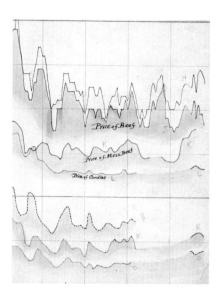

FIGURE D Stanley Jevons, detail of untitled watercolor showing world commodity prices. Marshall Library, Cambridge University. Reproduced with the kind permission of the Marshall Librarian.

In her reading of Bourdieu, Fraser argues that cultural elites are part of a dominant class in the broader society. But within that dominant class, economic elites have *more* power that cultural elites. Thus, cultural elites – art critics, artists, university professors – are a *dominated* class within a *dominant* class. They have power in determining what is aesthetically and philosophically significant, but economic elites – the 1 percent, the hedge-fund class – have power more absolutely. Bourdieu described this energy among cultural elites as "the logic of resentment."[13]

Theories of the intersection of art and economics take root in the sociologist Viviana Zelizer's studies of how money intersects with family and children. Zelizer characterizes two competing views: Hostile Worlds or Nothing But. In the Hostile Worlds view, intimate family life must be firewalled from commercial life because otherwise commercial life will grow like kudzu and engulf what is personal and meaningful. In the Nothing But view, the commercial sphere is in fact capable of putting a price on anything and thus representing any form of value. In fact, Zelizer describes a third alternative, "circuits of commerce," in which the intimate and commercial interact.[14]

The cultural sociologist Olav Velthuis adapted Zelizer's work to the arts in his 2005 book *Talking Prices*.[15] Here, the commercial and intimate spheres can be replaced by economic and artistic ones. In the Hostile Worlds view, economic value must be kept separate from artistic value because otherwise economics will engulf and flatten all that is good and important in art. In the Nothing But view, economics is fully capable of reflecting artistic value. And without its "cultural camouflage," the art market is simply another ordinary market.[16] Here, the third alternative is the interaction and mutual dependency between institutional and commercial value, meaning the value conferred by museums, galleries, scholars, and critics, as compared by the value recognized by financial markets.

Probably the most extraordinary proponent of the Nothing But view is William Grampp, whose 1989 book *Pricing the Priceless* argues seamlessly for the capacity of economics to represent the value of art. It is a maddeningly eloquent read for anyone who disagrees with his ideas. Grampp writes not only that any form of artistic value – aesthetic, cultural, social – can be transmuted into price but also that artistic actors are motivated by money. Grampp writes,

> Pictures have a price, so do violins and violinists; painters want an income; theaters and museums must be heated and lighted; guards, ticket sellers, and curators must be paid.[17]

While most would agree that within the current organizational structures of society these activities require economic support, the idea that artists are *motivated* by money is less than palatable or relatable for most. Needing money to make work is not the same as being motivated by money to make art. Most artists create work before its market value is known, investing time and resources without any assumption about price or the certainty of sale. In this sense, artists are risk-takers and investors in their own practice. As the sociologist

Alison Gerber writes in *The Work of Art*, artists take on many forms of investment, only some of which are "pecuniary."[18]

The Hostile Worlds view essentially hangs on the belief that artistic value can never be fully represented by markets. One of the most eloquent scribes of this idea of art is Lewis Hyde, who writes in *The Gift* that all art originates in the idea of gift so that "when we are touched by a work of art something comes to us which has nothing to do with the price." Hyde's view allows for market participation but not complete market control. He writes,

> A work of art ... can be sold in the market and still emerge a work of art. But if it is true that in the essential commerce of art a gift is carried by the work from the artist to his audience, if I am right to say that where there is no gift there is no art, then it may be possible to destroy a work of art by converting it into a pure commodity.[19]

If a work of art is truly original, the outcome of the work is not known to the artist at the outset. Thus, the artist operates with risk, generosity even, putting things into the world before their value is known.

The observer of Grampp's work who may deserve the last word, for now, is the economist William J. Baumol, who was asked to write a dustjacket endorsement for the 1989 hardcover of *Pricing the Priceless*. Baumol trained as a sculptor and taught woodworking classes during his time on the economics faculty at Princeton University. He contributed highly influential studies of both arts administration and art markets, coining the term "cost disease" to describe the performing arts and calling the art market a "floating crap game" in a landmark 1986 paper that we discuss in Chapter 9.[20] Baumol's blurb describes Grampp's bracingly neoliberal writing as "An unpopular view on art prices, aesthetic value, and the justifiability of government support well presented and logically argued." Baumol then encouraged the reader, "Even those who disagree with Professor Grampp most strongly can benefit from a dispassionate reading of the book."[21]

THE MATERIALS OF ARTISTIC PRODUCTION

Luckily for us, the starting point of economics is not so theoretical. Our starting point is the time and resources that go into making art and managing organizations in service to art. We only have to ask the question: This person or organization wants to do something they believe is of value. How do they pay for it? How do they pay to invest in research? How do they build sustainable structures that support their work with ease and within their values? These questions become interestingly hard to answer, especially given how many experiments, research cul-de-sacs, hours devoted to preparation, and even failures can be involved in artistic process.

Artists' early work reflects the larger tension in market economies between exploration and learning, and efficiency and production. For example, the British artist Bridget Riley is probably best known for large abstract compositions and op-art (optical illusion) paintings. Before she developed those bodies of work, she drew and painted from the figure (see Figure E). Those paintings began with studies – with drawings that were gridded and transferred by the artist to canvas. Before that, in order to learn to paint, Riley copied older masterpieces. All of this time, labor, and material became an investment in her future work. It would be hard to define the economic value of those earlier studies tidily, and harder still to have done so at the time she was making them.

The economics of making a work of art can also be central to the artwork conceptually. For the Chinese artist Ai Weiwei's 2010 commission at Tate Modern, he blanketed much of the floor of the Turbine Hall with 100 million painted, life-sized sunflower seeds. To make the work, Ai hired 1,600 porcelain artisans in the city of Jingdezhen in southern China. The artisans painted the seeds by hand in a twenty-to-thirty step process that included two kiln firings. Altogether, they produced 100 cubic meters of seeds, weighing roughly 150 metric tons.[22] The visual effect of the installation was, in the words of *New York Times* art critic Roberta Smith, "oceanic," – a vast "indoor pebble beach."[23]

FIGURE E Bridget Riley, *Seated Nude*, in two studies and one painting. Left to right: *Tonal Study (Painting of a Seated Nude)*, 1949–52, black and white Conté and oil on paper; *Color Study (Painting of a Seated Nude)*, 1949–52, oil on paper; *Painting of Seated Nude*, 1952, oil on canvas board. Courtesy of the artist.

In the production process, the artist expressly declined to have the artisans apply a finishing coat of glaze to seal the black "slip" or liquid clay used to paint the telltale stripes of a sunflower seed. Without the glaze, the seeds were the chalkier, truer-to-life texture of a sunflower seed. Within days, however, the unglazed seeds started to kick up dust. The dust – from the "slip" – forced the closure of the installation on health and safety grounds. Visitors were limited to peering from the edge of a roped-off expanse. Smith, the *Times* critic, suggested the Tate allow visitors to take a few seeds or to package them in plastic bags. The artist declined. The production economics of the piece were part of the conceptual statement of the work: about the collective or the whole of society, not just the individual constituent seed.

The economic story of a work can also vary substantially across projects by the same artist. For example, the artist Kara Walker has very different production methods and scales for her cutouts and for her large-scale public works. According to Sikkema Jenkins & Co., Walker's gallery, for her wall-sized installations, such as in her 1997 work *Slavery! Slavery!*, the artist uses photo-backdrop paper – the kind rolled down the wall and directly onto the floor at photoshoots to give the appearance that a model is floating in space. After working through preparatory drawings, Walker draws directly onto the paper and then cuts it out. The paper is backed with wax and put onto a wall. The materials are relatively inexpensive but require the artist's intensive time, original thinking, and virtuosic hand.[24]

That story of production is obviously different for *A Subtlety*, Walker's sphinx-like sculpture commissioned by Creative Time in 2014 as an installation in a disused Domino Sugar factory in Williamsburg, Brooklyn (see Figure F).[25] The sculpture extended more than 10 meters high and 22 meters long. It contained 31 metric tons of granulated sugar held to an underlying polystyrene structure.[26] Then for her 2019 commission in the Turbine Hall at Tate Modern, Walker's production method differed still. She created a 13-meter fountain, *Fons Americanus*, made from wood, metal, recycled cork, and an acrylic-cement composite.[27]

FIGURE F Kara Walker, *A Subtlety*. Courtesy of the artist and Sikkema Jenkins & Co. Photograph by Mark Reinhardt.

The various economics of production of artworks are matched in complexity – and creativity and political resonance – by the economics of the institutions that commission, exhibit, or acquire these works, including their histories of patronage, their ethics of philanthropy, and their governmental support or lack thereof. Economics is important to understanding structural privilege and doing necessary repair work with rigor, imagination, and care. In its reliance on but also resistance of markets, art gives us a microcosm for considering the economics – and politics – of anything.

THE STRUCTURE OF THIS BOOK

The ten chapters of this book lay out the fundamentals of the economics of art. The first three chapters are the wax-on, wax-off parts: Chapter 1 introduces markets as the meeting point of buyers and sellers and as a way of managing for scarcity and resourcefulness. Chapter 2 introduces cost structure as the basic architecture of making things. Chapter 3 covers price, including the level of price in absolute terms, and also the structure of pricing strategy. Chapter 4 covers market failures, meaning places where price and value are not aligned, such as when a public institution creates substantial value that is experienced by the broader community more than it is captured directly by the institution. Chapter 5 covers whole-market structures including the duopoly between the rival auction houses Christie's and Sotheby's and their related price-fixing scandal. Chapter 6 covers what are called vertical markets or supply chains, meaning the ecosystem of buyers and sellers in sequence from the studio to the gallery to the auction house. The arrangement of vertical markets often follows from forms of market power, and so this chapter also introduces business-strategy frameworks to analyze those arrangements. Chapter 7 focuses on labor economics including the formation of unions and the role of pay in relation to diversity, equity, and inclusion in the arts. Chapter 8 covers law and intellectual property in relation to economics. Chapter 9 covers investment in relation to economics. Chapter 10 offers conclusions with a focus on the arts as a system unto itself – and the art world as part of the larger world. Each chapter after this Introduction includes a set of review questions. For economic concepts that are reinforced by calculation, the appendices at the back of the book give more detail. Where the figures are uncredited in the text, they are by the author.

Throughout, the basic logic of economics is that price equals value. When we see cases where price and value are out of alignment, we will try to build tools for aligning them – getting paid what something is worth – or for using other mechanisms such as property rights to design solutions. Where reasonable people can disagree on whether price can represent artistic value, we will focus on building structures of economic support regardless. Where these tools feel inadequate, we are likely either grappling with the difficulty of valuing early-stage creative work or with what William Davies calls the disenchantment of politics by economics.[28] Ultimately, art represents a broader human capacity to see, reflect on, engage with, and build toward the redesign of the world, far beyond the arts. I hope the tools in this book can lead to communities of support for artists and organizations, and to the design of the world itself as an art project.

1   **Markets**

> You can't use up creativity. The more you use, the more you have.
>
> Maya Angelou[1]

On March 5, 2010, the Finnish-Armenian-American artist Nina Katchadourian flew from New York to Atlanta, Georgia. Recollecting the flight later, she said,

> I thought, here I am with two and a half hours of time, and why am I not going to consider this time as time that counts? Why not think actively, be alert and attuned to possibility? I thought, okay, I am going to make things until I get to Atlanta and see what happens.[2]

Ten years and over 250 flights later Katchadourian has made hundreds of photographs and several video artworks as part of a larger, open-ended project called "Seat Assignment" devoted to making art while on airplanes.[3] "Seat Assignment" includes various subseries. In *Pretzel Meteor* from the "Disasters" subseries, an airline snack bag of crumbled pretzels are heaped like rubble over a meandering bridge in a travel photograph from an inflight magazine. In the subseries of imagined "Proposals for Public Sculptures," a folded drinking straw or a lemon peel is placed over a magazine photo to resemble jaunty abstractions rising from public spaces. In *Topiary*, an image from the "Landscapes" subseries, a column of green peas rises up from a manicured Italian garden (see Figure 1.1).

Perhaps the best-known subseries within "Seat Assignment" is *Lavatory Self-Portraits in the Flemish Style*, hatched on a January 2011 flight from New York to San Francisco. While in the airplane lavatory, Katchadourian placed a paper toilet-seat cover over

FIGURE 1.1 Nina Katchadourian, *Topiary*, 2012 ("Seat Assignment" project, 2010 and ongoing).Courtesy of the artist, Catharine Clark Gallery, and Pace Gallery.

her head and realized she looked not unlike a Flemish character in a fifteenth-century painting.[4] Three months later, Katchadourian decided to make all of the art for an exhibition at Dunedin Public Art Gallery in Auckland, New Zealand on the airplane on the way there.[5] Armed with an aisle seat and a cell-phone camera, she relied on materials already in her travel bag – a black scarf, a red shawl, an inflatable neck pillow. She added materials offered to her freely on the plane: toilet-seat covers and paper towels folded into ornate, white neck collars, a paper coffee cup placed over a ponytail, a plastic shower

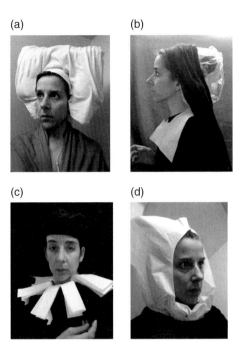

FIGURE 1.2 Nina Katchadourian, selected images from *Lavatory Self-Portraits in the Flemish Style* ("Seat Assignment" project, 2010 and ongoing). Courtesy of the artist, Catharine Clark Gallery, and Pace Gallery.

cap.[6] Of the many works that Katchadourian produced on that original trans-Pacific flight, she made twenty-six photos of herself dressed as Flemish characters (see Figure 1.2).[7]

On the airplane, Katchadourian *makes things*. Economists understand making things as *production* in the sense of a factory and prize the idea of making work efficiently. Katchadourian's work engages this story of production as resourcefulness and curiosity, not grind-it-out efficiency. Veronica Roberts, the curator of Katchadourian's exhibition *Curiouser*, likened Katchadourian's process to that of conceptual artist Sol LeWitt, who once wrote, "In terms of ideas the artist is free even to surprise himself."[8] Katchadourian's work is not simply produced. It is also discovered. This idea of art as a process of discovery frames this book's approach

to the initial economic tools around creating, exhibiting, and collecting art.

Think of all the decisions that go into making, selling, and
buying works of art: An artist purchases supplies (or finds them on
an airplane). A bidder at auction buys an antique table or lesser-known
Leonardo da Vinci. A tourist visits Madrid and buys a ticket to the
Prado. A visitor to an art fair falls in love with a photograph and, not
able to afford it, purchases a book of photographs instead. A group of
artists rents a space for an exhibition. The technician of an art school
purchases sketchbooks for all of the students in an introductory drawing class. A philanthropist decides to support one cause or museum
over another.

Economists view all of these decisions through the lens of
markets and map this meeting of buyers and sellers as the intersection of **supply** and **demand.** Demand describes all of the willing
buyers or audience members. Supply describes the sellers who offer
work. While markets are stories of exchange, at their most optimistic they also track back to a much more fundamental idea of
resourcefulness. As we will see in this chapter and the next,
Katchadourian's ability to make art on the airplane – in some
ways, making something from nothing – is both an explainer of
economic resourcefulness and a crashing counterexample to the
idea of markets as a way to manage scarcity.

1.1   STORIES OF BARTER AND EXCHANGE

Many broader histories of markets begin with stories of barter – people
coming together to trade one item, say, a cow, for something equivalent, say, five bushels of wheat. Anthropologists debate barter as an
origin story for markets. David Graeber, author of *Debt: The First 5,000
Years*, argues that if barter markets had existed historically, anthropologists would have found them by now.[9] Graeber argues instead that
neighbors extended credit – as potentially fraught or transactional as
the term "credit" or "indebtedness" is – within communities where
people were dependent on each other. No one magically spot-traded

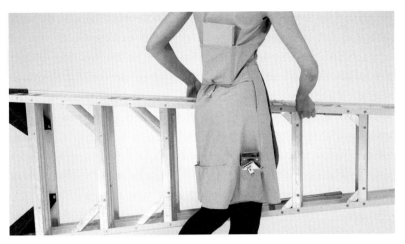

FIGURE 1.3 Caroline Woolard, *Work Dress*, 2007–13. Courtesy of the artist.

a cow for a coincidentally available quantity of wheat, but people did interact and trade in long-form webs of reciprocity.

On this idea of trade and reciprocity, in 2007 the artist Caroline Woolard made herself a "work dress," a wraparound utilitarian pinafore rimmed with large pockets which she wore as a uniform (see Figure 1.3). When people expressed interest in buying one, she agreed but only to barter. Trading for dresses, she mostly covered basic needs for five years.[10]

Those exchanges characterized Woolard's larger artistic practice. As John Haskell described her practice in *Bomb*,

> Artists generally fall into two groups: the makers (of objects) and doers (of activities) . . .. And then there's a third group, not creating objects exactly and not performing activities exactly, but working to change the way the doing of art gets done. Caroline Woolard is a member of this group . . .. [S]he . . . grounds [her art] in the practicalities of life – her life – along with anyone who's willing to join her. Part of the appeal of her work is the invitation to join the idealized world she's trying to create.[11]

In 2010, Caroline and a group of collaborators launched Trade School, a barter-economy school in which anyone could sign up to teach and request anything in return. The classes ranged from how to shoot in 35 mm film to "Justice! Justice! Justice!" taught by philosophy professor Matthew Noah Smith in exchange for Belgian beer and pickles. Trade School had the same material resourcefulness – of working with what is available – as Nina Katchadourian's "Seat Assignment." Paint buckets turned upside down and ringed with pocketed toolbelts served as student desks. By bringing together people with "haves" and "needs," the project approached exchange through a lens of resourcefulness.[12]

Although histories of currency are debated, it is intuitive that when parties could not trade their wares directly, they may have searched for some kind of equivalency – engaging in what sociologists call acts of **commensuration**, or the process of comparing the worth of two different things by reference to a third metric, in this case money.[13] If the person with the cow needs apples but a third person with apples needs hay, then some ledger or currency would help facilitate the swap by standing in as a marker of equivalence. *Relative Values: The Cost of Art in the Northern Renaissance*, a 2018 exhibition at the Metropolitan Museum of Art in New York, embraced this logic. The curator, Elizabeth Cleland, produced an array of seventeenth-century curiosities from the Met's collection, some in solid gold, and pegged each to its equivalency in cows. One object, a gift of financier J. Pierpont Morgan in 1917, was an automaton of Diana and the Stag. Hidden wheels propelled the wind-up mechanism forward, presumably across a dining table. The parlor curiosity doubled as a flask. In its day, it was worth seventy-nine cows.[14] Another object, a German chalice from 1608, jewel encrusted and solid gold – leaving little to the imagination on critiques of church spending – weighed in at 255 cows.[15] This relational logic of cow equivalency describes the central schema of economics: the idea that we can peg products to equivalency in cows, or money, and then bring together the willing

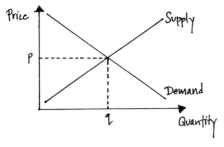

FIGURE 1.4 Supply and demand.

buyers and sellers at an agreed-upon price at the intersection of supply and demand (see Figure 1.4).[16]

Demand describes the audience, those who derive enough utility or satisfaction from the work to be willing to pay to acquire it. Supply describes all of the producers or offerers of products to the market. In theory, these lines – called curves, whether straight or not – intersect at the price that will prevail in the marketplace. At that price, a corresponding quantity will be sold.[17] Demand is based on tastes, income, prices of other goods, and beliefs about the future. Supply is theoretically based on the costs of production favoring whoever can make something most cheaply. Katchadourian's work complicates supply with its ingenuity of reclaimed labor and interstitial time, and it illustrates demand with its desirability to art collectors, museumgoers, and internet audiences alike.

The demand curve slopes down: the lower the price, the higher the quantity that will be purchased. The supply curve slopes upward: the higher the price, the more people who will want to produce. In theory, the market sets an equilibrium price at the intersection of these two lines, and the picture generalizes to any market – for oranges or orange *Balloon Dogs*. But the diagram will take different shapes depending on the circumstance. We will take demand and supply in turn and then talk about how they come together. (For a review of graphs, see Appendix A.)

I.2   DEMAND

Demand is a way of describing a person's or a whole group of people's willingness and ability to pay for something. Economists say **willingness to pay** as a shorthand to describe both the will and the financial means. Means includes both income and wealth, where **income** is used in the traditional sense of money made from a variety of sources, and **wealth** has a holistic meaning of savings.[18] Income describes flows of money in, and wealth describes stores of money already held, whether those stores are "wealthy" in absolute terms or not. The term **reservation price** is also used somewhat interchangeably with willingness to pay in order to describe the highest price a buyer will pay or the lowest price a seller will accept.

The demand curve is a flexible representative tool that can describe the willingness to pay for just one person – *individual* demand – or the willingness to pay for an entire group of people – *aggregate* demand. The rationale for the downward-sloping demand curve – the Law of Demand – is different for an individual person versus for a group of people. For an individual person, demand is downward sloping because of **diminishing marginal utility**. Under the rule of diminishing marginal utility, the *total* amount of satisfaction that one receives may increase with each unit consumed, but the additional or *marginal* utility will be less for each additional unit. If a trip to a museum brings me ten units of utility, a second visit might bring me six units, and a third visit might bring me two more. My total utility goes up (from 10 to 16 to 18) but the marginal utility (the additional +10, then +6, then +2) goes down. For aggregate demand, the demand curve also slopes downward because more people join in. Each person has a different ability to pay and derives a different level of utility from the work. For example, one person in the world is willing to buy Leonardo da Vinci's *Salvator Mundi* for $450.3 million, but perhaps ten people are willing to pay $100 million, and so on until 100 million people would have been willing to pay $50.

The diagram of supply and demand is a snapshot tool that can describe individuals or groups as long as the terms are defined. For this purpose, economists use the Latin phrase ***ceteris paribus*** to mean "all things equal." The phrase is used to mean that the diagram holds its ability to describe an interaction of buyers and sellers – producers and audiences – as long as no parameter is changed. For example, if we learned that that *Salvator Mundi* might or might not be by the hand of Leonardo da Vinci, the *ceteris paribus* assumption would no longer hold and our willingness to pay might change.

I.2.I   *Determinants of Demand*

If you think about one of your own purchase decisions, whether for a cup of coffee or an artwork, it is probably a holistic and even somewhat subconscious calculus including some analysis of price and some gut feel. Economists model that human algorithm into neat categories that together comprise demand. These determinants of demand are tastes, income, number of buyers and sellers, change in price of related goods, and change in expectations. Notice that some of these factors apply to individual and some to aggregate demand.

Tastes means whether you like something or not – what your "preferences" are. Of course, taste is extremely complex in the arts. Some of the foundational studies of taste come from Pierre Bourdieu, the French sociologist. For the five-year period from 1963 to 1968, Bourdieu conducted empirical studies of the cultural consumption habits of French people. His study, and the patterns he distilled from it, became the influential 1979 book *Distinction*, which was published in English in 1984.[19] Bourdieu argued that there was a class structure in which those with high cultural capital set taste and those with lower cultural capital were likely to follow them. Bourdieu defined "symbolic capital" as reputational capital based on honors, awards, prestige, or position as a critic.[20] Thus, while taste is straightforward in an economic sense, it is complicated in an artistic sense. What if more people like the Museum of Ice Cream, opened in New York in 2016, than documenta, the cerebral exhibition of contemporary art that takes place every five years in Kassel, Germany? The philosopher Theodor Adorno describes the "fetish" character of mass taste.[21] He argues that

the general population likes music that is comforting and monoton-
ously familiar. The same could be said for the ready appeal of popular
art. What people like is sometimes very different from what is artistically consecrated, and what is artistically consecrated evolves over
time.

The evolution of taste over time is well-documented and also
theorized.[22] Much pioneering art was so unfamiliar when it first
appeared that it seemed transgressively bad, or at least, in hindsight,
attractively priced. For instance, Betty Parsons, who was the early
dealer for New York–based abstract-expressionist artist Jackson
Pollock, sold his paintings in 1950 for $300. Those paintings could
be worth $100 million now – or be largely retired from market circu-
lation and held by museums.[23] In an interview in the 1980s, Parsons
recalled a visit to her Fifty-Seventh Street Manhattan gallery by the
New York Times critic Stuart Preston to see an exhibition of the later
canonized American abstract painter Clyfford Still:

> [Preston] came off the elevator [into the Betty Parsons Gallery], took
> one look at the Clyfford Still show, and started back into the elevator.
> I told him, "Please do me a favor." (We were friends, you know.)
> "Would you mind going into that room with a Clyfford Still and
> staying there for five minutes? I'll close the door and let you out
> afterwards." So he went in and sat there. When the five minutes were
> up, Preston walked out and reluctantly admitted that maybe, after all,
> I did have something.[24]

Critics have the power to set taste, but in Parsons's story they also
need time to metabolize new work. Parsons herself was trained as
an artist and lightly bemoaned the critic's tendency toward cre-
dentializing work by placing it in an historical context. As Parsons
told her interviewer, "A new work by a new artist is not history,
it's the present. Leave it alone, at least for a while, let it come to
life fully before you put it into this or that category."[25] It is hard
to parse genuinely new work and perhaps tempting to validate it
by placing it in an art historical context. The tendency to

credentialize may also support facets of the work such as social prestige or investment risk management.

Art also complicates "taste" because some moving or important art is not "enjoyable," per se. The idea of measurable utility or "enjoyment" could sound tone deaf toward difficult political work or could flatten the nuance of art that engages in anti-aesthetic, dematerialized, or willfully anti-capitalistic forms.[26] We lack good economic language to describe this unquantifiable importance of things – the utility of being challenged or made to think.[27]

The second determinant of demand is **income** or **wealth**. As described above, income which is typically derived from wages is distinguished from wealth as a descriptor of savings or net worth. The higher one's income or wealth, the higher one's willingness or ability to pay for something. A person with higher income or wealth is able to enter the marketplace for certain works of art – at the extreme end, the $450.3 million Leonardo da Vinci painting of *Salvator Mundi* sold at Christie's in 2017.[28]

Demand is sometimes mapped onto the social psychologist Abraham Maslow's 1943 hierarchy of human needs, described in the paper "A Theory of Human Motivation." At the bottom of the hierarchy, one must allocate budget to obtain basic survival before one can start to meet higher-order needs and wants, ranging from safety to love to esteem to, at the apex of the triangle, what Maslow calls "self-actualization" (see Figure 1.5).[29]

FIGURE 1.5 Maslow's hierarchy of need.

Maslow discusses some of the seeming reversals of these needs: Some people value esteem or recognition more than love. Some creative people seem to forego basic satisfaction to reach for self-actualization and expression. According to Maslow, the unambitious do not strive for achievement, and the psychopathic have permanent loss of love needs. People whose needs have long been met may underestimate the needs' importance; for instance, those who have not experienced food insecurity may vastly underestimate physiological needs.[30]

In a similar way, the concentration of very high prices at the top of the art market reflects an enormity of income and wealth inequality.[31] Although in market-based societies people arguably have autonomy to buy what they want, some observers have started to raise ethical questions about the price of art. In his 2017 book *The Orange Balloon Dog*, Don Thompson points out that the price of the Jeff Koons sculpture for which the book was named – $58.4 million in 2013, at the time the highest auction result for a living artist – happened to be equivalent in dollar terms to the US government's spending on Ebola vaccine development.[32]

The third determinant of demand is the **number of buyers and sellers** in the market. This factor describes aggregate demand rather than individual demand. A museum in a city of 60,000 people will almost invariably have less demand than a museum in a city of one million people, unless the small city has extremely strong tourism or an exceptionally desirable museum. One can liken this category of the determinants of demand to demographic trends. For example, as a population ages, demand surges for retirement communities. A university town has larger demand for products for students.

The fourth determinant of demand is **the relative price of related goods**. Economists classify goods into categories of **substitutes** and **complements**. Substitutes are goods that are interchangeable, to varying degrees. A pair of new size-ten blue Nike sneakers is a perfect substitute for another pair of the same style of size-ten blue Nike sneakers. (For a person who wears sneakers functionally, a wide range of shoes might be substitutes. For a collector of limited-edition Nikes, only an identical, perhaps rare pair of shoes would be a perfect substitute.) A complement is a good that goes together with another, where each enhances the other's value. A painting and a frame are complements. More speculatively, an artwork and its wall label are complements, though some people may read the label and barely glance at the work, making it a substitute.

The category of substitutes reflects the trade-off of one thing against another. If the Whitney Museum has a $25 ticket and the Museum of Modern Art has a free night, the free ticket might cause someone to substitute MoMA for the Whitney. On the other hand, complements are products that go together, for instance a museum and a nearby restaurant. If we imagined a curator visiting New York from out of town, the two exhibitions could also be complements, functioning together to build the curator's knowledge of exhibitions in New York at that time. Some activities that are not direct substitutes still compete for limited resources. An artist receiving a grant may need to choose between two projects, or the artist may be struggling to pay rent and invest in an artwork.

Complements and substitutes reflect the larger economic calculus of **cost–benefit analysis** – the weighing of a benefit against an associated cost. Imagine a small gallery is deciding whether to attend an art fair. That gallery may have a limited budget for art-fair attendance and be able to attend only one of the five fairs to which it could easily apply. That gallery has to weigh the costs and benefits of attending these fairs. Economists map "indifference curves," which describe the relationship between trade-offs across the two options. (See Appendix B for more on indifference curves.) As we will see in Chapter 2, the gallery could also collaborate and share booths or otherwise try to change their cost structure in order to be able to attend more fairs.

Art itself does not always have a neat substitute or complement. Technically speaking, the third print and the eighteenth print in a series of Albrecht Dürer engravings are not perfect substitutes because the plate from which they were printed may have been altered between those prints. The works may also be in very different condition or have distinguishing **provenance**, meaning history of ownership if, for instance, one had belonged to a public figure or the family of the artist. Many works of art are without substitute, falling under the economics of singularities described by Lucien Karpik in *Valuing the Unique*.[33] Even for unique objects, the body of work of one artist can function loosely as a brand, especially in cases such as Andy Warhol flowers or Damien Hirst spot paintings in which the canvases are particularly closely related.[34] And, as in Karpik's theory, when objects are unique and therefore hard to compare, we rely heavily on credentials such as rank-order lists and awards.[35]

The last determinant of demand is **change in expectations**. Do you expect to have more money in the near future? Do you expect that another Leonardo da Vinci painting is likely ever to come to auction? Have you already passed through the security checkpoint at the airport and expect that it will be impossible to find a less expensive bottle of water for sale anywhere in the terminal? According to economists, we are assessing our demand based on the ideas we have about the future. A business school student may have the same debt as an art school student but spend differently while in school out of belief that there will be higher paying jobs on offer in a few years. A bidder who believes a comparable artwork will not come to auction again in the next decade may stretch more in price. A city visitor who may never get to see a museum again may be willing to pay more to see it.

All of these determinants of demand are already somewhat artificially separated strands of decision-making relative to the ways most people determine what to buy. Demand for art is also complicated by the fact that what one is really buying may not be an artwork but something related: social standing, connection with other people, gratification of supporting an organization, or entertainment. Demand for art also depends on the appraisal of an artwork's qualities.[36] Some of these characteristics pertain to the artwork itself:

its size, medium, condition, and placement within an artist's body of work.[37] Other characteristics apply to the broader context of the work: its provenance, its authenticity, and the circumstance in which it is being sold. Some artworks have particularly acute scarcity and almost no substitute. Thus, if the artwork goes to auction and two bidders really want it, the price is set entirely by the willingness to pay of the winner and the underbidder.[38] (For a more detailed discussion of auctions, see Appendix D.)

Economists describe things that sell as **goods** and classify goods into different types, some of which reflect these ideas of status and social position. Broadly speaking, many consumer goods are what economists call **normal goods**. A normal good is one for which an increase in your income leads to an increase in demand. If you make more money, you might buy more plane tickets or eat more meals in restaurants. An **inferior good** is one for which an increase in income leads to a decrease in demand. If you have been economizing by eating canned beans or instant ramen noodles, an increase in income will lead to a decrease in consumption of those goods because you will replace them with normal goods that you are increasingly able to afford.

In his 1899 book *Theory of the Leisure Class*, Thorstein Veblen described goods – that now take his name – for which an increase in price leads to an increase in demand.[39] For a **Veblen good**, the more you pay for it the better you feel about the purchase. The purchase is a form of social signaling of status or a form of **conspicuous consumption**, and the information conveyed to others about the purchase is part of the value of the good. One might call a Jeff Koons sculpture a Veblen good.

Luxury goods, including art, can also function as **positional goods**.[40] A positional good shares some similarities with a Veblen good. However, its value is not just in its expense but in its exclusivity. It generates demand by not being available to everyone. Here, a Koons sculpture is also an example. Very few are made. If you want to have one in your atrium, there is a zero-sum chance that someone else can have the same one you have. Thus, the price you are willing to pay increases because of the conjoined Veblen and positional nature.

In *The Orange Balloon Dog*, Thompson underscores this positional nature of Koons's work when he quotes an email that Brett Gorvy, then chairman and Christie's international head of postwar and contemporary art, sent to collectors in advance of the sale of said sculpture at Christie's in 2017. Gorvy wrote,

> The *Balloon Dog* is the Holy Grail for collectors and foundations. In private hands, the work has always communicated the prominence and stature of its owner. To own this work immediately positions the buyer alongside the very top collectors in the world and transforms a collection to an unparalleled level of greatness.[41]

That the work went on to set an auction record for a living artist only reinforced its positional function.[42]

1.2.2   Constructing a Demand Curve

To build a demand curve for an individual, we find their schedule of preferences. To build a demand curve for a group, we put those preferences together. Let's say you are considering buying a cookie. You really like cookies and you are hungry. You are willing to pay $5 for the first cookie. The first cookie tastes delicious. It tastes so good that you consider buying a second cookie. You would probably enjoy that cookie slightly less than the first because you are already starting to feel a little full. The cookie would bring you less utility than the first cookie – diminishing marginal utility. You therefore would be willing to pay less for the second cookie. You can imagine a demand curve in which you would pay $5 for one cookie, $4 for a second cookie, $3 for a third cookie, $2 for a fourth cookie, and $1 for the fifth cookie. The demand curve shows all of these prices as a **schedule**, that is, a chart of your hypothetical cookie consumption.

The demand curve has an important property of *horizontal adding*. The different prices you are willing to pay are added together across the quantities so that the demand curve can reflect the total quantity you would buy at each price if the marketplace had only one price on offer. For instance, in a marketplace with a single price of $4,

Table 1.1 *Horizontal adding*

Price	Horizontal adding	Quantity
$5	1 =	1
$4	1 + 1 =	2
$3	1 + 1 + 1 =	3
$2	1 + 1 + 1 + 1 =	4
$1	1 + 1 + 1 + 1 +1 =	5

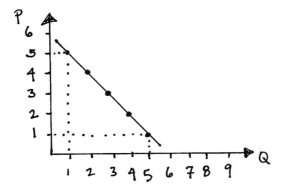

FIGURE I.6 Constructing a demand curve.

how many cookies would you buy? If you would be willing to buy the first cookie at $5, then it follows that you would still agree to purchase it for $4, saving $1 from your true willingness to pay. We can put these numbers into a chart (see Table 1.1).

We can draw the demand curve as shown in Figure 1.6. This demand curve shows a hypothetical person's individual demand for cookies. This assumption of demand is *ceteris paribus*, meaning we have held the circumstances equal.

I.2.3 Consumer Surplus

Notice what happens when the price in the market for cookies is set at $3. You would have been willing to pay $5 for the first and $4 for the second cookie, but you were only asked to pay $3 for each of those. That positive difference between your willingness to pay and the price in the market is called **consumer surplus**. Consumer surplus is the amount of money that buyers would have been willing to spend but were not asked to because their willingness to pay was higher than the market price. It is easier to see consumer surplus when we look at aggregate demand.

Aggregate demand takes this same concept of demand and applies it to what a group of different people are willing to pay. Suppose that the Museum of Modern Art is undertaking research on what to charge to attend the museum. In this simplified example, they study five different museum visitors: Allan, Beatriz, Charlie, Damien, and Elaine. Each person's willingness to pay for one ticket is shown in Table 1.2.

We still add horizontally here so that we understand the total number of people who would attend at a given price. The shaded

Table 1.2 *Willingness to pay for a museum ticket*

Visitor	Reasoning	Willingness to pay	Total tickets sold at this price
Damien	A New Yorker on his lunch break who only wants to stay 15 minutes but has significant wealth	$40	1
Allan	A tourist from Toronto, would never miss seeing MoMA unless it were truly expensive	$25	2
Beatriz	A schoolteacher who loves art but has a limited ability to pay	$12	3
Charlie	A New Yorker on his lunch break who only wants to stay 15 minutes	$8	4
Elaine	A former museum worker who is habituated to free staff tickets	$5	5

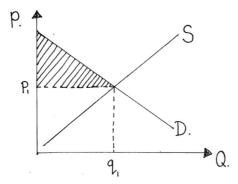

FIGURE I.7 Consumer surplus.

triangle in Figure 1.7 shows the consumer surplus of everyone whose willingness to pay is higher than the offered price.

In Chapter 3, we will look at the pricing strategies that follow from different willingnesses to pay and how to charge different prices to different people. For now, we will assume one price in the market, at the intersection of demand with supply.

I.3 SUPPLY

If demand describes all of the potential purchasers in a marketplace, supply describes all of the potential sellers. In classical economics, supply is easiest to describe for manufacturing because it is based on the cost of production. In theory, the supply curve represents the cost of producing the marginal additional unit, within the confines of the **short run**, which is what economists call the time frame in which decisions about the commitment of resources such as signing a factory lease have already been made. In contrast, the **long run** is the time frame in which all decisions about allocating resources – for example, signing a lease – are open.

In the arts, supply only occasionally reflects costs of production, in cases of extreme labor intensity, need to cover the cost of out-sourced manufacture, or use of precious underlying materials. If an artist spends six months creating a painstaking photorealist work, we hope that the artist is paid enough to cover that labor. When the minimalist artist Donald Judd outsourced fabrication of his giant aluminum boxes to Lippincott in Connecticut, one would intuit that he tried to sell the work for more than he paid the fabricators. When an illuminated manuscript was sold in the Middle Ages, the price had to cover the expense of gold within its decorated pages. And when Damien Hirst produced the diamond-encrusted human skull – titled *For the Love of God,* allegedly after what his mother said to him when he unveiled the piece – one would expect the price to be higher than the market price for that quantity of diamonds. Otherwise, someone could buy the artwork, disassemble it, and resell the diamonds at a profit.[43]

1.3.1   The Determinants of Supply for Art

What determines the supply of art? If we imagine this question from the perspective of artists, dealers, and museums, we get different answers. Although Grampp would take the economist's view that artists are motivated to produce because they get paid, many artists would object to this economic frame being placed over production. Many artists produce work without getting paid.[44] They make work because they are driven to make work and then figure out how to pay for it otherwise. From the perspective of an auction house, the supply of consigned works to auction often comes from what are referred to as the "four D's": death, divorce, debt, and disaster. For museums, the supply of exhibitions comes from a delicate combination of curatorial interest, reputation of artists, consideration of audience, and other factors.

For dealers and auction houses, the ability to control the supply of art is a huge determinant of price. If all of the works by a given artist flooded the market, the price would go down. Economists refer to this kind of over- or undersupply as **surplus** or **shortage**, respectively. When either occurs, the price in the marketplace adjusts accordingly. Surplus drives prices down so that the oversupply can be absorbed. Shortage drives prices up because there is competition for something desirable.

1.3.2 Constructing a Supply Curve

For our purposes, supply is what it sounds like. It is a schedule of how much of a given product – works of art, museum tickets, educational programs – is available at a given time. By the law of supply, the higher the price offered, the higher the quantity of works supplied. If artisanal beer sells for $30 per case, people who know how to make beer will produce it. If artisanal beer starts to sell for $2,000 per case, I might learn to produce it. The supply curve implies a kind of predictive power that if the price in the market went really high, more suppliers would join in. The logic does not hold in the arts for many reasons, including the premium placed on novel and original work. A price increase for a Banksy artwork does not imply that there will be a strong price for a copy of a Banksy or demand for interventionist graffiti.[45]

In the case of masterpieces, the supply curve for art can be dramatically constrained at one unit. To return to the case of the *Salvator Mundi* which sold for $450.3 million, sales of masterpieces at auction have a particular structure because the supply is constrained to one. Thus, the supply curve is vertical at one (see Figure 1.8).

The price is set by two bidders in the room, the underbidder and the winner. The sale of the *Salvator Mundi* was an unusual auction. The bidding lasted nineteen minutes. The bidding shot up quickly

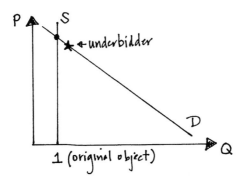

FIGURE I.8 Leonardo da Vinci, *Salvator Mundi* auction.

past the $200 million mark, and then slowed through the roughly $280 million mark. The bidding was at that point believed to be between only two parties. At $286 million, the price went straight to $300 million as the other party placed a **jump bid**, meaning the bidder skips over a number of increments, usually to make a point by show of bidding force. The price continued to climb, then jumped from $320 million to $350 million and landing at a $400 million **hammer price**, with $50.3 million in added fees. This price was set exclusively by the two bidders (see Appendix D).[46]

We will never know if the winner would have been willing to pay substantially more because the auction mechanism only discovers the price above the underbidder. We also do not know if the winner came to experience the "winner's curse" of successfully purchasing the piece, realizing they did so because they were willing to pay more than everyone else, and then coming to regret having overpaid (see Figure 1.9).

The winner's curse curve shows the distribution of willingness to pay around an average price. By definition, the winner of an auction is the highest bidder and thus the farthest out at the right tail of the curve. It is the terrific scarcity as well as the excellence of these works that makes them expensive. In this sense, many commentators describe the arts as "supply driven," meaning it is the supply of desirable artworks itself that drives the market.[47]

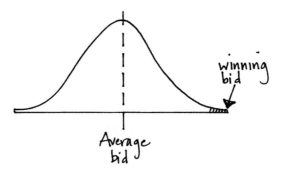

FIGURE 1.9 Winner's curse.

1.3.3 Producer Surplus

In traditional manufacturing economics there is a concept of producer surplus that parallels consumer surplus. Here, the producer receives a price per unit that is set by the market, for example, $10. If that producer can make units for less than $10, that producer holds this surplus, which one can think of as profit. To describe producer surplus requires explanation of what is called the **marginal cost curve,** a line that tracks the cost of producing each additional unit in the short run. In theory, the supply curve is based on the manufacturing costs of a firm, specifically on the **marginal cost** of producing one additional unit. By market logic, the competitive firm produces where marginal revenue (price) is equal to marginal cost (the cost of the last unit produced). This logic does not easily apply to the arts. Rarely is anyone producing a standardized good in quantity. One might think of yellow paint as such a commodity, but not all yellow paints are the same: The yellows based on cadmium are restricted for toxicity. The ones in Edvard Munch's *The Scream* have turned brown, much to the consternation of art conservators.[48]

In theory, the supply curve essentially represents the marginal cost curves of all of the firms. Each marginal cost curve is shaped like a hockey stick that dips down slightly then pegs up to the right. The profit-maximizing firm produces where the marginal cost curve intersects price, which is, for the firm, the marginal revenue. The supply curve goes up because it describes the frontier of each firm's capacity if the firm is so focused on profit that it is manufacturing against the limits of the resources – factories, staff, materials – that it has committed to in the short run. The supply curve in the arts is much more likely to serve as a snapshot of other circumstances – entirely artistic decisions to produce, calculated decisions to keep work scarce, or personal circumstance such as debt that brings a work of art back to the market.

1.4   SUPPLY AND DEMAND TOGETHER

Supply and demand together intersect at a price that prevails in the market. This intersection of supply and demand is the diagrammatic realization of Adam Smith's "invisible hand." This picture maps a relationship of price and quantity and the behavior of buyers and sellers *ceteris paribus*. We can see consumer and producer surplus, and we can see buyers and sellers – at the right side of the drawing – who are not able to participate in the market at the prevailing price (see Figure 1.10). If no assumptions change, *ceteris paribus*, then price and quantity move along these lines. An over- or undersupply causes a dislocation.

However, shocks to the picture overall create shifts in supply and demand, and the picture gets redrawn (see Figure 1.11). Anything that changes a determinant of demand shifts demand. Anything that effectively raises or lowers the price, as experienced by the consumer, shifts supply, for instance, the addition of a tax. One example in the arts that has this characteristic of added cost from the buyer's point of view is **resale royalties**, the distribution to artists in some jurisdictions when their works are resold.

An increase in an artist's popularity or expansion to a new market can shift the demand curve, as happened for the Chinese artist Zao Wou-ki (1920–2013) over the course of his career. Zao studied at

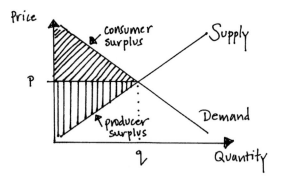

FIGURE 1.10 Summary of supply and demand.

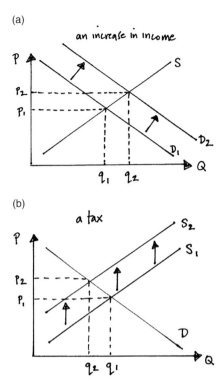

FIGURE 1.11 Shifts in supply and demand.

the National Academy of Fine Arts (China Academy of Art) in Hangzhou.[49] He became known in China for his experimental paintings, works on paper, and prints. After Zao moved to Paris in 1948, his work became better known to a European audience. In fact, Zao's work was already popular in France in the 1960s and 1970s before it subsequently gained recognition in China in the following decades. By 2018, Zao's work accounted for a full 4.3% of worldwide auction sales in the postwar and contemporary category. (His was the top market share, ahead of Jean-Michel Basquiat at 3.6%.) Different inflection points in the reception of his art would correspond to shifts in demand.[50]

In practice, pricing is often controlled by dealers and not only market mechanisms. For example, if an artist such as Katchadourian

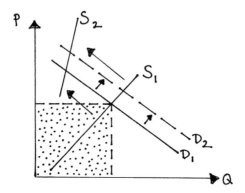

FIGURE 1.12 Shift in demand for editioned prints.

had an edition of ten photographs each selling for $100, at the point at which four had sold her dealer could decide whether to raise the price. If the artist receives a public commission or exhibition – news that disrupts the *ceteris paribus* condition in a positive way – demand often shifts to the right (see Figure 1.12). More people join the aggregate demand curve, and the willingness to pay of various individual collectors goes up based on a change in taste and perhaps also a change in expectations (believing the work to have become more valuable). At the same time, supply has become scarcer. There are no longer ten works for sale but six.

If you were the dealer in this situation, what would you do with the price? Some dealers would change it, and some would not. Some would honor the price to collectors who had already inquired and raise it for newcomers. In addition, those dealers might decide not to sell for the highest absolute price but instead to "place" the work in the best collections reputationally and to avoid the risk of speculative resale. Collectors who resell works customarily give the gallery first right of refusal, but many speculators head straight for auction markets instead.

1.5 CONCLUSIONS

If markets ask cost–benefit questions – how do you trade off finite resources and compete for scarce prizes? – artists often start with questions of resources and possibilities: What do you have and what do you need? If markets are about exchange, art is often about putting something out there before you can expect to get something back. Thus, supply and demand comprise the central metaphor of markets, but they do not fully describe the motivation of actors in art markets. Both the drive to make work and the desire to purchase – support, live with, speculate on – art are untidy in a market sense. Still, the ideas of supply and demand are useful to describe the coming together of offers and acceptances, and we can talk not only about markets for artwork or for labor but also for donations, grants, and other forms of philanthropic support.

The underlying first principle of markets is still this management of resources. Economists describe resourcefulness as efficiency – in the allocation of resources and, as we will see in the next chapter, in the production of goods and services. Here we might rethink efficiency as agility and ingenuity. As in Katchadourian's "Seat Assignment," the plane takes off and lands. The time in between is an open-ended experiment that may later find private markets, human joy, and civic import. But on the plane, the artist engages in resourcefulness – toward passengers, seatbelts, pretzels, and lavatory wares – with the utmost seriousness of curiosity and care.

QUESTIONS

1. Why is the demand curve downward sloping?
2. What is the difference between individual and aggregate demand?
3. The idea of complements and substitutes can extend to any area of life. For instance, texting and driving are substitutes but listening to the radio and driving can be complements. Experimental theatre and restaurants are complements but being in the audience and talking are not. Brainstorm as many complements and substitutes as you can. Compare lists.
4. Draw supply and demand for the following case: At a charity auction, an artist has donated a work of art. Of the ten people in the room, their willingnesses to pay (in $) are: 1,000, 900, 800, 700, 600,

500, 400, 300, 200, 100. There is one artwork. Where (give a range) will the price fall? (Hint: Supply is a vertical line at quantity of one. Demand intersects it between the two highest prices.)

5. Survey your classmates or another population of people on what they would be willing to pay for da Vinci's *Salvator Mundi*. (Set constraints so that the exercise is *ceteris paribus*, for example, set a point in time before or after the auction revealed a price and before or after the revelation that the work might not be by da Vinci's hand.) Make a chart of each person's willingness to pay. Now use the horizontal adding technique to find the total number of people who would purchase the work at each price. Construct a demand curve. What do you find in this graph relative to the actual price paid at auction? If you had held an auction with only these people present, what would have been the price? Repeat the same exercise for any work of art.

6. Find data on attendance for a museum in your area. Imagine the people who would attend if the museum were cheaper, and the people who are patrons who pay more. Draw a demand curve that includes them all.

7. You are the dealer of an artist who works in limited edition prints. You have ten prints to sell and have priced then at $1,000 each. Now five of them have sold. How will the picture of supply and demand shift? What decisions will you make about raising or maintaining the price? Why?

8. Draw the following shifts in supply and/or demand:

    a. Ticket sales at the Prado museum when there is a mass airline strike and tourists cannot travel to Madrid.
    b. Demand for Carolee Schneemann's work in September 2019, six months after she passed away.
    c. The European Union announces a tax on all art exports. (Draw supply and demand for the EU and again for an art market outside the EU.)
    d. An obscure drawing in a day sale is identified as a late Rembrandt sketch.

2   Cost

> Even his favorite activity, walking the city, is costless and in turn has
> repeatedly given him artistic ideas.
>
> Martin Herbert, on the artist David Hammons[1]

Massoud Hassani was born in 1983 in Qasaba, Afghanistan, on the
outskirts of Kabul near the airport. As children, he and his brother
Mahmud entertained themselves by racing handmade toys that the
wind would cause to roll and bounce along the flat terrain.[2] Their toys
occasionally veered into controlled areas with active landmines.
From the Soviet occupation of Afghanistan in 1979 and subsequent
armed conflict, Afghanistan is home to a dense number of unexploded landmines; projections range up to ten million unexploded
devices.[3] Despite substantial demining activity, in 2017 a likely 640
square kilometers of Afghan land remained unusable because of
mines.[4]

   In 1993, after the death of Massoud's father, the family left
Afghanistan as refugees, eventually gaining asylum in the
Netherlands.[5] There Massoud, who had been unsure of his direction
in school, followed his early interests in drawing and making things.
He enrolled in the Design Academy Eindhoven, an interdisciplinary
arts school located about eighty miles south of Amsterdam in the
Netherlands' fifth largest city. For his final graduation project,
Massoud was searching for a topic when one of his professors sug-
gested he explore something related to his upbringing. Initially,
Massoud collaborated with his mother on a cookbook that supported
a charity for women's education.[6] Then he started thinking about
landmines – and reimagining his childhood wind toys at scale.

FIGURE 2.1 Massoud Hassani with *Mine Kafon*, 2011. Installation photo, Museum of Modern Art, New York, 2013. Photograph by Mahmud Hassani. Courtesy of the artist.

What Massoud created was Mine Kafon, a wind-powered deminer, shaped like a giant dandelion (see Figure 2.1). Rolling with a diameter of several feet and a human-like weight of 70 kilograms, Mine Kafon's bamboo arms radiate out from a dense iron core. Each arm is capped with a biodegradable plastic disk that resembles a flattened toilet plunger. Light enough to roll in the wind and heavy enough to trip a mine, Mine Kafon was designed to traverse flat terrain exploding landmines as it went. A tripped mine would only blow up a few of the bamboo arms. Because the arms were modular, the device could be repaired and reused. Each deminer was fitted with a GPS chip that allowed it to exit a field safely for repairs. The GPS also saved a map of the demined areas for future reference. The busted bamboo arms and disk were biodegradable and could be left where they fell.

In 2011, the Museum of Modern Art in New York acquired Mine Kafon for its design collection.[7] While the deminer sat overlooking the MoMA garden, the Dutch Ministry of Defense ran tests on the device.

They found that Mine Kafon fell short of the United Nations' stringent standards – at least 98% certainty all mines have been removed. But even with this limitation, Mine Kafon could be used for preliminary scouting and assignment of a safety perimeter.

In most news coverage of the device, its cost is listed as $50. That number includes the materials needed to build one, but in an economic sense it does not represent many other forms of cost. These other costs include the overhead of the studio, the time of both Massoud and his brother Mahmud, who works with him, or the production of all of the rewards that were offered in the Kickstarter crowdfunding campaign attached to the original Mine Kafon.

In this chapter we explore different economic categories of cost and how they come together to form the structural engineering of art projects and organizations. Because cost is sometimes integral to an artwork's meaning, politics, or market defiance, we will also explore art projects that consider cost as part of their subject. The first distinction we cover – between fixed and variable cost – is the structural support of accounting statements and tools such as breakeven analysis, which we will cover by the end of this chapter.

Mirroring Katchadourian's work as described in Chapter 1, cost structure begins with a story of resourcefulness. The plot structure of production begins with raw materials – which are assumed to be scarce – and extends through making something of value and then selling it. Economists categorize these inputs as factors of production: land, labor, and capital. **Land** encompasses all facets of the natural environment, including trees or minerals, beyond the general usage of "land" to mean an area of the earth's surface not covered by water. **Labor** includes work done by people, whether mentally or physically. **Capital** includes money but more strictly resources such as factories and machines that can transform "land" by use of "labor." Some economists add a fourth resource, entrepreneurship, to represent ingenuity.[8] These factors of production come together in replicable and wholly original ways to tell the story of objects, organizations, and artists' working lives.

2.1 FIXED AND VARIABLE COSTS

In her book *Double Entry*, on the history of accounting, Jane Gleeson-White credits the distinction of fixed and variable cost to Josiah Wedgwood, the ceramicist to the queen of England (see Figure 2.2). In the 1770s, Wedgwood was fending off throngs of carriages of the elites who swarmed his stores in a "violent Vase Madness." Then a staggering credit crisis, the 1770s equivalent of 2008, dried up those sales and forced many of Wedgwood's competitors out of business. Struggling to stabilize his business, Wedgwood analyzed his financials. He began to notice a pattern in his expense ledger that there were some costs, such as making molds for vases, that never changed with the quantity of vases he produced, but other costs that did. He drew the distinction between those costs that never changed and were fixed and those costs that did change and were variable.[9] This distinction between a **fixed cost** (overhead like rent and utilities) and a **variable cost** (materials and part-time labor) underlies the fundamental architecture of production economics. Much of business strategy follows from this core distinction. (We will explore these business structures more in Chapter 6.)

Like Nina Katchadourian in the last chapter, Massoud Hassani's work begins with what economists call **resource costs**, meaning the pre-market cost, whether monetary or not, of the materials needed to realize a project. Some of these materials will have **explicit costs**, meaning they will have a price paid in the marketplace, like pencils bought at an art supply store. Some other materials will have **implicit**

FIGURE 2.2 Wedgwood teacup and saucer. Courtesy of Wedgwood.

costs, in that they, like the toilet-seat covers, are used up in the process of making the work. Katchadourian uses a strikingly low number of objects with explicit cost. She is using up resources, such as toilet-seat covers, that the airline technically pays for. For the airline, toilet-seat covers are an explicit cost, though probably a very low one. She also uses materials that might get thrown away or consumed – a paper drinking cup or a bag of pretzels.

The chief cost Katchadourian or Hassani encounters is the metaphysical category of cost at the heart of economics: **opportunity cost**. Opportunity cost is the imagined cost of the best alternative use. If you were not using the resources for the project at hand, what else could you be using them for? Whatever you are doing, you not only face the costs at hand, but also the imaginative cost of what you would be doing instead.

In the case of Mine Kafon, the opportunity cost of resources used is relatively low – the space in the art school or the bamboo. The opportunity cost of not doing the project is very high – failing to remove landmines at cost of life or limb, and at cost of hundreds of kilometers of land that could be used for farming or roads or other purposes.

When we evaluate the cost of making Mine Kafon, we can look at the explicit cost of materials, the total per-unit cost to make each deminer, or more philosophically at the opportunity cost of doing or not doing the project. The $50 cost of Mine Kafon is really only the variable cost – that is, the direct cost of manufacturing each unit. What is the fixed cost or overhead? It depends on whether Hassani is using the resources of his school or of an overall design studio. Even if he does not have to pay explicitly, from an economic perspective, he is using resources: space, time. For the total cost, we would need to know the quantity of output. For example, if each Mine Kafon costs $50 in materials, and their overhead is $1,000, and they produce twenty Mine Kafons in that time period, then we can apportion $50 of the overhead to each of the twenty objects (20 × $50 = $1,000). In economics that $100 for materials and share of overhead is called the

average total cost per unit. In managerial accounting it is called a **fully absorbed cost** of production. We can consider the opportunity cost as well. If Massoud and his brother work full-time, the opportunity cost of their time is the salary they are forgoing to do this work.

Questions of cost structure have long affected the working lives of artists. Historically, Renaissance patrons covered these costs. For the Impressionists painters in the second half of the nineteenth century, their dealer Paul Durand-Ruel often bought work from them in advance, in what was effectively a patron relationship, according to Harrison and Cynthia White in their 1965 book *Canvases and Careers*.[10] Artists such as Edouard Manet, Camille Pissarro, and Claude Monet lived outside of Paris. Their overhead or fixed cost included rent, household staff, food and wine, and transportation for regular travel to Paris. Their variable cost included paint and materials.

However, it is complicated to account for the variable cost of making work. Manet's story is not unusual in that he made 286 artworks in his lifetime but only sold 58 of them while he was alive. (A further 67 paintings were sold in the year after he died.) Although Manet made over 75,000 francs from the sale of his work over the course of his lifetime (around $320,000 in today's dollars), most of that was made in the later years of his life, and thus he worked for decades covering the costs of making his work – including living his life – before the revenue from the sale of art came to him.[11] We have more information on the fixed costs of his life than the material costs of his art, but it is the fixed costs that would most drive artists, particularly those who did not have access to family wealth as Manet did, to agree to sell work to Durand-Ruel exclusively in order to receive a more reliable income.[12]

As you read the rest of this chapter, keep in mind your own projects and jobs, and the production of artworks or exhibitions or other projects. Fundamentally, what are the costs? If we start by thinking of the resources – materials, time, thought, space, labor, fabrication – we can then place those costs into economic and accounting categories to build and diagnose the business structure of anything. What is your opportunity cost right now? What other costs in time and energy do you experience?

In addition to these fixed, variable, and opportunity costs, there is also a broad category of **transaction costs**, which one can mentally model as the economic representation of friction – finding things, negotiating things, or managing people and processes, for instance.[13] Transaction costs exist in a number of categories including:

Search costs: the cost in time or resources to find something, whether lost keys, an obscure product on the internet, or a specific artwork.

Contracting costs: the cost, implicit or explicit, of entering into informal negotiation or formal legal arrangements whether for employment or art sale or something else.

Monitoring costs: the cost in time or resources of enforcement and management, for example, having to supervise work, proofread or fact check a deliverable, or make sure an employee is productive.

Explicit commissions: the surcharge or percentage commission applied to a transaction, for instance, a broker's fee or ticket fee. In the arts, this could be the seller's commission or the buyer's premium charged by an auction house.

Slippage: the transaction cost incurred when your behavior changes the price. Technically slippage refers to a change in the price of a commodity or security based on buying or selling a large volume. If Warren Buffett or another highly respected investor purchased or sold a position, the volume of the sale and reputation of the transactor could affect the price in the market overall. In the arts, collectors such as Don and Mera Rubell can move markets for emerging artists and thus would want to complete a purchase before their ownership became known, so as not to experience slippage.

Switching costs: the cost in time and resources of changing from one service provider or circumstance to another, for example, switching bank accounts or learning new software.

Some transaction costs show up in explicit costs while others are implicit. Transaction costs determine whether an activity is organized within a firm or outsourced – an area of economics founded on Ronald Coase's 1937 work on the theory of the firm.[14]

2.2 COST STRUCTURE AS INTEGRAL TO ART PRACTICE

Not only does cost structure enable the work to be made, sometimes cost structure becomes integral to the conceptual meaning of the work or inseparable from the work's operating politics.[15] Here I want to cover two artists whose practices illustrate a range of conceptual connections to cost structure: Charlotte Posenenske, who conceived of a way of making art that could not function in art markets, and the artist Lenka Clayton, whose typewriter drawings are beautifully, willfully inefficient.

2.2.1 Manufacture As Co-creation

As Martin Herbert writes in his book *Tell Them I Said No*, the German artist Charlotte Posenenske formally disengaged from the contemporary art world in 1968, amid the political protests of that year.[16] Posenenske had been making minimalist tubular shapes out of industrial air ducts – the kind used in building-ventilation systems (see Figure 2.3). As Posenenske wrote in a statement published in *Art International* in May 1968, "It is painful for me to face the fact that art cannot contribute to the solution of urgent social problems."[17]

Starting in 1968, at the age of thirty-seven, Posenenske refused all commissions, declined all exhibitions, put her art in the attic, and began a degree in the sociology of labor. She wanted to understand how factory labor could be seen through the lens of co-authorship with workers. Instead of seeing factory laborers as cogs in the machine of efficient manufacture, Posenenske saw them as autonomous collaborators.[18] Prevailing ideas of labor efficiency had been popularized both in the mass-manufacturing methods of Henry Ford with his model A car and in the writings of American researcher Frederick Winslow Taylor who propagated a theory of "scientific management," based on observing factory workers and optimizing efficiency of

FIGURE 2.3 Charlotte Posenenske, *Square Tube Series*. Courtesy of Peter Freeman, Inc., New York, and the Estate of Charlotte Posenenske, Frankfurt am Main, Germany.

output.[19] These top-down studies in which someone else told workers how to be efficient were antithetical to Posenenske's interest in, as phrased by her second husband, Burkhard Brunn, "breaking asunder the rigid standardization of factory labor."[20]

Posenenske maintained her refusal to practice art until the last year of her life. When she was dying of cancer in 1984, she and Brunn agreed that her work could be produced again. But it would be produced in open editions, meaning the work inherently did not have scarcity. She hoped this lack of scarcity would keep the works from trading in the art market. Administered by Brunn, Posenenske's estate arranges for the manufacture of works from *Vierkantrohre* or *Square Tube Series*. The work is sold at its manufacturing cost plus a small charge to cover the overhead of the estate. Enacting some of Posenenske's research on factory labor, the estate invites collectors to co-determine the configuration of their sculpture.[21] (The work is "sanctioned ... in whatever shape or form the buyer desire[s]."[22]) As Herbert writes, "Equal in 'producing' the sculptures, her 'co-authors' included collectors, promoters, steel workers, transporters, installers, and 'spiritual and financial supporters.'"[23]

The works she made in the 1960s, which do have scarcity, have become known as "prototypes." The estate only sells proto-types to public institutions, which typically have restrictions on **deaccessioning**, that is, reselling into markets.[24] As Alexis Lowry, a co-curator of Posenenske's 2019 retrospective at Dia:Beacon in New York state, noted, the early and later works are visually distinguishable because of advances in the manufacturing of gal-vanized steel.[25] The project separates out and covers the costs of production while disabling the work's ability to circulate in finan-cial markets. A new work can always be made and so an existing work is limited in its ability to gain in value by means of scarcity. In this way, the strategy of pricing to cover costs enacts what is essentially a moral view of labor.

2.2.2 *Willful Inefficiency and Technology in Artistic Production*

In traditional stories of cost structure, one generates an economic production function or model of how much it costs to produce one unit under different conditions of manufacture. For example, if pick-ing strawberries by hand costs $1 per pint and picking them with a machine costs $0.75 per pint once the cost of the machine is figured in, then economics would tell you to use a machine. A technological improvement that lowers costs is automatically adopted as econom-ically efficient. A make-or-buy decision is similar: if it is cheaper to outsource something, economics would say you should. But in the case of art, what is the value of the hand of the artist, and what are the other trade-offs in embracing outside manufacturing or new forms of efficiency?

In the arts, many forms of artistic production are willfully, even beautifully inefficient. The cost structure is not the point. The artist Lenka Clayton made a whole series of typewriter drawings (2012– ongoing) – drawings made by hand using only characters found on a 1957 Smith-Corona Skywriter to render a folded letter or a Welsh blanket or an antique Chinese pot (see Figures 2.4–2.6).[26]

FIGURE 2.4 Lenka Clayton, *Three Hundred Year Old Pot 06/02/2020*, from "Typewriter Drawings." Courtesy of the artist and Catharine Clark Gallery.

FIGURE 2.5 Lenka Clayton, *Traditional Welsh Blanket 05/03/17*, from "Typewriter Drawings." Courtesy of the artist and Catharine Clark Gallery.

An economic production function would take the work, analyze how long it took to make it, and figure out the most efficient method. However, Clayton is not making the same drawing twice, and so it is hard to know how one would plan. As with Katchadourian's and so many other artists' works, the process of discovery runs counter to a science of efficiency, and what is of value is not valuable because of its economic process engineering. The usefulness of cost structure is to ask how the artist, Clayton in this case, creates sturdy supports for her practice. How does she have the ability to sit down to the blank page in the typewriter

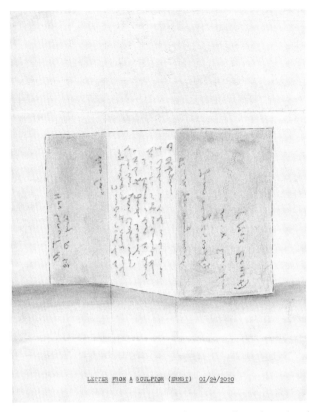

FIGURE 2.6 Lenka Clayton, *Letter from a Sculptor (Ernst) 01/24/2020*, from "Typewriter Drawings." Courtesy of the artist and Catharine Clark Gallery.

and to spend however many hours of her life in that process of discovery, exploration, and making?

Clayton is not the first artist to choose an inefficient means for an artistic reason. In the late eighteenth century, the British graphic artist and textile designer William Morris continued to make woodblock prints (see Figure 2.7), even though Thomas Bell had invented a much more efficient, cylindrical-copperplate printing technique in 1783.[27] Morris preferred the aesthetics of the more labor-intensive method. More recently, the British artist Paul Chiappe makes photorealistic drawings that are so intricate it

FIGURE 2.7 William Morris, *Tulip and Willow Printed Fabric Design*, 1873–5 (detail). Photograph by Birmingham Museums Trust, licensed under Creative Commons (CCo).

takes him six months to complete a small piece.[28] He could use available technology – for instance rephotographing his source images instead of drawing them – but drawing them laboriously is the work.

Although the idea of the production function – the high-tech strawberry-picking machine over the day laborer – does not have much place in the economics of art (and the day laborer example is not politically neutral), there are in fact some cases in which technological innovation does streamline and alter artistic practice. Cristóbal Valenzuela links two examples of this in the essay "Machine Learning in Plein Air": the invention of the paint tube, which allowed Impressionist painters to work outdoors, and the invention of some machine-learning tools, which give individuals access to technologies they might not have.

The paint tube was invented by John Goffe Rand in 1841 (Figure 2.8).[29] The paint tube spurred the movement of painting "en plein air," supporting the Impressionists' ability to travel outside to capture landscapes.[30] Where artists had previously needed to keep powdered pigments in jars and to suspend them in their own paint

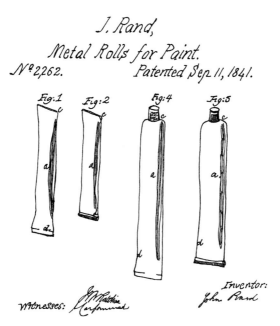

FIGURE 2.8 John Goffe Rand, drawing accompanying patent application for paint in tubes.

mediums, the paint tubes removed the need for this laborious process of drying pigments, gave artists access to a greater variety of colors, and eliminated the problems of paint drying out in open jars.[31] In an economic sense this invention did lead to greater cost efficiency – less loss of dried-up materials – and to flexibility in the "manufacture" or making of works on canvas.

Valenzuela argues that machine-learning programs such as Runway ML create access to technologies in ways that will – at the scale of the paint tube – alter contemporary art practice. As artist R. Luke Dubois has said, "Every civilization will use the maximum level of technology available to make art. And it's the responsibility of the artist to ask questions about what that technology means and how it reflects our culture."[32] These changes in technology not only create options for cheaper production; they offer new forms of creative expression and new choices about whether cheaper production enables new aesthetics or compromises them. The artist has autonomy to decide whether the technology serves the art.

2.3 TOOLS FOR ORGANIZING COST STRUCTURE: THE INCOME STATEMENT AND BREAKEVEN ANALYSIS

The purpose of labeling costs is to help make decisions about whether to produce, how much, by what technology, and within what structure of business. The fixed and variable cost distinction maps onto the accounting template of the income statement (also called a profit and loss statement or P&L).

2.3.1 *The Income Statement*

The income statement is one of three financial statements produced in accounting: the income statement, the balance sheet, and the cash flow statement. The **income statement** shows the firm's revenue, expenses, and profits over a period of time, separating the expenses into direct and overhead costs. The **balance sheet** is analogous to a statement of wealth at a point in time. By convention it shows assets in order of liquidity, meaning convertibility to cash, on the left and debt and equity on the right. The **cash flow statement** is analogous to a checking-account ledger, showing the liquid-cash position of the firm.[33] The income statement is useful because it shows us the margins, meaning the degree to which the firm has financial leeway once production, overhead, or all costs have been met. The margins show the likely sustainability of the business and the shape or type of business structure overall.

The income statement begins with revenue, which is the total inflow of money. From that, the variable costs are subtracted ("cost of goods sold" or COGS) to give a subtotal called gross margin. From there, the forms of overhead ("selling, general, and administrative" or SG&A) are taken out to give a new subtotal called operating margin. From there, details – some technical – are taken out to reflect tax, interest payments, depreciation, and one-time adjustments, giving a profit line of net income. (Depreciation is an accounting tool to

Table 2.1 *Sources of revenue for the artist*
Camille Pissarro, c.1884

Category	Price (FF)[1]	Quantity
Oil paintings	900	8
Watercolors	200	5
Pastels	150	0
Painted fans	100	15

[1] All figures are in French francs.

take an asset like a computer and reflect its use over time. It has the effect of making it seem that you rented on an annual basis an asset which was purchased every several years.) While the formal income statement used in accounting has very specific definitions of terms – beholden to international accounting rules and tax concerns – our goal here is to use the income statement in a more general way to see the structure of an organization's fixed and variable costs and its margins.

To give an example, consider a simplified version of the artist Camille Pissarro's life around 1884. We know from White and White the amount Pissarro, a Danish-French Impressionist painter, was paid for each type of artwork, and we can, for the sake of the example, suppose the number of each type of work he sold that year (see Table 2.1).[34]

According to White and White, most of the Impressionist painters spent somewhere between 500 and 2,000 francs on "color-and-canvas bills," meaning the expense of procuring supplies.[35] We can consider these supplies our main variable cost. (Even if the artist might buy the supplies in bulk and keep them in inventory, in both an economic and an accounting sense, the supplies are used up when the artist produces and are not used when the artist is idle, making them a variable cost or a cost of goods sold.) In practice, Pissarro bartered for supplies by trading paintings to the Parisian art supply store owner Père Tanguy in exchange for new paints, but for the sake

Table 2.2 *Overhead expenses of the artist Camille Pissarro, c.1884*

Category	Overhead (SG&A)[1] Monthly	Annual
Rent		1,000
Groceries	200	2,400
Wine	282	3,384
Train tickets	10	120
Impressionist dinners	26	312
Housekeeper		400

[1] All figures are in French francs.

of the example, we can presume that Pissarro spent 1,500 francs on supplies and a further 500 francs on framing the works that were sold.

Pissarro's overhead is the cost of his family life. With six children, these costs were not insubstantial. White and White also make the point that the Impressionists lived by a more bourgeois rather than bohemian lifestyle, for instance having a housekeeper.[36] In one month in 1883, the Pissarros seem to have spent 200 francs on groceries and 282 francs on wine. We can use those figures along with White and White's estimate that Pissarro would have traveled to Paris for Thursday suppers with other Impressionist painters. We can make the working assumption that those suppers were biweekly and then use White and White's data that the train ticket cost 5 francs and the dinner cost 13 to 15 francs, modeling it in Table 2.2.[37]

We can now place these numbers into the format of a simplified income statement (see Table 2.3).

As we can see in the income statement, Pissarro's economic stability was precarious, even this far into his career. In fact, he struggled with debt and needed to pay creditors along the way. Even if we modified these assumptions – taking out expenses for supplies gained by barter – we can see from the margins that Pissarro does not have a lot of leeway. In this example, if he had failed to sell just one of

Table 2.3 *Pro forma income statement for the artist Camille Pissarro, c.1884.*[1]

Income statement, 1884 (FF)[2]	
Revenue	
Oil paintings	7,200
Watercolors	1,000
Painted fans	1,500
Total revenue	**9,700**
Cost of goods sold	
Supplies	1,500
Framing	500
Total COGS	**2,000**
Gross revenue	**7,700**
Gross margin	79%
Selling, general, and administrative	
Rent	1,000
Groceries	2,400
Wine	3,384
Train tickets	120
Impressionist dinners	312
Housekeeper	400
Total SG&A	**7,616**
Operating revenue	84
Operating margin	1%
Net income	84
Profit margin	1%

[1] "Pro forma," meaning "for the sake of form" in Latin, is used to describe income statements that are formalities projected forward rather than detailed snapshots past of accounting. They are used most often in business plans, including for museums, to show the mechanics of an institution that has not yet been founded. Here, I use the term because we do not have full information on Pissarro's life.

[2] All figures are in French francs.

the painted fans, he would have run a loss. Of course, this analysis is limited; surely the family had other expenses not included here, and the artist may have sold many more works. What the income statement can do is to organize the shape of the overall operation. This shape is best seen in the margins. Each margin is a ratio taken against total revenue. Gross margin is the ratio of gross revenue to total revenue. It includes cost of goods sold (our proxy for variable cost). Operating margin is the ratio of operating revenue to total revenue. It includes the selling, general, and administrative expense (our proxy for fixed cost). The profit margin is the ratio of net income to total revenue. These margins allow for helpful comparison across comparable operations.

Income statements take different shapes in different parts of the arts. These shapes vary substantially for fixed-cost-intensive galleries, museums, and auction houses and for more variable-cost-intensive forms of artistic production. The relative relationship of fixed and variable cost to revenue paints a picture of risk. Does the business have very narrow margins the way that a restaurant might? Does the business mostly have fixed cost but need to operate at a large scale in order to make enough money? The income statement can help us start to see these patterns of business model and risk (see Figure 2.9).

2.3.2 The Breakeven Point

A breakeven analysis can get at the same connections of cost structure that an income statement does. Instead of focusing on margins, it solves for the quantity or scale of production. In a breakeven analysis, one starts with the overhead of a project or organization. The analysis serves to identify the **breakeven point,** which is the quantity at which the operation is able to cover all fixed costs and starts to turn a profit. The way of calculating the breakeven point is to quantify all of the fixed costs and then to identify the variable cost *per unit.* Breakeven analysis is based on the **unit contribution**, which is the amount of money contributed toward covering fixed cost each time a unit is sold,

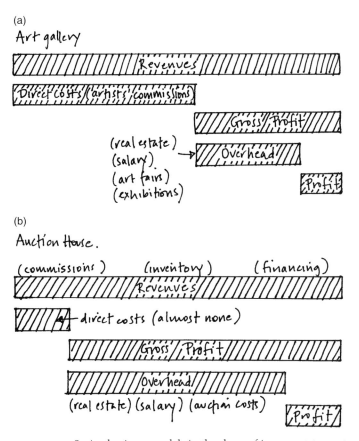

(a)

Art gallery

Revenues

Direct costs (artists' commissions)

Gross profit

(real estate)
(salary)
(art fairs)
(exhibitions) → Overhead

Profit

(b)

Auction House.

(commissions) (inventory) (financing)
Revenues

direct costs (almost none)

Gross Profit

Overhead

(real estate) (salary) (auction costs)

Profit

FIGURE 2.9 Seeing business models in the shape of income statements.

defined as the price minus the unit variable cost. The general equation for breakeven is the total fixed cost divided by the unit contribution.

For example, suppose that each individual Mine Kafon costs $50 in materials. We use this amount as the variable cost per unit. Suppose that the Hassani brothers rent a studio for two months paying $10,000 total in overhead. If the price for one Mine Kafon is $120, then the unit contribution – the price ($120) minus the unit variable cost ($50) – is $70. Each time one Mine Kafon is sold, the brothers have $70 to contribute toward covering overhead. If the overhead is $10,000, what is the breakeven point? To solve for the breakeven point, we divide the total fixed cost ($10,000) by the unit contribution ($70) and arrive at an answer of 142.86. This number is in units of output – meaning quantity of Mine Kafons sold. Breakeven is always rounded up. We still lose money at 142 units, and we cannot sell partial units. Thus, we break even at 143 Mine Kafons sold.

One way of picturing breakeven visually is to imagine that the fixed cost is a wall with the height, in this case, of $10,000. We then imagine that the unit contribution is a brick with the height of $70. The equation tells us how many bricks we would need to stack in order to clear the height of the wall. Any bricks above the wall would represent profit. If we had not included the Hassani brothers' time fully in the overhead, we would make other adjustments or know that we needed to pay them out of the profits (see Figure 2.10).

Although breakeven is designed best for uniform objects – all Mine Kafons the same – it can be readily adapted to encompass grants and donations. Let's say Massoud had received a $5,000 grant from the Dutch government. He could imagine that grant as a large brick that gives him a leg up on clearing the $10,000 wall. Now his remaining fixed cost is only $5,000. Thus, his breakeven point is $5,000/$70 or 72 units (rounded from 71.43). See the end-of-chapter questions for more analysis of Mine Kafon.

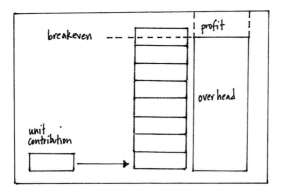

FIGURE 2.10 Breakeven calculation as "bricks" of unit contribution.

The key idea of breakeven analysis is the role of marginality. One does not have to seek maximum profit, but one does have to clear the wall of the overhead. The key to this sustainability is market size. If a project breaks even at one million units but only 10,000 people work in the field, then the market size is problematic.

2.4 THE CROSS-SUBSIDY

Many projects and organizations cannot meet a breakeven calculus and would run a loss. Some of these entities are legally structured as nonprofit organizations allowing them to receive grant funding or government support in different jurisdictions. Other entities – for-profit or nonprofit – engage in what is called cross-subsidization. A **cross-subsidy** is an amount of income from one area that is used to support another. For example, a museum with a blockbuster show can use ticket revenue from that exhibition to support smaller, riskier shows. An artist can support having a studio by teaching. As Xavier Greffe writes in *Art and Artists from an Economic Perspective*:

> No matter what country they live in, artists are forced to look for alternative or supplementary sources of income through non-artistic activities, as their principal income is inadequate to satisfy their basic needs.[38]

Greffe is describing a cross-subsidy.

A gallery employs a cross-subsidy when it supports ephemeral or unsalable art by selling documentation of the work or salable objects by other artists within the gallery roster.[39] A gallery could also produce a non-selling academic exhibition and cross-subsidize the costs of mounting the show by making related private sales. Some of these strategies may not be politically neutral, or they could have substantially different impact for individual artists on a gallery's roster. For instance, as Camila Nichols argues, the work of a well-known artist could cross-subsidize the work of an anti-market artist. And possibly, the fact that the gallery represents an anti-market artist might actually drive the gallery's overall sales by presenting an art-focused ethos. Paradoxically, the anti-market artist could serve a marketing function. The two artists would receive very different sales proceeds from this strategy.

In a museum, the idea of a blockbuster show cross-subsidizing a scholarly show reinforces the idea that exhibitions with broad appeal are automatically less rigorous. The Hilma af Klint exhibition at the Guggenheim Museum in 2018 provides a counterexample. An exhibition of paintings by a Swedish artist – who died in 1944 and stipulated that a large body of her work not be seen until twenty years after her death – drew record-breaking attendance.[40] That is to say, the cross-subsidy is not always predictable.

One last category of cross-subsidy that bears particular mention is the role of family wealth or income in the history of art. This subsidy is not politically neutral in its function as a barrier to inclusion, but it is important to acknowledge for our purposes in studying structural economics. Some stories are better known. For instance, Leo Castelli, who started his eponymous gallery on the Upper East Side of Manhattan in 1958, had the advantages of having married into a wealthy family and having hosted his first exhibitions in a family-owned townhouse. (Ileana Sonnabend, Castelli's first wife who later remarried, also happened to have a brilliant art-historical eye and would also go on to found her own gallery.) Yet even Castelli – later in his career when he had opened rented gallery spaces downtown – would face the breakeven moment of not being able to make rent and needing to call a collector to buy something.[41]

Johannes Vermeer, whose paintings are among the most valuable in the world, was, according to his biographer, John Michael Montias, "not poor by the standards of his day."[42] But Vermeer had eleven children, lending substantial overhead expense to the income statement of his life. Vermeer received substantial family support, including a bequest when his sister Gertruy died in 1671 as well as some rental income from a family-owned property. He likely also received some further subsidy from his mother-in-law. Montias argues that it was only these subsidies that allowed the artist to stay

in Delft after many of his fellow guild members had to relocate. As
Montias writes:

> The financial independence Vermeer enjoyed, partial and
> precarious as it was, gave him a greater opportunity to follow his
> own artistic inclinations than most of his fellow members of the
> guild, who had to adapt their art to suit market demand. He could
> also paint fewer pictures than he might have had to if he had been
> forced to support his family exclusively from his art.[43]

Vermeer's earnings also fluctuated substantially, and his sales
declined precipitously in the 1670s, at least in part owing to a war
with France.[44] Even with family support, when Vermeer died, he was
in debt. One of the most striking debts at the time of his death was to
his baker for an amount of money equivalent to the cost of
8,000 pounds (3,600 kilograms) of bread. Montias estimates that
amount to have been two-to-three years' worth of bread delivery.[45]
To put the bread debt – totaling 726 guilders – in context, it is larger
than the proceeds from the sale of three major works that took place in
1696, twenty years after Vermeer's death.[46] In that sale, *Young Lady
Weighing Gold (Woman Holding a Balance)* sold for 155 guilders,
Maid Pouring Milk (The Milkmaid) for 175 guilders, and *The City of
Delft in Perspective (The View from Delft)* for 200 guilders.[47]

This story underscores the differential between the economics
of breaking even while working as an artist and the later investment
returns to collectors of the work. Although it is hard to know investment returns for Vermeer paintings given that most of the artist's
known works are now in museum collections, the most recent
Vermeer to sell at auction was *A Young Woman Seated at the
Virginal c.*1670, which, even after a lengthy process of attribution to
Vermeer, was sold via Sotheby's London in 2004 for £16,245,600, then
equivalent to $30 million. The painting in question is only 8 × 10 inches
(20 x 25 cm). This archetypal story of artists – the difficulty, even with
family privilege of breaking even in the artist's lifetime – will also
surface in Chapter 9 when we discuss investment.[48]

2.5   ECONOMIES OF SCALE AND SCOPE

The last piece of cost structure is the role of economies of scale and scope. An **economy of scale** is an advantage conferred by doing something in bulk. An economy of scale occurs when the per unit cost goes down as quantity produced goes up. An **economy of scope** is an advantage conferred by doing something with breadth. An economy of scope occurs via joint production.[49] A factory that produces many pairs of blue jeans has an economy of scale. The legal department of a university that can help the biology department as well as the athletic department has an economy of scope. The photography department or the shipping department of an auction house also has an economy of scope – the ability to provide a service across a range of artworks of many sizes, shapes, genres, and periods (see Figure 2.11).

Where an economy of scale represents depth – doing one thing over and over again, at a lower and lower unit cost – an economy of scope represents range – having a department that can serve a wide variety of functions. Arts organizations are more likely to experience economies of scope than scale, owing to the unlikelihood of producing standardized units en masse.

Consider the difference in scale between a Leonardo da Vinci painting and an installation by Japanese collective teamLab, a group of architects, mathematicians, and other designers who build immersive

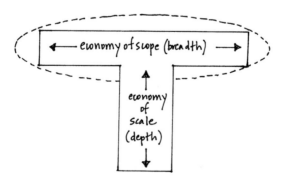

FIGURE 2.11 Depth and breadth in economies of scale and scope.[50]

installations.[51] The Leonardo painting is difficult to scale. Once it is made, it is still a singular work. It can be placed on a mug or a t-shirt, but it cannot be made in bulk in the same way that Uniqlo fleece jackets can be.[52] In contrast, the teamLab installations at Pace Gallery do have some dimension of scale, as well as scope. Once the project is developed, it can be extended to be experienced by many people at the same time. A digital installation could theoretically be replicated in hundreds of buildings all over the world with some adaptation to the new spaces. The collective also enjoys economies of scope in its ability to apply knowledge, skill, and previous programming to new projects. In 2018, when Pace Gallery installed the teamLab works in three Pace locations over fourteen months, they sold upwards of one million tickets, at $20 each.[53] Thus, this strategy can generate revenue as well.

Consider how economies of scope apply to the phenomenon of the mega-gallery.[54] The largest galleries in the world have multiple locations in numerous countries and also have extended themselves into a variety of related areas. At the time of writing, the Gagosian Gallery has nineteen locations worldwide. The press department within the gallery has an economy of scope in serving multiple locations. The same department can write press releases and liaise with journalists for the whole gamut of gallery exhibitions. The gallery can stagger these openings so that the department works consistently at a relatively full staff utilization. The fact that an artist represented by Gagosian has a worldwide audience functions as an economy of scale – allowing access to the work across locations. Although the fact artworks are often original objects complicates a pure scale economy, one can imagine Damien Hirst's dot painting event across Gagosian locations in 2012 as constituting an impressive economy of scale and scope.[55]

Art fairs also exhibit these economies of scope through global franchise operation. For example, 1–54, the contemporary African art fair, operates not only in London and New York but in Marrakech.[56] Art Basel operates not only in Basel, Switzerland, but in Miami Beach,

Florida, and in Hong Kong.[57] These companies spread expertise in managing art fairs – and expand the reach and recognition of their brands – across multiple locations. Because the fairs happen at different times of year, the company also smooths the usage of its overhead, with staff being able to shift between fairs seasonally – while also maintaining a roster of dedicated staff for each location.

2.6 CONCLUSIONS

Cost structure is the engineering of economics. The structural relationship of fixed and variable cost determines the *species* of business model. The presence of scale or scope and the sensitivity of the margins tell us if the business is sustainable. Often the difference between sustainable and precarious is a narrow margin. Even a canonized artists such as Vermeer can fall into bread debt. Many others still face profound economic precariousness or are excluded from becoming artists altogether.

These strategic and structural economics coexist with human stories, even in the upper echelons of the art market. In his recent book *Boom*, Michael Shnayerson writes about the gallerist Larry Gagosian's relationship with the artist Cy Twombly. A Twombly would sell for $5 million, meaning a single show could pay for the renovation and opening of a new gallery location.[58] At the same time, Gagosian and Twombly, the people, had a real relationship. When Gagosian visited Twombly in his US home, they "indulged in their favorite Virginia pastime: going to Walmart." Gagosian said, "We would wander up and down the aisles for a couple of hours. [Twombly] just liked looking at the stuff. It was a kind of Zen thing. And Walmarts in these rural areas are almost like civic centers, people come and congregate."[59] The tools of cost structure enable business modeling and sustainability. And the questions of overhead, production cost, and opportunity cost serve human decisions about values, priorities, and investment – in aisle-strolling with artists or the production of art.

QUESTIONS

1. What is the key difference between a fixed cost and a variable cost?
2. Compare the cost structure of a large encyclopedic museum to that of an artist's studio. What patterns do you notice?
3. Define scale and scope in your own words and think of as many examples of each as you can.
4. Almost any work of art, however anti-market or ephemeral, has a cost of production in the economic sense. As a thought experiment, can you think of an artwork that has zero cost of production? Or, what art projects come to mind that are unusually resourceful? For instance, John Cage's *4'33"* sonata consists of the ambient sound that occurs during that time period. Even that work requires the resources of a timekeeping device and the mental energy to record it. Jenny Odell made a piece while an artist in residence at Facebook that entailed taking objects contributed by Facebook employees, researching and archiving them, and returning the archival record to the employee. The main implicit cost of this project was the artist's time and the use of office space and supplies. (Odell is the author of *How to Do Nothing*, which she argues convincingly is a vital and important form of doing something.[60])
5. Little–big: Find two businesses that do the same thing but at different scales – a grocery store and a fruit stand, for instance. How are the businesses alike and how are they different? Can you imagine their cost structures and compare them? Can you apply concepts of scale and scope?
6. The cake project (with thanks to Hugh Musick): Divide into teams of roughly four people. Each team must make and sell a cake. (You can choose to define "cake," for example, gluten-free snacks, cookies. You can also have everyone bring in a recipe and trade recipes.) Each team must sell the cake and try to make a profit. The hitch is that the team can only spend $1. They must find an investor and try to return a 15% profit to the investor. (For instance, if the investor gave them $10, they would want to return

at least $11.50, or the principal plus 15%.) Have teams present their projects to the class. How did they account for costs? Was it per-unit or as an overall income statement? How did the idea of marginality come up? Did they almost make a profit or, conversely, make an enormous profit? Did any teams come up with creative solutions to the problem? Past teams have, for instance, found an "investor" by crowdsourcing a "Cakestarter" by wearing a sandwich board in a train station and offering to make caricatures of passersby in exchange for money, in order to get capital. Another team, cheerfully yet darkly, offered to teach after-school design classes to children and then used the children's drawings as their packaging. Discuss ways this assignment bridges thinking about resources (as in Nina Katchadourian's work) and thinking about costs (both explicit and opportunity costs).

7. To practice the income statement format, choose an art gallery – large or small. Based on available public information, sleuthing, and inference, build a working financial model for the gallery. You can focus on the gallery overall for a time period, for example, a year, or choose a specific project such as an exhibition or a trip to an art fair. Estimate the gallery's gross margin and operating margin and compare these numbers to the margins discovered by peers studying other galleries. Compare the gallery to benchmarks in the field, for example, using data from Clare McAndrew's annual *Art Market Report* published in partnership with Art Basel. This project can double as an Excel primer and an opportunity to build a "spreadsheet bank," sharing financial models with each other. Alternatively, students can study nonprofit organizations and, for US nonprofits, use Form 990 tax returns.

8. The artist's studio P&L: Choose any artist you are interested in and try to model their studio costs of production. Write a 1–2 page memo on how the idea of efficiency or inefficiency does or does not apply to their work. To use this question for class discussion, consider the artist Lenka Clayton as a case study. How do her "Typewriter Drawings" relate to the notion of efficiency? How

would you map out the cost structure of other projects of hers such as *Local Newspaper* and *Unanswered Letter?*[61] For *Local Newspaper*, the artist took a small-circulation newspaper from Hamburg, Germany, and tracked down all 312 individual people mentioned by name in a single issue. For *Unanswered Letter*, Clayton discovered a letter sent in 1978 to Anne d'Harnoncourt, then curator and later director of the Philadelphia Museum of Art, asking why Brancusi's *Sculpture for the Blind* was more valuable than an artwork the letter writer's great-grandfather had made. The letter writer, a man named Brian H. Morgan, never received a reply. In 2017, Clayton sent a copy of the letter to 1,000 curators, museum directors, and other arts professionals. She exhibited and published the 179 responses. What are the explicit and resource costs of these projects?

9. Both Lenka Clayton and Mierle Laderman Ukeles, who is discussed in Chapter 7, have made art in response to motherhood. Clayton created *An Artist Residency in Motherhood*, making work about her child.[62] Ukeles created *Maintenance Art*, elevating the mundane to the level of art. Compare and contrast the two approaches and consider the cost structure of each. Feel free to include in the discussion the work of other artists concerned with time and resources, for instance, Tehching Hsieh's *Time Clock Piece (One-Year Performance 1980–1981)*, in which the artist clocked in and out of the studio, punching a time clock every hour for a year.[63]

10. Mine Kafon problem set: Look at the original Mine Kafon Kickstarter campaign, which raised £119,456 (against a £100,000 goal) from 4,169 backers. (www.kickstarter.com/projects/massoud hassani/mine-kafon). Create an income statement for the Kickstarter campaign itself. For each reward level, estimate the cost of producing that reward, note the quantity of rewards, and use that quantity to determine revenue and cost of goods sold. For instance, the £12 reward is a PDF of a ferfrak (wind toy) with an instructional video. Suppose it cost Massoud £200 in time to make these resources, but once made they have no variable cost. There

are forty-one backers at this level. Thus, revenue is 41 × £12. Cost is £200. Variable cost is zero. However, in the case of the prize with a hand-cut ferfrak, you would need to estimate their time. In Part A, build the income statement. In Part B, advise Massoud on how to streamline production and on which prizes are most popular and/or cost effective. What would be your recommendations for future Kickstarter campaigns and why? After you make your recommendations, look at the webpage for Mine Kafon's subsequent Kickstarter campaign for a Mine Kafon drone.

11. Costs of producing an unusual artwork: Choose an unusual artwork – whether social practice or large-scale sculpture. What did it cost for the artist to make the work? Structure the costs into an imagined income statement. Then, in addition, consider all of the opportunity costs or other implicit costs, whether of time or in-kind use of resources. If you would like inspiration or a starting point, consider Argentinian artist Marta Minujín's *The Parthenon of Books*, a large replica of the Parthenon made out of plastic, steel scaffolding, and 100,000 banned books, in Kassel, Germany, as part of the art exhibition documenta 14.[64] The work was first created in 1983, marking Argentina's fallen military dictatorship by erecting a monument with 25,000 books banned by the dictatorship. When the work was recreated in 2017, it was made, in the words of scholar-critic Andrew Stefan Weiner, "under conditions in which the industrial-scale manufacture of 'fake news' poses much more of a threat than censorship does."[65] The site in Kassel was where, in 1933, the Nazis burned 2,000 books. For the recreation at documenta 14, a group of students from Kassel University worked to identify more than 150 books that had been banned in various countries around the world. How would the artist have covered the costs of making the work? For other examples, consider various works by the artist Michael Mandiberg, such as *FDIC Insured*, an archive of the logos of failed US banks, exhibited with the logos burned, using a laser cutter, onto the covers of remaindered library books on investment topics.[66] You can also consider the cost

structure of Mandiberg's other works, such as printing 106 of the 7,473 volumes of all of Wikipedia in book form *(Print Wikipedia)* or *Postmodern Times* (2016–18) in which he hired freelancers on the app Fiverr.com (where all work costs $5) to recreate scenes from the Charlie Chaplin film *Modern Times* as "'stories of industry' for the digital age."[67]

12. Milton Friedman, quilter (practice cost-structure fictional case study): It is a little-known fact that, after his retirement as a noted free-market economist, Milton Friedman took up crafting as a hobby. A pioneer of the "upcycling movement," he bought old men's suits and ties from charity shops and fastidiously turned them into quilts. Working under the assumed brand name Free Market Love Quilts, his work gained popularity, spanning an unusual cross-section of the nostalgic, suburban, *Mad Men*-loving set and stalwarts of the maker movement. He had to make a decision about scaling up his business and took some time to model his financials to help him evaluate his choices.

   Milton currently does everything himself. He goes to the local Goodwill store each month and purchases ten suits and thirty-five ties. The suits cost $10–$25, on average $15. The ties cost $2–$10, on average $3. He then sets to work sewing at home. His other materials – thread, backing, cotton batting – cost him $55 per month. He works very consistently, producing five whole quilts each month. He sells them directly over his website for $900 each. His nephew manages the website for $100 per month, and Milton pays an additional $10 each month for hosting and $25 each month for his online sales platform.

   Demand has surged after an article in *The Brooklyn Rail,* and he is faced with a decision. His inner hobbyist wants to keep producing himself, scale be ignored. His inner free-market economist feels he should hold up his half of the bargain – providing enough supply to meet demand. To do this, he would need to hire other workers. And those workers aren't cheap. Milton has three neighbors, Rosa, Esther, and Frank, who are retired dressmakers and tailors. If he pays them $30 an hour, they will work for him forty hours each week making quilts. Rosa can make a quilt in thirty hours. Esther can make one in twenty hours, and Frank can make one in twenty-five hours. They would use Milton's garage, for which he refuses to charge rent in either scenario.

What are his new production economics if all four of them can make quilts, Milton included? How many will they now make each month? How much will it cost to make each quilt? If you were Milton would you hire other workers? Why or why not?

3 Price

One of the greatest attributes we assign to a cultural good is to describe it as "priceless". Yet many gallery aficionados can confirm that such "priceless" works usually do have a price, albeit a high one.

Thomas M. Bayer and John R. Page[1]

In Bayer and Page's book *The Development of the Art Market in England*, the authors wanted to compare the prices of different paintings, and so they constructed a metric: price per area. They use the square inch (6.45 square centimeters) as their reference. What did they find? They found that the artist Edward Burne-Jones saw the price per square inch for his works decline from £1.04 per square inch to £0.50 from 1897 to 1910. In contrast, the price for a work by James McNeill Whistler increased from £0.60 per square inch to £1.90 per square inch over the same period.[2] What does a number like that tell us? It helps us understand the past but not plan or price for the future.

The story of pricing artworks is often complicated, opaque, and unpredictable. The sociologist Olav Velthuis, whom we encountered in the Introduction, has studied how artworks are priced. In what became his 2005 book *Talking Prices*, Velthuis engaged in an ethnographic study. In the book's opening pages, Velthuis recounts a visit to a dealer. When Velthuis questioned the dealer about pricing, his inquiries were met with a wall of rhetorical resistance. Velthuis did not interpret the dealer's deflection as "anxiety to disclose business secrets" but as the appearance of "a sheer disinterest in prices."[3] Yet after the interview, something curious happened. The dealer invited Velthuis into his home. Velthuis turned off his recording device and accepted a glass of wine. While giving Velthuis a tour of his personal art collection, the dealer changed how he spoke about art:

> The same dealer who had so carefully avoided invoking mundane interests before, turned out to remember precisely how much he had paid for the works in his collection in the past, and was also up to date about their present price level. Moreover, he eagerly and proudly emphasized that the current market value of his collection surpassed the past acquisition prices dramatically.[4]

Velthuis concluded that prices had a symbolic function well beyond their economic explanation. The pricing of art, while still mysterious to most people, even those who practice it, could be understood within social customs and "scripts" or stories. In these scripts, prices were presented in context of other prices for art. Stories of the artist – honorable, superstar, prudent – cast the prices in a narrative arc.[5] Dealers spoke not about money but about people and about art.

The complexity of art pricing often derives from the lack of definable value. As we will cover in Chapter 9, artworks cannot be valued by the traditional tools of finance because they do not have cash flows. As Aswath Damodaran, finance professor and corporate valuation expert, states, it is not possible to *value* a painting, only to price it.[6] Pricing art is further difficult in that art is both a consumption good and an investment good, meaning that it can be lived with and enjoyed but also treated as an asset.

In this chapter, we will – in spite of art's slipperiness and pricing mystery – consider how people price art and other goods such as museum tickets. We will look at both the *level* of price and the *structure* of pricing strategy. We will see how people respond to price – whether by consuming less, willingly paying more, or changing habits to consume more cheaply in different ways. We begin with price elasticity, a measure of sensitivity to changing price, and then shift to price discrimination, arguably the worst-named yet most compelling strategy on offer both to raise revenue for arts organizations and to include wider audiences.

While these tools help inform how we think about tastes and trade-offs and also how we strategize what and how to price, we still may be left in the same place as Velthuis, figuratively or literally, holding a glass of white wine while someone who remembers purchase prices in actuarial detail also waxes poetic on the transcendental value of art.

3.1   PRICE ELASTICITY

In 2007, Maxwell Anderson, the former director of the Whitney Museum of American Art, arrived in Indiana to become director of the Indianapolis Museum of Art. He dropped the museum's $7 general admissions fee all the way to zero, making the permanent collection of the museum free, though visitors still paid for parking and special exhibitions. Within a year, the museum's attendance, as it was measured at the time, rose from 185,000 to 462,000 people. Three years later, in 2010, Anderson oversaw the opening of a long-planned 100-acre art park. The park (formally the Virginia B. Fairbanks Art & Nature Park: 100 Acres), the museum, and various historically donated houses and gardens together began to operate under the name Newfields.

In 2014, under the leadership of Anderson's successor, the museum started charging a general admissions fee again. Visitors started to pay $18, which included parking and exhibitions.[7] The museum cited financial need relative to endowment spending. The museum had substantial debt obligations from building projects that dated to before Anderson's tenure. The 2008 financial crisis had also hurt the museum's endowment.

At issue in the decision of whether and what to charge for museum entry is a philosophical as well as economic question of museum ticket prices. On the one hand, ticket sales generate revenue. Beyond its function to fund the museum, the revenue can signal, sometimes to a museum's own board and staff, a sense of its own worth. On the other, ticket prices can exclude audiences, and this exclusion is harder to measure.

From an economic standpoint, the change in ticket price at the Indianapolis Museum of Art is a story of how sensitive consumers are to a change in price. When the price of museum admission dropped, customers noticed and changed their behavior. But was that change proportionate to the change in price? The measure of this sensitivity to a change in price is the **price elasticity of demand.** Price elasticity measures the percentage change in quantity demanded given a percentage change in price. (For more detailed treatment of the calculation, see Appendix C.)

Elasticity is synonymous with sensitivity. If consumers were insensitive to price, a store could generate revenue by raising the price of bottled water slightly and people would still buy it. For a life-saving medication, people tend to be insensitive to price as far as they can be, a factor that is widely debated in health-care policy and the ethics of pharmaceuticals pricing.

If we look at the Indianapolis numbers, it appears that attendance has skyrocketed, more than doubling. But if we look at the change in price it is even more dramatic. The price to see the permanent collection has gone from $7 to zero (ignoring momentarily the other pieces of the ticket structure, such as temporary exhibitions). Even though the attendance numbers look dramatic, visitors to the museum actually appear to be insensitive to price. If the ticket price had been discounted by $1, from $7 to $6, there may not have been a big change in visitor behavior. In calculating the price elasticity (see Appendix C), we find that the price elasticity of demand is 0.42. If elasticity is less than one, consumers are said to be **price inelastic**, or insensitive to a change in price. If elasticity is greater than one, consumers are said to be **price elastic**, or sensitive to a change in price. If elasticity is exactly one, consumers are said to be **unit elastic**, meaning that their sensitivity to a change in price is exactly proportionate (see Figure 3.1).

The price elasticity of demand essentially tracks the slope of the demand curve, though the calculation will yield different results at different points along the curve (see Figures 3.2–3.3). If the slope of the

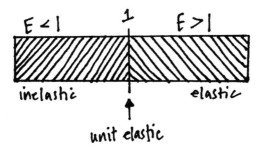

FIGURE 3.1 Elastic, inelastic, and unit elastic.

demand curve is steep, demand is more inelastic – a greater move along the price axis relative to the quantity axis. If the demand curve is more horizontal, there is proportionately more change in quantity relative to change in price. (To remember these features heuristically, you can think of the middle bar of the "E" for "elastic" in shape of the flatter curve. When demand is inelastic, the demand curve looks more vertical like the "I" in "inelastic.") By convention, price elasticity of demand is always expressed as a positive number, even though mathematically the calculation yields a negative number, owing to the downward-sloping demand curve. (See Appendix A for a review of the slope of a line.)

The Indianapolis case is not quite as straightforward for a reason that is common in the arts: reliability of data. The measures of attendance varied over time. In 2005 and 2006, the museum was undergoing renovation, depressing typical visitor numbers.[8] Thus the starting figure – 185,0000 – was lower than the recorded long-term average of 350,000 visitors annually. Our *ceteris paribus* assumption – all things being equal – does not hold. Second, after the renovation, the heat-sensitive counters that museums commonly use counted staff as well as museum visitors. Either change could intensify the effect, meaning that the drop in admissions charge had even less effect on attendance. After the return to an admissions charge – and a restructuring to go from a $7 to an $18 ticket – the reported visitor numbers stayed roughly the same, but the count changed to include visitors to the

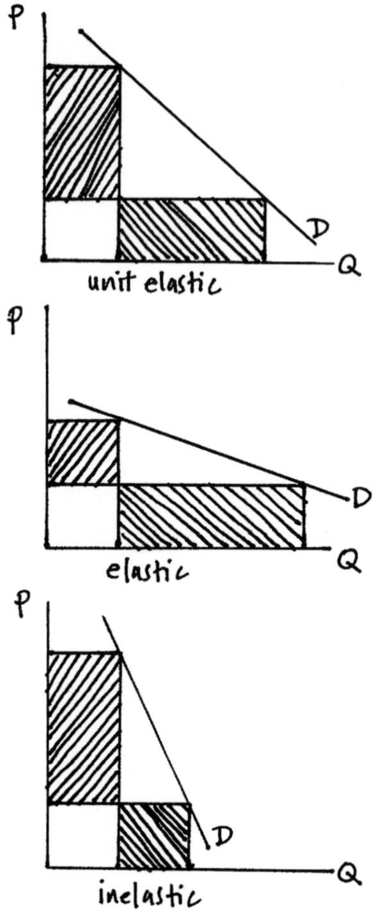

FIGURE 3.2 Elastic and inelastic slope in demand.

grounds and to Winterlights, a seasonal display of lights throughout the Newfields grounds.[9]

In any of these cases, what we see is that museumgoers are price insensitive and that decisions around ticket pricing are political as well as economic. Economically, visitors will not change their behavior if the price is dropped by a dollar. It may take dropping the price all the way to free to have an impact on attendance. The ticket revenue is arguably critical to the museum. As Michael Rushton, pricing

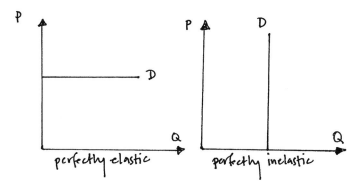

FIGURE 3.3 Perfectly elastic and perfectly inelastic demand.

expert and professor at Indiana University, told the local newspaper at the time, "The money has to come from somewhere. A museum needs funds to operate. It has to have different sources."[10] Others would argue that free admission is not only mission-critical in reaching more inclusive audiences but that it more than pays for itself in generating audience metrics that, in turn, support successful grant applications – often for sums of money larger than what would have been earned at the gate.

In the arts, price elasticity can be useful in a number of ways. In a commercial setting such as an art fair, where a dealer has one object to sell, elasticity can guide whether to drop the price slightly to sell the piece at all. In a nonprofit setting such as a museum, an analysis of price elasticity can help the institution further its mission to reach many people. If making an admissions ticket free helps a museum to bring in more visitors and a wider array of visitors, then the museum can focus on making itself free for those who would not attend otherwise. Bringing in larger audiences can also help the revenue of a museum in indirect ways. An increase in attendance is its own metric, one that may help the museum to demonstrate its reach, bringing the institution far more holistic funding opportunities than the ticket revenue could. Lastly, price elasticity can be used for revenue generation in hybrid or charity settings. For instance, the Danish-

Icelandic artist Olafur Eliasson created Little Sun, a solar lamp shaped like a cheerful flat yellow sun that he sold in arts institutions in the United States and Europe in order to subsidize their sale in parts of the developing world. It would help Eliasson to know the price elasticity of people shopping for Little Suns in the MoMA Design Store because maximizing his revenue there supports him to realize his mission of sharing solar lamps with people in other parts of the world.[11]

The traditional use of elasticity is to maximize revenue. If customers are price sensitive, then dropping price can cause an increase in total revenue. If customers are unit elastic, revenue stays the same. And if customers are price insensitive, then dropping the price does not lead to a proportionate increase in purchasing and so revenue goes down. Here, if the goal is revenue generation, there are other strategies. For instance, the museum can charge a variety of price points. This strategy is called price discrimination.

3.2   PRICE DISCRIMINATION

In actual fact, the Indianapolis Museum of Art was not entirely free. It was free to see the permanent collection, but there was an extra ticket for special exhibitions. Most museums do not have single prices or only one structure of price. An adult entry ticket to the Musée du Louvre currently costs €17, but admission is free for people under eighteen, people between eighteen and twenty-five who live in the European Economic Area (the European Union, Norway, Iceland, and Liechtenstein), art teachers, schoolteachers holding a "Pass Education" card, various members of associations for artists and museum professionals, visitors with disabilities and their caregivers, and job seekers or others on income support. Members of the Louvre also receive free admission if they have paid €80 for one adult or €15 for one youth card.[12] Tourists pay the sticker price of €17 online in advance or €15 at the door. (The €15 ticket has the added cost of waiting in line.)

Those with significantly higher "consumer surplus" over the €17 ticket, and with a desire to support and be affiliated with the Louvre, can join the Patron's Circle, which costs €2,000 for members under thirty-five years of age or €3,000 to €5,000 for patron levels above that. Granted philanthropy and museum access can be viewed by some observers as distinct products, in a broad sense this continuum from paid ticket to donor support uncovers a greater spectrum of willingness to pay. This patron level is not only a ticket to the museum but a transformed, related product – what we will shortly call a versioned good – that includes "privileged encounters with key players at the museum" and other benefits.[13]

Forms of charging different prices for the same good – and charging different prices for closely related goods – fall under the umbrella of **price discrimination.** Price discrimination requires the ability to segment customers, either through self-selection or external marker, in order to charge them different prices. It also requires safeguards to prevent resale of the cheaper product to another segment. This possibility of resale is sometimes described, perhaps jarringly, as a form of "cannibalizing" sales at a higher price.

In this section, we will look at price discrimination in two regards: charging different prices and creating pricing structures, such as versioning and bundling, that allow people to vote their personal willingness to pay. Although price discrimination is traditionally taught as a revenue-maximization strategy, it can be used in the nonprofit fields to increase access and audience inclusion or to increase revenue to support mission. By the end of this section, you hopefully will begin to form your own politics of the trade-offs – and sometimes creative responses – between free access and sustainability of organizations.

Price discrimination – charging different prices for the same or related goods – is categorized as first-degree, second-degree, and third-degree price discrimination.[14] Many pricing strategies in the real world combine aspects of each. **First-degree price discrimination** is the ability to charge each customer their individual willingness to pay. **Second-degree price discrimination** is based on offering customers a set of options and letting them select into the one, or ones, they want. **Third-degree price discrimination** involves segmenting the audience based on a signal or external categorization, for instance, a student discount. All forms of price discrimination require market power, meaning the ability to set price. We will discuss this power in Chapter 5.

First-degree price discrimination requires strong information (theoretically, perfect information) about the customer's willingness to pay.[15] Sometimes first-degree price discrimination is done imperfectly by relying on the customer to reveal their own price. For instance, financial aid for university education is an example of first-degree price discrimination. The university or government requires disclosure of financial circumstance and then uses their own systems of measurement to decide how much a student can afford to pay. Pay-what-you-wish policies in art museums are an example of self-reported first-degree price discrimination. In a field adjacent to the visual arts, the Flux Theatre Ensemble in New York has experimented with pay-what-you-wish through its "Living Ticket." In this program, the company publishes three budgets, labeled current, minimum wage, and living-wage pay to dancers. They then publish three ticket prices ($26, $70, and $91) that allow them to cover the three budgets, respectively. The main difference is in the artists' fees, though other production costs ramp up as well. The ticket purchaser can see these budgets and then choose a corresponding ticket price. Flux does not call it a "pay what you wish" ticket because, in their words, "We don't use the word pay because we want the Living Ticket to be an ongoing relationship of mutual support, not a one-time transaction, and we define mutual support more broadly than just show me the money."[16]

If first-degree price discrimination is conducted through information about individual customers, second-degree price discrimination is done through the revealed characteristics of the product. Here, the drink at 4pm is a different, if related, product from the drink at 7:30pm. These options are presented to the customer, who then selects into one or the other based on preference and budget.

If second-degree price discrimination is done through revealed characteristics of the product, third-degree price discrimination relies on external, verifiable characteristics of the customer as part of a group. If a bar offered discounted drinks based on the ability to show a student or senior ID card, that would be third-degree price discrimination. The crux of price discrimination overall is that the seller has to find a way to get through the noise of the marketplace to reach individual buyers. The seller must be able to segment their audience – via individual knowledge, product characteristics, or group membership. Then the seller must also be able to prevent resale by someone purchasing at a discount to someone who is not.

Second-degree price discrimination merits more attention in its application to art through the strategy of **versioning**. Versioning is the selling of related goods at different prices. A first-class plane ticket is a version of an economy-class ticket. A flight with a Saturday night stay is a version of a midweek flight, but one intended to appeal less to a time-sensitive business traveler. In fashion, some designers have versions of their offerings that range from couture to runway to bridge and even mass market, for instance, through a Target collaboration. These goods are all versioned. The price discrimination occurs by virtue of which product the purchaser selects. In the arts, a painting can be a version of a print, or a larger print is a version of a smaller print. Some artists intentionally create versions of their work so that more people can be included in the audience. The conceptual artist Sol LeWitt, known for his large-scale wall drawings, also made artists' books, which were much more accessible (see Figure 3.4).[17] Some photographers or printmakers intentionally create works in smaller print sizes with larger editions to increase accessibility.

Another structure of pricing is the bundle. A **bundle** is a collection of goods sold under a single price, for example, a soup-and-salad lunch deal, an all-inclusive vacation with airfare and hotel, an album of music, or even a packet of ten postcards in a museum gift shop. Bundles are intended to address the problem of heterogeneous demand, meaning variety in willingness to pay and therefore difficulty

FIGURE 3.4 Sol LeWitt, *The Autobiography of Sol LeWitt*, 1980. Courtesy of the estate of the artist and Pace Gallery. Image from the Metropolitan Museum of Art and Art Resource.

in setting uniform prices. For example, say that a graduate student named Picasso really likes to eat soup for lunch and his colleague Matisse really likes to eat salad. Picasso loves soup and is willing to pay $6 for it. He sort of likes salad and would buy one too if it were $3. Matisse loves salad and is willing to pay $6 for it. He sort of likes soup and would pay $3 to add it. If the restaurant they both frequent tries to win them both over while offering uniform prices, they can only charge $3 for soup and $3 for salad. (They would make $12 in revenue for the two soups and two salads, which is the same amount of revenue – $12 – that they would make from selling one soup and one salad at $6 each but with higher production costs.) However, if the restaurant charges $9 for soup and salad as a *combination*, both Matisse and Picasso will buy it. (The restaurant will make $18 in revenue for the two soups and two salads.) The two students like different things within the combination, but they value the bundle equally.

Bundles are nearly ubiquitous: The assorted postcard packet in a museum gift shop offers a bundle compared to purchasing postcards individually. Say the packet of ten postcards costs $7.50 and each postcard individually costs $1.00. If the purchaser likes at least eight postcards, the bundle becomes an $8.00 value, so a deal at $7.50. If there is variety in taste and everyone dislikes two postcards but never the same two, then the museum can especially benefit from selling the bundle. Equally, you see strategies of unbundling. Airlines offer basic economy tickets so that travelers must reveal their preference to bring an extra bag and pay for it separately. The advantage of this pricing is that the airline can include people who do not wish to bring a bag and for whom the price savings on the bag is meaningful to their ticket-purchasing calculus. The airline may also be engaging in behavioral pricing to woo people with low basic rates and then have them dissociate the actual total price of the bag and seat because they have paid for them separately.[18]

Another form of price discrimination is the **two-part tariff**.[19] In this structure, the customer pays a single lump-sum price upfront and then a second price per use. Common examples would include amusement parks for which there is an admissions price and a price per ride or private clubs with a joining fee and later fees to use services. The core identifier of a two-part tariff is a pricing structure that includes both a lump sum and a fee per use. A wide range of products have this structure, including computer printers and ink cartridges, razors and blades, or coffeemakers and pods.

One can say that museum memberships share some of these characteristics: A member pays a lump sum up front and then attends the museum a number of times that corresponds to that person's willingness to pay per visit. Members may also spend money on each visit, if only at a gift shop or café. In practice, however, a museum membership tends to function more like a bulk discount. Owing to diminishing marginal utility, a museum member is likely to value the visits to a museum less over time. For example, consider a museum that has a $20 admissions price. An individual visitor has the following schedule of demand: $30 for one visit, $15 for a second visit, and $10 for a third visit. Suppose the museum has a membership price of $50. The visitor would purchase a first ticket at $20, pocketing $10 in consumer surplus. If the visitor has diminishing marginal returns and only values the second visit at $15, if faced with the choice of purchasing a second $20 ticket, the visitor would not. If the visitor values the third visit at $10, then the visitor receives $55 worth of value on the $50 membership. The museum could not have made more money on the tickets because the visitor would have stopped at one $20 ticket. Here, the bundle serves both visitor – in enjoyment of the museum – and museum – in receiving $50 rather than $20 in revenue.

Structures of price discrimination have some unusual applications in the arts. For example, for the VIP opening days of art fairs, the tickets are time-stamped with entry at, for example, 11am, 3pm, and 7pm. The most exclusive ticket is the earliest. The time-stamped tickets to the "preview" are usually given for free by the fair to a VIP list or by galleries to their important clients. Later in the run of the fair, members of the public can also purchase entry. This form of price discrimination is not direct. The best customers are given the earliest tickets and therefore the greatest advantage buying works that are in demand before others arrive. Those customers who could most afford the ticket are given it for free. In addition, the "product" for sale is not only the art but the relational aspect of bumping into people, which the early ticket enables. (As we will see in Chapter 4, the attendance at the preview day creates a network externality – a benefit conferred by collective action.) The VIP ticket is also a positional good because not everyone can have one. Its value rests on some attributes of art markets and the art world that are exclusive and confer status.[20]

There also may be simple cases of discounts. While a bulk discount falls under second-degree price discrimination, a discount offered to a specific group would fall under the third-degree category. In art sales through galleries, art advisors are commonly offered a 10% discount. Many advisors charge their clients 10% of an artwork's price, and so this arrangement has the effect of covering the advisory fee.

Some forms of price discrimination are political, in providing access or fairness. Many are designed to include some audiences for free without losing the ability to charge other audiences. And still others are aimed at generating income. A museum could look at the demand curve and try to develop a pricing strategy that captured as much consumer surplus as possible from those to the left of the market price and that included audiences to the right of the market price through discounted or free tickets. In this way, price discrimination is a strategy for both income and inclusion (see Figure 3.5).

For artists, inventive pricing strategies may also originate in trying to cover fixed cost. The artist Elisabeth Sunday's work is a case in point. A third-generation artist, Sunday lives in a sixteenth-century manor in northwestern France, having realized it was cheaper to live in France and purchase $1,000 plane tickets each year than to continue to live as an artist in Oakland, California. For the past few

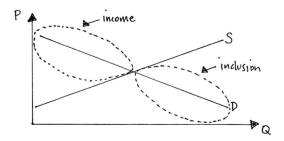

FIGURE 3.5 Pricing for income and inclusion.

decades, Sunday has managed to cover her costs by what she calls a "Collectors' Circle." Sunday determines her annual cost of living and then invites a group of collectors to each take a share of that cost, in exchange for credits toward purchasing her work. When Sunday first started the Collectors' Circle in the mid-1980s, she needed $25,000 per year to live. She now needs $50,000 to cover her annual expenses. Ten collectors each pay $5,000 annually to support her artistic practice.[21] Sunday is very clear that the plan is "not a get rich quick or a buy a house" venture and that "the success is predicated on it only supporting what I need." Each member of the circle receives a studio credit double the amount of their support – $10,000 in the case of a $5,000 donation. The arrangement mirrors the consignment structure of most galleries, which would split proceeds 50:50 between artist and dealer, leaving Sunday with $5,000 for a work priced at $10,000.

Sunday's strategy is an interesting mix of covering her fixed costs – an application of breakeven thinking – while offering a discount that corresponds to what she would have been paid through a gallery. Sunday also works with collectors to raise funds for some research-based projects, for instance, traveling for a photo shoot. Members of the Collectors' Circle have two to three years to choose a work and typically replace themselves with a new member when they leave the circle. One might describe her arrangement as a modern-day, crowdfunded version of traditional patronage. The group functions socially, with Sunday, an eloquent and authentic presence and lyrical speaker, making introductions and hosting. As Sunday says, "It's important for everyone to win." She sums up the ethos: "It has to be generous or it won't be appealing. Art has to be limited or it won't be appealing."[22]

3.3 PRICING SCRIPTS

Many pricing strategies in the general world would be highly unusual in the arts. Ivan Karp, the right hand to gallerist Leo Castelli in the late 1950s and early 1960s in New York, used to make jokes in his previous job working at the Green Gallery that "The paintings are all twenty percent less on Wednesdays."[23] The crux of the joke was that the paintings were not on sale on Wednesdays. Even if Wednesdays had been slow days, discounting for a midweek lull would fall outside the cultural norms of selling art.

This story of pricing art follows Velthuis's idea of pricing scripts more than it does the economic narrative of efficiency. In competitive markets, firms do not set price. They are "price takers." The market sets the price. This is the story of allocative efficiency – that price is connected to the cost of materials and so allowing markets to set price manages for the efficient allocation of underlying resources.

The silent, slippery architectural support of this idea is the marginal cost curve. The premise of the marginal cost curve is to be inside the decisions of the firm – here the gallery or artist's studio – in the short-run world in which you have made resource-allocation decisions. You have hired staff, paid rent, and so on. If you look at the cost to produce each additional unit, you will see a curve that dips down and then shoots up to the right. The story behind the curve is that as you get started producing, you first experience economies of scale. It becomes cheaper to produce an additional unit as you advance beyond producing just a few units. This makes sense. You may have idle space or employees with spare time. The cost to add a tenth unit is less than to add a second one. What is less intuitive is why the curve goes up so much to the right. Here, I imagine the adage that things can be fast, cheap, or good, and rarely more than two of the three. In this story, you produce something that is covered in the news. It is put on the Oprah gift list or worn by a member of a royal family. You can just sell out of what you have and stop. Or you can try to meet at least some of the increased demand. If we suppose you are profit-maximizing, you will produce up until the point at which your marginal cost is equal to the price. At that inflection point, you have made as much money as you possibly can.

I have never met anyone in the arts who prices this way, though the logic of the marginal cost curve is sometimes invoked to answer questions of pricing. For example, should museums have free entry or charge for general admission? Rushton, the researcher we encountered earlier in this chapter regarding the Indianapolis Museum of Art, argues that museums, despite the social benefits of free admission, must make revenue somewhere and so realistically must charge admission. As Rushton points out, museums are quasi-public goods, a concept we will get to in Chapter 4. To say museums are a quasi-public good is to acknowledge that they can be enjoyed by multiple people simultaneously but only up to a point. Two or twenty people can look at *Starry Night*, but the view of the painting becomes rival-rous – that is, limited and therefore competitive – at some point. At the same time, museums are fixed-cost-intensive businesses. Most of the costs of an exhibition are incurred whether a few people or many people attend. Thus, museums have very low marginal cost associated with adding one additional visitor. If one priced at marginal cost, one would price close to zero. For Rushton, the ideal alternative is to strongly advocate for becoming a museum member, so that one pays a membership fee and then in fact the marginal cost of the additional visit is zero. We will return to this conundrum in Chapter 4, when we look at public goods.[24]

3.4   PRICING OPACITY AND GENERAL MODELS

Pricing in the arts tends to be opaque and difficult to understand, and the difficulty or opacity often seems intentionally so.[25] Even if prices cannot be predicted or compared apples to apples, the structure by which they are charged tends to remain constant. In the **primary market** – when a work of art is sold for the first time – galleries tend to take work on consignment, meaning they do not purchase it for inventory but instead split the proceeds with the artist when the work sells. The typical artist–dealer split is 50:50. In the **secondary market**, meaning when a work is resold either privately or via public auction, galleries might actually buy the work outright (from a collector or at auction) and resell it at a markup, or they might serve as brokers arranging two sides of the transaction and taking a commission. Like dealers, auction houses also operate in private secondary markets, selling some works outside of public auctions.

In 1981, approximately twenty years into their artist–dealer relationship, the artist Robert Rauschenberg sent a letter to his dealer Leo Castelli simply stating that their artist–dealer split would change from 50:50 to 60:40 in Rauschenberg's favor. At that stage, the artist had the power to set that price (see Figure 3.6).

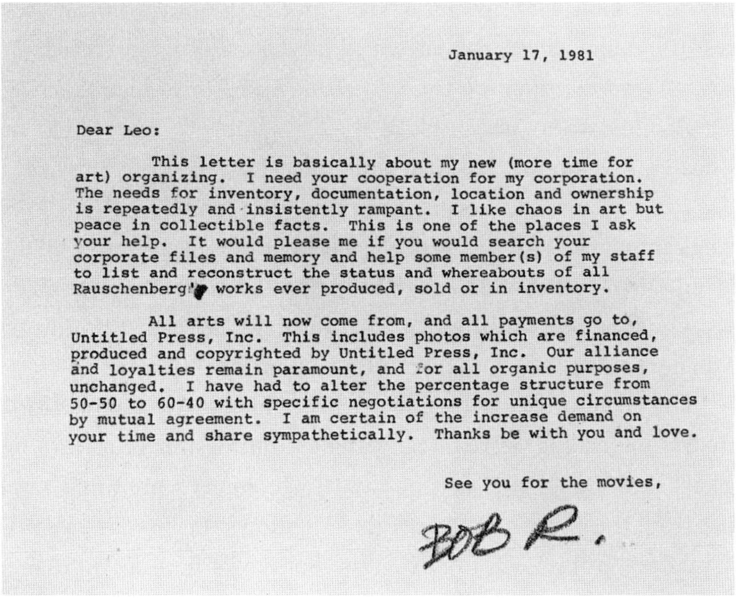

January 17, 1981

Dear Leo:

   This letter is basically about my new (more time for art) organizing. I need your cooperation for my corporation. The needs for inventory, documentation, location and ownership is repeatedly and insistently rampant. I like chaos in art but peace in collectible facts. This is one of the places I ask your help. It would please me if you would search your corporate files and memory and help some member(s) of my staff to list and reconstruct the status and whereabouts of all Rauschenberg works ever produced, sold or in inventory.

   All arts will now come from, and all payments go to, Untitled Press, Inc. This includes photos which are financed, produced and copyrighted by Untitled Press, Inc. Our alliance and loyalties remain paramount, and for all organic purposes, unchanged. I have had to alter the percentage structure from 50-50 to 60-40 with specific negotiations for unique circumstances by mutual agreement. I am certain of the increase demand on your time and share sympathetically. Thanks be with you and love.

See you for the movies,

BOB R.

FIGURE 3.6 Robert Rauschenberg letter to Leo Castelli. Courtesy of the Archives of American Art, Washington, DC.

When a gallery or auction house resells a work privately, there is often no disclosure of the price or the markup. For example, in 2014 Dmitry Rybolovlev – an art collector and the former owner of an extremely successful potash fertilizer business – purchased an Amedeo Modigliani painting called *Nude on a Blue Cushion* for $118 million. His dealer and art advisor, the free-port owner Yves Bouvier, told Rybolovlev that the price included a $2.36 million commission. What Bouvier allegedly did not tell Rybolovlev is that the price also included a markup of some $25 million over what Bouvier paid. Rybolovlev discovered the markup by chance when he dined with the art consultant Sandy Heller, who told him that Heller had sold the work on behalf of hedge-fund manager Steven Cohen for $93.5 million, a fact which revealed to Rybolovlev the markup. A substantial lawsuit ensued.[26]

In other cases, a price is advertised but no one is sure if it was really paid. Don Thompson's book *The $12 Million Stuffed Shark* takes its name from the artwork by Damien Hirst titled *The Physical Impossibility of Death in the Mind of Someone Living*, otherwise known as the shark in the formaldehyde tank. Hirst and his dealer, Jay Jopling, publicly announced the sale of the work to hedge-fund manager Steven Cohen – the same seller of the Modigliani above – for $12 million. Yet that price was not verifiable. The only firm public offer was from Nicholas Serota, then director of Tate, who offered £1 million, at the time equivalent to $2 million.[27] We do not know what actual amount Cohen paid.

The structure of pricing in auction houses is to charge fees to both the buyer and seller. The **seller's commission** is private and negotiable. Some clients do not pay it. The **buyer's premium** rarely varies from the published rates. Table 3.1 shows the buyer's premium at Christie's from 1975 to 2020. The Sotheby's fees are similar (of which more in Chapter 5).

The key to applying the buyer's premium is to understand that the fee is charged on each tranche or slice of the price. For a work over $4,000,000, the fee is not 13.5% of $4,000,000 but still 25% of the first tranche, 20% of the second tranche, and then the last percentage of the price above the upper limit. Table 3.2 gives an example of the buyer's premium for an artwork that costs $1 million.

Prior to a public auction, an auction house typically publishes estimates in the form of price ranges, for example $4,000 to $6,000. The seller almost always has a **reserve price**, meaning the minimum price at which the auction house is allowed to sell the work. By custom, the reserve is usually around 75% of the low estimate. For example, in

Table 3.1 *Christie's buyer's premium 1975–2020*[1]

Date range	First increment	Second increment	Third increment
1975–92	10% of all lots		
1993–9	15% up to $50,000	10% above 50,000	
2000–3	20% up to $10,000	15% between $10,000 and 100,000	10% above $100,000
2004	20% up to $20,000	15% over 20,000	
2005–7	20% up to $200,000	12% above $200,000	
2007–8	25% up to 20,000	20% between $20,000 and $500,000	12% above $500,000
2008–13	25% up to $50,000	20% between $50,000 and $1,000,000	
October 2013–September 2016	25% up to $100,000	20% between $100,000 and $2,000,000	12% above $2,000,000
September 2016–September 2017	25% up to $150,000	20% between $150,000 and $3,000,000	12% above $3,000,000
September 2017–February 2019	25% up to $250,000	20% between $250,000 and $4,000,000	12.5% above $4,000,000
February 2019–2020	25% up to $300,000	20% between $300,000 and $4,000,000	13.5% above $4,000,000

[1] Ekelund, Robert B., Jr., Jackson, John D. and Tollison, Robert D. (2017). *The Economics of American Art: Issues, Artists and Market Institutions.* New York: Oxford University Press, p. 48, updated with press accounts and Christie's' own figures. See, e.g., Boucher, Brian. (2016, September 6). Christie's Hikes Buyer's Fees for First Time in Three Years. *Artnet News.* https://news.artnet.com/market/christies-hikes-buyers-fees-636194.

Table 3.2 *Buyer's premium example ($1 million artwork)*

Tranche of artwork price	Percentage of the hammer price	Amount of the purchase price in each tranche	Buyer's premium in this case
Up to $300,000	25%	$300,000	$75,000
From $300,000 to $4,000,000	20%	$700,000	$140,000
Above $4,000,000	13.5%	$0	$0

the price range above, the reserve might be $3,000, that is, 75% of the $4,000 low estimate. In many jurisdictions, the auctioneer is allowed to open the bidding with momentum by taking fake bids up until the reserve price. Then any bid at or over the reserve must be real. This practice is often called **chandelier bidding** because the auctioneer may stare intently at the back curtain or the chandelier as if it is the source of the bid. (For an overview of auctions in theory and practice, see Appendix D.)

3.5   CONCLUSIONS

The price at which artworks sell also depends on the relationship between cultural institutions and commercial art markets. Inclusion in museum collections or exhibitions validates artworks, often leading to an increase in price. Dealers are typically willing to sell to museums at a discount. Dealers also generally sell to collectors who will steward the work, even if a speculator offers a higher price. The dealer has an interest in controlling prices for the artist's work so that prices do not go down. As such, it is customary in the arts, and not in other industries, for a collector who wishes to sell a work to return to the gallery that sold it to them and give them first right of refusal.

The artwork may sell via the pricing strategy of a dealer who swears, as Velthuis's subject once did, that he sells artworks to people who are interested in art for spiritual growth. Or the artwork may be a gift from one artist to another or a trade for supplies. Or the artwork may sell through the masterful energy of an auctioneer. Even with these idiosyncratic and human features of the art sale, the pricing strategy can still follow these mechanics concerning the sensitivity of the customer to pricing level and structure.

Ultimately, the art market is full of pricing that is hard to generalize and sometimes does not make sense. Art is worth what someone is willing to pay for it and is priced at what someone is willing to try to ask for it. That reality likely serves to reinforce the art market's insularity. Prices are not listed and asking for them is hard to do. Those who are interested in art and have the means to acquire it at some level may fear being taken advantage of or hesitate at the cultural mores, which are often opaque to newcomers. What it is to buy art in the primary market now is very different from what it was to buy art in the primary market when Jasper Johns or Frank Stella was first selling work. Still, pricing helps to frame the ways in which art becomes an investment, a theme we explore in Chapter 9.

Pricing is important to the revenue needs of nonprofit institutions like museums, and pricing strategy can be used to include audiences. The balance is in trying to price all the way up and down the demand curve, to capture people who can afford to support the arts while also including those who cannot. (Pricing of salary in the arts can also exclude people from the workforce, a topic we cover in Chapter 7.)

In all of these cases, pricing has a structural mechanistic nature, while also being socially significant. It is socially significant to the people who brag, sometimes silently, about the positional goods they purchased at the top of the art market, and it is socially significant to the people trying to build community governance and participation in art museums. The next chapter addresses what is essentially a failure of pricing – of forms of value, for the greater good, that markets cannot easily compute.

QUESTIONS

1. What are the ways in which artists can engage in price discrimination for income and inclusion? Auctioneers? Museum managers?

2. Find a museum in your community or elsewhere that has free days. How is this policy structured? Are the free days limited to local residents? Is there a very long line to enter the museum those days? What other pricing strategies can you imagine to make the museum as accessible as possible, while finding sources of funding?

3. Paid admissions tickets are often cited as a key barrier to inclusion of audiences in museums. Similarly, low pay of museum staff is cited as a barrier to inclusion in the museum workforce, a topic we cover in Chapter 7. If you were lobbying a museum to make its admissions free on these grounds, how would you go about doing it? Does such a strategy require governmental support? Could museumgoers who could afford it be asked to contribute more than the ticket price to offset others? Would you distribute free tickets through schools or social-service organizations or include entry via local library cards? You are encouraged to think as creatively and also as precisely as possible. One point to remember is that the metric of attendance numbers can be an important driver of successful grant applications. Consider what other metrics, in addition to attendance numbers, would support mission and fundraising.

4. Research the history of artists' books and the founding of Printed Matter, the non-profit store for artists' books started in New York by Sol LeWitt, Lucy Lippard, and others. How can you frame the role of versioning and price discrimination in this project? Do you see digital projects now that try to accomplish similar forms of access to art as Printed Matter does via books? How has Printed Matter's own approach evolved since its founding?

5. How do you think brand and versioning are related? What artists can you think of who use branding to create an aura that hangs over their work so that they can sell related objects at different price points? Are there examples from outside the arts that also come to mind?

6. Some more populist artworks are sold through highly sophisticated versioning strategies with many different products of the same image at different price points. See, for example, the painting of a cat *White Persian in Pansy Patch*, sold by the platform Fine Art America.[28] Customers can buy wall art in various forms and sizes, stationery, phone cases, beach towels, and as of 2020 the original painting itself. Compare and contrast this pricing strategy with the ways you observe artworks being priced at the high end of the art market. Do you think price-discrimination strategies dampen the ability to sell art at very high price points? Why or why not? What is the most careful, interesting, and precise answer you can give to why the price of this work on Fine Art America is $175 and the similarly sized Vermeer in Chapter 2 sold for $30 million?

7. Choose a museum with publicly available financial records, for instance, US Form 990 tax returns or annual reports. Estimate the museum's annual attendance and revenue from ticket sales. Given this information, in the context of their larger budget, what do you think is the pricing strategy that would most support their mission? Research the institution's history of ticket pricing, for instance the Museum of Modern Art in New York's jump to a $25 ticket with one building expansion and the decision to make the ground-floor space free in the next.

8. Keep a diary of prices for one week. Notice every time you encounter price-discrimination strategies in everyday life. Do you notice attempts to extract information about customers' price elasticity? Some stores will discount one brand of seltzer over another or change the price of bottled water slightly, seemingly as an experiment. What were the most successful and the least successful strategies that you saw? Did you experience any interaction where you would have bought something for more or less than it was offered? If you purchased a bundled good, notice how you valued the parts, relatively speaking. Do you know anyone who purchased the same bundle who valued the constituent parts differently?

4   Failure

Specificity is everything.

Alex Beard, chief executive, Royal Opera House

In 1972, Nicholas Serota was walking across Green Park in London with his Arts Council colleague Francis Pugh, who would later become Serota's brother-in-law. As Pugh recalled, "We were really bemoaning the state of things. And then Serota said: 'What we really need in London is a museum of modern art.'"[1] Serota would go on to serve as the director of the Tate from 1988 until 2017, where he was the founding force behind Tate Modern, the museum of twentieth- and twenty-first-century British and international art that also revitalized the Southwark area of London. But as Serota and Pugh crossed Green Park, Tate Modern would not open for another twenty-seven years.

In this chapter we consider the founding of Tate Modern, a public institution that both depends on economic analysis and creates forms of value that markets have a hard time recognizing and delivering back to the value's creator. This condition is called market failure. In this chapter, we investigate two broad categories of market failure – externalities and public goods. We investigate two methods – economic impact studies and contingent valuation – that some economists use, however valiantly, to attempt to quantify the unmeasurable. We explore strategic responses to market failure, ranging from governmental intervention to philanthropy to speculative design around taxation and community governance.

Serota's early biography is not only a backstory to Tate Modern but a parallel. Like the "Tate Gallery of Modern Art" as the project was initially called, Serota's trajectory went through its own process of formation and junctures where the outcome was not certain. In this way, the long arc of creative process becomes a story of market failure as well, though also a story of democratic success, urban renewal, and a project so successful in general terms that it is now hard to imagine Tate Modern existing in different form or not at all.[2]

4.1 THE BEGINNINGS OF TATE MODERN

The notion of a museum of modern art in London was not a new idea when Serota and Pugh found themselves crossing Green Park in the early 1970s. In the late 1930s, the collector and philanthropist Peggy Guggenheim had proposed such a modern art museum in London. The efforts were scuppered by the war though her collaborator, Herbert Read, became involved in the founding of the Institute of Contemporary Arts (ICA) in 1946.[3] In the 1960s, the incoming director of the Tate Gallery, Norman Reid, tried to convince Peggy Guggenheim to donate her many modernist and surrealist master-pieces to the Tate.[4] From December 1964 through February 1965, the Tate hosted an exhibition of almost her entire collection. The British government funded the exhibition, and the Tate held a lavish dinner in the galleries. As Guggenheim wrote in her autobiography, "My only rival was Churchill's funeral," which took place on January 30, 1965.[5]

The year 1965 was also when Nicholas Serota arrived at Cambridge University to begin his studies in economics. He had taken a gap year from 1964 to 1965. During that time, he spent six months traveling around India to look at dams and engineering pro-jects being used to create hydroelectric power and to improve agricul-tural production. He was interested in the model of the United States' Works Progress Administration, which created jobs for artists as well as funding infrastructure works in the 1930s and 1940s.[6] Serota's father, Stanley, was an engineer who built earth structures and dams across the United Kingdom and in Africa. Although Serota acknowledged that approaches to land and community economic

development have changed since the time of his own formal education, he entered the study of economics with a firm interest in structural development of communities.

The economics course – which like other undergraduate courses
and examinations at Cambridge is called a tripos – consisted of two
parts split across three years. Art history had only been a discipline at
Cambridge since 1963. One could only study art history secondarily
after switching from another field. After completing the first part of
the economics tripos, Serota switched over, joining students coming
more commonly from English, history, or foreign language courses.

Serota credits his decision to study art, at least in part, to the
program of Kettle's Yard, the "house museum" in the town of
Cambridge, founded in 1958 by Jim and Helen Ede, a curator at the
Tate Gallery in the 1920s and an art teacher, respectively.[7] Having
become friends with influential British artists such as Ben Nicholson,
Jim Ede would buy artworks from them so that they could afford to
buy new supplies.[8] When the Edes opened Kettle's Yard, visitors could
use the house as a house – nap in the bed, use the toilet, or sit in the
chairs.[9] When Serota was a student, the Edes opened Kettle's Yard for
undergraduates every afternoon and lent works for students to let
them live with art in their own rooms (see Figure 4.1). Serota lived
with a Henri Gaudier-Brzeska drawing on his wall for three months
before his switch to art history.

Kettle's Yard embodied the same grand mission of a large public
museum but in the form of a more purist philosophical statement on
the role of art in everyday life – and a place to spend the afternoon.
Mr. Ede's own biography echoes this sense of mission and service.
During World War II, Ede gave art lectures in hospitals in war zones.
From December 1944 to March 1945, he gave 145 lectures on art to
patients in the wards of a British base hospital in Marseilles and
broadcast a further thirty-five talks over the hospital's public address
system.[10]

Serota bookended university with a second gap year, this one
spent working on a Mellon Foundation catalogue of British art and

FIGURE 4.1 Poster for Kettle's Yard, University of Cambridge. Courtesy of Kettle's Yard.

studying French in Paris. He then enrolled in the one-year MA at the Courtauld in London. In 1970, Serota joined the Arts Council before becoming director of Modern Art Oxford in 1973, and then becoming director of the Whitechapel Gallery in east London in 1976.[11] The Whitechapel Gallery is located directly across the street from a shop that Serota's grandmother had run in the 1950s.[12] The shop sold wholesale clothing to smaller retailers. Although it closed more than a decade before Serota arrived at the Whitechapel, Serota's own sense memory of the shop rooted what were otherwise extremely experimental exhibitions of that period – Carl Andre to Anselm Kiefer to Eva Hesse[13] – in the footprint of the neighborhood. This ethos – the cantilever into risk-taking art from the steady base of connection to place – followed Serota's career.

When the job as director of the Tate was advertised in 1987, Serota was not a frontrunner. Each candidate was asked to deliver a seven-year plan for the organization. Serota's two-sided A4 report, titled "Grasping the Nettle," became quietly legendary. Written in compact typewritten form, words neatly but densely laid out on the page in the manner of "you may bring one index card of equations to this science exam," Serota reimagined the institution across categories of the collections, the exhibitions, the buildings, fundraising, and management. The conclusions centered the future plan of the museum with artists when Serota wrote:

> The Tate is loved, but not sufficiently respected. Artists continue to regard it with ambivalence, though their support is the key for an institution which should safeguard the future by attention to the present. A Gallery cherished by artists will eventually be appreciated by all.[14]

When Serota started work as director in 1988, he held a party for artists in the first week.[15] Then he began to implement much of what was written on those two A4 pages.

When Serota began his appointment, a new building plan on the Tate's existing site – called the "hospital site" – had been approved, but Serota had doubts about the essence of the plan, which proposed separate buildings for a museum of sculpture and a museum of new art, creating complicated questions of what went where and making it easy for a skeptical visitor to give a whole building a miss. "There will be people who don't visit that part of the museum because they'll think that they are not interested in new art," Serota said. "We were also going to end up in London with a museum of twentieth-century art that was smaller than a museum of twentieth-century art you would have found in a provincial city in Germany."[16]

Serota hired Richard Francis, the outgoing director of Tate Liverpool, who conducted an imaginative yet also analytic feasibility study of what it would take to exhibit the Tate's collection with the proper amount of space. Describing Francis's study, Serota said,

"There was this rather lovely diagram of notional galleries filled with art showing the whole collection as you would want it to be. These galleries started on the hospital site and they went over the Clore [Turner wing] and out across the river until they reached the other side of the river" – what is currently the headquarters of the Secret Intelligence Service, MI6. It became clear to Serota that pleading with government to fund more space would not be as effective as persuading them by showing the collection well enough for the need for space to reveal itself. The Tate started to rehang its permanent collection every year.[17]

By 1992, the trustees were convinced that a second site was needed. Numerous sites received serious consideration. It is easy to forget the "before" picture and to assume the current Tate Modern was always meant to be, but in fact many sites received detailed feasibility studies, including the aptly named "Project Moby Dick" which evaluated the Billingsgate fish market as a site. The current site – the former Bankside Power Station – became a contender in 1993 after Francis Carnwath, then Tate deputy director and also a member of the London Advisory Committee for English Heritage, visited the decommissioned power station as part of a BBC program on historic buildings that needed to be saved.[18] Designed by the architect Giles Gilbert Scott, Bankside was planned in the 1940s, completed in the 1960s, and decommissioned in 1981. On that visit, someone suggested to Carnwath that Bankside could be a potential Tate site. Carnwath initially thought it was too large and derelict, and said so. That afternoon, he and Serota happened to bump into each other in the hallway. When Serota asked about his day, Carnwath described the morning's visit and the idea of Bankside as a Tate site.[19]

That very evening, Serota stopped by to see the power station on his way home. The building was surrounded by walls and difficult to access. From the river side, Serota paced out the length, walking from the central chimney to one end and then doubling his measurement. The structure, although vast in scale, likely aided by the chimney – which rises to 99 meters (325 feet), just shy of the dome height of St. Paul's Cathedral across the river – was not as overwhelmingly large as it seemed. It was in fact the rough size of the current Tate, just with four stories instead of two. Serota was immediately attached to the site.

Alex Beard, now chief executive of the Royal Opera House, joined the Tate in January of 1994 as the director of finance and operations. (He would go on to serve as deputy director.) Beard was immediately tasked with undertaking a review of the four final potential Tate Modern sites for the board and asked to advocate for one. In the first draft report Beard identified Jubilee Gardens as the preferred option, now the site of the London Eye. The site was close to the Southbank Centre complex of arts facilities and had good public transport links, a riverfront location, and space for a new-build museum. As Beard tells it, "Basically Nick's [Serota's] response to that was 'very interesting, tightly argued but you haven't actually been inside Bankside Power Station have you?' I went, No." Beard visited Bankside and was convinced. And in a mythic story that seems also to be true, when Bankside was first being considered in 1993, the trustees had piled into a large minivan and were driven to see the site. Instead of winding through the narrow roads of its Southwark borough, the trustees approached the building from the north bank, stopping by St. Paul's to see the chimney rise through the break in the buildings.[20] It is the sight line now occupied by the Millennium Bridge, the pedestrian crossing that connects the north and south banks on the river side of Tate Modern.[21]

In 1992, the UK government had announced a newly formed National Lottery that would begin in 1994, part of the proceeds of which would support the construction of large building projects to celebrate the new millennium. This development gave them a deadline and the implication that large-scale government funding would not be available otherwise. Dennis Stevenson, who had become chair of the Tate trustees in 1989 and who was working hand in hand with Serota on the project – and who would be the only individual mentioned by name in Serota's preface to the first edition of the

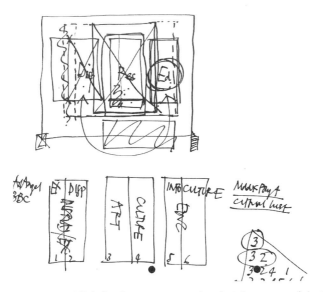

FIGURE 4.2 Nicholas Serota, concept sketch, ink on copy of the Tate Masterplan June Report, June 1991, from Tate Modern Project: Early Concepts, Jan 1991–June 1992. Courtesy of Tate Archives.

Tate Modern Handbook in 2000 – persuaded McKinsey & Co. to undertake an economic development study.[22] An architectural competition was organized. Tate Modern – still called the Tate Gallery of Modern Art – received £50 million from the Millennium Commission. The project had a planned budget of £137 million. What included concept sketches from 1991 started to take built form (see Figure 4.2).

Many things went wrong. Beard recalled, "We discovered asbestos in a place that it wasn't expected to be that led the site to be shut down for six months, the steel work contractor went bust, the construction manager went bust." Many tough decisions had to be taken to stay on budget. "We made a rule that the financial decisions were never taken in the same room as the artistic ones and that any artistic decision with regard to scope or design was subject to it being affordable, which took the emotion out of it," Beard said.[23] Level 4 of the museum was taken out of the plan and only added back at the last minute when the gallery received £6.2 million from the Arts

Council's Lottery Fund.[24] A full bank of elevators was taken out to save £5 million. Tate staked its reputation on the project, soon to be named "Tate Modern" by the branding firm Wolff Olins. As Beard said:

> Nick is a visionary who's massively pragmatic . . .. He wanted to realize his vision . . . starting from the position that we were more or less a startup. Tate Modern was more than twice the size of Tate Britain in terms of scale and impact and therefore the reputation of the institution was going to be forged by whether we did this right or not. In a way that is very liberating because you've just got to get on with it.[25]

The winners of the architectural competition, Herzog and de Meuron, were also staking their careers on the project. Rather than choose the most celebrated candidate as if it were a prize, Tate chose a partner for whom the building would also be a career-defining project.

True to the ethos of Serota's early work, Tate Modern combined an economic and community focus from the outset. The first person hired was the community liaison. In the lead up to the museum's opening in May 2000, parties for special audiences included one for London taxi drivers, a group who would most need to find the venue. The museum expected two million visitors each year and instead received five million. By 2017, Tate Modern had opened a second, adjoining building.

In the creation of artistic, cultural, and local economic impact, Tate Modern has been an enormous success. In this general sense, it is anything but a failure. In the market sense, however, it is not possible to support Tate only by earned income. To their credit as public and civic institutions, museums do not ask that their visitors – tourists, local community members, Londoners – pay their full apportioned cost of operations as the price of attendance.

Thus, if we wore an itchy, ill-fitting economics hat, we would call Tate Modern, and most other art museums, market failures. That is not to ascribe failure to a person or an institution – or even to economic theory – but to say that Tate Modern cannot itself operate solely on its revenues.[26] What is interesting though is that Tate Modern has generated so much economic or financial value for the surrounding area and for London as a whole. The institution generates many forms of civic and cultural value that are not easily represented by price.[27] It has also generated increased property values from which it does not benefit.

To investigate Tate Modern's position more, we examine two core categories of market failure – externalities and public goods. **Externalities** are a category of market failure in which all costs or benefits are not included in a price. **Public goods** are those for which markets have difficulty getting users to pay because many people can use the good simultaneously and without being forced to pay. In a pure public good such as air, everyone can breathe at once. In a quasi-public good such as a museum exhibition, many people can see it at once but not all people. After we explore these concepts, we return to the methods, however quixotic, that economists use to try to measure these broad forms of civic and cultural value anyway.

4.2 EXTERNALITIES

An externality is a cost or benefit that is not priced in. A **negative externality** is a cost that is not priced in, and a **positive externality** is a benefit that is not priced in. The arts often create positive externalities. They revitalize economic areas, beautify and regenerate neighborhoods, and offer bright spots in urban centers. A classic textbook example of a negative externality is a factory that produces more cheaply by polluting water downstream or a very loud nightclub that keeps its neighbors awake. The factory and nightclub benefit in ways whose costs are borne by other parties. They save money by not mitigating pollution or installing soundproofing. Others bear the cost. A textbook example of a positive externality is a beekeeper who lives next door to a flower grower. The bees pollinate the flowers, and the flowers feed the bees. Neither pays the other. This beguilingly pastoral example was published by James Meade in 1952 and then somewhat debunked in 1973 by Steven Cheung, who found that there is in fact a thriving business in hiring hives of bees to pollinate flowers. That said, the concept stands that there can be match-ups of complementary positive externalities in the manner of the fable of the bees.[28]

A special category of positive externality is a **network external-ity** in which the benefit comes about specifically from collective action. For instance, the value of a social media platform comes about from the fact that everyone is on it. Similarly, because there is a cluster of galleries in a given neighborhood, an individual gallery might benefit from the network effect that the larger destination attracts people. A week before Nicholas Serota started his job at the Tate, the artist Damien Hirst first organized a group exhibition of his and his Goldsmiths classmates' work. The show is credited with launching the phenomenon of the Young British Artists (YBAs). Imagine if Hirst had told Serota to come visit a distant dockland in east London only to see Hirst's own work. The fact that there was a critical mass generated a network effect.

4.3   PUBLIC GOODS

Some goods that generate positive externalities, such as public art or Tate Modern, are also public goods. A **public good**, in contrast to a private good, is one that is non-rivalrous and non-excludable. **Non-rivalrous** means that it can be used by more than one person at a time and that one person's use does not prevent another person's use. If I walk by a public sculpture today, I have not taken away from someone's ability to see the sculpture tomorrow. But if there is only one donut today and I eat it, it is gone. **Non-excludable** means that it is not possible to stop someone from enjoying the good. It may be technically possible to wall off a public sculpture, but in the case of pure public goods such as the air that we breathe, it would be hard to exclude someone from access to it under normal circumstances. If we return to the donut, it is easier to exclude someone, for instance, by building a glass case for the donuts within a donut shop.

Knowledge, in the broad sense, is a public good. A physical book is a private good. The ideas it contains are a public good. In fact, knowledge also has network externalities. For example, in a democracy, the more people who have knowledge of the government's workings, the better the democracy functions. The open access movement in science, and increasingly in the humanities, has supported the sharing of academic research without paywalls. In that case, my reading an article online is non-rivalrous – I do not stop others from reading at the same time – and it is non-excludable if the paywall has been removed. Many museums have placed substantial digital representations of their collections online in order to create image repositories as publicly accessible resources.

4.3.1 The Tragedy of the Commons

A special category of market failure is what, in a December 1968 essay in the journal *Science*, Garrett Hardin called "the tragedy of the commons."[29] Hardin imagined a pastureland shared by a local community. Each person in the community would have an incentive to add an additional animal to their fold. The benefit of the animal would be positive because the grazing would be free. However, if every person in the town got an extra animal, the entire pasture would be overrun and there would be no more grazing. Hardin encapsulated a structural problem in which an individual person's incentives, if followed by all individuals, would lead to a suboptimal group outcome. If one hiker drops an apple core, perhaps no one notices. If all hikers drop apple cores, the forest is covered, and apple trees start to grow. If one person at the airport has an intrusively loud phone conversation, they create a negative externality for others, but the intrusion is much more manageable than if everyone in the gate area has a loud conversation. The temptation to intrude on public quiet can be manageable if only one person does it, but if everyone does it, the circumstance becomes a tragedy of the commons.

In Hardin's original essay, the subject is actually population growth. In the late 1960s many people were worried that a growing world population would lead to overpopulation and famine. Some of this theorizing is problematic in its White-centered overtones and unmetabolized colonial histories. The broader idea of the tragedy of the commons has, however, outlived the context of its gestation and can be applied in decolonialized ways to describe these cross-purposed incentives of the individual and the collective. The tragedy of the commons describes everything from climate crisis to the oversaturation of art fairs or the desire to benefit from public arts programming without paying for it.

When it becomes especially difficult to align payment with use for a public good, we also use the term **free-rider problem.** A free rider is someone who benefits from something without paying their fair share. Public art can be viewed by all who pass by, including those who contribute taxes and those who commute in. In fact, much public art is erected with that express purpose. Depending on the jurisdiction, the public art is paid for by government, philanthropy, or other support. A more contemporary example would be a boutique in a town. A person could visit to see clothing or try on shoes and then go home and order that size online. The customer is a free rider on the boutique, which has offered a benefit that is not priced in. Over time, if everyone shops but does not buy, then the boutique may close.

4.3.2   Adverse Selection and Moral Hazard

Two other related market failures concern forms of market offering that over-select from less desirable behavior or below-average goods. In George Akerlof's 1970 article "The Market for Lemons," the economist describes marketplaces such as those for used cars which select inherently for faultier products than found on average in the larger world. If one has a broken car, one is more likely to sell it because it does not work. Thus, the market for used cars has an average level of quality that is below the level for the overall population of cars in use. The market adversely selects for worse than average cars, creating a market for lemons or duds.[30] Bayer and Page make the same argument about the art market for old masters, that the worse the works, the more likely they are to come to market.[31]

A **moral hazard** is essentially a type of risk-related negative externality borne by others. I might engage in riskier behavior if I knew that the safety net was provided for me without having to pay. This argument is most commonly applied to something like going heli-skiing in a country with publicly funded rescue and health care. In the arts, one might imagine taking risks on shipping or under-insuring works of art if another party would help cover a possible loss.[32]

4.4 PUBLIC ART, ECONOMIC IMPACT, AND NONMARKET VALUE

Economists still try to measure the impact of public goods or positive externalities. They have two main tools: economic development analysis and contingent valuation method. The first takes a top-down approach, mapping the overall impact. The second takes a bottom-up approach, attempting to estimate what individual people would have been willing to pay and summing those values. Although these methods are considered very differently within economics, we consider them together because they are attempts to understand the value of something not easily represented by markets.[33]

4.4.1 Economic Impact Studies

In 1994, Tate commissioned McKinsey & Co. consultants to conduct an economic impact study pro bono for what was then still called the Tate Gallery of Modern Art. McKinsey used a method devised by Peter Johnson and Barry Thomas in 1992 and summarized here from Johnson and Thomas's 1998 article "The Economics of Museums: A Research Perspective."[34] They essentially looked for the value of museums beyond "turnstile" demand," that is, beyond the demand to enter the museum as a visitor.[35]

The McKinsey study estimated that turning Bankside Power Station into a modern art museum would bring £30–£90 million of economic impact to London, creating 790–2,400 jobs. Of those, the McKinsey team estimated that £13–£35 million of impact and 400–1,000 of those jobs would benefit Southwark, the local borough of London in which Tate Modern is located. When McKinsey redid the study in 2001, a year after Tate Modern had opened (in May 2000), they found that the impact was substantially higher. They estimated that the new museum had brought £75–£140 million in impact to London (£50–£70 million to Southwark), creating 2,100–3,900 new jobs (1,390–1,890 jobs in Southwark).[36] The increase was accounted for by greater than estimated numbers of visitors.

These studies essentially try to assess and quantify the positive externality that the cultural destination, in this case Tate Modern, creates for the local environment – generating jobs, bringing people to the area who also make hotel reservations or purchase meals, increasing property values, or otherwise bringing income and economic growth that is catalyzed by but not directly captured by the arts organization. Often, the audience for these studies is the government whose support the organizations seek.

Scholars such as Arthur Sterngold have suggested that economic impact studies are advocacy work toward this end.[37] Where Tate Modern differs is in a much larger and abstract sense: Tate Modern arguably led to five-fold increases in neighboring property values – notable even if overall property values were rising – and a host of other economic benefits that accrued to other parties. The criticism of economic development that it is solely for advocacy risks underestimating the broader impact of such ventures. Instead, Tate Modern's economic impact story invites curiosity and creativity: How do we understand value creation that is not structurally contained within value capture? At the time, Tate explored creative solutions. One can imagine a share of property or sales tax given back to a nonprofit organization based on certain metrics or change compared to a city-wide benchmark. These solutions may become more tenable in the future, but in the case of Tate Modern they were not possible at that time.[38]

4.4.2 Contingent Valuation Methodology

Contingent valuation methodology (CVM) is a technique that uses survey methods to try to elicit someone's willingness to pay (WTP) or willingness to accept (WTA) a compensatory payment, in order to measure the economic value that an individual places on something.[39] For example, if the British Library has a reading room that is open to researchers for free, one can tell researchers that the library is closing for a period of time and ask what payment they would need to receive as adequate compensation for the closure. The compensation is defined as **compensating surplus** (CS), which is the amount of money that makes whole the person's welfare after a change in service, here the closure of the library.[40] When researchers did this study in 2004, they found an average willingness to accept a monthly payment for closure of the British Library of £273 (£431 present day). Summing those values and adding them to other values in their study, they arrived at an annual value of the British Library of £363 million per year (£573 million present day).[41] These estimates can be especially useful in cases such as the library, for which there is no stated price.

In a willingness to pay study, researchers might try to identify both **use value** and **nonuse value**. For a museum, the use value is the amount a visitor is willing to pay to attend a museum when that museum might otherwise be free. For nonuse value, a survey might try to uncover what the person would donate to support the institution's work. As Beatriz Plaza et al. argue, the brand value of major museums – especially those that also double as significant architectural monuments – has an economic impact and this impact is part of the nonuse value.[42] One other form of nonuse value is **option value**, meaning the nonuse value of having the possibility of attending even if one does not go. National parks and monuments often fall into this category. The use and nonuse values are summed to find **total economic value**.[43]

In 2015, the Arts and Humanities Research Council (AHRC) in the United Kingdom performed a contingent valuation study of Tate

Liverpool and the Natural History Museum in London.[44] In asking for the use value – how much someone would pay to attend if the museum were not free – the average use values were £6.65 for the Natural History Museum and £10.83 for Tate Liverpool.[45] When asked for nonuse value, in the form of what donation a visitor would be willing to pay on top of the ticket price in order to fund the research activities of the Natural History Museum and Tate Liverpool's work in the broader community, the average top-up donation was £2.78 for the Natural History Museum and £8.00 for Tate Liverpool.[46] A separate online survey gathered more information on nonuse value from non-visitors.

Contingent valuation studies are sometimes blended with survey questions about well-being, lending some of the survey questions a sharply existential mash-up of meaning and measurement:

> Take your life as it currently is, but now imagine that you have visited the Natural History Museum [once every [frequency] months (in other words, about [frequency] over the year)] alone or with your family/friends. Assume that you usually spent one to two hours there per visit and vary the activities each time. Overall how satisfied would you be with your life?[47]

Other questions ask, "How happy were you feeling in the last hour or so?" One imagines that in the midst of a busy day visiting a museum, perhaps with friends or small children or navigating crowds of strangers, it would be hard to pause and gather the first answer – how happy you are in your life – so that you can measure the change brought by two hours at Tate Liverpool. At the same time, the survey results can also underscore charmingly predictable human preferences. For instance, the top attractions at the Natural History Museum are, in order, dinosaurs, whales, and volcanoes.[48]

CVM can be controversial among economists because of its hypothetical nature and reliance not only on self-reported but subjective information. There is often no external benchmark for comparison. For instance, if asked to pay what I wish to visit the Metropolitan

Museum of Art in New York at the admissions counter, I would hand over one dollar. If a student presented the Metropolitan Museum of Art as a business plan and asked me what I would be willing to pay to attend, the amount would be much higher. While self-reporting in the abstract is problematic, the method is still considered the state of the art, absent other ways of attempting to put a price on the priceless, whether cultural heritage, art museums, protection of endangered species, or national parks.[49]

In 1989, the public-interest attorney Bryan Stevenson founded the Equal Justice Initiative (EJI), in Montgomery, Alabama. EJI aims to challenge systemic poverty and racial injustice, initially by focusing on legal representation of those facing excessive prison sentences or wrongful conviction. In 2018, EJI opened the Legacy Museum and the National Memorial for Peace and Justice. The Legacy Museum charts the line from slavery to mass incarceration. The National Memorial for Peace and Justice is dedicated to those lynched in acts of racial terrorism. The memorial displays 800 six-foot monuments honoring and listing the lynching victims by county. The coffin-like, corten-steel boxes hang in an open-square formation so that visitors may walk around and then under them. As part of the memorial, EJI launched the Community Remembrance Project to support communities wanting to engage in the work of reflection and remembrance of their own necessarily broken stories, past and present. As part of that work, EJI made two of each sculpture so that communities can go through a process of reclaiming theirs to "reflect a community's ongoing commitment to truth-telling and racial justice."[50]

Within that story, it may seem a footnote, or a neoliberal detail, to say that in 2019, the year after the museum and memorial opened, sales tax revenue in Montgomery was up 23%.[51] One can imagine – in the same way that Tate Modern tried to but was not able to realize – designing a system by which some of those funds flowed back to the institution, not just as a donation but as a claim on a percentage of sales tax in the neighboring area. As we will consider in Chapter 9, these complicated forms of value can sometimes be represented by property rights, as in the case of equity that artists might retain in their artwork.

4.5 DIFFERENT MODELS OF ECONOMIC DEVELOPMENT

Tate Modern is one of many museums credited with economic revitalization of a perhaps neglected area. As Sandy Nairne, then Tate's
director of programmes and later the director of the National Portrait
Gallery, notes, the area was "still recovering from structural changes
in the loss of commercial river traffic and associated warehousing and
light industry."[52] In the same time frame as Tate Modern, in 1999,
Mass MoCA (the Massachusetts Museum of Contemporary Art)
opened in a revitalized factory in North Adams, Massachusetts. In
1997, the Guggenheim Bilbao opened in the Basque town, with
a Frank Gehry marquee building that, in the words of writer Chloe
Wyma, turned a "decaying port town into an elite tourist
destination."[53] The Basque government paid a reported $100 million
in construction costs, $50 million for acquisition of new artworks, and
$20 million "licensing fee" paid to the Solomon R. Guggenheim
Foundation in New York annually, in addition to the Guggenheim
Bilbao's estimated $7 million yearly operating budget.[54]

There are a variety of models for economic development projects, with some stemming from artists' use of abandoned spaces and
others coming about through explicit partnerships among governments, collectors, philanthropists, and other private-sector actors.
For instance, the 798 Art Zone in Beijing grew around an anchor
institution, the Ullens Center for Contemporary Art (UCCA), founded
by Guy and Myriam Ullens in 2007, and also via the earlier initiative
of artists who found studios nearby. The area of Beijing, an old Soviet-
style, Bauhaus-inspired set of factory buildings, had been used by
artists from the nearby Central Academy of Fine Arts (CAFA) as
studios in the early 2000s. The area received municipal government
support to avoid demolition, and the Seven Stars Group still manages
the complex.[55] UCCA operates as a nonprofit under the Beijing Bureau
of Civil Affairs and Hong Kong government and receives one million
visitors per year.[56] The 798 Art Zone is home to commercial galleries
including Long March Space. Pace Gallery opened and then closed

a Beijing location there. Commercial rents have increased tenfold from 2005 to 2014.[57]

At the same time, recent years have seen other forms of museum development that include more complex public and private interests. China is home to an estimated 1,500 private museums.[58] Some of those museums were developed in areas such as the old Longhua Airport in Shanghai's West Bund that serve some similar urban revitalization purposes.[59] Some of the museums such as the Long Museum and the Yuz Museum are founded by philanthropists who are substantial private art collectors. Questions remain in practice regarding the ways in which those museums potentially increase the value of private art collections that may not in all cases belong to the museum exclusively. If institutions are not governed by international museum policies on deaccessioning, collectors can sell works back into the market without restriction.[60]

Whether public or private, some museums have also been criticized for neoliberal expansion, for example, the Guggenheim's expansion in Abu Dhabi. Saadiyat Island, a $27 billion development on a reinforced sandbar in Abu Dhabi, includes a Guggenheim Museum and an outpost of the Musée du Louvre as well as a campus of New York University. As Wyma writes in *Dissent*, "Sprinkled among these bastions of liberal arts and culture will be two golf courses, three yacht-friendly marinas, and several shopping centers, as well as luxury apartment complexes."[61] Organizations have publicized the working conditions under which the museums have been built, including recruiter fees, which can have the effect of locking international workers into long-term exploitative labor contracts.[62] Wyma quotes the twentieth-century American art critic Clement Greenberg, who famously described the arts as connected to the oligarch classes by an "umbilical cord of gold."[63]

Artists have also undertaken projects connected to urban revitalization, in diametrically different ways. On the one hand, the artist Theaster Gates's Rebuild Foundation and Dorchester Art + Housing

Collaborative in Chicago and Rick Lowe's Project Row Houses in Houston have revitalized communities.[64] At the other end of the spectrum, after the 2016 terrorist attacks in Paris targeting the Bataclan music venue and other sites, the artist Jeff Koons offered a self-described gift to the people of Paris – a sculpture of a hand holding flowers. However, Koons gifted the work itself but not the installation costs, which were covered by private donors. Some observers viewed the gift as a Trojan horse full of Koons marketing by means of a permanent, seemingly altruistic presentation in the Parisian cityscape, at Le Petit Palais near the Champs Élysées. Some also viewed the work as potentially cynical, a giant human hand punched up through the earth sprouting floppy tulips in shades of blue, red, yellow, green. Koons's studio wrote that the flowers "represent loss, rebirth, and the vitality of the human spirit."[65] Writing in *L-Obs* magazine, Yves Michaud described the monument to the 130 killed and hundreds wounded as (translated from the French) "eleven colored anuses mounted on stems."[66] In any of these scenarios, one can map the ecosystem of value around the sculpture, the museum, the art collection, and the community to ask the question of who benefits.

4.6 CONCLUSIONS

After the runaway success of the Guggenheim Bilbao in 1997 and Tate Modern in 2000, cities all over the world – and for Tate especially in the United Kingdom – approached the institutions to ask for their own "Bilbao" or "Tate Modern." The two institutions took very different approaches. Tom Krens, the Guggenheim Foundation director, collaborated with different cities and sponsoring institutions to explore other Guggenheim branches – opening outposts for a time in Las Vegas and Berlin, and exploring projects in Helsinki, Abu Dhabi, and Guadalajara, among others.[67] When Krens left the Guggenheim in 2008, he launched a consulting company to help start museums, many of them in China.

When organizations across the United Kingdom approached Tate to bring a Tate to one town or another, Tate took a different tact. Tate had already in 1999, under Nairne's oversight, started to create a national network complementing Tate Liverpool (founded in 1988) and Tate St. Ives (founded in 1993). When they were increasingly approached in the wake of Tate Modern's success, the Tate team essentially said, your town likely already has an arts institution. Instead of parachuting in with a Tate Modern, we will work with you to best support and amplify the institution you have. Tate started convening arts organizations across the United Kingdom, sharing Tate's own resources and bringing people together to learn from each other. The project resulted in a book called *On Collaboration* and in 2008 became a longer-standing consortium Tate Connects, later renamed Plus Tate. The name described the idea that towns and cities were getting their local gallery "plus Tate." Organizations pay a membership fee, currently ranging from £500 to £2,000. The gathering itself created a network externality, and then the overall project also led to sharing knowledge on economic impact.

In 2015, Plus Tate produced a book profiling the economic impact of the member organizations.[68] Working with Regeneris consultancy, they measured impact based on full-time equivalent employees of the organization and then an extrapolated figure they called "gross-value added" (GVA) impact, which tried to model a larger increase in employee wages and company earnings within a twenty-mile radius. In a separate measure that shares sympathies with contingent valuation methods, they modeled what they called "consumer surplus," which they defined to include the benefit of free visits, the value of advertising and positive media for the area, and different measures of education, health, community cohesion, and civic pride.[69] For individual arts organizations, they found overall that for every £1 invested, the arts commonly generated between £1.20 and £3 of GVA-calculated return.[70]

Although these measures are hard to model precisely, the larger impact has been a wave of interest in contemporary art. In 2018, Serota told *Guardian* interviewer Charlotte Higgins, "The most exciting development of the past 15 years has been that you can get 400,000 people a year going to a gallery in Margate, 200,000 to a gallery in Nottingham, 600,000 to a gallery in Liverpool. Compared with what people thought was possible 25 years ago, it's astonishing."[71]

Tate was able to lend its reputation to amplify and to credentialize these efforts. Higgins accompanied Serota to Nottingham where he would "lend endorsement" to a charity auction. In addition to the network externality produced by sharing information across organizations, Serota could essentially lend the aura of Tate Modern, and his own of course, to create a rising tide that lifted all boats. The goal was not only to create economic development through the arts but to persuade people of art itself – in Higgins's words, to "convince the English to value the arts as fundamental to ordinary existence, not just as branches of industry or drivers of tourism, or aspects of social policy, or flourishes of fashion."[72]

To say Tate is a market failure is to mean several different things at once. It is a failure in that it created value that is bigger than the institution itself. The value accrues to many people and organizations, not only to Tate which, being free to visit the collection, gives much more than it takes in. It is government support and private philanthropy that make the museum possible. In the case of mission-driven organizations that essentially function as common pool resources – public cultural trusts in physical spaces – the economic impact does not capture the value, and the reliance on philanthropy and government support should not determine the program.

When Tate Modern opened an extension in 2017, it needed to name the two linked but different buildings. The new extension is named for Sir Leonard Blavatnik, the Russian-born, British business titan whose fortune came from energy companies and whose family foundation offered substantial funding for the Tate Modern extension. In 2018, the original Tate Modern building that opened in 2000 was renamed for Natalie Bell, a single parent and resident of the surrounding borough of Southwark who was recognized by her neighbors for her work as the head of youth and community programs at Coin Street

Community Builders. When Tate Modern was in its mid-1990s planning phases, Bell was homeless before finding cooperative housing in nearby Oxo Tower Wharf. The naming was part of an art project – a Turbine Hall commission undertaken by the artist Tania Bruguera.[73] Bruguera's artistic intervention harkens back to the first hire at Tate Modern: the community liaison. As Serota wrote on the gallery's 1988–90 Biennial Report, "nothing can be achieved without sound planning and imagination, but progress depends on the creation of a partnership between Government, the private sector and the Gallery itself."[74] In that process, the gallery became a public good, in the noneconomic sense as well.

QUESTIONS

1. In your local community, find as many examples as you can of public goods and externalities. Do an audit of the source of each. Where does a positive or negative externality come from? Why is something a public good?
2. Choose an organization anywhere in the world that either operates as a nonprofit or that you think performs a public benefit. Write a proposal for grant funding or governmental funding based on the benefit provided but not directly supported by a market.
3. Consider the case of both Tate Modern, London, and the Equal Justice Initiative, Montgomery, Alabama. As in the chapter, Tate Modern has led to the revitalization of the Southwark area of London, leading to substantially increased property values for neighboring owners. The opening of the Equal Justice Initiative's museum and memorial has coincided with a substantial rise in sales tax revenue for the surrounding area. What are speculative proposals that you could make to help these nonprofit institutions claim part of the value that their existence has helped to create? Or, do you think these institutions do not have a claim? Be as imaginative and speculative as you can. Consider returning to this question after reading Chapters 8 and 9 to see if you can apply tools of property rights.

4. In an unusual recent use of an economic development study, the managers of documenta 14 cited such a study in 2017 when the art event that has taken place in Kassel, Germany, every five years since 1955 encountered financial difficulty.[75] Amidst press reports that the event was nearly insolvent, CEO Annette Kulenkampff and artistic director Adam Szymczyk, along with over two hundred artists, signed a set of open letters in defense of the exhibition. In their second letter, they cited an economic impact study conducted by the University of Kassel crediting documenta with €130 million in economic impact on Kassel. The deficit was estimated at €7 million ($8.3 million).[76] In the rhetorical context of art criticism and of much art that is expressly resistant to market commodification, this reference to an economic rationale was striking. Ultimately, the shortfall was covered by the city and regional governments, and the CEO of documenta stepped down without implication of wrongdoing. The story is still unfolding though some more creative financial arrangements seem to be under consideration, such as guaranteeing debt in place of additional outright funding.[77] Discuss the role of economic development around exhibitions that have expressly noncommercial purposes. Do you agree with the response of the documenta organizers? Why or why not?

5. Compare and contrast the process of Tate opening Tate Modern and the Guggenheim opening in Bilbao and exploring other locations. What are the similarities you observe and what are the differences? Agree or disagree with the idea that Tate is a federation and the Guggenheim was, at the time, operating as a franchise.

6. The Guggenheim project in Abu Dhabi was one of a number of large museum projects in the geographic area of the Arabian Peninsula that is referred to as West Asia or the Middle East. Consider other ventures within the Saadiyat Island Cultural District itself, such as the Louvre Abu Dhabi, and also those projects elsewhere in the region, such as the National Museum of

Qatar in Doha. What similarities and differences do you notice in strategy, funding, sources of art, and civic aspirations? Consider the role of architecture and related construction labor.

7. In 1981, the American artist Richard Serra erected a public sculpture called *Tilted Arc* across the plaza of a federal government building in Lower Manhattan, New York. A curved and leaning wall of corten steel, the work rose 12 feet (3.7 meters) tall and extended 120 feet (37 meters) in length. It bisected a pedestrian plaza on a diagonal, diverting foot traffic around itself. The work had been commissioned in 1979 as part of the US General Services Administration Art-in-Architecture program, but once it was in place, protests arose to lobby for its removal. Over 1,300 employees of the General Services Administration of the US government signed a petition. The sculpture spurred a conversation on how much role the public should have in choosing public artworks.

This debate became understood under the umbrella of public choice theory, a school of thought concerning the ways in which economic tools can be brought to bear on political processes and decisions.[78] In the case of *Tilted Arc*, a panel of experts convened by the National Endowment for the Arts had recommended the artist. The removal of the work in 1989 came about from a court case in which the artist sued to protect his First Amendment or free speech rights against the government's arguments to remove the work in the interest of security. Serra lost the case when the Second Circuit determined that the government's property rights allowed "content neutral" removal of the work.

In the context of this chapter and considering the difficulty of valuing public goods or analyzing the public's utility derived from them, research this case and related ideas of public choice theory. Present an argument for how, ideally, you would have designed the decision-making process at different junctures from the 1979 commission to the intervening petitions and hearings and then the eventual court case. What are ideal ways for the public to participate in these curatorial decisions? Does everyone have an equal vote, or do some stakeholders have more concentrated interests that need to be represented? How do you weigh the opinion of experts against the feelings of the public? Consider in your response the argument of Grace Glueck, then critic for the *New York Times*, who wrote in 1985,

> To this viewer, who admires Mr. Serra as a sculptor, *Tilted Arc* is still one of the ugliest pieces of public art in the city, a domineering work that bullies, rather than enhances, the open plaza .... Yet there *Tilted Arc* stands, awkward and stubborn, conveying to the viewer the important message that, unlike politics, a work of art is not about compromise.[79]

8. The ideas of this chapter are commonly applied to climate change and to the study of the environment. In addition, they apply to structural issues such as systemic racism or intersectional forms of exclusion and inequity. Consider questions of racial and socioeconomic participation in the arts workforce. How can you apply the lenses of this chapter – the misalignment of price and value and the tragedy of the commons – to analyze questions of exclusion? Write a speculative proposal in response to your analysis. Consider Claire Bishop and Nikki Columbus's review of the reopened Museum of Modern Art as a potential model.[80] Consider revisiting this question in tandem with Chapter 7's themes on labor economics. What other disciplines besides economics – history, political science, critical theory – do you draw on in your analysis?

5 Structure

> The chap next door who worked as a butcher's assistant earned more than my father.
>
> Christopher Davidge, Christie's CEO and third-generation Christie's employee[1]

On Wednesday, February 8, 1995, Christopher Davidge, the CEO of Christie's auction house, arrived by Concorde at John F. Kennedy Airport in New York at 9:25am.[2] He was met by Dede Brooks, the CEO of Sotheby's auction house, who picked him up at the British Airways terminal in her personal car, a dark-green Lexus.[3] They drove to the short-term parking lot and sat in the back seat so that they could look at files together. After a few hours, Davidge flew back to London on the 12:30pm flight.[4] That meeting was one of several that they held in order to hammer out details of a price-setting agreement between Sotheby's and Christie's.

The two auction houses that currently control about half of the global auction market for fine art were started in the eighteenth century.[5] In 1744, Samuel Baker, a bookseller, founded Sotheby's in London. The first recorded sale, on March 11, 1744, was of several hundred books, which all told brought in £826. In 1766, James Christie resigned his post in the British Navy to become an auctioneer. The first recorded sale at Christie's, on December 5, 1766, featured hay and alcohol instead of books. Christie himself socialized with many artists including his next-door neighbor, the celebrated British nineteenth-century painter and founding Royal Academician Thomas Gainsborough.[6]

Despite their stature and centuries-long tenure, by the early 1990s the auction houses were struggling financially. What had for a long time functioned as a kind of friendly rivalry became a cutthroat competition.[7] Around March 1995, not long after Davidge's airport meeting with Brooks, the fierceness of the competition, especially for higher-value works, eased. As subsequent criminal and civil litigation would reveal, the auction houses had conspired in a price-fixing scheme. Beginning as early as 1993, the chairmen of the two auction houses had been meeting for breakfast in each other's home, allegedly bringing in their respective CEOs to implement their plans.[8] In fact, Christie's and Sotheby's had likely engaged in price-fixing in the 1970s, but they had resolved the lawsuit brought by the Society of London Art Dealers and the British Antique Dealers' Association by paying £75,000, or half of the dealers' legal fees. This time, the litigation would result in a $512 million settlement.[9]

In this chapter, we will toggle between the people operating these firms and the ways in which their highly idiosyncratic human behavior animates the theoretical economic structures of markets. What would happen in the litigation would separate out the four actors – two CEOs and two chairmen – and the two auction houses, with radically different outcomes for all of them. The case would highlight two aspects of economics: that industries can have overall *market structures* and that these structures, however much they can be described as objective, are ultimately inhabited by people.

Theoretical economics begins with an ideal of perfect competition, but most actual market structures involve imperfections, which is to say market power. **Perfect competition** is a bland and fictional state in which all goods are interchangeable, there is perfect mobility of resources, and the market sets the price. Other market structures start to complicate that anodyne and frictionless personality with quirks, needs, and unfair advantages that range from the unavoidable to the strategic to the illegal. In the market structure of an **oligopoly**, a few firms exert power over an industry. A **duopoly** is a special form of oligopoly, as in the case of Christie's and Sotheby's, in which instead of rule by the few there is rule by two commanding firms. In **monopolistic competition**, which characterizes the vast majority of markets, there is some product differentiation, often through brand, and therefore some pricing power but still the availability of a range of substitutes. In the arts, most participants, whether artists or dealers, are monopolistically competitive. They have some, but not total, market power.

The narrowest definition of market power is the ability to set price. In any of these cases, firms with some pricing control are still beholden to the market demand curve. They can maximize profits, but they are not omnipotent. When they raise the price, they lose some customers. Oligopolies, including duopolies, can achieve these benefits of pricing power, but to do so they must act together. For firms to collude and conspire in anticompetitive practice is illegal in the United States under the Sherman Antitrust Act of 1890. At the time of the Sotheby's and Christie's case, collusion was illegal in the United Kingdom, though as a civil and not criminal offense.[10]

As we will see in this chapter, market structures are identified by a group of factors: the number of firms, the presence of high or low barriers to entry, the presence of market power (again, defined narrowly as the ability to set price but also marked by more general attributes of power), and the uniformity or differentiation of goods on offer. **Barriers to entry** describe factors that keep new firms from joining an industry. These barriers may include start-up costs, patents or other intellectual property, trade secrets and professional relationships, regulatory limitation or advantage, or the existence of partnerships and contracts. This study of market power is one of the inflection points at which economics shifts from the mechanics of cost, price, and markets into complicated environments operated by people.

5.1 THE FOUR CHARACTERS: TWO CEOS AND TWO CHAIRMEN

The price-fixing scheme at Sotheby's and Christie's – a story inimitably told by Christopher Mason in the book *The Art of the Steal* – hinges on the lives of four people: Alfred Taubman, the chairman of Sotheby's; Diana (Dede) Brooks, the Sotheby's CEO; Anthony

Tennant, the chairman of Christie's; and Christopher Davidge, the Christie's CEO.[11] Whether by virtue of legal settlement or personal wealth, by the end of the story only one of them will have worked for a paycheck they have not had to return.

Alfred Taubman (1924–2015), the Sotheby's chairman, came from Detroit, Michigan, and was the *inventor* of the shopping mall. A man with what Mason describes as "the prodigious girth of a well-fed German burgher even as a young boy," Taubman carried an awareness of the need for self-reliance likely instilled as a boy watching his father fall on hard times and their house get repossessed.[12] Having built a real-estate empire by the early 1980s, Taubman married Judith Mazor Rounick, a former Miss Israel, in the summer of 1982 and then bought Sotheby's in 1983. The Taubmans were a power couple who entertained dignitaries and later, as Taubman was about to go to prison, loyal close friends.

When Taubman purchased Sotheby's in 1983, he rescued the company from financial crisis. Not only was Taubman rescuing them financially, he was also rescuing Sotheby's executives from the presumed indignity of being taken over in a hostile bid by Stephen Swid and Marshall S. Cogan, the co-chairmen of General Felt Industries, Inc., a carpet-lining company based in New Jersey. Through social connection, Sotheby's' dazzling efforts to court Taubman during his visit to an auction, and favorable downward social comparison from mall- to carpet-mogul, Taubman became the majority owner and chairman of Sotheby's. He paid $139 million, $38.5 million of which was his own money. At Taubman's first all-hands meeting at Sotheby's, he lectured the staff on their insufferable snobbishness which he had also experienced as a customer. He told them to do better.[13]

Dede (Dwyer) Brooks was the CEO of Sotheby's under Taubman's chairmanship. Brooks started working at Sotheby's in 1979. A Yale graduate – tall and with the demeanor of an avid runner – Brooks had grown up with six siblings including two older brothers. She honed her stoical caretaking abilities in her teens when her oldest brother was killed in a motorcycle accident, leading Brooks to tend to her younger siblings – and her parents.[14] Her fortitude was tested again in college when she faced a serious health battle that required several rounds of surgery. After graduation, Brooks worked as a lending officer at Citibank for five years before leaving her job to spend more time with her baby daughter.[15]

In 1979, Brooks decided she wanted to go back to work and asked Sotheby's chief operating officer, Fred Scholtz, for a part-time job. He told her they did not have any jobs, to which she replied, "Well you don't have to *pay* me. I just want to work three mornings a week." She was hired on the spot and tasked with collecting late payments from wealthy clients. She excelled at this task and was put on the payroll shortly thereafter.[16] In 1987, at age thirty-seven, she was appointed president. In November 1993, Sotheby's announced her appointment as global CEO.[17] Brooks's husband, Michael, whom she met in college, went on to become a very successful banker. One could wonder if this fact was known when, under the later investigation, Brooks would be required to return every dollar of post-tax pay she had ever received from the auction house.[18]

Taubman's counterpart in the chairman's role at Christie's was Sir Anthony Tennant, the former chairman of the brewery Guinness. Tennant had famously doubled Guinness's profits under his leadership. Tennant had joined Guinness in 1987 to replace a CEO who left under a veil of scandal regarding manipulation of Guinness' share price and who would ultimately serve a prison sentence. Tennant was credited with restoring the company's reputational standing and building out its business internationally. At the time he was appointed chairman of Christie's, Tennant was receiving an annual pension of £500,000 (equivalent to about $758,000).

Tennant came from family wealth – his ancestors had invented bleaching powder in 1799. He was described as "unmistakably upper-class," as sometimes "a cold fish," and also as enjoying "schoolboy humor – slipping on bananas, that sort of thing."[19] Tennant spoke little. A peer of his in the drinks industry Lord Sheppard once said,

"You can see him thinking. I might say 5,000 words, he will say just 10."[20] Upon first meeting Tennant, Taubman described him as "a tall, rather attractive English gentleman ... [with] very strange glasses like two big windshields."[21]

The Christie's CEO, Christopher Davidge, had the longest family ties to – and the most complex class dynamics with – the auction business. Davidge was the third generation of his family to work at Christie's. His grandfather Wilfred Davidge had gone to work at Christie's in 1904 at age twelve, rising from the rank of trainee porter to senior cashier. Wilfred died of a heart attack at his desk at the age of forty-one. Christie's offered Wilfred's widow, Eva, a small pension of thirty-five shillings a week, as well as a job for her seventeen-year-old son Roy, Christopher's father. Roy left school to take the position in 1932. Roy met Olive Fowle, a secretary in the Decorative Arts Department. When they married, Olive's family disinherited her. Roy worked at Christie's for thirty-four years, rising to the position of company secretary before dying at age fifty-one of a heart attack. When Christopher was in school, his best friend Jason moved in with the Davidge family after Jason's mother's suicide, which he had been the one to discover. Later, Christopher's mother left his father to be with Jason.[22]

Christopher Davidge technically went to work at Christie's at age eight when the firm was returning to its bomb-damaged King Street offices after World War II. Christopher, because he was small, was paid to stand inside an overloaded elevator and push the buttons to move furniture around.[23] In his twenties, after an interlude selling men's shirts in the Petticoat Lane market in east London – a job at which he did well but which provided only seasonal income – his father ordered him back to Christie's under threat of being kicked out of the family home. Christopher's father had first sent him on an interview at Christie's a few years earlier, but when the interviewer, a senior director called Guy Hannen, asked Christopher if he had any questions, Christopher had said, "I can see there's a future if you are the grandson of one of the partners, but as the grandson of a clerk,

I don't see any future." In Christopher's telling, Hannen told Christopher's father, Roy, that he was, "the most arrogant young man he had ever met."[24]

This time working at Christie's, Davidge became a printer for White's, the catalogue publishing business that Christie's had just acquired. Davidge was twenty-one. He rose to run White's and he dedicated himself to it tirelessly. From 1976 to 1983, Davidge flew from London to New York forty times each year to manage the production of auction catalogues.[25] Even though Davidge rose to the CEO role, he was still dogged by criticism of his appearance, personality, and class position. Some people called him "the butler" behind his back.[26] Some called him "the golden hamster" after his immaculate coiffure and his diminutive stature.[27] By accounts, Davidge was fastidious about his appearance. One colleague who shared a two-bedroom flat with him once said he was surprised to see Davidge hanging out at home without trousers. Davidge said he waited to put on his trousers just before leaving so that they would not crease.

However Davidge's upbringing affected him, one thing was clear: He was the one among the four who decided to keep notes of the meetings. He would become the informant and, unlike Brooks, he would leave the story with a substantial multimillion-dollar payment that assured his participation as a cooperating witness, allowing Christie's to seek amnesty.[28]

By the early 1990s, Taubman, Brooks, Tennant, and Davidge were ensconced in their roles. The chairmen met at a party in 1993 and began to meet for breakfast periodically at Taubman's London pied-à-terre.[29] Brooks and Davidge started meeting later in 1993, not long after Brooks's appointment as Sotheby's CEO was announced in November 1993.[30] Over the next couple of years, the two CEOs agreed to commit to various non-price terms. For instance, they would no longer offer zero-interest loans to collectors. Previously, they would loan money to a collector without charging interest in advance of the auction to which the collector's artwork was consigned. They stopped donating to charities to motivate consignments.

And they stopped offering "straight guarantees." In a straight guarantee, the consignor keeps all of the proceeds above the guarantee. For instance, if an auction house guaranteed a collector $10 million for a painting, the collector could keep any amount that was bid above $10 million. By the new agreement, now the auction house would split the proceeds with the consignor and receive some percentage of any amount above the guarantee.[31] The purpose of these agreements was to stop the auction houses from undercutting each other in the task of winning business. Theoretically they could compete with each other to the quick, so that neither of them was making any profit. (For an overview of auction theory, see Appendix D.)

The agreement on price happened in the first quarter of 1995. In January 1995, Davidge finally broached raising commission rates with the Christie's board. They asked him for a formal proposal before their next board meeting on March 7. Davidge called Brooks and said they had to meet. The next day was their famous parking-lot meeting at the airport in New York. Davidge told his colleagues he was at the dentist.[32]

On March 9, 1995, Christie's announced a new seller's commission. On April 13, 1995, Sotheby's announced that it would follow.[33] Sotheby's offered a small discount to museums, and two weeks later Christie's confirmed that it would do the same. In June and July, Davidge and Brooks met in Brooks's London flat to trade "grandfather lists" of clients already in negotiation. They were agreeing who would be exempt from the new fees and laying claim to certain consignments or relationships.[34]

By the end of 1995, the economy was rebounding, but it was clear the new commissions had had an impact. Sotheby's revenue was $1.67 billion in 1995, up 25% from the $1.3 billion revenue in 1994.[35] Christie's revenue in 1995 was $1.5 billion, up 17% from the $1.3 billion in 1994. Christie's pretax profit was up 32%.

In 1996, the United Kingdom's Office of Fair Trading noticed the near-identical rates and launched an inquiry under the Fair Trading

Act of 1973 and the Competition Act of 1980.[36] Both Christie's and Sotheby's received letters dated June 25, 1996, making "informal enquiries."[37] The investigation was probably unsettling but not as existentially worrisome as the later overtures under the more punitive US law.

By 1997, the two firms were not as actively colluding. They were either beginning to cheat on their deal or inadvertently straying from the arrangement by having uncoordinated staff negotiate deals. The agreement simply eroded over time. The problem was that one auction house would find out the other had cheated or offered unaligned terms because the clients would try to play off the deals against each other. For instance, Sotheby's waived the seller's commission for the John Langeloth Loeb collection of Impressionist paintings, but then the Loeb estate asked Christie's to match the offer.[38] It is not known whether the person who waived the seller's commission knew of the collusion or just really wanted the business.

In 1997, the US Department of Justice, the governmental agency tasked with enforcing antitrust laws, began to investigate the auction houses. They subpoenaed any documents related to correspondence or meetings between the two houses since 1992. The investigation spun its wheels until two years later when Patricia Hambrecht, an attorney who served as Christie's general counsel before assuming the role of president of Christie's North and South America, told lawyers that in fact she thought there had been price-fixing. Hambrecht had been close to Davidge, close enough that some rumors of an affair had risen to the level of insinuation in the UK press that Hambrecht was a codefendant in Davidge's second divorce. Both parties strongly denied the claim.[39]

The two worked closely together, and Hambrecht told lawyers about her prior experience calling out Davidge on the collusive arrangement, just up to the point where each of them still had plausible deniability. Hambrecht had to resign her job, most likely because of her role in an entirely separate lawsuit, one in which Michael Ward Stout, the executor of the estate of the photographer Robert

Mapplethorpe, had sued Christie's for defamation when the auction house said Stout had misled them, as a way of explaining away a very high 1989 appraisal of Mapplethorpe's estate. Stout sued for defamation over the insinuation that he had misled anyone. After Christie's paid a reported $2 million settlement to Stout, Hambrecht resigned, and it was weeks later that she met with Christie's lawyers and said that there had in fact been a price-fixing conspiracy. When the lawyers flew to London to interrogate Davidge based on Hambrecht's claims, he again denied any untoward conversations or agreements with Christie's. But then the attorneys happened to speak with Davidge's executive assistant, Irmgard Pickering, who recalled that Davidge and Brooks had met multiple times not long before the announced changes in the seller's commissions.[40]

Christie's legal team strongly encouraged Davidge to get his own counsel, which he did in the form of an American criminal defense attorney named Joe Linklater.[41] With his attorney, and a letter Davidge already had from Tennant's successor as chairman, Lord Hindlip, promising certain terms, Davidge negotiated his resignation and severance agreement and then turned over his papers and confessed his role. Davidge had enormous leverage given that Christie's own immunity from prosecution rested on his testimony and notes. Because Davidge resided in the United Kingdom where the offenses were only civil, his appearance in US court was not a given.

The Sherman Antitrust Act had recently been amended regarding the claiming of amnesty by one party in a price-fixing scheme. Prior to 1993, one could only claim amnesty by coming forward before an investigation had begun.[42] The investigation had begun in 1997, and Davidge and his employer were coming forward in 1999. The standard was changed so that a party could still come forward provided they could prove that they were not the instigator nor a coercive influence in the price-fixing. Thus, when Davidge confessed to the lawyers, they raced against the clock to be the first in the door at the Department of Justice to plead for amnesty from prosecution. A set of dominoes fell in late 1999 into early 2000: On Christmas eve, Davidge's severance agreement was completed and he received his first $3.2 million payment.[43] His attorney, Linklater, emailed Cliff Aronson, Christie's antitrust counsel, to say there were some documents.[44] The new Christie's CEO, Ed Dolman, and general counsel, Jo Backer Laird, received the documents and had to decide swiftly to come forward to the Department of Justice. On December 29, 1999, at 1pm, Aronson delivered the documents to the Department of Justice and asked for immunity for Christie's.[45]

On January 12, 2000, the Department of Justice invited Aronson to Washington, DC, where they peppered him with skeptical questions about Christie's' amnesty plea.[46] Christie's had to promise that Davidge would testify. In exchange, Davidge's lawyer negotiated favorable protections. The Department of Justice tipped off Sotheby's by issuing a new round of subpoenas, but Sotheby's thought it might just be a routine flurry of activity in advance of the expiry of a convened grand jury.[47]

On January 24, 2000, the Department of Justice finally confirmed provisional amnesty for Christie's. On January 27, 2000, Brooks learned from Sotheby's' attorney that Christie's had mysteriously called off their joint-defense agreement without explanation. The next day, on January 28, the head of the Sotheby's press office asked Brooks for comment on an article the *Financial Times* was planning to run the next day that Christie's had been given amnesty from antitrust prosecution. That is essentially how she found out. By chance, Brooks already had a meeting scheduled with an outside attorney, John Siffert, who happened to be at Christie's that day separately, prepping Christie's executives for their appearances before a grand jury. Among many famous cases, Siffert represented the author Truman Capote in a libel case again the author Gore Vidal. Brooks hired him on the spot as her personal attorney.[48]

Under criminal prosecution, Brooks returned to Sotheby's all of the post-tax money she had been paid since 1993, approximately $3.25 million. With forfeited stock options and payment of her own legal fees, it was that Brooks returned or forfeited $13.25 million in total compensation. She was sentenced to six months of house arrest, three years of probation, 1,000 hours of community service, and a \$350,000 criminal fine. Taubman was sentenced to one year in jail and a \$7.5 million criminal fine.[49]

In civil litigation, Christie's and Sotheby's paid a combined \$512 million to the class-action plaintiffs, defined as anyone who had *bought* an item from Christie's or Sotheby's between January 1, 1993 and February 7, 2000, as well as anyone who had *sold* an item through Christie's or Sotheby's between September 1, 1995 and February 7, 2000.[50] A separate suit, settled for \$30 million, addressed anyone who had bought class A common stock in Sotheby's between February 11, 1997 and February 18, 2000.[51]

One piece of the prosecution not related to market structure but of worthy economic note was an innovative structure designed by Judge Louis Kaplan to choose the attorneys who would represent the class of plaintiffs. Under this novel bidding system, Judge Kaplan asked each legal team to bid the minimum amount they thought they could win for the plaintiffs. The lawyers' fee would be 25% of the amount *above* whatever minimum they had bid. David Boies and his team won by bidding \$405 million, only to learn that most other firms had bid closer to an average of \$130 million.[52] With the \$512 million settlement, the lawyers were paid 25% of the \$107 million above their \$405 million bid, or \$26.75 million. Christie's – its owner Francois Pinault – paid \$256 million. There was substantial concern that paying its share would bankrupt Sotheby's. Taubman personally paid \$186 million, so as not to bankrupt a firm in which he was a majority stakeholder. Sotheby's paid the rest.[53] The class of plaintiffs had included buyers and sellers. Whether the auction houses fixed the buyer's premium when it was raised in 1992 was never confirmed and also vehemently denied.[54]

5.2   PERFECT COMPETITION

The null hypothesis of market economics is a structure called perfect competition. In perfect competition, the price of a good is set by the market itself, and firms compete to produce in a

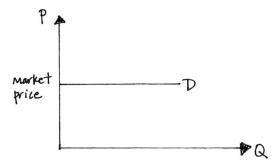

FIGURE 5.1 Demand from the point of view of a perfectly competitive firm.

cost-effective and efficient manner. Market power is synonymous with being able to set price. In perfect competition, all firms are "price takers." The demand curve for the market overall has its typical downward slope. The demand curve faced by each firm in a perfectly competitive market looks like a flat line at the market price (see Figure 5.1).

Perfect competition is the Platonic ideal of the market according to an economist. The market brings together buyers and sellers efficiently, as the story goes, to use scarce resources in the best possible way. Under the assumptions of perfect competition, we would have to have perfect information, as in, we could know exactly what it cost to make, for example, a pencil, down to whether Bob in accounting was slacking off on the job. We would have to have perfect mobility of resources, meaning that the entire pencil factory could – as if Harry Potter donning an invisibility cloak – just up and become a pharmaceuticals company, if there were profits to be had in medicinal pills but not in pencils. The rationale is that the threat of other firms entering the pharmaceuticals industry is what keeps those producers working efficiently and not gouging anyone on the price. In reality, huge barriers to entry and exit exist and pharmaceuticals production is also a highly regulated industry.

Notice that under perfect competition, the firm that makes the pencil is an amorphously unified actor. The firm is like a cow, not like a bunch of people inside a cow costume trying to act like a cow. The firm is a magnetic constellation of market transactions, inside and outside its boundaries. As theorized by Ronald Coase in his 1937 essay "The Nature of the Firm," the firm exists to manage for the friction of the transaction costs of coordinating activities by placing a set of activities under this umbrella of the firm. Coase memorably quotes Dennis Robertson, an economist who worked closely with John Maynard Keynes at Cambridge, to describe "islands of conscious power in this ocean of unconscious cooperation like lumps of butter coagulating in a pail of buttermilk."[55]

5.3 MONOPOLY

A monopoly is a market structure in which one firm dominates. The monopoly holds the power to set price. The monopoly firm is still beholden to the market demand curve, but the firm is the entire market. The firm maximizes profits by pricing where marginal revenue equals marginal cost. The monopolist's marginal revenue curve extends below the demand curve, sloping more steeply than demand and falling below zero (see Figure 5.2).

As Figure 5.2 shows, the ability to set price does not mean that the monopolist is magically in control of demand. As the monopolist raises price, fewer people can buy the good because fewer people demand it at a higher price. But the monopolist still has power to set price to its best advantage.

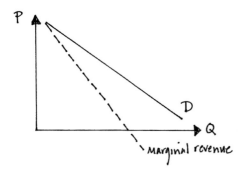

FIGURE 5.2 Demand curve and marginal revenue curve for the monopolistic firm.

In general terms, we perceive monopolies to be bad because they run counter to the story of efficiency and competition as serving the greater good. In many ways, this fear of monopolies is warranted. Monopolists can engage in predatory pricing to drive out competitors and then broad groups of people risk being left without choice, whether of software and computer-operating system or of search engines and places to purchase books online.

But there are also some monopolists with whom we tend to feel comfortable. For example, the company Brannock makes the Brannock device, which is used to measure people's feet for shoes. The company generally dominates sales of shoe-measuring devices, but it lacks structural market power: The Brannock company's webpage says one million of the devices, which currently sell for about $75, have been sold, but that is not such a large quantity for a product patented in 1929.[56]

We also have "natural monopolies," such as the post office or the utility company. These monopolies occur because the fixed cost of operating the overall system is so high that the marketplace cannot support two firms. The average total cost continues to become lower the larger the marketplace becomes. Rather than break up these firms, we tend to regulate them in order to control their pricing.

It is hard to imagine pure monopolies in the arts, outside of artists who technically hold monopolies in their own artistic output, but we will see many monopolistically competitive firms, those with brand differentiation and some but not total market power.

5.4   OLIGOPOLY

An oligopoly is a small group of companies or other entities that together, if coordinated, can behave as a monopoly. As before, a duopoly is a subset of oligopolies in which there are exactly two firms. A commonly invoked example of an oligopoly is OPEC, the

Organization of the Petroleum Exporting Countries, a group of oil-producing nations that have since 1960 worked together to agree a common price for oil. The OPEC member states benefit by cooperating to reduce competition. If each country tried to maximize its profit from oil, all of the countries would compete their profits away. By coordinating they reach a stasis in which everyone is as well off as they can be.[57]

The Christie's–Sotheby's price-fixing scandal follows a similar trajectory. If an art collector is deciding whether to consign a collection to one house or the other, they might ask Christie's for a benefit and then ask Sotheby's to match it. Over time, the consignor might be able to use this strategy of playing the auction houses off against each other to reduce their profit to zero. By coordinating prices and agreeing not to negotiate, the auction houses protect their profitability, though to the detriment of competition in the market.

The way in which governments typically evaluate whether there is anticompetitive practice is to look at the market concentration and at a related metric called the Herfindahl–Hirschman Index.[58] The **market concentration** is the percentage of the overall market that the top firms claim. The **Herfindahl–Hirschman Index** (HHI) is the sum of squares of the market shares. The advantage of the HHI, which is the most widely used contemporary measure, is that by squaring the market shares, concentration at the very top is emphasized. For example, if we had a market with the top four firms having the share 50%, 5%, 3%, 2% or instead a market with the top four firms having the share 15%, 15%, 15%, 15%, both would have a market concentration of 60%. But the HHI would be different – 2,538 and 900, respectively – because squaring the 50% allows us to see the relative concentration more clearly.

The HHI is calculated either by squaring the percentages as if they were full numbers, for example, 24 instead of 0.24, or by squaring the percentages and multiplying by 10,000. For example, in 2018, the top four auction firms worldwide were Christie's, Sotheby's, China Poly, and Phillips. Christie's reported sales of $7 billion. Sotheby's reported sales of $6.4 billion. China Poly reported sales of $1.2 billion, and Phillips reported sales of $916 million. These numbers show their

Table 5.1 *Market concentration analysis for Herfindahl–Hirschman Test, 2018*[1]

Auction house	Annual revenue (2018) in USD millions	Percentage market share ($29.1 billion auction market)	Market share squared
Christie's	7,000	24.1%	579
Sotheby's	6,400	22.0%	484
China Poly	1,200	4.1%	17
Phillips	916	3.1%	10
Total	**15,516**	**53%**	**1,089**

[1] McAndrew, 2019, pp. 146–147.

revenue rather than their profits.[59] According to *The Art Market 2019*, the worldwide auction market for art was $29.1 billion.[60] We can use this figure as the denominator to find the market concentration and HHI, as shown in Table 5.1.

To trigger a Department of Justice inquiry, the top four firms would typically have a market concentration in excess of 60% or an HHI of over 1800. Here, the market concentration for the top four firms is 53% and the HHI is 1,089. McAndrew notes in *The Art Market 2019* that, despite market concentration across the large auction houses, the overall auction business is relatively regional, which makes sense considering the difficulty of transporting large works of art or heavy pieces of furniture.[61] That said, we have made a few implicit judgment calls here. We have used a global art-market number, as opposed to looking at the concentration within New York or London. We have used the overall revenue numbers for the auction houses, including private sales. If we considered the options for someone selling a top-tier Mark Rothko painting at auction, their choices are realistically limited to Sotheby's and Christie's, though of course they could sell the work via private sale. These questions of defining terms characterize antitrust outside the arts as well. Companies like

Amazon and Google have such broad remits that they can argue for a definition of industry classification that does not acknowledge necessarily their full market power.

In the arts, we see a concentration in major organizations, even in the so-called "mega-galleries" such as David Zwirner, Gagosian, Hauser & Wirth, and Pace. However, it would be hard to imagine the dealers colluding to set prices across works of art. Following from Velthuis's work as cited in Chapter 3, pricing is set in such complex and sociological ways, it seems hard to imagine effective coordination. Furthermore, even though dealers can represent some artists exclusively, in practice there are other ways to secure that artist's work. Artists are commonly represented by dealers in different geographic locations with those dealers cooperating. And for some artists, a work could be purchased at auction if not available through the gallery.

Curiously, in the Sotheby's–Christie's case, Davidge seems to have told himself, according to his notes, that the auction houses were not in fact colluding to set price. He reasoned that artworks are singular and thus always have a different price. As Ashenfelter and Graddy point out, the houses were not conspiring to set price on artworks; they were conspiring to set price on the service of selling art. It is the commission rate that was fixed in the scheme.

The diagram of supply and demand for oligopolies is sometimes debated among economists but is essentially described as a kinked demand curve (see Figure 5.3). The kink shows the two alternate universes depending on whether participants in the oligopoly follow the pricing agreement or not.

5.5   MONOPOLISTIC COMPETITION

Most firms in the arts could be described as monopolistically competitive. They have relatively low barriers to entry and differentiated products. One can think of outlier examples immediately. For instance, it would be very hard to start a competitor to the Museum of Modern Art unless one had an unrivaled art collection already. It would be hard to start a competitor to a major gallery without relationships with artists and collectors. All of these enterprises are expensive to run, on real-estate grounds alone. And yet there are new entrants in the arts and relatively creative ways that new entrants are resourceful in clearing these hurdles. The gallery Signal in Brooklyn, which ran from 2012 until 2018, was an industrial live-work space that was only open on weekends because its purveyors had full-time jobs to support the gallery's expenses.[62] The gallery Norte Maar was founded by Jason Andrews and Julia Gleich in the living room of Andrews's apartment. He avoided the fixed cost of operating a gallery by foregoing a couch some of the time.[63] At the top of the market, it is hard to imagine competition with Christie's or Sotheby's for major consignments. Yet, in 2020, three large galleries – Pace, Acquavella, and Gagosian – formed a syndicate to sell the $450 million art collection of Donald Marron, the former chairman

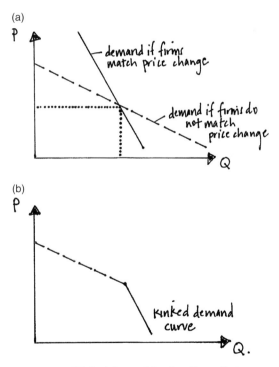

FIGURE 5.3 Kinked demand for the oligopolistic group of firms.

Table 5.2 *Summary characteristics of market forms*

Perfect competition	Monopolistic competition
Many firms	Many firms
No barriers to entry	Low barriers to entry
No market power	Some market power
Standard products	Differentiated products
Monopoly	**Oligopoly**
One firm	Few firms
High barriers to entry	High barriers to entry
High market power	High market power
Unique products	Standard or differentiated products

and chief executive of the bank PaineWebber and former president of the MoMA trustees.[64] (Marron was also instrumental in the formation of the PaineWebber now UBS art collection.) With Christie's, Sotheby's, and Phillips all having reportedly issued at least $300 million guarantees, it was assumed that one would win the business.[65] But the consortium of galleries won out instead.

Monopolistically competitive firms traditionally engage in non-price competition, most notably by focusing on brand. Even though the term "brand" derives from marketing and is dismissed derisively in some areas of contemporary art practice, here its first-principle meaning – of signaling the authenticity of something – captures the strategy of non-price competition. It matters that when an artwork is shredded at an auction, it is by Banksy, not in the style of Banksy.[66] And it matters that when a bisected dead animal is placed bracingly in a formaldehyde tank, it is done by Damien Hirst and not anyone's obscure creepy neighbor.

Table 5.2 summarizes the market forms.

5.6 GAME THEORY

To return to the Sotheby's–Christie's case, the resolution of the anti-trust inquiry is instructive both about the auction industry and about market power. If we go back to 1995, Christie's and Sotheby's published near-identical seller's commission tables. (They also both moved the buyer's premium from 10% to 15%, but whether this was coordinated has always been debated, and the auction houses have maintained their innocence.)

Here is where the nature of a cartel particularly surfaces. The collusion between the two firms required both firms to act in concert. Without their coordination, they would not have reaped the economic benefits of a monopoly. The two houses could be said to have been engaged in a **Prisoner's Dilemma game**.[67] In the original version of the game – and here "game" is used generally to describe an interaction in which each party knows the other party is trying to behave strategically – there are two prisoners, Al and Bob. They have been arrested for a crime they committed jointly, but they are being questioned separately. The best outcome for the two of them together is that neither caves under questioning and confesses to the crime. If neither confesses, both receive a one-year sentence for gun possession. However, the prisoners face opposing incentives. Their individual best outcome is to confess and accuse their co-conspirator of committing the crime. In that case, each would receive a sentence of zero years, but their co-conspirator would receive a full twenty-year sentence. However, if both of them try for the zero-year sentence, they will end up in a situation where neither receives amnesty and they both receive ten years. The prisoner's dilemma is usually depicted in a two-by-two matrix of outcomes. The pairs of numbers show the outcomes to (Bob, Al) for each circumstance (see Figure 5.4).

In this case, Christie's has confessed but essentially accused Sotheby's of the greater crime because they have been able to convince the Department of Justice that they were not the sole instigator of the price-fixing. They have been able to secure something analogous to the "0, 20" outcome – with more substantial cost but unequal consequence – by claiming amnesty first. As before, the outcomes for Taubman, Brooks, Davidge, and Tennant diverged wildly.

Many have observed the irony that an antitrust investigation intended to protect market competitiveness almost had the opposite

		AI	
		Confess	Don't Confess
Bob	Confess	10, 10	0, 20
	Don't Confess	20, 0	1, 1

FIGURE 5.4 Prisoner's Dilemma game.

effect – lending Christie's monopolistic power by forcing Sotheby's out of business under the weight of crushing fines. Today, both houses still dominate auction markets for large-value artworks. The seller's commission is not public and is generally understood to be negotiable. The buyer's premium is public and gigantic – much larger than at the time of antitrust. (See Tables 3.1 and 3.2.)

5.7 CONCLUSIONS

The Sotheby's–Christie's collusion was a story of people, protagonists in a complex novel. Yet from 30,000 feet, it was also a story of market structure. The unanswerable question was whether the people needed to collude in the first place. Whether the auction houses would have followed each other informally without collusion cannot be known. For price competition, it seems possible that the same outcome could have been achieved without coordination. For other contract terms, such as guarantee structures or grandfather lists, the houses would likely have needed an explicit understanding – a handshake deal. In addition, as auctioneer Barbara Strongin has noted, auction houses already coordinated with each other in a number of ways that arguably served buyers, for instance, coordinating their schedules so that auctions did not take place on the same evenings. From outside the industry, hosting competing events at the same time might sound like a form of more perfect competition. Yet from inside the arts, where singular works of art are on offer, the buyer could be served by the choice to be physically present at both sales, able to bid in the room each time.[68]

In addition to illustrating market power and structure, the story also serves as an example of pricing, including the pricing of auction fees, the estimation of damages, and the inventive pricing of legal services. In 2003, a group of economics professors including Orley Ashenfelter, Victor Ginsburgh, Kathryn Graddy, Patrick Legros, and Nicholas Sahuguet wrote a short essay in *The Art Newspaper* upending the entire logic of the legal settlement in this case. They wrote that the apportionment of damages completely misunderstood pricing. The settlement had, they wrote, compensated buyers at 5% of the sales price and had compensated sellers at 1% of the sales price. This division, they argued, was entirely wrong. By the logic of economics, buyers had information on the full price they would be paying when they bid. The buyer's premium, whether the result of collusion or not, was advertised ahead of time. Thus, buyers could plan their bid so that the hammer price plus posted premium would accurately reflect the buyer's full willingness to pay. Thus, if the buyer's premium was inflated as a result of collusion, it was the sellers who were really hurt. The buyer could still bid with full information, leaving the seller with a lower net sum after the premium was paid to the auction house. By this logic, the sellers were doubly shortchanged: They could potentially have been charged higher seller's commission initially and received a lower net price.[69] Given that the auction house's primary fiduciary duty is to the seller, this oversight would be that much more consequential. These points continue to be debated. Regardless, the price-fixing scandal remains a story of market power and of the role of individual leadership in setting strategy, legal or otherwise.

QUESTIONS

1. Who in the arts do you think are monopolists or oligopolists, if any? For example, do you think that an artist has monopoly power over their own work? Why or why not? Do the top commercial galleries have power either to act as monopolists or as oligopolists? Under

what circumstances would you say that an arts organization had gone from being monopolistically competitive – that is, having some brand differentiation – to behaving like a monopolist? You may wish to consider examples such as the pricing and contract terms around Jeff Koons's sculptures or the dealer consortium selling the Marron collection.

2. Since the price-fixing scandal, the auction houses Christie's and Sotheby's have diverged in strategy more than in the past. Under the leadership of Tad Smith, a former head of the concert and sports venue Madison Square Garden, Sotheby's diversified into a number of related areas. In 2016, Sotheby's acquired the advisory business Art Agency, Partners for $50 million (up to $85 million including structured bonus payments).[70] One might hypothesize that the acquisition allowed the auction house to build toward recurring revenue – not the lumpy revenue of big spring and fall auction seasons but the regular and ongoing payments of artists' estates seeking advisory support on the management and, perhaps, controlled sale of their assets. Select one of the companies that Sotheby's acquired during this time, for example: Art Agency, Partners; Orion Analytical, the forensic conservation lab; or the Mei Moses Art Indices, home of the art-market data analytics founded by researchers Jianping Mei and Michael Moses, whose scholarship we touch on in Chapter 9.[71] Researching the acquisition, what do you think was the auction house's strategy?

3. In 2019, Sotheby's was acquired by BidFairUSA, a company wholly owned by telecom entrepreneur and art collector Patrick Drahi. The acquisition took Sotheby's from being the longest-operating company on the New York Stock Exchange to being a private company again. With Christie's also a privately owned entity, in what ways does the dynamic between the two companies change? Note that because the Sotheby's acquisition was financed substantially with debt, the company is still required to make a number of public disclosures.[72]

4. Consider Ashenfelter, Ginsburgh, Graddy, Legros, and Sahuguet's argument that sellers were treated unfairly – doubly so – in the class-action settlement. Do you agree with their logic that buyers could still insure that they did not exceed their own willingness to pay? How can you tie this argument back to the concept of price elasticity of demand? Argue for or against the claim that elastic demand would lead to greater harm to the sellers.

5. According to Strongin, prior to the price-fixing scandal, Sotheby's and Christie's coordinated with each other to plan the schedule of sales. For example, the houses would take turns going first in the major seasonal sales. This alternation also allowed the houses to alternate which one would host a sale on US elections night.[73] Is this coordination in schedules an example of collusion that harms competition or an act of coordination that serves buyers by giving them maximum access to sales? Or would you argue for a third option that weighs various costs and benefits? What, in your view, would be the ideal way to coordinate the timing of sales? As a project, choose a city such as London or New York and find the schedule of auctions, ideally for a cluster of sales in May or November. Make a master calendar of sales across the auction houses. What do you notice are the advantages and disadvantages of the schedule for the different houses individually and for all of the houses overall?

6. In an auction, if the bidding does not clear the reserve, then the work is bought in, meaning it fails to sell. The fate of the artwork that is bought in depends on the arrangement that the auction house has with the seller. If the auction house has provided a guarantee, then the auction house has effectively bought the work at the guaranteed price and may resell it. If there is a third-party guarantor, then that party has bought the work. If there is no guarantor, the work simply fails to sell and goes back to seller – unless the auction house and seller later confer and try to sell the work privately at a lower price. (Other arrangements may be negotiated as well, for example, for the auction house to keep a work

that has been bought in but not guaranteed, with the auction house paying for storage and insurance in exchange for the ability to reoffer the work at a lower price point.) How would the consequences of guarantee arrangements have differed for Sotheby's and for Christie's at the time when Sotheby's was publicly traded and Christie's was owned by a deep-pocketed private company? What would have been the different risk profiles and worries of the institutions? How can you liken guarantees to insurance and investment decisions?

7. Consider the arts overall as an industry including the phenomenon of "mega-galleries" and any other concentrations of power that you observe. Read the section of Hans Abbing's *Why Are Artists Poor?* on "Informal Barriers Structure the Arts: How Free or Monopolized Are the Arts?" In discussion or in a written research memo, debate the extent to which the arts exhibit characteristics of monopolies. You may choose to consult Edward Winkleman's writing on mega-galleries or any number of other resources on concentrations of taste-making or gatekeeping in the arts.[74]

6 Power

In some ways [art is] the home decoration of capitalism and in some ways it's a search for meaning.

Maxwell Tetenbaum, circa 2019, Goldsmiths MFA student at a coffee shop

On Monday, September 15 and Tuesday, September 16, 2008, Sotheby's London hosted "Beautiful Inside My Head Forever," an auction of 223 new works by the artist Damien Hirst.[1] The Friday before, Lehman Brothers had lost 93% of its stock value and declared bankruptcy. Hirst had come to fame as a leader of the Young British Artists (YBAs) who were students at Goldsmiths when Hirst organized *Freeze*, their 1988 breakout group exhibition. Hirst later became an international art celebrity with his iconic work *The Physical Impossibility of Death in the Mind of Someone Living*, a preserved shark suspended in a tank of formaldehyde.[2] By 2008, Hirst was represented by both Jay Jopling of White Cube gallery and Larry Gagosian of Gagosian Gallery. For his Sotheby's auction, Hirst circumvented both dealers. Now a global brand, he sent his new work directly from his studio to the secondary-market auction house, bypassing his dealers. By skipping the step of first selling work into the primary market, Hirst disintermediated the supply chain – that is, the connected sequence of markets – of the art world. In enacting this supply chain strategy, Hirst exercised market power.

In this chapter, we will consider the supply chain of the art world. A **supply chain** is a manufacturing-centric model of production – a chain of steps or stages from raw material through production and distribution. Supply chains tell a few different stories simultaneously. The first is a structural story of this trajectory from raw material to finished good to distribution to customers. The second is a story of market power – of the interactions along the supply chain and the holders of negotiating leverage. The third is a story of systems in which the supply chain is not linear but part of a larger constellation of actors. In this third story, artists have opened their own galleries, galleries (and artists) have started residency programs, and many actors have blurred the lines of nonprofit and for-profit enterprises. The fourth and last story is one of strategy. Because supply chains form the spine of many industries, they also feature prominently in business strategy frameworks that are used to map competition and collaboration in any field. We will look specifically at the classic business strategy frameworks of Porter's Five Forces, Oster's Six Forces, and Brandenburger and Nalebuff's Value Net. We will conclude by considering very different supply chain interventions such as the artist Mark Bradford's opening of the gallery Art + Practice in his neighborhood in Los Angeles or Hauser & Wirth's opening of an artist residency program in the English countryside.

6.1   SUPPLY CHAIN AS STRUCTURE

An archetypal supply chain describes a manufactured product such as a breakfast cereal or a car. Cereal starts with farmed grains that are harvested and processed, then used as ingredients in factory production, magically transformed into flakes or shapes that are bagged, boxed, and shipped to wholesalers and grocery stores, then purchased by cafeterias and household shoppers. Various other functions – such as management and design – occur as a kind of overhead to the supply chain process. Historically, industries such as steel have been used to illustrate the supply chain: at the peak of the industrial revolution in the United States, Andrew Carnegie's US Steel owned almost all of the stages of the steel supply chain, from raw materials all the way through the distribution channel of the railroads.[3] By contrast, the art world supply chain appears looped and idiosyncratic. Before we turn to the art world, let us explore a manufacturing example in the adjacent field of luxury goods: the case of conglomerate LVMH, which adapted its factories to produce hand sanitizer for French hospitals during the coronavirus pandemic.

Moët Hennessy Louis Vuitton SE, aka LVMH, is a multinational corporation made up of seventy-five companies, including Christian Dior whose factory near Orléans, France, produces soaps and perfumes. In March 2020, as the pandemic was surging, the company shifted manufacturing from bottled soap to hand sanitizer in less than three days so that an estimated 12,000 kilograms of hand sanitizer could be distributed for free to Parisian hospitals.[4] In addition to requiring a certain form of decisive leadership, centralized control, and strong personal connections across public and private sectors in an upper stratum of French society, this move also engaged certain aspects of a supply chain. The factory already had bottle parts that could be adapted. The ingredients of hand sanitizer were already on hand and also not rare. The factory had the means to change its production and distribution relatively quickly.

In contrast to the linear manufacturing of cereal or Christian Dior soap or hand sanitizer, the art world has a complex, nonstandard, and overlapping supply chain. How would you apply this manufacturing-centric model to the arts? The "manufacture" of art includes education, making, finding an audience through sales or otherwise, and collections management, as well as parallel structures of sense-making via journalism, art education, scholarship, and formal art criticism. In teaching an introductory art-business course, I used to assign students to draw a supply chain of the art world. One student, Anastasia Loginova, drew a symbolic tree reminiscent of an Ad Reinhardt diagram (see Figure 6.1). Another student, Peter Bahr, offered a stick figure who sells a picture of a tree that gains a gilded frame to symbolize its progress from one supply chain stage to the next (see Figure 6.2). Importantly, the stick figure dons a bow tie between the roles of art advisor and auctioneer.

We could probably agree that the art world supply chain goes something like this: It begins with research and learning for the purpose

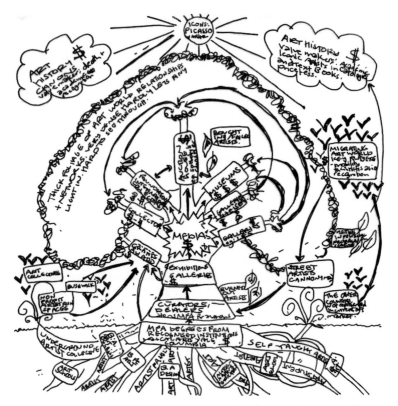

FIGURE 6.1 Anastasia Loginova, *Supply Chain of the Art World.*
Courtesy of the artist.

of informing an artist's work, capacity building to hone their craft, developing ideas, making work, finding suitable outlets to exhibit and distribute the work, and then sales through various distribution channels including art galleries, art fairs, and Instagram (see Figure 6.3). Some artworks might eventually be resold through private dealers or auction houses such as Sotheby's or Christie's. Some works complete their supply chain journeys with inclusion in museum collections.

While we speak of the primary market, in which works are sold for the first time, and the secondary market, in which works are resold, these market categories overlap. Auction houses are almost entirely concerned with the secondary market while art fairs and

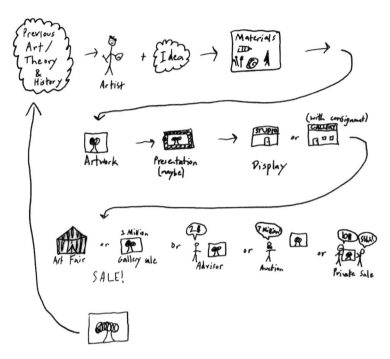

FIGURE 6.2 Peter Bahr, *Supply Chain of the Art World*. Courtesy of the artist.

galleries typically deal in both primary- and secondary-market sales. Thus, in introducing primary market activity into Sotheby's auction house, Damien Hirst broke with a very long-standing convention. The trailblazing two-day single-artist auction not only brought Hirst $201 million, but has, in the words of art-market critic Tim Schneider, "come to symbolize both an inflection point in the world economy and a source of dramatic irony for anyone looking back."[5] (For an overview of auctions, see Appendix D.)

The supply chain of the art market has evolved over time. For her book *Rembrandt's Enterprise*, the art historian Svetlana Alpers studied the Dutch artist Rembrandt (1606–69), examining the artist's

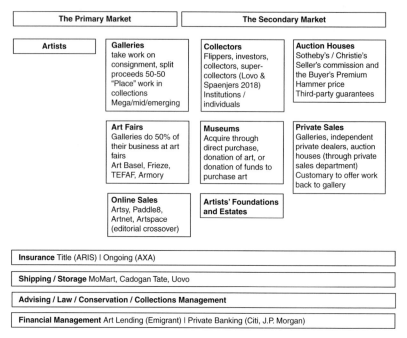

FIGURE 6.3 A working supply chain of the art world.

studio practice and connection to the market. Even Alpers's art historical observations can be mapped onto a supply chain. For instance, Rembrandt strongly separated out his drawing, painting, and etching practices. He required very long sittings from the subjects of his portraits. Apparently, Rembrandt kept a number of nearly finished works in his studio so that he could finish them to order for collectors. He also, according to Alpers, retooled his etching plates with small changes so that he could sell the images as new.[6]

For most contemporary artists operating within the constructs of the art world, the supply chain looks very different from that of Rembrandt. Artists typically make work in their studios on spec. Those artists with gallery representation consign those works to dealers, meaning the artist still owns the work but has given the gallery contractual rights to sell it. This system is in contrast to buying the work as part of inventory. If the works sell, the artist and gallery typically split the proceeds 50:50 unless negotiated otherwise.[7] The collector then keeps the work indefinitely. Customarily, if the collector wishes to sell, they give the original gallery first right of refusal before listing the work at auction or otherwise trying to sell it privately.

Regarding these dynamics of collecting and resale, Stefano Lovo and Christophe Spaenjers have proposed that collectors behave according to various motivational patterns. They model four different types of collectors, whom they call flippers, investors, collectors, and super-collectors. Essentially, flippers will always auction work if it is to their advantage. Investors are driven most by macroeconomic factors. Collectors only sell under distress. And super-collectors never sell as they are insulated from market forces and motivated to hold onto the art.[8]

In addition to the trajectory through primary and secondary markets, supply chains have overhead functions to support these sales. These functions include storage, insurance, and financial management. The latter includes, for instance, art lending – pledging a collection as collateral to secure loans with which to invest in other activities.[9]

6.2 SUPPLY CHAIN AS POWER

The supply chain not only shows how something gets made but also allows for the study of power and control of **vertical markets**, which are the sequenced set of marketplaces along a supply chain. Imagine that a supply chain is a stacked set of marketplaces, a chain of supply-and-demand interactions. For instance, there is a market of artists consigning work to dealers, followed by a market of dealers selling to collectors, and so on.

Along that line of markets in a supply chain, there are distinct power differentials. Sometimes, in order to harness market power, firms will engage in **vertical integration**, or the move (by acquisition, competition, or partnership) into adjacent stages of the supply chain. For instance, LVMH is, in the story above, able to create hand sanitizer within seventy-two hours because it is a highly vertically integrated firm. It manufactures and distributes its own goods. In this sense, vertical integration is a study of market power. While power in the most traditional economic sense means the ability to set price, here it also means the ability to operate strategically, to secure advantages, and to protect against various forms of operational risk.[10]

6.2.1 Vertical Integration and Risk

Power in a vertically integrated supply chain can also derive from risk. The journalist Patrick Radden Keefe's 2012 investigation of the North American drug-trade supply chain provides a compelling example.[11] As Keefe writes, there is a reason that drugs "cost more on the street than at the farm gate: you're not paying for the drugs; you're compensating everyone along the distribution chain for the risks they assumed in getting them to you." Keefe tracked the price of one kilogram of cocaine from Peru to its US market value. What cost $2,000 in Peru was worth $10,000 by the time it got to Mexico. It trebled in price to $30,000 as it crossed the US border, and then it more than trebled again to $100,000 street value.

Keefe was studying the Sinaloa cartel, the Mexico-based empire then headed by Joaquín Guzmán, better known as El Chapo, before his arrest in 2014 (and escape in 2015 and rearrest in 2016). In Keefe's telling, the supply chain for cocaine radically reset its power structure in the 1980s when the United States began policing smuggling routes through the Caribbean so strongly that the Cali and Medellín cartels in Columbia started to contract middlemen in Mexico. This route became so important and high volume that the Columbians began to pay the Mexican contractors in drugs, giving the latter enough capital to start their own operations and to transition from being intermediaries to being principals themselves. By 1990, the Sinaloa cartel was transporting an estimated three tons of cocaine through Mexico into California each month, inventively relying on everything from Boeing 747s to submarines. In all seriousness, El Chapo has been commended for the creative ingenuity of his supply chain management, including building a tunnel from Mexico to the United States.

Hirst's sale at Sotheby's perhaps lacks the ingenuity of Guzmán's tunnel – or of Hirst's original procurement of the shark, an animal Hirst sourced by calling coastal Australian post offices, which placed "shark wanted" flyers on the artist's behalf.[12] Nonetheless, Hirst's auction strategy demonstrates the same core principles of control and design of a system. In hindsight, we know that Hirst's sale took place on the precipice of collapse of the global economy that had just been signposted by the bankruptcy of Lehman Brothers. In Hirst's sale, only two lots failed to sell by auction, though were sold privately in short order. Hirst himself – his holding company Science (UK) Limited – made $172 million.[13] The reversal of fortune came later: Although the auction was successful, Hirst's career subsequently suffered. In 2008, the average auction price for his work was $831,000, compared to 2010 when the average price dropped to $136,000. Hirst's gallery relationships were also destabilized. In 2012, he left Gagosian Gallery, though he did return a few years later.[14] Hirst's supply chain intervention may have benefited him in the short term, but it arguably destabilized the supply chain for his work. Still, his story is unusual because few artists would have the market power – and wherewithal – to try to intervene so pointedly in the structures by which their works are curated and sold.

6.2.2 Vertical Market Failure

Vertical integration can be a strategy to amass power or also an attempt to avoid forms of market failure. What we call "market failure" here is not a failure in the sense of externalities or public goods in Chapter 5. In those cases, market mechanisms fail to align price and value. Either people could use a public good without paying or something generated externalities, positive or negative, for which there was not compensation. Here, we use the term in the sense the economist Oliver Williamson did when he wrote in 1971, "What are referred to here as market failures are failures only in the limited sense that they involve transaction costs that can be attenuated by substituting internal organization for market exchange."[15] The failure is that two firms cannot interact without an overwhelming transaction cost, or risk, and so it is easier for one firm to acquire the other and to internalize the market.

For example, in the earlier story of making hand sanitizer, notice that all of the parts of making the hand sanitizer fall under the umbrella of one company, LVMH. We could imagine an alternate story in which sanitizer is made by one company in bulk, then sold to another company that bottles it, and then sold to a wholesaler that distributes it. Instead, LVMH is a vertically integrated business. While it has suppliers – for instance, entities from which it purchases bottles or raw ingredients such as glycerin – the company, broadly speaking, controls the entire supply chain from inputs through manufacturing through sales and distribution.

Similarly, the clothing company Uniqlo is generally a vertically integrated business. While the company outsources the manufacture of fabrics, including its innovative heat-tech thermal layering textile, the company controls design, manufacture, and distribution through its own stores.[16] In contrast, an artist's studio is not typically a vertically integrated business. An artist may singlehandedly produce the work, but it is rare for an artist to distribute the work as well. Social media complicates the supply chain for art by encouraging artists to represent their work directly to collectors.[17]

In a 1993 article, "When and When Not to Vertically Integrate," John Stuckey and David White studied vertical integration as a response to various categories of market transaction failure.[18] In their view, companies acquire businesses adjacent to them or form partnerships – quasi-integration strategies – in order to avoid these forms of transaction failure and market risk. In a pure sense, integration means acquisition or purchase of the other resources, but it can also mean entering into long-term contract or other formal collaborations. In the parlance of vertical integration, to acquire toward the buyer end of the supply chain is **forward integration** or integration

downstream. To move backwards toward suppliers is **backward integration** or integration **upstream**. For example, LVMH entered into a quasi-integration strategy by establishing a long-term contract with its bottle manufacturer; Uniqlo did the same with its fabric suppliers. Some artists have handshake deals with their galleries, while others have formal, exclusive, even long-term contracts that also function as quasi-integration strategies, connecting artists downstream to the distribution of their work.

Broadly speaking, transaction failure occurs when there are too few buyers and sellers, when buyers and sellers need to transact often, and when they have to commit substantial resources first before transacting. In markets with monopolies or monopsonies, there can be too few sellers. (A **monopsony** is a market with only one buyer, for instance, WalMart as the buyer of wholesale medicine and household goods.) A powerful company could change the terms of an agreement suddenly, leaving less-powerful participants without recourse. For example, in 2017 the Artist Pension Trust announced that it would start charging storage fees to the artists who had placed artworks in the trust as savings for their retirement. Although there was an outcry, artists had little power to negotiate those terms that were newly introduced by a much larger entity.[19] There was not another fund artists could move to. The field of competitors is not yet developed.

Another reason vertical markets fail is from frequent transactions. Although we could assume goodwill of individual people, in theory frequent transactions present opportunities to cheat. Even if people do not cheat, there is too much uncertainty if one party can renegotiate.[20] For instance, imagine a donut-and-coffee cart that receives a delivery order each morning. They would not want to have to negotiate the price of donuts daily or to risk not receiving the full quantity of their order. Thus, they have long-term contracts with their suppliers, who also would not like the donut orders refused or renegotiated at a discount on a daily basis. Similarly, if you were working as a development officer in a museum, you would not want your employment contract and pay negotiated on a daily basis. You would rather have a general contract and negotiate for a raise or promotion periodically.

Vertical markets can also fail because of required commitment of resources. If an actor is required to invest in a specific asset without commitment from adjacent stages of the supply chain, then a risk is involved. This risk of investment is described as **asset specificity.** Asset specificity is the commitment of an organization to invest in something of value that has a limited range of use. **Site specificity** is the commitment of resources geographically. For instance, if a factory that manufactures parts for an Apple iPhone must locate right next to an Apple factory, that supplier to Apple would be risking a strong commitment of site specificity and therefore would want to have a long-term contract. **Technical asset specificity** is the commitment to the customization of machinery or tools for a specific purpose. If the above factory has also engineered its manufacturing line to fit Apple parts, it has a commitment of technical asset specificity. The third category, **human capital asset specificity**, is the training of a workforce for a particular task needed by a supply-chain-adjacent firm. Training workers to make specific products is an investment. In all these categories of asset specificity, the firm investing in specific assets is left exposed to the risk of the outside firm reneging on an arrangement after the firm's commitment to location, tools, and training.

In the art world, artists commit to developing material for exhibitions in galleries and museums. Artists could therefore wish to have a contract to cover their risk of committing time and materials – various forms of asset specificity – to the project. Similarly, a gallery or fabrication shop that is paying for the work to be made might also wish to have a contract. The arts ecosystem is also full of many long-term partnerships that are more human than economic in nature.[21]

Vertical markets may also fail in the final stage of reaching the buyer. If a product is innovative enough, an existing supply chain may not be able to sell it. For example, when CAT-scan machines were first developed, the inventors had to forward integrate into sales because they had to explain why the machine was useful. Artists can face this same problem of needing to develop a market for their work or having their work only slowly find its audience.

6.2.3 Quasi-Integration Strategies

Overall, vertical market strategy depends on questions of risk, power, and collaboration. These factors can be managed through forms of commitment that fall short of outright merger. These quasi-integration strategies include long-term contract, joint venture, licensing arrangement, and even franchising.

The collaboration between the Museum of Modern Art New York and the clothing company Uniqlo illustrates a quasi-integration strategy. Clothing featuring MoMA-licensed images from the museum's collection are sold at Uniqlo's flagship Fifth Avenue store, down the street from the museum. Uniqlo became a sponsor of MoMA's program of offering free admission on Friday nights in 2013 and then formed the partnership SPRZ in 2014, the following year, to produce the clothing.[22] They offered Warhol flowers on windbreakers or Keith Haring characters on pocketed t-shirts. This quasi-integration strategy through licensing arguably serves both parties. Especially if the museum retains rights to design approvals, the partnership furthers the store's sales and anchors its art-friendly brand. The museum benefits from this marketing. At its best, the clothing even educates a shopping audience about art.

Franchising is not as common in the arts because of the needs of the dealer–critic system to control points of taste-making and because of the focus on scarcity of singular objects. One related example of a franchise model would be the case of the American artist Thomas Kinkade, whose sometimes-mocked but incontrovertibly successful landscapes were once described by Joan Didion as having "such insistent coziness as to seem actually sinister."[23] Kinkade created approximately twelve new works each year, then made versions of them for a broader market, sometimes applying touches of paint to signal the "hand of the artist." (Note this versioning strategy from Chapter 3.)

Distributed through a large network of partner galleries, the works were so ubiquitous in the United States that circa 2002 the works reportedly hung in one of twenty American homes. However, the enterprise arguably overexpanded. The business reported a - $16.2 million profit in 2000 and a $16.6 million loss in 2001.[24] In the context of this kind of overexpansion problem, various forms of franchise, strategic partnership, and license can help someone like Kinkade to distribute work without taking on the risk.[25]

Some relationships which would be quasi-integration strategies in other industries are kept distinct in the arts. This separation is sometimes necessary because of the relationship of institutional and commercial value. For example, the writing of a scholar or of a critic has an impact on the market for an artist's work, but the scholar and the dealer need to be independent for that impact to occur. Mukti Khaire theorizes this role, which she terms that of **intermediaries**. An intermediary can be a person or an institution – a museum, a scholar, a critic – that provides information, signals merit, or otherwise curates, champions, or evaluates work in ways that affect markets.[26] This role of intermediaries happens across cultural areas. As Khaire writes in *Culture and Commerce*:

> Although such discourse is particularly influential in the so-called high culture segment (art, literature, classical music, and dance), ... the so-called low culture segment (film, pop music, genre fiction) is not entirely immune to these standards either, because consumers enjoy the emotional security that comes from knowing that a credible source has validated the quality of the work according to some widely accepted criteria.[27]

These intermediaries render the work visible – for instance, culling a gallery guide of must-see shows; they instruct and introduce art – through educational programs and prizes; and they simply compile listings.[28] These actions are perceived as independent of the market, thus serving an primarily informational rather than marketing function. Following from Velthuis's work, intermediaries may sometimes signal independence but really mask the reality of joint venture between, for instance, an artist's commercial gallery and a national pavilion at the Venice Biennale.[29] The commercial gallery may have paid for the exhibition, but the venue projects the critical distance and separation from commercial interests that museums have from the market.

This role of taste-making in supply chains is also explored in White and White's pioneering work *Canvases and Careers*, tracking the development of the dealer–critic system in France during the rise of the Impressionist painters.[30] Artists were no longer validated by their inclusion in salons but by their presentation by dealers. This historic shift from the French Academy system to the validating forces of art dealers and taste-making critics has been interpreted as an art historical and sociological change. It is also a structural transformation of the supply chain for art, one that is still in some state of ongoing evolution.

6.3 SUPPLY CHAIN AS ECOSYSTEM AND SITE OF CREATIVE INTERVENTION

Supply chains are linear tools but also maps of ecosystems. In 2014, Hauser & Wirth, one of the largest galleries in the world, opened an artists' residency program in Somerset, England. The gallery also founded the Hauser & Wirth Institute, a separate nonprofit organization which gives grants to scholars for archival research in art history.[31] The gallery also started a publishing imprint that produces around twenty-five titles per year and also a quarterly magazine.[32] This kind of lateral and organic expansion of a commercial gallery is interesting to consider in a supply chain context. Theoretically, a residency could be placed on a supply chain as a feeder to a gallery, but that is not the case here. The residencies are by invitation and typically for artists not represented by the gallery. The residents also create educational programming for the local community. These questions are complicated where mission and money coincide.

At the same time, there are other ventures founded by artists that can be interpreted in the supply chain context much more purely in a sense of audience development, giving back to communities, and supporting other artists who are making their way. This work exists in a historical context of creative placemaking with such ventures as Rick Lowe's Project Row Houses, a transformation, beginning in 1993, of a five-block area in the historic Third Ward in Houston, Texas, into a community campus.[33]

In 2014, the artist Mark Bradford, who is represented by Hauser & Wirth, founded Art + Practice (A+P), an exhibition space in Leimert Park, the Los Angeles neighborhood where he grew up (see Figure 6.4).[34] Bradford founded the space, which operates as an incorporated 501(c)3 nonprofit organization, in collaboration with the collector and philanthropist Eileen Harris Norton and the activist Allan DiCastro. Art + Practice aims to encourage "education and culture by providing life-skills training to foster youth" in South Los Angeles and also by holding "free, museum-curated art exhibitions and moderated art lectures" for the community.[35] Essentially, Bradford stretched the supply chain, making it more elastic to pull people in. He uses the

FIGURE 6.4 Art + Practice exhibition space exterior, Los Angeles, CA. May 6, 2019. Photograph by Natalie Hon. Courtesy of Art + Practice.

authority of his artistic position to bring a museum-like space to the neighborhood. When he speaks about it, Braford intends the gallery to honor the neighborhood, to bring the same kind of value that Tate Modern or other public goods do.

Bradford relayed some of his story to curator and museum director Thelma Golden in a 2015 interview. Bradford grew up around his mother's hair salon, learning the craft himself. He did not study for an MFA in art until age thirty-five. He joked that he got "a PhD in night clubs" but one that trained his sensibility about presentation and form.[36] Braford's vision for the gallery was one of bringing art to the community instead of expecting the community to come to the museum:

> It would be great if it could be in a local neighborhood. We are always asking people to come to the mountain. Go out of your communities. Drive on the bus, and feel really uncomfortable in the temple of art. Well if it was just in the neighborhood, contemporary, full of expansive ideas, little A instead of a big A, you know, we would probably find more practitioners early – the thought, I get this. I can own this too. It can belong to me too. Oh I get this. I just wanted to have the contemporary – right around the corner from the … local businesses. They can go in there and they can have a relationship with something that is local ….. I make it accessible. I don't change anything. I just make it accessible.[37]

Visiting the gallery, if you exit and stand with Art + Practice to your back, the building across the street, which is not part of A+P's campus, has a giant sign which reads, "There is a free art gallery across the street."

6.4 SUPPLY CHAIN AS THE SPINE OF BUSINESS STRATEGY

Supply chains often form the spine of business strategy analysis. As defined by the economist Sharon Oster, "a strategy is a commitment to undertake one set of actions rather than another."[38] A strategy takes into account the behavior of other organizations, the opportunities (or rivalry) in the field, and the ease with which other organizations can compete. That ease is usually measured in two ways: by the availability of substitutes – the power buyers have to purchase other goods – and barriers to entry – the difficulty that other firms would have getting into the industry and making it more competitive.[39] The other key factors include the power of one's suppliers and of one's buyers, a dynamic which maps onto a supply chain.

Various business strategy "frameworks" or tools serve as shorthand ways of considering questions of strategy. In the most archetypal of these business strategy tools, Michael Porter offered in 1979 his iconic Porter's Five Forces (see Figure 6.5). The spine of the diagram is from suppliers to buyers. Is the industry itself rivalrous? Do suppliers or buyers have market power? The intensity of rivalry depends on a few different factors: If the industry is fragmented with many different organizations, it can be hard to coordinate the firms, thus making it harder to marshal market power. The arts do not have standard products, lending an unusual dynamic in which suppliers can have more substantial power and price competition is not so simple because the products are not interchangeable.

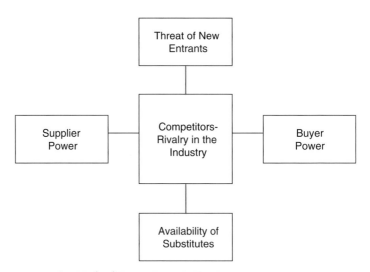

FIGURE 6.5 Michael Porter, Porter's Five Forces.

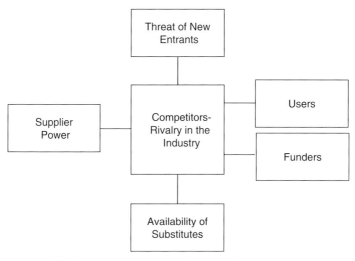

FIGURE 6.6 Sharon Oster, Six Forces framework.

In 1995, Oster created a variation of Porter's framework for nonprofit organizations (see Figure 6.6). She split "buyers" into "users" and "funders" in order to distinguish those directly using the services from those who might be users but are fundamentally intending to support the institution philanthropically.[40] The core idea is that donors are a special kind of customer of the organization. Even though the framework allows for application to nonprofit management, the framework is still based on the assumption of competition.

Around the same time, in 1996, Adam Brandenburger and Barry Nalebuff devised a new framework, the Value Net, that models firms as competitive and cooperative simultaneously (see Figure 6.7). They called their approach "co-opetition."[41] Their business strategy framework keeps the spine of the supply chain but replaces barriers to entry with the *availability of complements*. The framework still captures competitive dynamics but adds the question of complements.[42] By adding complements, the framework allows for collaboration – for things that support, not just replace, each other. The question becomes – not just how do I compete well but – if I succeed who succeeds with me? This question of collaborative strategy perhaps

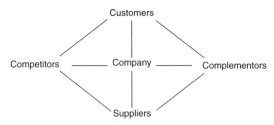

FIGURE 6.7 Adam Brandenburger and Barry Nalebuff, Value Net.

informs gestures such as Bradford's Art + Practice: imaginative philanthropic ventures that are field-building.

One takeaway of co-opetition is a reorientation toward value and the possibility that value is not zero-sum but potentially generative. One tool of game theory that Brandenburger and Nalebuff explore in *Co-opetition* is the idea of added value. Added value is the benefit one party brings to a group or situation, defined as the change in circumstance or monetary value when that party is subtracted out of the situation.[43] For instance, a key sales director in a commercial gallery or a museum financial officer who negotiates an advantageous vendor contract has added value that they might use to negotiate their salary. This framework of added value supports a way of reorienting from the competitive frameworks of traditional economics to the promise of shared value creation.

6.5   CONCLUSIONS

Supply chain strategy has become more kaleidoscopic and sometimes artist-driven. Where Damien Hirst leapt over his dealer to sell works directly to collectors, other artists have opened up supply chains in different ways. Consider the artist Kehinde Wiley, who runs a studio in Beijing and also founded an artist's residency in Senegal.[44] Called Black Rock Senegal, the residency center gathers writers, filmmakers, and visual artists in an architecturally striking building designed by Senegalese architect Abib Djenne with interiors made collaboratively by Wiley and Senegalese designer Aïssa

Dione.[45] Three selected artists stay at a time, to make work and also to engage with the local arts ecosystem in the surrounding area. In 2020, Yinka Shonibare announced the opening of the G.A.S. Foundation, an artists' residency in Lagos, Nigeria, also aimed at supporting international exchange and individual artistic practice. The foundation includes studio and exhibition space as well as access to a 30-acre farm in Ijebu, a rural community a few hours' drive from Lagos. Shonibare's initiative supports artists and also places the arts in a context of local food security and economic growth.[46]

Supply chains, which originate as linear tools of a manufacturing mindset, are also narrative arcs of how work comes into the world, how reputations are made, and how forms of commitment – asset specificity – can be balanced with forms of collaboration and flexibility. Supply chain interventions can transform who is included in artmaking and art audiences. We may benefit when a philosopher-king-style informed owner of a factory can retrofit it for hand sanitizer production in mere days, but we also can observe less vertically integrated supply chains with many actors necessarily coming together in concert. The field exists as an ecosystem of connected parts, and a rising tide lifts all boats.

QUESTIONS

1. Draw a supply chain or ecosystem map of the art world. You can choose to draw it for the overall art world or choose an organization, artist, or other actor in the arts and map the ecosystem in which they operate. Who are all of the people and what are all of the institutions in their orbit? How much can you shoehorn the supply chain into a linear structure, and how inventively can you imagine it nonlinearly?

2. Damien Hirst's 2008 sale at Sotheby's is an example of supply chain disintermediation. In hindsight, do you think this decision worked well or poorly for Hirst, or had no effect? Why do you think other artists have not tried this strategy since?

3. In 2016, Sotheby's acquired Art Agency, Partners.[47] Research this firm and describe the acquisition within analysis of supply chains. Draw a diagram of Porter's Five Forces or the Value Net for Sotheby's with this acquisition.

4. Consider an area of social justice, museum governance, or diversity and inclusion in the arts. How can you approach this topic as a supply chain problem? Can you use the supply chain itself or one of the strategy frameworks to identify points of entry, collaborators, or pinpointed challenges?

5. Lack of transparency characterizes many art-market transactions. Companies such as Artnet shed some light on the operations of the market by providing the public with pricing data from auction results. However, much of the art market still operates in private ways. Describe two or three changes which would potentially make the art market more transparent. Imagine a start-up company trying to bring transparency to the art market. Draw a Value Net from the start-up company's perspective, showing competitors and complementors.

6. National and international trade bodies such as the US organization AAMD (Association of Art Museum Directors) and ICOM (the International Council of Museums) publish guidelines on museum deaccessioning, the process of selling works from a museum's collection.[48] Draw Oster's Six Forces for a museum of your choosing. How would this picture change if the AAMD or ICOM changed its deaccessioning policies?

7 Labor

Something weird about the art world is how one of your friends lives in
their van and your other friend makes 6++ figures like [no big deal] and you
have 5$ in checking but stay in 5 star hotels/fly first class on collector's
coin and you're all making the same art.

Addie Wagenknecht, artist, Twitter December 22, 2019[1]

In 1951 in New York, three artists without a gallery – Wolf Kahn, Jan
Müller, and Felix Pasilis – decided to host their own exhibition in
a loft that Kahn and Pasilis shared as an art studio. The show – called
813 Broadway after the building's address – led a larger group of
artists to found the Hansa Gallery the following year. Located at
70 East Twelfth Street, Hansa would become canonical in the story
of mid-twentieth-century artist-run spaces in New York City. The
gallery would also encapsulate an economic story of labor. The early
days of Hansa relied almost entirely on collective free labor, followed by paid labor that was still precarious, interspersed with
generosity and gifts.[2]

In this chapter we explore the applications of economic principles to markets for labor – both for artists and for other art workers –
including the systemic prevalence of low pay in the arts. We will lay
a foundation for the current state of pay in the arts and then apply
economic principles of labor supply, unionization, and the design of
work. As a starting point, consider the early days of Hansa Gallery as
a case study in labor. See if you can notice in Hansa's story the
opportunity cost of time, the motivation to make money (or lack
thereof), and the possible presence of wealth or income from other
sources.

FIGURE 7.1 William Powhida, *Why Are (Most) Artists (So Fucking) Poor?* Courtesy of the artist and Postmasters Gallery.

When the group of artists founded the Hansa Gallery in 1952, they contributed their time for free, pitching in to paint walls and install lights.[3] Initially, the gallery was staffed by a rotation of artists who took turns working twice each month. The artists staffed the desk six afternoons a week, 1:00–6:00pm, Monday through Saturday. When this voluntary arrangement became unreliable, the group hired a recent college graduate, Anita Coleman. By some reports, they paid her $7 a week – equivalent to $68 per week or $3,536 per year in 2019 dollars.[4] By other reports, she was a recent graduate of Sarah Lawrence College who volunteered.[5] The fact she was paid at all was noteworthy at the time. As Melissa Rachleff, a scholar of artist-run spaces and curator of the 2017 exhibition *Inventing Downtown: Artist-Run Galleries in New York City, 1952–1965*, notes, most of the artist-run cooperative galleries of the time had no paid staff.[6]

In 1954, Hansa moved uptown to a small and "spiffy" space on the second floor of 210 Central Park South where they hosted their first show that December.[7] When Anita Coleman married and left her job, Hansa hired Anneta Duveen, a woman who shared a name with the legendary English art dealer Lord Joseph Duveen on account of having married and divorced two of the dealer's nephews.[8] Duveen was not paid a salary at all but was promised a 25% commission on sales. Six months later, when few sales had been forthcoming, she left the gallery to pursue a graduate degree at Columbia University. (She went on to illustrate a 1966 textbook, *Essentials of Astronomy*.)[9]

Hansa next hired Richard "Dick" Bellamy in September 1955.[10] Bellamy's biographer, Judith Stein, records his pay as $25 per week plus a 25% sales commission, while Rachleff pegs his pay at $40 per month, based on Bellamy's recollection in an interview.[11] Whether it was $25 per week or $40 per month, Bellamy's pay was much higher than Coleman's $7 per week and Duveen's zero dollars per week plus commission. Still, Bellamy's pay was very low. As Stein points out,

Bellamy was paid about a quarter of the average 1955 annual wage. For personal reasons, Bellamy did not have a home at the time. He mostly slept on the artist Alfred Leslie's studio sofa or in the Hansa space itself. (Bellamy had separated from his wife and likely sent her some of his income.) Bellamy argued for the professional benefit of sleeping at the gallery. Waking in the mornings at Hansa during Jan Müller's exhibition, Bellamy claimed, "I felt I was seeing what the artist was putting down, his life going on in the work. I was able to see these paintings in an unguarded moment that art dealers rarely have."[12] Artistic benefit or not, his circumstance also spoke to economic precarity.

Bellamy supplemented his income from the gallery by painting houses at night and on the weekends.[13] In September 1956, on Bellamy's recommendation, Hansa hired Ivan Karp to work with Bellamy as the gallery's codirector. Bellamy and Karp shared the salary. Karp, who would later become Leo Castelli's right hand, was presumably able to accept such a low-paying job because his wife Lois worked full-time for the *Village Voice*, which had just been founded in 1955.[14] Ivan published occasional pieces in the *Voice* as their art critic.[15]

Hansa Gallery operated as a cooperative (co-op), with artists contributing monthly dues and making decisions collectively. At first, each member contributed $21 per month, an amount that dropped to $15 per month, then went up to $35 when the gallery moved uptown.[16] In parallel to the revenue from dues, the explicit costs of running the gallery were $70 per month at the East Twelfth Street location, and $150 per month once the gallery moved to Central Park West. The gallery operated until June 1959, when it closed because it could no longer meet its operating expenses.[17] The gallery was an institutional equivalent to an artist ahead of prevailing tastes. For all of its – and its dealer's – economic instability, its art historical contribution has not since been in question.

The cooperative structure of the Hansa Gallery included a proper governance model with formal by-laws and twice-yearly elections.[18] As in many situations, the same person – perhaps with the curse of competence – was repeatedly asked to serve the community. Here it was the sculptor Richard Stankiewicz who, as Rachleff describes, was known for his "passion for parliamentary order," his irritation with "irrelevant group conversations," and the fact that he was "an adept handyman."[19] (It's hard to imagine such an all-rounder or cooperative gallery decathlete, so to speak.) The gallery charter also recognized certain economic concepts, such as the free-rider problem. They called these people "riders" who wanted to join socially without investing the effort to contribute toward the gallery's administration.[20] It is possible that the closure of the gallery followed from the departure of key people. Stankiewicz resigned in the summer of 1958 to move to the Stable Gallery. Karp left in the fall of 1958 to work with Martha Jackson Gallery, going on after that to work with Castelli.[21] While the Hansa Gallery was operational, it had reliable purchasers, whether volume collectors such as Horace Richter of a North Carolina textiles family or institutional collectors such as architect and former MoMA curator Philip Johnson, MoMA founding director Alfred Barr, artists Elaine de Kooning and Dan Flavin, and the Museum of Modern Art itself.[22]

Bellamy's experience at Hansa, and Anneta Duveen's before him, and Anita Coleman's before her, and the collective of artists before that are all lessons in the labor economics of working in the arts. As we have seen, the arts does not have tidy measures of labor productivity against which to set wage rates – whether because the work of a museum is fixed-cost intensive with little measurable marginal output or because the labors of an artist are often not recognized in the time frame of the artist's efforts. The pricing of labor tends to be done based on the going rate, what an institution feels it can afford or get by with, or in the case of unionized workforces, the wage rates agreed through collective bargaining.

FIGURE 7.2 Artist Jan Müller standing in front of his painting *Faust, II,* at the opening of his solo exhibition at the Hansa Gallery, 1957. Photograph by Robert Frank. Courtesy of the Museum of Modern Art Archives.

7.1 PAY IN THE ARTS

Labor economics in the arts rests on an uneasy history of an arts workforce that did not necessarily need to work. Museum employee manuals once had sections on what to do ethically if one were in the position of bidding against the museum at auction. And one notable museum used to have a standard form one could use to donate one's salary back to the institution for tax benefit.[23] This history of pay has also served as a barrier to diversity, equity, and inclusion in the arts.[24] In a study by Mathew Britten and Kerry Grist of museum workers who self-identified as "working class," three-quarters of them said that low pay was a reason they considered leaving their job.[25] This class problem is exacerbated, Taryn Nie argues in her research, because arts workers identify as politically progressive and inclusive and thus are potentially not as vigilant about their own potential bias.[26]

Various data sources support these claims. In the United States, statistics on salaries in the arts have been collected by groups including the Association of Art Museum Directors (AAMD), the American Alliance of Museums (AAM), the Professional Organization for Women in the Arts (POWarts), and the Art + Museum Transparency group. The AAMD administers a detailed annual survey of its members that covers salaries as well as other expenses and revenues, but the organization generally does not share the findings publicly beyond a top-line report. The AAM, which includes nonart museums as well, published a detailed salary survey in 2017. POWarts published a salary survey in 2019 that included both nonprofit and commercial arts workers. In 2019, the Art + Museum Transparency group crowd-sourced over 5,000 salaries in a spreadsheet that the group shares freely with researchers. Historically, the National Endowment for the Arts (NEA) commissioned studies of gender, racial inclusion, and pay disparity from the 1970s to the 1990s, and more recently the Mellon Foundation and Ithaka S+R partnered in 2015 on a study of diversity and inclusion in the arts. The US Bureau of Labor Statistics also publishes information on pay in the arts.

Working with the AAM 2017 salary report, Taryn Nie found that, of ten representative large museums, on average the institutions spent 40.4% of their operating budgets on staff compensation.[27] Nie also analyzed five entry-to-mid-level positions across curatorial and education areas and found substantial gender pay disparity. The workers in those roles were predominantly (more than 80%) women. On average, the salary for female workers in those roles was $3,000 less than for men, on an average pay scale of $37–$40,000. The national "living wage" was $32,947, while the living wage in New York City was closer to $52,000. (For comparison, the US federal minimum wage of $7.25 per hour equates to a $15,080 annual salary assuming a forty-hour work week and no vacation; the New York City minimum wage of $15 per hour corresponds to $31,200 annually.) While some average pay levels in the arts approach the living wage, in the case of the New Museum in New York City, the $52,000 minimum living wage is comparable to the museum *median* salary, meaning roughly half of the museum's employees made below this living wage, with that institution's entry level pay closer to $35,000.[28]

In tandem with low pay, these groups of arts workers are generally not representative of their communities. In 2019, the New York City Department of Cultural Affairs announced that 61% of nonprofit cultural sector workers were non-Hispanic White, compared to 33% of the New York City population. In 2015, the Mellon Foundation and Ithaka S+R found that of the workforce of AAMD member institutions, 72% were non-Hispanic White, as compared to 62% of the general population.[29] The pipeline of students studying fine art in school mirrors these statistics. According to the Strategic National Arts Alumni Project (SNAAP), which collects data from art school graduates in the United States, 84% of art school graduates are White.[30]

These disparities in pay equity and inclusion across gender and race are reflected in historical reports as well. In 1970, the NEA found that male artists were paid $12,000 per year as compared to $5,500 for female artists. In addition, twice as many men were classified as "established artists" for this study as compared to women. Without gender breakdown, the comparable pay for Black artists was $8,200, as compared to $9,050 for Hispanic artists, $8,000 for Native American artists, and $10,700 for artists of Asian descent.[31]

Contemporary reports on the level of pay of artists show that it is still very low, perhaps even lower in real terms than it was in the 1970s. According to the *Creative Independent*, the journalistic out-post of the crowdfunding company Kickstarter, the median income for artists was $20–$30,000 per year, based on a 2018 survey of 1,000 artists. Most artists ranked themselves a "5" on a scale of 1–10 for financial stability.[32] The Arts Council England released similar find-ings in the report *Livelihoods of Visual Artists: 2016 Data Report.* Based on a survey of 2,000 artists, the report found that in 2015 the average total income for artists in the United Kingdom was £16,500, only £6,020 of which was from art directly. A full 69% of artists held other jobs to support their practice.[33]

7.2 LABOR SUPPLY

The supply of labor parallels some of the determinants of consumer demand – tastes, expectations, and income or wealth – but with a backward-bending curve. The backward-bending supply curve is accounted for by two effects: a substitution effect and an income effect. Theoretically, workers offer themselves into labor markets because of a desire for income. As that wage offered for their labors goes up, the opportunity cost of leisure increases because taking an hour off of work means forgoing that higher wage. The **substitution effect** describes the tendency of a worker to replace hours of leisure with hours of work as the wage rate increases. However, the labor supply curve bends backwards because as one moves along the curve, the substitution effect is followed by an income effect. As the wage rate increases and a worker starts to make more money, the marginal benefit of the extra income decreases, and scarce leisure time becomes more valuable. Thus, the opportunity cost of each additional working hour becomes higher because it is traded off against increasingly precious leisure time. The **income effect** describes this area of the labor supply curve over which the worker trades back work hours to gain leisure time (see Figure 7.3).

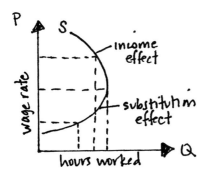

FIGURE 7.3 The backward-bending labor supply curve.

This phenomenon of the backward-bending supply curve takes many different forms depending on the supply of labor. The supply curve for labor of a famous actor is severely constrained by that person's time relative to the demand for it. Their labor supply curve is thus quite vertical, constrained at twenty-four hours in the day, in the manner of the supply of a masterpiece painting that is constrained at a quantity of one. However, if demand for labor is at a wage rate below a living wage, then the demand for a worker's labor intersects the supply curve before its inflection point to bend backwards. In these cases where wage rate is structurally low, many industries and increasingly the arts have labor unions.

7.3 LABOR UNIONS AND COLLECTIVE BARGAINING

Although the Museum of Modern Art in New York has had a labor union since around 1970, a wave of other US museums have formed unions much more recently. In New York, UAW Local 2110 represents workers at the Shed, MoMA, the Bronx Museum, the Tenement Museum, and the New Museum.[34] Workers have also unionized at numerous other museums including the Solomon R. Guggenheim Museum, the Frye Art Museum in Seattle, Washington, and the Museum of Tolerance in Los Angeles.[35] A complicated and ill-fated early unionization effort at the Marciano Art Foundation in Los Angeles is credited as one instigator of the wave of union formation, though this political activism is also a response to much larger factors in both the arts and the broader economy.[36]

The theoretical premise of a union is that workers can bargain better on their collective behalf. Suppose that supply and demand for labor intersect at 100 jobs each paying $10 per hour. A union might be able to bargain for $15 pay. According to economic logic, there will be fewer total jobs at this higher wage rate because of the higher pricing. That is, pay to workers supplying their labor must still follow the demand curve.[37] Critics of unions argue that there is a loss because more total money could have been paid to the larger number of workers employed at the lower rates. However, if those lower rates are under a living wage, then substantial issues arise ranging from worker human rights to diversity, equity, and inclusion. In addition, the wage rate may be elastic, so that paying workers more may not actually in practice decrease the number of workers. The structure of jobs in arts organizations is not tied to production functions as it is in the case of the theoretical strawberry picker in Chapter 2. Pay in the arts is part of a larger system in which nonprofit organizations are uniquely authorized and arguably even compelled to make mission-driven decisions about pay and related questions of equity and inclusion. Failure to pay workers equitably can have negative knock-on effects for organizations. These costs may be implicit, for instance, high staff turnover or breaking of trust with workers, audiences, and communities. Yet even if they are not explicit, the costs can be profoundly consequential.

On the artist side, the organization W.A.G.E. (Working Artists and the Greater Economy) has advocated for union-like treatment of artists, using the mechanism of certification. In 2014, W.A.G.E. launched a program of certifying organizations that agree to pay at or above set minimum rates to artists who exhibit work in those venues. The premise is that artists' labor has been overlooked. Artists have been told that they receive exposure or some other benefit and thus their labor preparing for a museum exhibition does not need to be directly compensated. W.A.G.E argues that the artist's labor is a transaction that must be compensated regardless. The actual rates of compensation vary from institution to institution. They are set based on a percentage of the organization's operating budget.

W.A.G.E. has unapologetically taken a very focused view of artists' economic sustainability, looking mainly at the narrow question, "Why don't nonprofits pay artist fees?" In writing about their mission, Lise Soskolne, a core organizer of W.A.G.E., uses the word "myopic" when describing the organization's work. Within W.A.G.E.'s focused work on artists' fees as a form of advocacy, they encounter some deep ambivalences between artistic practice and markets. Soskolne recounted one common contradiction she encountered as, "The real value of my work is non-monetary but I want to be paid for my work because my work requires time and labor and I need to earn a living."[38] This paradox is in fact an encapsulation of the market question: Are people motivated by money or is economics just a form of structural engineering to make the work possible? W.A.G.E. sees labor compensation – not rewards to artists but pay for time – as essential to artistic sustainability.

In fact, Soskolne highlights the complexity of museums' claim that artists donate their time because they will be paid later in art markets. Soskolne writes:

> it is precisely the non-profit's moral authority that increases the monetary value of the art and artists that pass through it in the form of exhibitions and programs. The logic is that if it's exhibited in a non-profit institution, it serves the public good and therefore must have value beyond commerce – and it is exactly this perception that adds economic value to art when it reaches the commercial auction and sales markets.[39]

Her observation raises the same questions that Velthuis introduced concerning the complicated power relationships and interdependency between institutions and commercial markets.[40] But even if the institutional value conferred by a museum exhibition leads to increased commercial value, Soskolne argues that artists should be paid for their labor regardless. Many artists who show work in museums will not go on to commercial success, depending on the salability of their art, or sheer chance. The museums are making an "exposure" argument often used to solicit free labor whether from writers or artists or others.

W.A.G.E. has also experimented with certification of artists directly instead of certification of venues. Under that plan, if an artist were approached to exhibit work with a museum that was not willing to pay fees according to W.A.G.E.'s schedule, the artist would generally need to decline the opportunity. If the purpose of W.A.G.E. certification is to support artists and to do activist work to normalize and make universal the practice of paying proportionate artists' fees, then that plan seems to place substantial responsibility for structural work on individual artists. What is clear is that W.A.G.E. has had impact; numerous venues are certified. And W.A.G.E. has been very clear that it is not trying to build a new world but to make the current system healthier and more functional.

Other ventures have been even more ambitious in imagining new systems of support within the arts and also new economic models *as art themselves.* One initiative, founded by the Center for Cultural Innovation (CCI) in Los Angeles, in fact takes its name from this intention and is called AmbitioUS. The initiative grants money to working groups both that self-identify as artists and that take an artistic view of the overall economy as if it were itself a canvas and paint. As Angie Kim, the director of CCI and founder of AmbitioUS, described it, her ambitions are to rethink the entire "cultural paradigm in economic systems."[41] AmbitioUS is considering the pricing of all labor, raising the existential question of why domestic labor has not been priced in while also raising the governance question: Who decides what is labor? These questions of self-determination of labor are hard to answer. They raise fundamental critiques of what is important, what is leisure, what is work, what is paid and recognized as work, and who decides.

7.4 INVISIBLE LABOR AND MAINTENANCE WORK

The artist Mierle Laderman Ukeles engaged these questions viscerally and poetically in the body of her work that followed from a piece of her writing, "Manifesto for Maintenance Art 1969!" Ukeles had trained as an artist but was forced to drop out of art school at Pratt in New York City in 1962 after male administrators complained that her abstract relief works – bulbous forms tied down with ropes – were "over-sexed."[42] She enrolled in an art education program instead, gave birth to her first child, and encountered the crossroads of being a mother and an artist. The "Manifesto for Maintenance Art 1969!" doubled as a proposal for an exhibition on the subject of care, specifically care as labor.

Ukeles described "two basic systems" of work, which she called "Development" and "Maintenance." Development concerned new ideas, creativity, and what one might artistically associate with

an avant-garde ideal of bleeding-edge progress. In contrast, maintenance concerned the more domestic and caretaking duties of sustaining, nurturing, and renewing other living beings and spaces.
Development was deemed more culturally valuable. In Ukeles
ineffable language (semi-colon included):

> Maintenance is a drag; it takes all the fucking time
> the mind boggles and chafes at the boredom.[43]

Although the manifesto was rejected as an exhibition proposal, over
time it led to her life's work. In 1976, students in the Whitney
Independent Study program in New York invited Ukeles to participate
in an exhibition called *Art < >World.*[44] For the project, Ukeles collaborated with the maintenance workers in the building that housed the
Independent Study Program at 55 Water Street in lower Manhattan.
She asked the workers to designate one hour of their labor each day as
"maintenance art." Ukeles's project – *I Make Maintenance Art One
Hour Every Day* (September 16–October 20, 1976) – consisted of a grid
of Polaroids showing workers engaged in their work-as-art. She simply
asked the workers when she saw them if they were working or making
art, and then categorized the Polaroids accordingly.[45]

The leap in her career came about from a letter she wrote in
response to something of a joke that the art critic David Bourdon
included in a review of that exhibition. Writing in the *Village Voice*,
Bourdon proposed that if maintenance could be classified as art, then
New York City, struggling through a deep budget crisis in the late
1970s, could perhaps apply to the National Endowment for the Arts
for city funding.[46] Ukeles clipped the newspaper article and sent it to
the commissioner of the New York Department of Sanitation,
Anthony Vaccarello, who invited her for a meeting.

That meeting led to Ukeles's appointment in 1978 as the first
artist-in-residence at the New York City Department of Sanitation. At
a time when New York City had been brought to its knees economically, Ukeles spent more than a year of her life traveling around the city
shaking hands with over 8,500 sanitation workers thanking them

FIGURE 7.4 Mierle Laderman Ukeles, *Touch Sanitation Performance,*
July 24, 1979–June 26, 1980. Citywide performance with 8,500 sanitation
workers across all fifty-nine New York City sanitation districts. Date
unknown. Sweep 3, Manhattan 3. Photograph by Robin Holland.
Courtesy of the artist and Ronald Feldman Gallery, New York.

individually for their work "keeping the city alive." In documentation
of the project, called *Touch Sanitation Performance* (1979–80), Ukeles
exudes authenticity and a fearless presence that both transcends and
embodies charm, her voluminous red hair cascading around her as she
laughs, listens, and connects with people (see Figure 7.4).[47]

Although Ukeles received a 2017 retrospective at the Queens
Museum of Art in New York, curated by Patricia Phillips, she never
received money for her residency. The Department of Sanitation gave
her "in-kind services and assistance, including personnel labor and
time" and a desk at the Department of Sanitation starting in 1977. By
2016, she had two offices there, with space for a "staging area and
archives."[48] The fact that Ukeles was not paid is of course not politically
neutral. She was supported financially by the work of her husband, Jack
Ukeles, who was employed by the New York City Department of City
Planning. The lack of pay excludes others from having created the same

position for themselves, at the same time that, in a way, it reinforces the themes of the work itself. Maintenance is often underpaid or invisible labor. It shares the formlessness and constancy of care that held together the early days of the Hansa Gallery.

As Ukeles conceptualizes them, development and maintenance have different footprints artistically but also economically. Development entails the risk of investing time and resources in new projects before value is known. Maintenance entails the ongoing labor of overhead, of the silent care required to nurture things, whether museums or parks or human beings. Neither development nor maintenance is well protected economically. Development requires risk and investment. It explains histories of patronage and archetypes of the starving artist. Maintenance has an opportunity cost in development – the invisible domestic labor that interferes with the time to become the hero artist of a new frontier.

Maintenance often comes with little bargaining power. Maintenance is a fixed cost in ways that are often problematically under-recognized within families and undercompensated when in the form of paid domestic labor. In 2019, Palak Shah, the director of social innovation for the National Domestic Workers Alliance, spoke as part of a program called Workspheres, number 31 in a series of "MoMA R&D Salons" hosted by Paola Antonelli, the senior curator of architecture and design at the Museum of Modern Art. The overall series has aimed to frame museums as the research and development (R&D) function of society by approaching different topics.[49] These salon topics have ranged from anger to dogs to plastics to philanthropy. Shah argued that domestic workers – childcare providers, hospice workers, housekeepers – have some of the least protected labor conditions while providing what Shah termed the "economic scaffolding" of everything. Shah said, "As we say in our movement, 'they do the work that makes all the other work possible.'"[50] Yet the workers are not well compensated and struggle in ways that parallel, at least in part, the predicament of the maintenance labor that instigated Ukeles's work.

From an economic standpoint, domestic or maintenance work does not scale. It is difficult to outsource beyond hiring a person and it is so far impossible to automate. Shah recounted a visit to a Californian innovation lab that had been trying to teach a robot to fold a towel for eleven years. The work of care is mostly done by people. These workers benefit from collective action. That could be unionization to secure stable wages, or as the National Domestic Workers Alliance has done, creating a centralized portal through which domestic workers collect portable benefits.[51] This platform, Alia, drastically reduces the transaction costs faced by workers holding multiple jobs. Not just eager to improve private labor markets, Shah asks whether we "should reconceptualize in society access to the labor market as fundamentally a public good."[52]

In this larger context of labor markets, the motivation to work can stem from both necessity and preference, in varying combinations. Economists model the income people make from work as consisting of both their pay and their **psychic income**, meaning nonmonetary benefit associated with their work.[53] Mission-driven work, as in the arts, is often saddled with this idea of psychic income. By this idea, because workers enjoy their jobs, they do not need high pay. Even in commercial galleries where work is sold, sometimes at very high price points, one is still seen to be working in part for psychic income. This line of thinking excludes people from the field. If pay is below a living wage, then psychic income is only an option for those who can either drastically economize or rely on forms of compensatory privilege like independent wealth or income from a spouse.

Apart from this question of securing a living wage, researchers outside of economics have theorized other motivations to work. Daniel Pink, synthesizing research for his book *Drive*, found that most people were propelled less by the "carrot" of money and more by autonomy and intrinsic motivation.[54] The psychology researcher Carol Dweck identified two general frames – a fixed mindset and a growth mindset. She found that those with

a fixed mindset encountered work as a referendum on their intelligence whereas those with a growth mindset approached everything as an opportunity for learning.[55] The influence of Dweck's
research is perhaps best felt in the change in parenting advice from
praising the child, which encourages the fixed mindset, to praising
the effort, which reinforces the growth mindset. More broadly, her
work characterizes cultures in which workers can discover autonomy in constant learning.

7.5 CONCLUSIONS

One art project on the subject of labor frames the themes of this
chapter. In the spring of 2016, the Chisenhale Gallery in east London
hosted an exhibition by the artist Maria Eichhorn entitled *5 weeks, 25
days, 175 hours.* Alongside preparatory meetings and a publication,
the work consisted primarily of the closure of the gallery for the five-
week run of the show. The staff were paid but did not work.
The building was closed, but signs informed visitors of the artistic
purpose of the closure. The preparatory process included taking an
inventory of the "particular likes or dislikes" of their jobs for the eight
members of the gallery's staff.

As Polly Staple, the gallery's director at the time, wrote in the
exhibition catalogue, the staff largely liked their work though disliked
"repetitive tasks, intrusive emails," and the challenges of time
management.[56] One could grapple with the bundling of tasks into
jobs, or reconsider the overhead of the gallery and the necessity of
each part of the team's work. One could frame the exhibition as
vacation or as receiving wages while having free time, a kind of
magic wand toward the income and substitution effects of the labor
supply curve. Functioning as a form of litmus test for conceptual art or
willful degradation of audience trust, the project was both "a gift and
a burden" that freed the workers of their work.[57]

In context of the adjunctification of academic labor and the
complexity of managing freelance work in the creative sector, the
project also called attention to the steady, secure employment that

was the subject of the piece. Writing in the catalogue, Staple framed the project: "Eichhorn presents a challenge – to Chisenhale staff, its Board of Trustees, stakeholders, funders, partners and programme participants, but also to its audiences – to ask questions and reassess assumptions about work and leisure and the expectations we may have of arts organisations, artists, and how we all work together."[58] The project documented the structural solidity of their work, made visible by its absence.

QUESTIONS

1. Research museums in your area. Is the staff at any of the museums unionized? Over social media or in person, try to speak with employees to understand how they feel about unionized labor.
2. Draw a supply curve for your own labor. At what salary levels do you anticipate working? At what levels of pay would you seek more work and then trade off work for more leisure? Does the logic of the backward-bending supply curve seem to apply to you? Why or why not? Try to list the wage rates that accompany the backward bend in your own labor curve.
3. Choose a salary report such as the POWarts salary survey, the Art + Museum Transparency working group spreadsheet, or the Arts Council report. Selecting a lens such as living wage, gender, or inclusion, what observations can you make of the data? Write a fact sheet on your findings. Include diagrams of labor supply if you can.
4. Select an institution such as the High Museum in Atlanta, Georgia, that has made concerted efforts to diversify both its workforce and its collection and exhibition program.[59] What strategies have worked best? What other strategies would you recommend?
5. Interview an art worker who is employed full-time by one organization to learn about that person's job. Try to inventory, as far as possible, all the different facets of that person's work. Reverse engineer a job description that encompasses all of the tasks that have been bundled into this position. Compare job descriptions

with other people completing the same exercise. What patterns do you notice about the construction of individual jobs in the arts? Are they specialized or broad? Do relatively senior staff handle their own administrative labor? Are the jobs well defined?

6. Interview an art worker who specifically has a freelance or adjunct structure of working life. Now bundle all of their tasks into one job. What do you notice about the transaction costs and the time spent shifting between roles and organizations? What do you imagine would be different if this person's job were pulled under the umbrella of one organization? In particular, focus on the transaction costs, for example, coordination costs, of their freelance working life. As an additional project, if possible, try to interview two arts workers – one full-time and one freelance – whose jobs are as similar as possible. Examine the ways their time, salary, and risk profiles are similar and different.

7. Speaking about her body of work in maintenance art, Mierle Laderman Ukeles said, "If I am the boss of my freedoms and I name what I name art, I name my life. I name maintenance art."[60] What would it look like for you to do a labor assessment of your overall life? Which areas are paid externally? Which areas of labor go unpaid? Which areas would you consider development, and which would you consider maintenance? Are there areas of your life you could designate as art, or areas of labor you could embrace symbolically or also refuse? As Ukeles said, "A human being always has the freedom to say 'no,' but a human being can also say 'yes.'"[61]

8. Considering the working lives and salaries of arts administration workers and artists, how do you interpret the pros and cons of legislative initiatives for universal basic income (UBI)? Debate the pros and cons conversationally and write a proposal brief either recommending or discouraging UBI. Reconsider this question in Chapter 9 in the context of shared equity – that is, investment shares that serve as property rights rather than recurring payments of universal basic income.

9. As in many other sectors, arts organizations increasingly rely on contingent or contract labor. These labor arrangements are made visible in times of crisis when those workers are laid off first. Consider the parallel case of lower-commitment hiring in academia. Reportedly over 75% of faculty positions in the United States are nontenure line, and many of these jobs are for adjunct instructors who are contracted to teach individual courses. In one valiant artistic encapsulation of this phenomenon, Dushko Petrovich raised just over $5,000 on Kickstarter to launch a short-lived newspaper called *Adjunct Commuter Weekly*. With a target audience of those professors navigating adjunct appointments in New England's "Northeast Corridor" commuter schedule, editorial features included titles such as "Blur of Chobanis" after the yogurt well stocked in train station snack cases.[62] Discuss this phenomenon of contingent labor. What are approaches that would help? Would unionization help? Would activist interventions – from Petrovich's newspaper to protest – help? What strategies come about from collective action? What creative interventions can you imagine here?

8   Property

Should there ever be a question about artists' rights in reference to their work, the artist is more right than anyone else.

Seth Siegelaub[1]

On January 3, 1969, Panayiotis Vassilakis, the Greek artist better known as Takis, removed his own artwork from an exhibition at the Museum of Modern Art in New York.[2] A self-described "instinctive scientist"[3] whom the artist Marcel Duchamp once called the "happy ploughman of the magnetic fields,"[4] Takis was known for his kinetic sculptures and abstract canvases. What looked like a color-field painting was sculptural, with a metal plane stretching the canvas forward toward a metal nail suspended from the ceiling and held in tension mid-air by magnets. What looked like wildflowers swaying in a breeze was a scattering of wispy metal stems activated to sway by a hand-swung magnetic pendulum suspended from the ceiling. John Lennon, of the Beatles, bought a Takis sculpture in 1966.[5] John and Dominique de Menil, the art patrons and founders of the Menil Collection in Houston, Texas, bought one which they donated to the Museum of Modern Art in 1962.[6] It was this donation from the Menils that Takis had come to see.

The artwork in question, *Tele-sculpture*, consisted of a motorized spinning base and two pendants – a ball and a cork on cords – that rotated around the spinning base in circles, aided by magnets. Takis did not like how the curator Pontus Hultén had contextualized the artwork in an exhibition titled *The Machine, As Seen at the End of the Mechanical Age*.[7] Even though the museum owned the work – gifted to them but the museum's property all the same – Takis felt he still had a say over how his work was exhibited.[8] Thus, in a bold symbolic gesture, Takis stood in the museum's sculpture garden with the artwork he had taken down waiting for reassurance that it would be formally removed from the exhibition. A few hours later, Bates Lowry, then MoMA's director, confirmed that the museum would respect Takis's wishes. The work was taken out of the show.

Takis's action led to the founding of the Art Workers' Coalition (1969–71), an activist group who made poetic and sometimes economic demands of museums on behalf of the rights of artists and citizens more generally.[9] One enduring manifestation of this assertion of artists' rights has been the Artist's Contract – formally "The Artist's Reserved Rights Transfer and Sale Agreement" – a private contract that allows artists to retain rights to borrow their own work, to veto exhibitions, and to claim a portion of accrued value when their work resells.

In this chapter we explore the economic idea of the work of art as *property*. We consider the rights that artists and others have in relation to their work. Property is both a deeply enabling and a deeply problematic concept. In the case of the Artist's Contract, defining property is enabling to artists. More broadly, many notions of private property mask land theft and cultural appropriation.[10] We discuss these ideas in more depth later in this chapter.

Microeconomics has to this point tended to give us tools to look at "goods" – that is, at objects that can be made, sold, traded, or exhibited. Art is an "unusual form of property."[11] Art can be conceptual, performative, or ephemeral. Even in the case of traditional objects such as paintings and drawings, artworks are not just objects but also bundles of rights. The physical art object, when it exists, is only one aspect of this stack of rights.[12] All of these rights – moral rights, copyright, and rights to control exhibition or resale – are typically intact in the artist's studio. How they are split when a work is sold depends on the jurisdiction and the contract of sale.

In this chapter, we will focus on property rights granted to artists and collectors. We will begin with intellectual property rights such as copyright and conclude by considering fractional equity as a speculative form of artistic property. This discussion of rights leads into Chapter 9 on art investment because the idea of art as an asset stems from the application of property rights.

The Siegelaub–Projansky Agreement

As Lauren van Haaften-Schick, a leading scholar of the Siegelaub–Projansky agreement,[13] has pointed out, the Artist's Contract sits so squarely across art and law that people do not even agree on what to call it.[14] The contract was drafted by the exhibition planner and art dealer Seth Siegelaub and the attorney Robert (Bob) Projansky. Instigated by the Art Workers' Coalition, the contract was published in 1971. It gives artists a number of different rights, depending on the artist's use of the contract. The most famous of those rights is a 15% share in the accrued value of the work when it is resold. This right replicates resale royalties, which are paid by law in many jurisdictions. The Artist's Contract also allows artists to veto exhibitions, to receive half of rental income from loaning the work, to borrow the work themselves at regular intervals, or to restrict the work's sale. The artist Hans Haacke has used this contract consistently for works of substantial value. The artist Adrian Piper has used the Artist's Contract along with a Solo Exhibition Agreement to prevent her work from being resold at a discount.[15] As Piper told the artist Maria Eichhorn in an interview about the Artist's Contract, Piper included a "Discounts to Purchasers" clause which reads, "No single work by the Artist shall be sold by the Dealer at a percentage discount ... since it is already subject to the 50% Off Black Artists Discount and the 25% Off Women Artists Discount."[16] In addition to Piper's and Haacke's uses of the contract, other artists have devised further applications of the thinking behind the contract. For example, the artist Lawrence Weiner placed some works in "public freehold," meaning the works were not sold but offered to the public so that anyone could execute and possess their own.[17]

8.1 COPYRIGHT AND BUNDLES OF RIGHTS

Copyright is the protection offered to artists and other creators against copying or undue adaptation of their work. In the United States and United Kingdom, an Anglo-Saxon tradition roots copyright in a logic of economic incentive for innovation – known as "economic rights." In contrast, the continental European rationale for copyright stems from the innate "moral rights" of the artist.[18] The economically rooted example of US copyright is granted in Article I Section 8 of the US Constitution, which gives Congress the power to "promote the progress of science and useful arts, by securing for limited times to authors and inventors the exclusive right to their respective writings and discoveries."[19] It is noteworthy that copyright is not simply inscribed in law but in the Constitution itself. The provision grants an economic monopoly for a fixed period of time in order to incentivize the risk of investing in new work in the arts and sciences.

Copyright is one of three branches of intellectual property along with patent and trademark. Patent law protects inventions, which in the United States must be registered with and approved by the US Patent and Trademark Office.[20] Trademark protects the visual identity used to sell wares, including registered names, logos, or specific brand identities (even colors). Copyright is the most common of these three branches of intellectual property law in the protection of artworks.

Copyright covers works that are fixed in a tangible medium of expression. Copyright exists automatically. It does not require registration. For works made in the United States today, or any time after 1977, the copyright term is the artist's (or author's) life plus seventy years. When copyright expires, works fall into the public domain. For **works made for hire**, an employer or other commissioner of the work owns the copyright. In the United States, works made for hire are protected for 95–120 years.[21]

While US copyright law protects artists and authors and offers penalties or remedies for infringement, there are limits to what is secured by copyright. These limits stem largely from the protections for free speech and the understanding that building upon or referring to prior work is necessary for creative progress. One of the main carve-outs is an exemption for "fair use." **Fair use** is described in the 1976 Copyright Act by the following four factors:

(1) the purpose and character of the use, including whether such use is of a commercial nature or is for nonprofit educational purposes;
(2) the nature of the copyrighted work;
(3) the amount and substantiality of the portion used in relation to the copyrighted work as a whole; and
(4) the effect of the use upon the potential market for or value of the copyrighted work.[22]

In an influential 1990 essay in the *Harvard Law Review*, Judge Pierre N. Leval argues that the central purpose of fair use was that "the use must be of a character that serves the copyright objective of stimulating productive thought and public instruction without excessively diminishing the incentives for creativity."[23] The first factor – the purpose and character of the work – identifies the intent. Does the work "stimulate creativity for public illumination?"[24] Relying especially on this first factor, Leval emphasizes what he terms "transformativeness." Does the work "transform" the original by having a "different purpose from the original" that adds value more than simply repackaging the underlying work.[25]

The second factor – the nature of the copyrighted work – concerns the intentions of the original author, whether for fact or fiction, secrecy or broadcast. For instance, is the copyrighted work a private piece of correspondence or an intentionally published work? Leval argues that if copyright exists as an incentive to authorship, then the copyrighted work should be *more* protected if it is a public work.[26]

The third factor – amount and substantiality – describes the portion of the whole or the fraction of the copyrighted work that has been used.[27] The rationale is still economic: the greater the proportion of the work used, the higher the likelihood of an impact on the market for original copyrighted work. Judges, Leval included, have cautioned against too rigid an interpretation of fractional math. Leval writes, "Too mechanical a rule, however, can be dangerously misleading. One can imagine secondary works that quote 100% of the copyrighted work without affecting market potential."[28]

The fourth factor – the effect on the market – considers explicitly any empirical evidence of market impact that a secondary work has on the sales of the original copyrighted work.[29] Demonstrated impact on the market can support a claim of copyright infringement – that is, not fair use – but the lack of demonstrated market impact does not automatically mean the secondary work is okay.[30] Taken together, these factors aim to protect the public good by safeguarding incentives to creativity. As Leval writes, "Copyright is not a reward for goodness but a protection for the profits of activity that is useful to the public education."[31] This connection of personal profit to public benefit may seem a peculiarly American story, and one based on a logic that is more than a little libertarian.

The application of fair use has become increasingly contested, and therefore nuanced, in fine art especially as digital technology has made sampling easier. The legal scholar Amy Adler has proposed that we do away with fair use because all artists copy.[32] Consider two different recent cases: that of the appropriation artist Richard Prince, who has become ensnared in various lawsuits based on his use of other people's images, and that of the artist Shepard Fairey, who used an Associated Press (AP) photograph to make the iconic *Hope* poster for Barack Obama's 2008 presidential campaign.

In 2014, Richard Prince created a series "New Portraits" in which Prince found Instagram posts he liked, interacted with the posts by adding his own comments, then screenshotted the posts, blew up the images, and sold them through Gagosian Gallery at roughly $90,000 each. The people who had taken the underlying images were not credited, financially. Two commercial photographers whose images were included in Prince's works, Eric McNatt and Donald Graham, sued Prince and his gallery.[33]

In addition to the works from Graham and McNatt, Prince also used images from an "alt-pin-up" collective of models and performers called Suicide Girls.[34] Selena Mooney, founder of Suicide Girls, who goes by Missy Suicide, announced that they would be responding by reprinting Prince's $90,000 works and reselling them in an unlimited edition for $90.[35] Mooney wrote on the group's website, "If I had a nickel for every time someone used our images without our permission in a commercial endeavor I'd be able to spend $90,000 on art."[36] The Suicide Girls reportedly sold 250 prints the first day. The sales benefited the Electronic Frontier Foundation, the organization championing internet freedom and privacy.[37] A few months later, the dealer Magda Sawon, who runs Postmasters Gallery in New York, included one of the Suicide Girls reappropriations in her exhibition of "#WCW: womancrushwednesday." Sawon's son had bought the print, which Sawon included in the show as not for sale.[38] Sawon received inquiries from other owners of the $90 prints wanting to flip their works. She rejected the offers, summing it up, "The art market is a disgrace to humanity."[39]

The study of fair use raises questions not only of economic incentives to creativity but also of economic complements to copyright. The fourth factor of the fair-use test – often described as the market test – is actually a "market and value" test. If we remember the core rationale of economics – that price represents value – then we can think through ways to support copyright with flexible economic tools. The "value" test can include an analysis of added value – meaning the extent to which the work would be transformed if any one contributor were imagined not to have participated.[40] Consider, for example, the artist Shepard Fairey, whose *Hope* poster became an emblem for Barack Obama's campaign for the US presidency in 2008. The inputs begin with an Associated Press (AP) photo taken by Mannie Garcia, who was contracted by the AP to attend an event on April 27, 2006. Garcia was hired to document Barack Obama, then a US senator, in conversation with Senator Sam Brownback and the actor George Clooney about humanitarian work in Darfur, Sudan.[41] Garcia opportunistically took the iconic shot of Obama because he had the angle. Garcia took 251 photographs during the almost hour-long event. He included the Obama photograph as one of the sixteen images he gave to the AP to complete his assignment.[42]

Fairey, in turn, discovered the photo online some eighteen months later while volunteering his time in support of Obama's campaign efforts. Fairey worked on the poster for two days in January 2008, at his own expense.[43] The poster went on to earn over $1 million in revenue, bringing enough media attention that a blogger, Tom Gralish, identified the underlying AP photo.[44] The AP sued Fairey and the parties went to court before ultimately settling.[45]

Although some of the machinations of the case are highly specific – Fairey lied and arguably destroyed evidence – we can also consider the circumstances from an economic standpoint. Through an economic lens, the earlier photograph is an input to Fairey's work but at a stage when the artist is in the studio, so to speak. Fairey is investing time and resources before value is known. It is only later when the $1 million has been earned that the AP wants its share. If economics is based on price equalling value, Fairey and the AP could have negotiated a zero-fee, future-upside-only percentage royalty at the outset. Fairey would have been free to use the image, and only if that use led to outsized gains, the AP would have received a share of them. This contract would have led to the same outcome minus the legal fees.[46] A technological system would be needed to mitigate search costs for images and transaction costs where permissions clearance can be automated.[47]

As fair use and copyright law try to catch up to and offer clarity around the nature of digital images, one can remember that these questions of copying have existed in other eras. Even at the Great Exhibition at Crystal Palace in London in 1851, there was a strict prohibition on *drawing* the exhibitions. The organizers wrote, "No drawing of any article exhibited can be taken except upon a written authority from the proprietor, countersigned by an officer of the Executive Committee."[48] That anxiety about drawing might seem antiquated now, but drawing was sensitive at the time in a way taking photographs or posting them to social media might seem now.

The cooperation and shared agreements of different nation states are laid out in a series of international treaties and bilateral agreements (between two countries). Although no "international copyright" exists, these agreements set forth obligations related to intellectual property rights for signatory countries, including the protection of foreign works or the designation of jurisdiction in cases of dispute.[49] Table 8.1 summarizes some key treaties and conventions.

Table 8.1 *Membership to international intellectual property treaties, 2019*

Convention or treaty	Number of members
Berne Convention for the Protection of Literary and Artistic Works, Paris, 1886 (amended variously up to 1979; United States joined 1989) [Berne]	178
Convention for the Protection of Producers of Phonograms against Unauthorized Duplication of Their Phonograms, Geneva, 1971 (US 1974) [Phonograms]	80
Convention Relating to the Distribution of Programme-Carrying Signals Transmitted by Satellite, Brussels, 1974 (US 1985) [SAT]	38
Universal Copyright Convention, Geneva, 1952 (US 1955) [UCC Geneva]	100
Universal Copyright Convention, Paris, 1971 (US 1974) [UCC Paris]	65
The Marrakesh Treaty to Facilitate Access to Published Works for Persons Who Are Blind, Visually Impaired, or Otherwise Print Disabled, 2016 (US 2019) [VIP]	79 members (covering 105 countries)
World Intellectual Property Organization (WIPO) Copyright Treaty, Geneva, 1996 (US 2002) [WCT]	109
WIPO Performances and Phonograms Treaty, Geneva, 1996 [WPPT]	108

| World Trade Organization (WTO) Agreement on Trade-Related Aspects of Intellectual Property Rights (TRIPS), 1994 (US 1995) [WTO] | 164 |
| Beijing Treaty on Audiovisual Performances 2012[1] | 39 |

[1] The Beijing Treaty on Audiovisual Performances 2012 went into force on April 28, 2020. The United States has not yet acceded to the treaty (US Copyright Office, 2021).
Sources: US Copyright Office, 2021. World Intellectual Property Organization (2021, March). Beijing Treaty. www.wipo.int/beijing_treaty/en.

These organizations are connected informally and formally not only via treaties and but also intergovernmental agencies. The World Intellectual Property Organization (WIPO) is an agency of the United Nations established in 1967 for the coordination of intellectual property across a membership that currently includes 193 countries.[50] The 193 member states oversee the Berne Convention, which was first passed in 1886.[51] The Berne Convention was the first international copyright agreement, and it generally recognizes copyright for a fifty-year term. The Berne Convention has three core provisions: "national treatment," in which member states agree to give citizens of other member states the same rights that their own citizens receive; "automatic" protection, in which copyright exists regardless of whether the author has explicitly added a copyright notice; and "independence," through which countries with longer-term copyright protection may not have to grant rights to citizens of origin countries with shorter-term rights.[52] The United States did not join the Berne Convention until much more recently, effective March 1, 1989.[53]

Many of the member states of WIPO and signatories of the Berne Convention are also part of the World Trade Organization, which administers the Agreement on Trade-Related Aspects of Intellectual Property Rights (TRIPS), the agreement for protecting intellectual property in the context of trade.[54] Various other copyright treaties have broad application, including the WIPO Copyright Treaty and the Marrakesh Treaty to Facilitate Access to Published Works for Persons Who Are Blind, Visually Impaired, or Otherwise Print Disabled.

8.2 MORAL RIGHTS

Drawn from a French legal tradition of imbuing the artwork with the humanity of the creator, moral rights offer strong and broadly inalienable rights to what is essentially a form of guardianship over the dignity of one's work. Although the innate moral rights of artists do not unequivocally exist in the United States, some core tenets of moral rights were adapted meaningfully in the Visual Artists Rights Act of 1990 (VARA).[55] Under VARA, moral rights fall into broad categories of attribution and integrity – that is, for the artist to receive credit and to have control over the life of the art. The rights of attribution can be complicated for conceptual art. A wall drawing by Sol LeWitt is typically executed by other artisans, even during the artist's lifetime. And the work travels with a certificate of authenticity. The instructions for the drawing are the work. The wall is not signed but the certificate is, and the certificate becomes a central part of the artwork, emphasizing the importance of the integrity and attribution aspects of moral rights.[56]

Rights of disavowal or refusal can be especially complicated in an industry which has operated historically on good faith and handshakes. For example, in 2006, the Swiss artist Christoph Büchel conceived a vast installation *Training Ground for Democracy* at Mass MoCA (the Massachusetts Museum of Contemporary Art) in the small northwestern Massachusetts town of North Adams. It was Büchel's first US museum commission and one of the largest gallery spaces in the United States – an open multistory structure called Building 5 that is almost 100 meters long.[57] The installation was scheduled to open in December 2006 but was postponed to 2007. The artist and museum had a falling out over the completion of the work. Their agreement had been that the museum would pay for the materials and the installation. By the time the artist and museum parted company, the museum said it had spent double the $160,000 budget. The artist did not believe the work was completed. The museum created an alternate exhibition by charting a visitor pathway through the unfinished work. The path was flanked by large tarps obscuring much but not all of an installation that included among other things a full-sized small house, a leaflet-bomb carousel, part of an old movie theatre, and a bus.[58]

The alleged cause of the impasse was the artist's request for the fuselage of a Boeing 737 aircraft.[59] The exhibition – what *New York Times* art critic Roberta Smith called "the shrouded non-Büchel" – included a list of items the artist had requested, which in Smith's recounting reads:

> Requested are accoutrements for Mass and Baptism; a hospital bed and related medical equipment; eight voting booths; hundreds of old tires; piles of old computers; 1,000 beverage cups from a race track; 1,000 feet of barbed wire; 12 grenades and 35 pounds of bullet casings; eight body bags and 75 white protective suits; four prosthetic legs; decorations and campaign buttons from election rallies; a concession stand, popcorn and popcorn buckets; Christmas lights; and 16 large bags of corn leaves and husks.[60]

In addition to contemplating the costs of acquiring and transporting these objects, one can also appreciate the "museological car crash" (Smith's term) between the vision of the artist and the economic constraints of the museum. Mass MoCA is a giant museum in square footage but a modest, even scrappy one in budget; its annual budget in 2006 was less than $7 million.[61] Mass MoCA's 2007 annual tax filing shows a decrease in net assets of $232,247, labeled as "Extraordinary Loss – Abandoned Exhibition."[62]

The vision of the artist turned out legally to be less gauzy than structural. The appeals court (the US Court of Appeals, First Circuit) found that the museum had violated the 1990 Visual Artist Rights Act (VARA) by failing to protect the artist in "the event of a distortion, mutilation or other modification of the work."[63] The conclusion that Büchel's integrity rights in the work had been violated seemed a victory for artists' rights generally. However, other observers thought the effect could be that museums, seeming to have operated in good faith, would increase the robustness of their contracts and potentially require artists to give up rights as a condition of exhibition.

Other recent cases have brought up additional aspects of artistic control and responsibility in relation to the institutional power wielded by museums and market power wielded by collectors and dealers.[64] In 1990, the artist Cady Noland created a large sculptural work titled *Log Cabin*.[65] In 1995, the collector Wilhelm Schürmann lent the work to the Suermondt Ludwig Museum in Aachen, Germany.[66] The museum displayed the work outdoors, and some of the wood rotted. The work was conserved by replacing it with logs from the same source in Montana. Then, in 2014, Schürmann sold the work to an American collector, Scott Mueller, for $1.4 million.[67] The sales contract included a provision in which Schürmann agreed to buy back the work if the artist disavowed it within the first twelve months. Noland did disavow the work, leading to a lawsuit, dismissed in 2016, between the collectors. The artist then filed her own lawsuit alleging that the museum was negligent in exhibiting the work outdoors and that the work could have been conserved less intrusively. (Noland had granted permission to display the work outdoors and to stain the wood, but she argued that the museum was negligent to place the structure directly on the ground without a protective base.) Thus, she was claiming that the defendants "destroyed" the work by leaving it outside and "copied" it without authorization by replacing the wood.[68]

The conservation of the work occurred exclusively in Germany, but Noland sued under US copyright law and VARA. Noland argued that the collector's purchase of wood from the United States and attempt to sell the work to an American collector allowed US law to apply. The extraterritorial standard was met but the court also had discretion to dismiss the matter, and it did.[69] These cases are significant to artists because they concern ongoing authorial control. They are significant to markets because the artist has the power to reduce the value of the work practically to zero by disowning it.

8.3 RESALE ROYALTIES AND DROIT DE SUITE

A resale royalty is a right that grants an artist a percentage of the proceeds when an artwork is resold in the secondary market. Resale royalties, called *droit de suite*, originated in France in 1920 and have been adopted in over seventy jurisdictions worldwide, including the members states of the European Union as well as the United Kingdom.[70]

Resale royalties in the European Union and United Kingdom follow the European Union directive 2001/84/EC. The legislation was ratified in 2001 but nation states were given a grace period for implementation. The resale royalty, called the Artist Resale Right (ARR), has been operational in the United Kingdom since 2006 and is managed by DACS, the UK rights management body, which also handles copyright. Artworks that sell for under €1,000 are exempt from the ARR. The ARR rate is charged on a sliding scale from 4% down to 0.25%. The maximum resale right per artwork is €12,500.[71] Since 2012, the ARR has covered both living artists and artists' estates in the UK. The resale right expires seventy years after the artist's death. Under the EU rules, if two friends who did not work in the arts sold a painting between them, there would be no ARR. The resale must be done by an "Art Market Professional (AMP)," generally defined as an auction house, private dealer, or gallery.[72] The EU regulation does not include a cost basis but instead takes the ARR based on the full purchase price, creating a "cascade effect" in which artworks with multiple intermediaries in a single transaction are subject to the ARR multiple times. In that case, the ARR functions more like a tax or surcharge than a claim on an investment return.[73]

Although federal resale royalties have been proposed numerous times in the United States, they have not passed. The only state to have resale royalties was California, but that law was subsequently challenged and substantially gutted.[74] The US Copyright Office has undertaken large-scale study of resale royalties twice in recent decades, first in 1992 and then in 2013. In the first study, the

Copyright Office recommended that there were not yet sufficient policy or economic justifications for resale royalties. However, they reversed their opinion in 2013, writing in the report, "The Office agrees that, under the current legal system, visual artists are uniquely limited in their ability to fully benefit from the success of their works over time."[75]

Yet some scholars disagree with resale royalties on principle. For example, Guy Rub, a law professor, describes them as a form of welfare for artists. He argues that artists are unfairly singled out as a group of people and given a special benefit.[76] Writing with another intellectual property law professor Christopher Sprigman, Rub also argues that resale royalties help artists who are already wealthy, while putting emerging artists at a disadvantage.[77] Some economic arguments against resale royalties rely on the concept of price elasticity of demand from Chapter 3. As the argument goes, a resale royalty functions as a surcharge on the price a collector pays. (Or it functions as a discount to the previous owner's sales proceeds.) If purchasers of art are price sensitive, this circumstance will cause them to buy less art. Chanont Banternghansa and Kathryn Graddy studied this problem empirically and did not find an effect of resale royalties on art prices though their study concerned data very early into the existence of resale royalties in the United Kingdom.[78]

Some experts see resale royalties not as a special benefit but as a structural correction for the difficulty artists face reaping rewards of their own work. A common art-market parable invoked to support resale royalties is the Scull sale. In 1973, the taxi-magnate couple Robert and Ethel Scull sold their art collection at what was then Sotheby Parke-Bernet. Among other works, the Sculls sold the Robert Rauschenberg piece *Thaw* (1958), which they had purchased from the dealer Leo Castelli in 1959. The Sculls had paid $900, with half or $450 going to the artist. At the 1973 sale, *Thaw* sold for $85,000. Rauschenberg, who had only been paid his $450 share originally, was not eligible to receive any of these proceeds.[79] At the Scull sale, Rauschenberg legendarily showed up slightly drunk and was recorded somewhat playfully shoving Scull and telling Scull he would need to buy more of Rauschenberg's work in the future.[80]

In a strictly theoretical sense, many parties, in this case including both the artist and his dealer, helped to create the value of the sale without owning upside, that is, without claim to any potential gains. Rauschenberg represented the United States at the Venice Biennale in 1964, with the American pavilion winning the Golden Lion or top prize. When his dealer, Leo Castelli, first hosted a solo exhibition of Rauschenberg's work in 1958, only one work from the exhibition sold – *Bed* (1955) – and only because Castelli himself bought it.[81] If we imagined all of these actors as cofounders and early investors in a start-up company, they would have owned shares in the company. The artists, dealers, and collectors were all creators of value. Here, only the Sculls profited directly. In practice, sometimes artists address this concern by "holding back" earlier work to sell later, but storing work can be expensive.[82]

Whether someone agrees or disagrees with the idea of resale royalties or their legislative design, their financial impact on artists has been not inconsequential. Since the inception of the ARR in the United Kingdom in 2006, DACS has distributed over £80 million. In 2018, DACS distributed £18 million to over 58,000 artists and artists' estates.[83]

8.4 COASE THEOREM AND RETAINED EQUITY

One alternative to resale royalties is to directly assign fractional ownership in art. This proposal applies Ronald Coase's theory of property rights from his 1960 paper "The Problem of Social Cost" to works of art. Foundational to the understanding of property rights in economics, Coase's work would go on to be awarded the Nobel Prize and to form the basis of tradable emissions permits in environmental science.[84] Coase argued that it mattered less that one could assign a price to something like pollution and mattered more simply that one could create a property right around it. So long as the property rights were distributed into the marketplace and transaction costs were not too high, the market itself would be able to set a price. In the case of tradable emissions permits, a governmental authority sets the total level of pollution and distributes a corresponding number of permits. Those firms for which pollution is especially cost-saving will purchase other firms' permits, provided they can transact with reasonable ease and low enough transaction costs. This idea of property rights can be applied to art, recreating the effect of resale royalties but in a more flexible way. If artists owned fractional equity in their work, those shares would function as property rights that could be traded anytime, allowing artists access to capital and investors more tools for diversification in their holdings of art.[85]

In this framework, instead of regulating resale royalties, artists can retain fractional equity in their work by contract when it is first sold. For instance, if an artwork normally sells for $100, with the dealer taking $50 and the artist taking $50, instead the work can sell for $90 with the dealer taking $50 and the artist taking $40 in cash and retaining 10% in equity. If the work later resells, whether at auction or privately, the artist receives 10% of the new price. If the artwork goes down in value, the artist receives nothing.[86]

These applications of the Coase Theorem are still speculative. They require forms of tracking technology and widespread cultural adoption, a problem that the Artist's Contract also faced. But the empirical results are noteworthy. In an early study with Roman Kräussl, we found that if artists from the 1950s and 1960s had retained equity in their work they would have substantially outperformed US stock markets. Jasper Johns and Robert Rauschenberg would have outperformed the US S&P 500 Index by up to 1,000 times. Even taking a larger sample – works sold by Green Gallery and Betty Parsons Gallery – the pooled fractional equity would have substantially outperformed US equities markets, even if we assume the gallery "bought" all of the works and only realized an investment for the roughly 10% of works that went to auction (see Figure 8.1)[87]

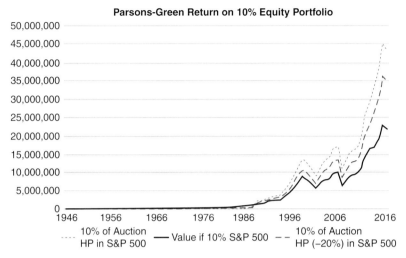

FIGURE 8.1 Performance of retained equity portfolio, from Amy Whitaker and Roman Kräussl (2020). Courtesy of *Management Science*.

8.5 CULTURAL HERITAGE AND OWNERSHIP

These ideas exist in a field in which many forms of cultural property were acquired through colonialism or theft. In 1801, Thomas Bruce, 7th Earl of Elgin, acquired the Parthenon marbles from the Acropolis in Athens. The British Museum claims that the marbles were taken lawfully by the British explorer with sign-off of the Ottoman Empire, which had control over Greece at the time. Greece claims the marbles as their legitimate property.[88]

In 2018, Felwine Sarr and Bénédicte Savoy published *The Restitution of African Cultural Heritage: Toward a New Relational Ethics*, a report commissioned by the French President Emmanuel Macron. In the report, Sarr and Savoy found that over 90% of African cultural artifacts are located outside the African continent and that over 90,000 significant objects are held by French museums.[89] New technologies such as blockchain open up novel approaches to these restitution questions. For instance, it is possible to separate out the "rights stack" of ownership, exhibition, and revenue streams using blockchain to manage these records without having to trust a single, centralized authority. For a group of objects held in a museum, one can imagine, for example, granting ownership back to the source country with the source country then gifting some objects to the museum, reclaiming some objects physically, and for others negotiating to receive revenue streams in exchange for exhibition rights. These potential solutions raise difficult but nonetheless important questions and depend on fair negotiations that center source countries. The structure of blockchain – allowing trust in information without reliance on a central recordkeeper – would support such experimental arrangements and potentially leave all stakeholders better off.[90]

Researchers are actively questioning and reorienting understandings of property and authorship, whether building communal frameworks for ownership, protecting indigenous data sovereignty, or recognizing the authorship of indigenous communities within library records.[91] In this last category, professors Jane Anderson and Kim Christen have started an organization called Local Contexts which allows indigenous communities to catalog and write reference texts for their own materials using Traditional Knowledge (TK) Labels. A universal set of pictorial icons identify different aspects of the work, which can then be populated by whatever text the indigenous group chooses, in their own language. One tag describes material that is considered sacred. The tag can require the library to restrict access to the material. Such initiatives provide a novel angle on these threads of economic and cultural ownership. They also animate questions of ownership as cultural as well as economic.[92]

8.6 CONCLUSIONS

These questions of intellectual property have added layers to the economic nature of art as a "product." The logic of property varies substantially across jurisdiction, community, and culture. In the same way that one may doubt that artists or arts workers are profit-seeking, one may doubt that creators of copyrighted work are economically motivated. Even in jurisdictions such as the United States in which intellectual and creative progress is economically incentivized, the private incentive serves a deeper rationale of public benefit. The themes of this chapter encapsulate the awkward pull between authorship and market structures, and the nature of property as both an asset and a representation of the dignity and autonomy of artists. These cases underscore the complex interplay between artists, museums, and markets in the construction of value.

Returning to the Art Workers' Coalition (AWC), the 1969 group catalyzed by Takis's removal of his work from MoMA, the AWC made demands of museums that are still resonant today. Their demands root artists' rights – economically and intellectually or legally – in larger ideas of how societies should be. In 1969, the Art Workers' Coalition convinced a number of New York museums to close for a day – Moratorium Day on October 15, 1969[93] – to protest the Vietnam War. Of their list of demands to Bates Lowry, then MoMA director, the AWC demanded numerous protections of the arts ecosystem that activists still advocate for today. They demanded healthy board governance including representation by staff and artists. They argued each institution strive to become "a more open-minded and democratic museum" and that culture "belongs" to – is the property of – the people. They argued that museums should be free and also "decentralized" with locations in neighborhoods of poorer people and of people of color. They argued that those communities should have some control over events. They argued that museum collections should have greater representation in gender and race and that museums should keep registries of local living artists. They wanted museum workers to take political positions on issues of the day, whether rent control or other artists' rights.[94]

The members of the Art Workers' Coalition seemed to understand that believing one can maintain neutrality in the face of injustice is a fallacy, that passivity in the face of injustice is a support of injustice itself. Stating the core dignity of artists' rights, they wrote, "Artists should retain a disposition over the destiny of their work, whether or not it is owned by them, to ensure it cannot be altered, destroyed, or exhibited without their consent." At the same time, artists should receive exhibition fees, a percentage of profits on the resale of their work should a museum deaccession a piece, and the distribution of stipends, coverage of health insurance, and other benefits that could be funded by the tax collected on artists' estates.[95]

These conversations about rights and property and the responsibilities for governance and inclusion are simultaneously conversations about politics and economics. If museum board seats are for sale, are they priced too cheaply? If activists want to pressure board members to step down, does forensic analysis of their finances help? To what degree should artists influence the institutions that present their work? With the different kinds of financial precarity, what responsibilities do museums have toward artists and what responsibilities do artists, and other members of the community, have as citizens of museums? Fundamentally the idea of artists' rights straddles this notion property rights as economic incentive and property rights as the designation of the citizen, of the protected space in which to act. These stories of ownership, activism, and determination have profound effects on markets, and markets in turn are petri dishes for how we understand broad currents of nearly unanswerable questions about the value of art.

QUESTIONS

1. The artist Adrian Piper adapted the Siegelaub resale royalties contract to prohibit the selling of her work at a discount. Piper explained that this was because her work already sold doubly at a discount on account of her being female and black. Using the concepts from economics – inclusive of pricing methods in the art world, price discrimination, and the function of resale royalties – analyze and frame Piper's decision in both economic and artistic terms. Write a 1–3 page response, in the form of a memo to the trustees' acquisitions committee of the Museum of Modern Art, to contextualize Piper's dealer's inability to offer a standard 10% museum discount on a piece that the museum is trying to acquire.

2. Lauren van Haaften-Schick analyzes Benjamin Buchloh's and Alexander Alberro's writings on the ways in which conceptual

artists use administrative contracts. In "Conceptual Art 1962–1969: From the Aesthetic of Administration to the Critique of Institutions," Buchloh suggests that artists' use of contracts is an indication that artists have been subsumed by market structures.[96] In *Conceptual Art and the Politics of Publicity*, Alberro contemplates the artist's signature on the contract. Both writers focus on the aesthetics of administration.[97] Van Haaften-Schick emphasizes instead the performative and subversive use of these contracts. She writes of Buchloh's and Alberro's critiques of administration that their "negative assessments *assume* that the use of certificates and other administrative forms can only indicate subsumption under capitalism and bureaucratization, rehearsing a scenario where art is helpless before market flows."[98] Read the Buchloh essay and van Haaften-Schick's argument. In the context of the Hostile Worlds and Nothing But views of Zelizer and Velthuis covered in the Introduction, what relationships of art and economics are Buchloh and van Haaften-Schick espousing? Choose a conceptual artist who uses contracts or certificates in their work or in the sale of their work (e.g., Hans Haacke, Felix Gonzalez-Torres, Jenny Holzer, Adrian Piper, Cameron Rowland). Write a research paper on the use of contracts in this work and the relationship of conceptual artistic practice to contracts.[99]

3. Choose a work of art that has been contested from a copyright standpoint (e.g., works by Richard Prince, Jeff Koons, Shepard Fairey). Analyze the dispute using economic rights and moral rights. How is the outcome different?

4. Numerous scholars have debated the efficacy of copyright in a digital age of sampling. Discuss ways of developing fair-use approaches to sampling. Can you reimagine the application of the fair-use factors in any useful ways? You may wish to consider the College Art Association fair-use guide, or speculative proposals.[100]

5. Choose three countries anywhere in the world and compare/contrast their copyright schemes.

6. The study of artists' rights points to the ecosystem of "product" in which there is an artwork, a body of critical writing, and participation of audiences. As an experiment, see if you can draw a diagram of these interactions and the ways in which all of these actors might share rights.

7. Research the 5Pointz case in New York in which the longtime owner of a building in Long Island City decided to develop commercially and whitewashed over expansive graffitied murals without notice to the artists, who sued for damages and won both at the district court and on appeal.[101] In discussion or writing, what are your views on the key points of the analysis? How would this story have unfolded differently in different locations (e.g., Toronto, Beijing, Lagos, Sydney) or not? Recognizing that having artwork destroyed irrevocably is traumatic, how do you consider the psychological toll on artists as part of the analysis?[102]

8. If you could propose one new international copyright treaty, legislative action in a specific country, or private venture on behalf of artists' rights, what would it be and why?

9. In addition to artists' rights, one can imagine advocacy and participation for audiences, nonprofit organizations, and other actors in the arts. In the spirit of the Art Workers' Coalition, choose a group and write a manifesto or list of demands for them.

10. Read Felwine Sarr and Bénédicte Savoy's 2018 report considering the large number of objects of African cultural heritage in the possession of European museums.[103] How does Sarr and Savoy's work relate to the themes of this chapter? In addition to complex and contested questions of ownership, is it possible to separate out all of rights, for example, property, exhibition, claim to related revenue, authorship (as in the work of Anderson and Christen with Local Contexts), and so on?[104] For discussion or a written assignment, identify an artwork or group of artworks whose ownership is contested. Propose policy, contractual, diplomatic, or other approaches to address these questions of restitution.

11. The decentralized ledger of blockchain has been proposed as a potential registry of property. Read about the use cases of blockchain to the arts. Do you see applications of property or other rights management?[105] How might an art fair, such as 1–54, Art Basel, or the European Fine Art Fair consider using blockchain as a registry? If you believe the arts does not need or cannot support such a system, make the claim as to why not.[106]

12. Most art museums have a staff member who clears rights to reproduction – both for works in the museum's collection and for works from outside copyright holders – when the museum wishes to use images in its own publications. When Nick Pozek was working at the Carnegie Museum of Art in Pittsburgh, Pennsylvania, the museum commissioned a designer to create a catalogue. The design of the catalogue was so compelling that the Cooper-Hewitt, the New York-based design museum that is part of the Smithsonian Institution of national museums in the United States, acquired a copy for their collection. Consider all of the contributors to the design of the catalogue, from the hired designer to the underlying creators whose work was cited in the book. How would you apply principles of ownership to that work? What rights would you grant to the Cooper-Hewitt as owner of the book?

9 Investment

Gold is, give or take some major geopolitical drama, going to hold its value over time, whereas most art is gonna be virtually worthless in the very long term.

Julia Halperin, editor-in-chief *Artnet News*[1]

Werner "Wynn" Kramarsky and his wife Sarah-Ann, a math tutor, amassed a collection of over 4,000 artworks, a vast number of which they donated to museums.[2] Mr. Kramarsky, who was born in Amsterdam in 1926, began collecting art on his own in the 1950s and continued collecting throughout his marriage. He particularly loved drawings – any kind of work on paper.[3] As Kramarsky told *The Brooklyn Rail* in 2008:

> I really start out by looking at something and saying, "How is it made?" not, "Why is it made?" .... What happened when the artist put pencil or pen or brush to paper? And because it is almost impossible, when you work on paper, to correct it, that initial moment is crucial. It interests me that somebody had the courage and the idea to make that original mark.[4]

Kramarsky's first well-known acquisition was a $175 work on paper by Jasper Johns in 1959.[5] Kramarsky – who had served as a US Navy radioman, an investment banker, and later a New York State commissioner on human rights – spent rent money on it and paid in installments.[6] He said, "Although that $175 was two months' rent, if I missed the rent, I'd crash with somebody. It was easy; I was single." Several years later, when Kramarsky was married with small children, the Jasper Johns work needed $1,500 worth of conservation. Not able to afford it with their young family, the Kramarskys sold the work to someone who could. Despite that early sale, over six decades the Kramarskys were dedicated collectors of art and patrons of artists. Their donations to museums are exemplified by the eighty-one works they gave to the Museum of Modern Art, New York, in 2004.[7]

The Kramarskys' story takes us from the act of making art in a studio to the very human side of collecting art to the transformation of art into a financial asset. To go from the studio to the investment analysis of art is the aim of this chapter: to relate the principles of economics to those of finance and investment.

Mr. Kramarsky's parents had been art collectors. They had purchased Vincent van Gogh's painting *Portrait of Dr. Gachet* in the 1930s and brought the work with them when they fled the Netherlands in 1939, moving to the United States by way of Canada.[8] Van Gogh had made two versions of *Dr. Gachet*, both in 1890, shortly before his death.[9] The other version hangs in the Musée d'Orsay (now Valéry Giscard d'Estaing) in Paris.[10]

After Wynn's father died in 1961, the family kept the painting in trust and lent it to the Metropolitan Museum of Art for several weeks each summer and later for a period of years. After Wynn's mother suffered serious health difficulties, the family decided to sell the work. The sale took place at Christie's on May 15, 1990.[11] The *Portrait of Dr. Gachet* bore an estimate of $40–$50 million dollars. At the time, that was the highest estimate that an auction house had ever placed on a work of art.[12] (See Appendix D for an overview of auctions.)

Despite booming Impressionist sales in the late 1980s, markets had wobbled shortly before the sale. Even with this uncertainty, the sale of *Dr. Gachet* was a success.[13] Christopher Burge, the auctioneer, hammered down a bid of $75 million, resulting in a price, once the 10% buyer's premium was added, of $82.5 million. The purchaser was the Japanese gallerist Hideto Kobayashi, who only entered the bidding when the raising of paddles slowed around the $40 million mark. According to Peter Watson, who was given special access to the behind-the-scenes preparations for the sale, Mr. Kobayashi was known to Christie's in general terms but had told no one of his interest in this painting.[14] Kobayashi was raising his paddle on behalf of a client who had given instructions to bid up to $70 million. In the moment, Kobayashi had decided his client would be comfortable with $75 million.[15] Thus, that price – $75 million hammer, $82.5 million with premium – became the price of record for that work. It would be treated as the reference point, despite being set by the dynamics in the room.[16]

Microeconomics, the subject of this book, essentially fits on an income statement. It is about the efficient use of resources. It is about the system of thought that balances revenue – price times quantity or money in – against costs. Economics includes notions of investment. But whereas the central logic of economics is that price equals value, the central logic of finance is that risk and return move in lockstep.

Finance is important to the economics of creativity and of art specifically because markets from creative work often have difficulty setting price. In the artist's studio, the work is made through the investment of resources – time, materials, labor, ingenuity. The artist pays – in both explicit and implicit (opportunity) cost – to make the work. Most of the time, the artist is making the work on spec, without a purchaser known ahead of time.[17] The artist operates in this economic world of resource procurement and also in an investment world of taking risk. In both a market and an artistic sense, the artist is producing something of unknown value: Will the mark go down on the paper well? Will the work find an audience? Will the work one day hold financial value and be traded in secondary markets?

One of the first studies of art investment returns was conducted by William Baumol, the same scholar whose endorsement of Grampp's purist free-market view of arts economics we encountered in the Introduction.[18] In 1986, Baumol published an article in the *American Economic Review* titled "Unnatural Value: Or Art Investment As Floating Crap Game." Using a 1961 book by Gerald Reitlinger called *The Economics of Taste*,[19] Baumol found that, on average and adjusted for inflation, investments in art performed at an average rate of 0.55% per year. In comparison, he found that bonds – as measured by the interest-rate return on debt instruments – over the same time period returned approximately 2.5%.[20] If someone could have invested their money and received a 2.5% rate of return, why would they have bought art and received only a 0.55% rate of return? Moreover, why would someone purchase art when they could purchase something which they could more easily analyze financially using investment tools? Baumol calls the art market a "floating crap game" because it defies analysis by traditional financial methods, at the same time that art is considered an asset class and included in investment portfolio returns.

Although art investment happens in many nonfinancial ways – investment in art for art's sake – in order to consider the financial side of art investment, we will begin with background on the language and logic of finance. With this perspective, we will cover the methods by which scholars typically study art investment returns – specifically repeat sales and hedonic regression.

9.1 THE BASICS OF INVESTMENT

Financial investors – in art and in general – are typically trying to accomplish at least one of these objectives: capital protection and capital accumulation. **Capital protection** describes the necessity of putting money to work, as opposed to proverbially putting cash in one's mattress, in order to protect the money's spending power, given inflation. (In the same way that the term is commonly used, **inflation** is the macroeconomic tendency of currency to have less buying power over time; it is the explanation for why a candy bar that cost five cents in 1955 costs a dollar in 2021.) **Capital appreciation** means investing in order to increase wealth by taking a risk in order to achieve a return.

9.1.1 *Risk and Return*

The logic and language of finance derives from the economic concept of opportunity cost. In Chapter 2 we defined opportunity cost as the cost of your next-best alternative. In any scenario, what would be the highest and best use of a resource – of your time, talents, or equipment – if you were not using it already in the way that you are?

Finance is based on the opportunity cost not of time or factories but of capital. Here, capital essentially means monies – in the broad sense of cash, bank accounts, and assets – that can be securitized or transferred into money and used for investment. The **opportunity cost of capital** is the rate of return you would receive if you deployed money for your next-best alternative. This rate becomes the hurdle you are trying to clear, the benchmark you always try to best. Put simply, if you have $100 and you are asked to invest in a project that could give you a 10% rate of return a year later, is that a good investment? Is it better than your next-best alternative?

This is not an easy question to answer. It is a question that often gets answered in a spreadsheet, a format that has the effect of making the information look true. But figuring out the opportunity cost of capital – what percentage return you could get if you were doing another activity – would require a crystal ball. Instead, we agree on ways of thinking through this problem. These ways of thinking are based on another economic principle applied to financial markets: the principle of efficiency. The way that efficiency is applied in finance is different from how it is applied in economics. Whereas in economics efficiency generally describes the use of scarce resources to produce at the lowest cost, in financial markets efficiency describes the core belief that risk and return are aligned. Under this belief, it is not possible to get a big return without taking a proportionate amount of risk.[21]

At the heart of the assumption of efficient markets is the idea of **arbitrage.** Arbitrage is the act of trading in two different markets in order to take advantage of a mispricing between them. For example, if a chocolate bar cost $5 in one store and $10 in another store, I could theoretically buy the chocolate bar for $5 and stand outside the other store successfully selling chocolate bars for $9, at a $4 profit. In financial terms, if risk and return are priced out of lockstep, then investors will try to take advantage of this opportunity. The assumption of efficient markets is maintained by the constant activity of arbitrage, a regulation of mispricings by market actors seeking them out.

Although it is hard to know one's opportunity cost of capital beforehand, one can model these rates using historical data.[22] Rates that are commonly used take as their foundation the interest rate at which banks loan money to each other. For example, the rate at which US banks lend money to each other overnight – if they need to have a certain amount of money in hand to meet their reserve requirements – is called the Fed Funds rate. The most common comparable rate used internationally is LIBOR, the London Interbank Offered Rate. This rate represents time – the fact that one is borrowing money from one point in time the next. Investors also use the rate of return on US Treasuries. Analysts start with this base rate and then add a premium to account for risk. The idea is that this is a "risk-free" rate – one that simply reflects the time value of borrowing money. If there is risk that the money will not be repaid, then the rate becomes higher. That is, the lender is an investor who is receiving a higher return given the level of risk.

9.1.2   Discounted Cash Flows

Whatever rate one uses – the risk-free rate, the long-term return on equities – one applies the opportunity cost of capital as this benchmark or hurdle to see if something is a good investment. The rate used to represent the opportunity cost of capital is called the **discount rate**, because it is used to discount future cash flows so that they can be compared to money in the present. Discounting cash flows shows opportunity cost in mathematical terms.

The calculation is essentially the inverse of compounding-interest rates. **Compounding interest** is the mechanism by which an amount of money earns interest over time but also earns interest on the past interest paid. For example, if you invest $100 in an account that pays 10% interest per year, then at the end of the first year, you have $110. In the second year, you make 10% interest on $110 – both the original $100 and the $10 interest earned in the prior year. Thus, at the end of year two you have 110% of $110, or $121. And at the end of year three, you have 110% of $121, or $133. This principle of compounding interest is the rationale for investing early for one's retirement – to benefit from these compounded gains.

A discounted cash flow uses this principle of compounding interest in reverse. In the example above, if you are offered $133 at the end of year three, you can calculate whether that is a good investment. In this example, if you have a 10% opportunity cost of capital and are asked to make a $100 initial investment, we know that $133 exactly meets this 10% return threshold. The term **present value** describes the future cash flow discounted back to the present to reflect the opportunity cost of capital. The term **net present value** describes the difference between the initial investment one is asked to make and the present value. Projects that have a positive net present value make better than their opportunity cost rate of return. To calculate discounted cash flows and also to solve for an implied annual rate of return, see Appendix E.

The specific tools of discounting cash flows or solving for implied rates of annual return allow us to know whether our investments have met, exceeded, or fallen short of our opportunity cost of capital. Of course, art investing may be for financial or nonfinancial reasons. This enjoyment is often framed analytically as "aesthetic dividends" or "psychic returns."[23] Bruno S. Frey and Reiner Eichenberger point out that measurements of the return on art are usually considered by comparing two sales prices, when the enjoyment of art is really measured by what would be the equivalent of a rental of the art for purposes of enjoyment. Frey and Eichenberger focus on the need to evaluate this psychic income that comes from holding art.[24] For the purposes of investment background, we will focus on the financial logic and then return to the artistic one.

9.1.3   Asset Classes

The field of investment management uses specific language to describe the conceptual and mechanistic principles of finance. We introduce this language here in order to describe both art as an investment and art as part of a larger investment portfolio. Different categories of investment are called **asset classes.** An **asset** is something – whether an artwork, a share in a company, or a house – of potential value or worth that can be owned. The most common asset classes are equities, fixed income, cash or cash equivalents, real assets, and alternative assets. Asset classes can have different expected risk profiles, returns, and other characteristics.

Equities are shares in the ownership of something, for instance, stock in a company. Equity has no guarantee of payment. Theoretically, equity holders receive dividends when the company decides that they do not have enough projects to reinvest all of their profits at or above their opportunity cost of capital and thus should return those monies to investors. (In practice, investors in some larger "blue chip" companies expect regular dividend payments.) An equity investment can have theoretically unlimited upside or losses to zero. For instance, when Sotheby's was a publicly traded company, if the stock price had risen to $50 after you purchased one share for $45, you could have sold that share for a $5 gain less transaction costs. If the company had cratered, the value of your share could have gone to zero.[25] In a bankruptcy, anyone who had lent money to Sotheby's – owned debt not equity – would typically have been repaid before you.

Fixed income is an asset class generally based on debt instruments such as loans. The name comes from the fact that the investor receives monies that are agreed ahead of time as a recurring payment at a regular interval. Debt instruments can have fixed interest rates – for instance, a mortgage that is 4% each year over the thirty-year life of the mortgage. Or they can have floating rates – for instance, LIBOR (the London Interbank Offered Rate) plus 200 basis points (or 2%).[26]

Real assets are tangible things of value such as real estate – including commercial and residential property – and commodities such as gold, coffee, corn, or oil. These asset classes are all containerized in different kinds of **securities,** the hold-all name given to something formatted in such a way that one can invest in it. A stock is a security. A bond is a security. In the case of real estate, a security might be designed so that one could invest in it, for instance, as a real estate investment trust (REIT). These investment structures could include mortgages or derivatives based on mortgages. (In art lending, the art serves as collateral and collectors can borrow against it. The collector can borrow a percentage of the value of the work, usually at up to 50% of the work's appraised value. This percentage is expressed as a loan-to-value ratio. If one can borrow $50 on a $100 work, the ratio is 50:100 or 50%.)

If stocks and bonds are types of financial instruments, they are joined by another class of instruments called **derivatives**, meaning financial instruments whose values are based off of – or "derived" from – some underlying assets. For example, an **option** is a security that is a contractual right to buy (or obligation to sell) an underlying security at a set price either within a set period of time or on a set date.[27] Because the option is based on the underlying security, it is a derivative. Derivatives can be used speculatively and with intense risk, or they can help to mitigate risk, particularly for one party that has a concentrated exposure.

For instance, consider an orange farmer named Merlina. Her entire livelihood is tied up in how a crop does in a given year, but she does not have control over the weather. In a typical year, she sells her farm's output for $100. If there is an excellent year, she sells the output for $130. If there is a frost and a terrible year, she makes $80.[28] To cover the cost of the farm she needs at least $90 per year.

For Merlina, there is considerable risk. She is willing to trade off some additional income for the certainty of covering her costs. She might therefore enter into a contract by which she has a guarantee that she can sell her oranges for $95. This gives her certainty that she can cover her expenses with $5 profit. A large-scale financial operator would have an incentive to take the other side of the contract with Merlina. This operator deals with farmers with many different crops in many different weather areas. With such broad exposure, that operator expects that across its many investments an average crop return will prevail, giving the operator on average $100 for Merlina's crop. For Merlina, this contract functions broadly as insurance, to lock in gains and avoid losses.

I use the case of Merlina because agriculture and other industries have more developed futures contracts than art.[29] You could imagine a dealer going to an art fair – feeling unsure of whether the gallery will sell enough work to cover its costs – being interested in this type of arrangement, though it is not formally offered in the arts. Auction houses tend to have more developed financial practices in these areas. For example, if Merlina happened also to own an important Andrew Wyeth painting that she decided to sell in December, she could enter into a contract with an auction house to receive an advance or a guaranteed price at the next auction, the following May. If she were selling the work to cover debt on her farm, an advance or guarantee would help her do that. Merlina might be forced to give up some potential upside of the auction sale, but if she were selling the work to cover debt on her farm, she could structure the arrangement to be guaranteed at least the amount of her debt payment.[30] The auction house, in turn, assumes risk. If they guarantee the work and it fails to sell, the auction house must still pay Merlina. They may later be able to sell the work privately.

Art as an asset class tends to be grouped with other nontraditional asset classes including hedge funds, private equity, jewelry, and other collectibles. These categories are broadly known as **alternative assets**. Alternatives may perform very well on their own, or they also may serve a purpose in an overall portfolio by being uncorrelated to other assets. Because they do not always perform the same way that other assets do, they can lower risk by offering an internalized form of insurance. As we will come to see, portfolio diversification is difficult in the arts because of the relatively high price point of many investible individual works of art and because of the difficulty of buying works collectively, as in an art fund.

9.1.4 Portfolio Allocation and Diversification

One of the most profound theories of financial markets is the idea of a diversified investment portfolio. In 1952, the professor Harry Markowitz published a paper in the *Journal of Finance* called "Portfolio Selection."[31] Markowitz argued that the most efficient way to invest was to purchase a diversified portfolio of the whole market – the equities market – because the positions would not be perfectly correlated with each other and thus they would have some effect of insuring against one another, leading to a higher risk-adjusted return. This theory is the basis of the way most people invest in the stock market: by purchasing an index fund or mutual fund with a broad exposure.

This rationale of diversification extends to art funds. If one wanted to diversify while investing in art, one would either need to have a very large sum of money or to collect low-value works. It is difficult for one person to hold a diversified portfolio in art singlehandedly. To invest in art with some advantages of diversification, collectors have pooled assets and bought work together. In 1904, the Parisian financier André Level, who specialized in the shipping industry, assembled an art-buying club, La Peau de L'Ours club (the bearskin club), a buying syndicate that is often referred to as the first art fund. Members contributed 250 French francs annually – 2,750 French francs total across the eleven voting members of the club – in order to purchase works collectively.[32] The club bought roughly one hundred works over ten years. In 1906, they spent most of their money collecting works by Pablo Picasso. On March 2, 1914, the entire collection was auctioned off at the Hôtel Drouot in Paris. The sale brought 100,000 francs, or a 4x return. Some individual works, such as Picasso's *Saltimbanques* (1908), brought notable returns; that work was purchased for 1,000 francs and sold for 12,500 francs, or 12.5 times its acquisition cost, six years later.[33] The members of the bearskin club, who never apologized for being speculators, also implemented resale royalties, sharing proceeds of the sale with artists in 1914, six years before such droit de suite rights (see Chapter 8) were implemented in France.[34]

The relatively more recent example of a standout art fund is the British Railways Pension Fund, which invested in over 2,400 works of art from 1974 to 1980, selling off its collection over the 1980s and early 1990s. The fund returned 13%, or 6% after inflation. Those returns were above the fund's real-estate holdings and roughly even with its returns on UK bonds. Their returns were likely due to the timing of selling Impressionist works at the peak of that market in the late 1980s. As Marcus Linell, a specialist at Sotheby's, described the risk that British Rail Pension Fund took investing in art as a category: "You have to be offensively bad to be criticized for investing in stocks and bonds. But if you invest in works of art, 'if you win, you got away with it.' If you lose: 'We told you so.'"[35]

9.2 ART MARKET ANALYSIS

Art differs substantially from the ways in which companies are valued. The finance professor Aswath Damodaran, whom we encountered in Chapter 3, makes this point in his valuation classes by showing a picture of the Francis Bacon triptych *Three Studies of Lucian Freud*, which sold at Christie's New York for $142 million in 2013. Damodaran argues that, financially speaking, art cannot be valued, only priced. The art of valuation that Damodaran teaches draws on the underlying logic of discounted cash flows. The theoretical value of a firm is the present value of all of its cash flows – its profits – in perpetuity. In practice, this perpetuity is estimated using nearer-term – say, five-year – projections and applying growth rates, reinvestment rates, discount rates, and multiples. Art cannot be valued in this way because art does not have cash flows.[36] It is not like a firm making and selling sneakers. Financially, a collectible object is worth what one will pay for it at any given point in time. That price is supported by market comparables and expert opinion, but it is not grounded in valuation, per se. Nonetheless, art has been rigorously studied as an investment. The next section gives an overview of these research methods and findings.

There is in fact an economic dimension to purchasing these large value works in the navigation of US tax policy. For instance, the Francis Bacon triptych in question was purchased by Elaine Wynn. Instead of shipping the work to Nevada, she lent it to the Portland Museum of Art in Oregon. Oregon is one of a handful of US states that have no sales tax or use tax. By exhibiting the work there for three months, Oregon became the location of its first "use," lowering the tax bill for the work substantially. (In Wynn's case, experts estimated the Nevada use tax would have been around $11 million, though of course, as reporters noted, it is not known whether she intended to make use of the tax break.) For major value works, this strategy is common enough that the Jordan Schnitzer Museum of Art at the University of Oregon has a formal "Masterworks on Loan" program.[37]

9.2.1 Repeat Sales and Hedonic Regression

The two main methods of art market analysis are repeat sales and hedonic regression. In the repeat-sales method, one uses publicly available auction data and considers only the works that have sold at auction twice. One plots the return between these two price points for each individual work and then creates a combined portfolio of all of the works.

Baumol's 1986 study uses the repeat-sales method. A **repeat sale** is a work that has sold at auction at least twice, thus making it possible to infer a rate of return between two sales. Reitlinger's three-volume book catalogued the sales prices of "the best known painters of the world" over the period from 1760 to 1960. Baumol considered "the thousands of sales recorded between pages 241 and 506 of Reitlinger's book" and then narrowed those down to 640 transactions. Baumol only used records that corresponded to repeat sales. Baumol also excluded any sales that happened within a twenty-year interval. That is, the collector had to have held the work for more than two decades – a very long time in contemporary art market customs. Despite the title of the book – specifically referencing the two-century span of 1760–1960 – some of the sales dated back as far as 1652.[38]

Baumol wanted to answer the question of what annual return was received, on average, for an investment in art. More specifically, he wanted to know the return above the rate of inflation. Some art market studies such as Baumol's take inflation out, whereas others leave it in but use benchmarks such as long-term returns on the stock market that also include inflation. One can distinguish a **real rate of return**, which is adjusted to take out inflation, and a **nominal rate of return**, which is not adjusted and includes inflation. Thus Baumol's findings – 0.55% annual return for art against a 2.5% annual return for bonds – gave real rates of return.[39] In addition to Baumol's 1986 study and one by Anderson that preceded it (1974), the repeat-sales method has been used by William Goetzmann (1993) as well as by Jianping Mei and Michael Moses (2002 and 2005).[40]

The second main method of art market study is that of hedonic regression. In this method, one identifies variables for each work of art and then builds a multivariable regression analysis to connect those factors to appreciation in price. This method was pioneered around the mid-1990s and then built on by scholars developing hybrid methods.[41] A hedonic regression – named for the word "hedonic" meaning pleasurable – solves for what brings an art collector pleasure or utility, meaning what drives price. The multivariable regression combines many different attributes about an artwork – size of canvas, presence of a signature, whether the artist is living – and applies econometric techniques to determine what factors drive the price. Regression techniques vary substantially but typically consider attributes of the artwork, of the artist, and of the conditions under which it was sold.[42] Because both hedonic regression and repeat sales are based on secondary-market – that is, auction – data, they have the advantage of large data sets but also the disadvantage of selection bias and of heterogeneity – substantial variation – across individual sales within the data.[43]

To place these studies in context, the entire global art market is estimated at $64 billion, according to Clare McAndrew, author of the annual Art Market Report, cosponsored by Art Basel and UBS.[44] While that is a large number by some yardsticks, it is tiny by others; the entire global art market is roughly on par with the quarterly earnings of the company Apple.[45] The market also seems to have plateaued in size. From 2010 to 2019, the market grew 12% but nominally across a decade.-[46] As one might expect, the sale of art, especially at the highest registers of the market, is strongly connected to concentration of wealth. Scholars have also studied the ways in which overall returns on art mask a high degree of variability across individual works[47] and a high degree of structural bias in returns across gender and racial inclusion in markets.[48]

These art market returns also exist within a complex web of institutional and commercial value. **Institutional value** is the ability of seemingly nonmarket institutions such as museums or critical journals to lend credibility that supports market value. **Commercial value** is more straightforwardly the financial value of art in markets. For example, if an artist has a major museum retrospective, the artist's work typically jumps in value in markets. One might say, by very loose analogy, that museums serve a function in art markets that is analogous to the function of ratings agencies or equity researchers in financial markets.

In an influential 2011 essay, "The Venice Effect," Olav Velthuis theorizes the ways in which institutional and commercial value come together, sometimes invisibly and paradoxically. Velthuis cites the Venice Biennale, which stopped selling work and became "noncommercial" amid student protests of 1968. However, the Biennale still occurs just before the major fair Art Basel in Switzerland. Thus, one can see work in Venice and essentially buy it in Basel. Velthuis identifies paradoxes, including the silent financial backing galleries give to artists' nonselling installations in Venice and the appearance of nonmarket motivation by choosing the newest most emerging artists.[49] One commonly sees academic nonselling exhibitions – often of truly outstanding scholarly quality – hosted by commercial galleries or large-scale public commissions whose openings coincide in timing with exhibitions hosted by the artist's commercial gallery.[50] That is not to say these coincidences are categorically good or bad, just that it is very hard to untangle art markets from art criticism or from institutions such as museums. Perhaps the most substantial marker of this scholarly connection is the importance of catalogues raisonnés, the definitive collections of artists' work. If a work is not in the catalogue raisonné, it essentially cannot be sold. Questions of authenticity and provenance, that is, the history of ownership of an artwork, have a huge impact on whether a work can be sold and for how much.

Earlier, in Chapter 2, we visited the importance of provenance to the value of a work of art. Provenance, the history of ownership for an artwork, tells us whether the work has had noteworthy owners. It can also tell us the work's authenticity. Christopher McKeogh, the head of the art crime unit for the Federal Bureau of Investigation (FBI) in New York relayed a story of provenance. The invoices for gallery sales can be especially important as records of title to artworks. McKeogh shows invoices for the Betty Parsons Gallery in New York. Everything about the invoice looks right: the logo, the format, the address, down to the zip code. However, zip codes were not invented until a couple of years after this invoice date. On that basis, the FBI could rule out a whole group of documents (see Figure 9.1).

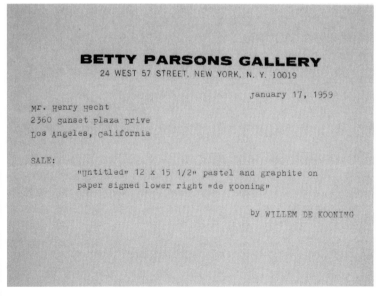

FIGURE 9.1 Betty Parsons invoice, forged. Courtesy of Christopher McKeogh and the US Federal Bureau of Investigation.

9.2.2   *The Longer Arc from Studio to Investment Return*

While financial studies of art investment typically start once the artwork has entered the secondary market, that is, when a work of art is resold, we need to look at the first sale, in the primary market, in order to connect economics and investment. In Chapter 8, we considered the 1973 auction price of $85,000 for Robert Rauschenberg's *Thaw*, a work for which the artist had only been paid $450 (his half of the $900 primary-market sales price) in 1959. Here, we might consider artists as the original investors in their own work and recognize that art markets may only come to value and prize artworks after they have left the artist's hands and the artist's financial interests.

As discussed in Chapter 8, it is possible to model artists as financial investors, via resale royalties or fractional equity.[51] Whether one ultimately agrees with or embraces these financial ways of recognizing artists as investors, we might better understand art markets if we rolled back the tape to before the first sale. Jasper Johns and Robert Rauschenberg would have – if they had retained 10% equity in their earliest work – received a 20%–40% annual return per year every year from 1959 to 2005 (see Figure 9.2).[52] Those artworks first entered the primary market starting around 1959, at which time Johns and Rauschenberg had been working in their studios for more than several years somehow covering their living expenses without much in the way of sales.

This type of story is even true of Pablo Picasso. Even though his works substantially lifted the returns of La Peau de L'Ours art-collecting syndicate, Picasso was himself at that time still struggling for recognition. He had moved to Paris from Spain around 1901 and was a genuinely impoverished, if talented and ambitious, artist for several years. That period contrasts sharply with his more recent market. According to the economist Clare McAndrew, in 2017, Picasso accounted for 11.5% of total global modern art sales by value.[53]

These early stories of art investment humanize the chance and risk involved in the creation of art well before it enters financial

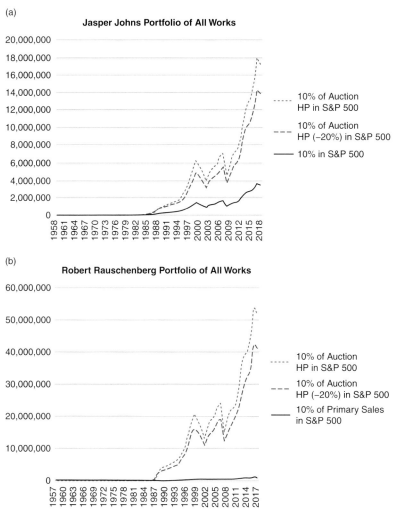

FIGURE 9.2 Jasper Johns and Robert Rauschenberg vs. S&P, from Whitaker and Kräussl (2020). Courtesy of *Management Science*.

markets. The working process of Jasper Johns or Robert Rauschenberg or Pablo Picasso or any other artist – of any form of artistic production – belongs to the world of economics. It fits on an income statement. It concerns using resources to make things of value. Although it is unfashionable and sometimes loathed to call artists investors, they are the original contributors of time and resources to their work. Those days in the studio are an act of investment, whether framed financially or otherwise.[54] These costs – explicit and opportunity costs – are hard to model but important to consider within the frame of art investment.

9.3 CONCLUSIONS

Even the sale of van Gogh's *Portrait of Dr. Gachet* back to the working economics of the artist. When Vincent made that work, toward the end of his life, he was supported by a monthly stipend sent to him by his brother, Theo van Gogh. Theo worked as a director at the art gallery Goupil & Cie. The monies Vincent received each month were between 100 and 150 francs, equivalent to one-and-a-half to two times what a Dutch factory worker was paid at the time.[55]

Of course, Vincent van Gogh is commonly used to invoke the archetype of the starving artist.[56] Yet even if his investment was not recognized financially in his lifetime, his courage was. When Theo and his wife had wife, Jo van Gogh-Bonger, a son, Theo wrote to Vincent to say they had named the child Vincent Willem after him. Theo acknowledged the risk-taking of art when he wrote to his brother, "As we told you, we'll name him after you, and I'm making the wish that he may be as determined and as courageous as you."[57] If Theo's family supported Vincent's courage economically, the "return" for his risk was experienced by collectors outside the family, even some who were early and important supporters. Still the courage carried through the family as Jo built the artist's career after his and Theo's deaths and Vincent Willem led the founding of the Van Gogh Museum in Amsterdam.[58]

Those acts of investment do not register on the radar of an international art market which is often dependent on both general and plutocratic wealth.[59] According to the 2018 Art Market Report, the top of the art market is defined as artwork sales over $1 million. In 2017, those sales made up 64% of the auction market by value, even though they only accounted for 1% of transactions by volume.[60]

This current reality may invite more cooperative structures that include artists and more inclusive structures that support broader access to art collecting. It may remind us of the attention that collectors pay to art. The artist Lawrence Weiner described Kramarsky saying that he was "not a philanthropist, not an altruist, but was completely sensually engaged in the work of art." As Kramarsky himself said, "Collecting is a little bit like making love. You don't know who your perfect partner is going to be. And you really don't make a choice that way."[61] That is to say, if making art is an act of investment and care, collecting of course can be too, regardless of the later financial footprints of those decisions. The story is one of value – however difficult to describe or model analytically or to know ahead of time. The studies of the market performance of art still track back to the starting point of resources and what to do with them.

QUESTIONS

1. Concept review: present value and future value
   Review Appendix E and answer these questions:

   – (a) You have $1,000 that you invest for three years at a return rate of 10%. What is your investment worth at the end of three years? (b) Your friend hires you to make him a website. He does not have a lot of money now, but he says he will pay you $1,331 in three years. If you assume that your opportunity cost of capital is 10%, what is this payment worth to you in today's dollars? (c) Explain the relationship between the answers in (a) and (b).
   – I offer to give you $50,000 today, if you will give me $100,000 in ten years. At a discount rate of 10%, would you take this offer? Would you take it at a discount rate of 5%? 20%?
   – What is the value in ten years of $1,000 invested now at a rate of return of 8%?
   – Would you invest $20,000 now in a project that would give you $40,000 in five years? Assume the opportunity cost of capital is 12%. Why or why not?
   – You bought a desk in 1943 for $200. It sells in 2013 for $15,000. If your discount rate is 8%, is this a good investment?

- You bought $1 worth of Sotheby's as a company in 1744. In 2010, you sold that stake for $1,000,000. Assuming a 5% opportunity cost of capital, was that a good investment?
- You allow a very good client of your gallery to borrow a work of art for five years. At the end of five years, he pays you $200,000. What is that amount equivalent to, if he had paid you at the beginning of the five years, before he took possession of the artwork? Assume a 10% discount rate.
- You work as a consultant. Your client engages you in a three-year project and offers you two payment options: (a) $300,000 now or (b) $50,000 now, $150,000 at the end of the first year, $100,000 at the end of the second year, and a bonus of $100,000 at the end of the third year. Assuming a discount rate of 10%, which of these payment options would you prefer?

2. In William Baumol's 1986 study, he excludes works with shorter holding periods. Why do you think this is? Discuss or write a short memo on what advantages and what distortions arise from only considering works with longer holding periods. How do you think shorter holding periods would reflect either speculation or forced sales from personal circumstance? Reread the Baumol essay to make your argument. For a longer research paper or in-depth discussion, read Lovo and Spaenjers's paper framing different kinds of collectors. Can you refine your hypotheses on how Baumol's exclusion of short holding periods affects these categories of art collector unequally?[62]

3. Choose an artwork that has gone to auction at least twice. What is the annualized rate of return for the period of time between the two auctions? Did you include the transaction costs of purchasing the work (i.e., the buyer's premium) and of selling the work (i.e., the seller's commission)?

4. Lack of provenance can radically alter the investment value of a work of art. Consider the Betty Parsons example in this chapter or research an example of a forgery. In an unusual case, the Scottish artist Peter Doig was sued in US Federal Court for failing to authenticate – that is, confirm his authorship of – a work someone was trying to sell. Signed "P. Doige," the work had been sold by an

inmate to a prison guard in 1976 for $100. With Doig's authentica-
tion, the work could have sold for around $10 million. Doig refused
and was sued for $5 million. Doig won the lawsuit but only after he
produced substantial evidence including family correspondence
proving he was in a school play, not in prison for LSD possession,
at the time.[63] What do you think of the responsibility of artists to
authenticate their work? Would it matter to your argument if
artists also held equity or resale royalties in their work? Why or
why not?

5. If someone asked your advice on whether to invest in art, what
would you say and why?

6. The finance professor Roman Kräussl ends his talks on the art
market with "Buy what you love." Do you agree or disagree?
How would you relate that sentiment to the ways in which Wynn
Kramarsky talked about art in this chapter?

10 Systems

I don't care for the term "art world." It's a useful term, of course, a kind of shorthand . . .. But the truth is, art is not a world unto itself. Art is part of the world.

Ben Davis[1]

The nonprofit and for-profit parts of the art world have been blurred for a long time. In 1959, Leo Castelli hosted the first solo exhibition for the artist Robert Rauschenberg and purchased the only artwork that sold. Three decades later, Castelli donated that work, *Bed* (1955), to the Museum of Modern Art. That donation was altruistic – of little tax benefit at the time. It was also strategic – reinforcing of Castelli's reputation and confirming Rauschenberg's place in the canon.[2] In 2013, the artist Ugo Rondinone received a commission from the Public Art Fund in New York. Concurrently, his dealer, Barbara Gladstone, mounted an exhibition showing miniatures of the gigantic Stonehenge-style figures he had erected in Rockefeller Center. Priced around $75,000–$200,000, the Gladstone Gallery works sold strongly.[3] The artist's public work likely boosted his private sales. In other cases, private galleries democratize access to art. To attend a Richard Serra show at the Museum of Modern Art costs $25. To see a "nonselling" Richard Serra show at the David Zwirner Gallery is free and open to the public.

These stories, like so many others, point to the intersections of art and economics as a system. That system in turn interacts with the much broader world. Thus, we end with these questions of how narrowly or broadly we define art, how analytically or creatively we practice economics, and how we engage with the politics of it all.

In the spring of 2020, Nina Katchadourian, whom we met on an airplane in Chapter 1, started an art school for children. More specifically, her cat Stickies did. Speaking with a *Washington Post* reporter, Katchadourian explained the backstory: The coronavirus pandemic and lockdown left Katchadourian with a "really strong impulse to make things, but not things that I think of as art – things that I think of as stuff I want to give to other people. Like, gifts." So her cat – who was mostly black with white paws and a white face – lounged at a Rubenesque angle on a sumptuous, richly colored fabric cushion and spoke to children in a deep, languorous, grumpy yet warmly monotone version of Katchadourian's own voice. Stickies's wide eyes never blinked and his mouth moved by artistic intervention when he spoke. Stickies welcomed students over a Facebook video. Their first assignment was to make a drawing of a transportation vehicle "just for Stickies":

> It can be anything. It can go into space. It can go in the water. It can go on the land, anywhere you want. But I want you to design it for me. Then I want you to make a drawing and then have a grownup post the drawing in the thread. And I will comment on them. We will have a group critique and you will see what I think. Okay? Welcome to Stickies Art School. Get working kids. Bye.[4]

A few days later, Stickies delivered feedback in the form of a ten-minute video in which he observed and appreciated each drawing. Seeing a drawing of himself on a boat, Stickies said, "I'm very pleased with this boat. I look very happy in this boat."[5] "The human," as Stickies called Katchadourian, made pillows to trade for drawings. She did not see Stickies Art School as an artwork: "I would not call [it] an art project. I just found it so relaxing to do this repetitive thing. I'm making something, but it's not this burdensome feeling of making art – of needing to have a point to make."[6]

The 2020 coronavirus outbreak brought into sharp relief the role of visual art in society. As doctors and nurses and other essential workers saved lives and kept societies running, people at home engaged in truly inventive creative projects, though few that were based in traditional categories of visual art. There was balcony-singing and TikTok video-making. Laura Benanti, the Broadway actress who had recently starred in *My Fair Lady* at New York's Lincoln Center, offered to be an audience, via video, for anyone whose high-school musical had been cancelled. The Metropolitan Opera streamed performances, and Yo-Yo Ma gave a cello concert on Twitter.[7]

Meanwhile, art galleries closed or operated by appointment. Museums closed and attempted virtual tours. Art fairs were cancelled and mounted "online viewing rooms." The Twitterverse joked that Shakespeare wrote *Lear* under quarantine and so everyone should expect great things from ourselves. Those great things tended toward home entertainment, such as from one apparently Italian gentleman armed with a mullet rocker wig, sunglasses, and a peerless talent for "deejay-ing" the burners of his stove to a techno beat. Governments, institutions, and individual people stepped up to catch the pass of financial need. The German government gave artists direct support. Arts Council England announced creative relief funds. The writers Roxane Gay, Yashar Ali, and others used social media to identify people in need and send money directly. Some public-health charts on "flattening the curve" rose to the level of design.[8] Then, the crisis itself demanded a combination of rational analysis and imagination not typically invoked. In this space between the art world and the world at large – the space between a painting in a closed museum and the expanse of visual culture – how narrowly or broadly do we define art? And second, when we speak of participation in relation to the art, do we mean democratized access or commerce? We can imagine broad audiences for art as part of a vibrant democracy or broad audiences for art as a form of consumption. We can also conceptualize democratic and economic repair and reimagination as art.

10.1   BROAD AND NARROW DEFINITIONS OF ART

In the course of researching this book, one of my favorite site visits was not an art museum per se but the International Table Tennis Federation

(ITTF) Museum in Shanghai, relocated from Lausanne, Switzerland, in 2018.[9] The museum may not be objectively hard to find, but it was only findable by me on a second attempt, after writing to a general email address and receiving a note and map back from Chuck Hoey, the founding curator. The museum's exhibitions begin with the origins of table tennis as a parlor game in nineteenth-century England. Life-sized mannequins in Victorian dress stand mid-swing around a repurposed dining-room table. A collection of hand-crocheted nets pulled taut between dowels show that any dining table will do. A wall of paddles doubles as a study of hues (see Figure 10.1). A visual explainer of ping-pong-balls' manufacture is revelatory of the small wonders of their construction.

During my visit, my excitement about the museum built so much as I progressed from room to room that I was shortly trailed by a kindly museum staffer seemingly at the ready for questions. The

FIGURE 10.1 The International Table Tennis Federation Museum, display. Photo by the author.

museum's upper floor began with a 3-D celebration of table tennis followed by black-and-white photographs of ping pong diplomacy between Chairman Mao and US President Richard Nixon. The museum's education program did not consist of well-written brochures with coloring activities but of virtual coaches on vertical screens offering lessons on one's backhand. On a nearby covered porch, people played actual table tennis. Downstairs near the exits there was virtual-reality table tennis and a 3-D film playing in a cinema outfitted with what seemed to be regulation bleacher seats. The museum store doubled as a pro shop. The variety of paddle surfaces was so large that it looked not unlike a CD store.

Why is the International Table Tennis Federation Museum not an art museum? Why does it fall outside the scope of this book? For all its governmental backing and diplomatic mission, it was a participatory museum, steeped in care, curiosity, and celebration of excellence and invention.

To consider this question more systematically, imagine a two-by-two matrix. On one axis is art – narrowly or broadly defined.[10] On the other axis is participation – civic at one end and economic at the other. Narrow definitions of art are those of the traditional art world: paintings, drawings, canonical art history, and other works that are metabolized through galleries, museums, and other institutions of the arts. The broader definition of art encompasses creative expression in many forms, including the immediacy and power of protest art, the thought processes of creative discovery in any field, and the excellence in craft of the International Table Tennis Federation Museum.

When we separate out these threads of how we define art, some veer toward the civic – broad public inclusion – and some toward the economic. We can imagine democratic access to art and commodified access to art. For narrowly defined art, democratic access is the museum and commodified access is the share of a Warhol sold on a blockchain platform next to a collectible pair of sneakers (see Figure 10.2). For broadly defined art, those sneakers are the commodified access. Democratically accessible and broadly defined art is wide

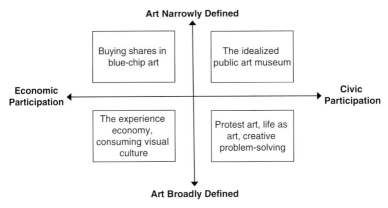

FIGURE 10.2 Narrow and broad definitions of art vs. economic and civic participation.

and inspiring. It is Stickies Art School. It is activism. It is novelty, usefulness, originality, arresting visual production, and creative courage in almost any area of life.

10.2 THE PROCESS OF LEGITIMATION

The broad and narrow definitions of art are related to each other through an ongoing process of legitimation. In her 2019 book *Entitled*, sociologist Jennifer Lena describes this process that brings popular culture into the realm of high art. She argues that the Works Progress Administration (WPA), the Depression-era US federal program that created jobs for artists, democratized access to art.[11] We saw this process occur more recently when the Museum of Modern Art collected the Pac-Man video game in 2012.[12]

These works are often legitimized through the process of curation which necessarily involves some claim on expertise, table tennis included. The curator of the International Table Tennis Federation (ITTF) Museum, Chuck Hoey, was a former player himself. In January 1965, he competed in the Central Ohio Intercollegiate tournament where he won his game but lost the tournament. (Hoey later became a chess player who once took a game off of Bobby Fisher.[13]) Hoey amassed a collection of table tennis memorabilia estimated to be

worth hundreds of thousands of dollars. When ITTF bought the collection and named Hoey curator, he moved to Lausanne, Switzerland,
from the United States, before the museum moved again to its current
home in Shanghai. In a series of articles in the late 1970s and early
1980s in *Table Tennis Topics*, Hoey compared collecting table tennis
objects to collecting stamps. He wrote:

> Stamp collecting can be a ravaging disease, whose possessed victims
> will do virtually anything short of armed robbery to fill a space in
> their collection. It has been known to reap great profits for some,
> financially ruin others; but for those of us somewhere in between, it
> is a source of constant relaxation and pleasure, worldwide
> friendships, and just plain fun.[14]

The legitimation of art can be conceptual and performative. Consider
Michael Tannenbaum, who is better known on Twitter as "The Art
Decider." He labels tweets as "Art" or "Not Art." For example, on
May 30, 2020, he labeled as "Art" a post by @dog_rates, a Twitter
account that normally rates dogs and had instead encouraged donations to the Minnesota Freedom Fund in the wake of the police killing
of George Floyd.[15]

Questions of "what is art?" and "why is that art important?" call
to mind an experimental gallery that the artists Ellen Letcher and
Kevin Regan ran from 2009 to 2012. Called Famous Accountants, the
gallery chose a name that calls into question why it matters that an
artist becomes famous as opposed to an accountant.[16] For our purposes, accountants and anyone else can make art or otherwise have
a relationship to their own creativity. But the arts are gatekept by
taste-making – what sociologists call "judgment devices" – which
can be people, institutions, prizes, or ranking lists.[17] While traditional
judgment devices such as art museums try to expand their viewfinders,
other ventures outside democratize access and refocus on structurally
under-recognized excellence. For example, in 2010 the filmmaker Ava
DuVernay founded ARRAY, a platform to champion and share arts
advocacy work and to amplify independent films "by people of color

and women filmmakers globally."[18] In DuVernay's words, "An artist and an activist are not so far apart." Both "use their imagination to envision a world that does not exist and make it so."[19]

10.3 ECONOMICS AS AN ART FORM

Economics too has a claim as art. In 2020, the economist George Akerlof (whom we encountered in Chapter 4 with his "market for lemons") wrote about his lifelong profession in an article, "Sins of Omission and the Practice of Economics," in the *Journal of Economic Literature*.[20] Akerlof argues that economics as a discipline favors "hard" over "soft" analysis. It prizes what can be measured and understood through the scientific method. In that process, economics sometimes overlooks important interdisciplinary questions and fails to address climate change or foresee financial crises. His plea is one for creativity – for the ability to sit with difficult questions before unfurling one's Inspector Gadget coat of quantitative tools. In describing the frontier of his field, Akerlof poses the question of art: of the construction of the world of economics itself.[21]

Other economists have certainly voiced a desire to modulate the strict application of economic theory. In his essay "The Economic Way of Looking at Life" (adopted from his Nobel acceptance speech), Gary Becker pulls back from the assumption of profit and utility maximization. He calls that way of thinking a "method of analysis not an assumption about motivations."[22] He suggests that people are utility maximizers but what utility means to each of us is subjective. One might be motivated by creativity or altruism, not only profit. This idea of self-determined utility challenges the ability of economics to reconcile many forms of value.

To return to the Hostile Worlds vs. Nothing But debate from the Introduction, the Nothing But argument is challenged by this problem of multiple yardsticks – of entirely subjective utility. If that utility still needs to be translated back into price, we will always struggle to measure value from many different viewpoints without distorting whose definition of value is heard. Value is already so hard to define in the arts not only aesthetically but over the long arc of time from studio beginnings to market stride or through market resistance. Where does that leave us with the Hostile Worlds dilemma? Should art be firewalled from economics to protect itself?

The problem of firewalling art from economics is that art depends on economics – less to explain its value than to support it structurally. It is here that the tools of this book intend to be useful. Is it hard to build a sustainable museum? Yes, and doing so actively engages critiques of philanthropy, reimagination of community governance, and the management of cost. As I often say when teaching, paraphrasing John F. Kennedy Jr., ask not what economics can do for you but what you can do for economics, which is to say: I hope the tools in this book support the economic sustainability of art and that artists help design systems that serve all of us leading lives and trying to make things of value.[23] These solutions are likely not individual but collective. As Maff Potts, the founder of the community Camerados, says, "The answer to our problems is each other."[24] In the arts and otherwise, the problems that feel the most isolating and insurmountable often have only collective solutions.

The Introduction to this book begins with a quotation from the scholar Leigh Clare La Berge: "It will not do to read only from economics to art. We must be able to read from art to economics as well."[25] To bring art toward economics is to marvel at the $100 million auction result or the museum ticket price. To bring economics toward art is to imagine equity, democracy, climate safety, and prosperity as art projects unto themselves. It is to design the arts as a hub for interdisciplinary collaboration and to support open-ended exploration in any field. In this way, economics is a hopeful system of managing value and a set of tools with which to build organizations and systems in the arts and far beyond.

QUESTIONS

1. What is your own working definition of art? If you were "art decider" for the day, what would you decide was art? Discuss

with friends and also write your definition down on paper. Compare notes. Where do your definitions overlap and converge? Try to find the most interesting challenges to your definition: a viral video, visionary work in science, or a creative life well lived. Consider as a case study the work of Richard Ankrom, who in 2001 built a highway sign as an art project – to better announce the interchange from the 110 Freeway to Interstate 5 north in Los Angeles. With technical skills in metalsmithing, he fashioned a near-perfect replica, then dressed as a workman and attached his sign to an existing highway sign. No one noticed the sign for nine months. According to researcher Nate Harrison, the sign remained in place for eight years until the California transportation department ran a sign audit and replaced Ankrom's sign with an upgraded version.[26]

2. What is your favorite concept in economics and why? What is art's greatest conceptual challenge toward economics and economics' greatest contribution toward art?

3. What is your greatest hope and greatest fear about the art world right now? What is the greatest contribution the arts can make to the broader world?

4. Consider the question raised in the Introduction of Hostile Worlds or Nothing But approaches to art and economics. Now at the end of this book, how do you define each in your own words? What is your own current view: Can economics describe artistic value? Why or why not? Think of a couple of cases that interest you – museums you follow, auctions of note, artists whose work you love or artworks that you yourself make). What are the ways in which economic value applies and does not apply to their practice? Draw a map of value across artistic and economic spheres. Where do they connect? Where are they least aligned?

5. Design a "value audit" of a specific artwork or institution. Can you map and explore all of the different kinds of value of the work? What about the work is valuable and to whom?

6. How would you describe the value of the arts in society? (You may wish to answer that question broadly in the manner of a mission statement or very specifically with a concrete story or example.) Consider who is served by the arts and who is excluded, what or who is valued or undervalued.

7. If you return in your mind to Nina Katchadourian's work – making art on the airplane for her ongoing project "Seat Assignment" – what have you learned that contributes to how you think about that project? If economics is about weighing and trading off costs and benefits, how does Katchadourian's practice of curiosity fit into or transcend concepts of this book?

8. If the economy were an art project, what would you redesign, based on the ideas in this book? Consider especially how opportunity cost and externalities come up in your work and life.

9. Take an idea of something you really want to do in the world, write it down, and go forth to build it.

Appendix A
Review of Graphs

A graph is a way of relating one variable to another or understanding the relationship between two pieces of information. We are generally looking at only one quarter – the upper-right quadrant – of the area of a graph. We are looking at the area with positive Y values and positive X values. The quadrants are numbered counterclockwise from the upper right (see Figure A.1).

In this case, we are mapping the relationship of price and quantity as a line. The horizontal axis is called the x-axis. The vertical axis is called the y-axis. The equation of the line that describes this graph is y = mx + b. In this equation, y is the number on the vertical axis. m is the slope (of which more soon). b is the "y-intercept," meaning it is the place where the line crosses the y-axis (see Figure A.2).

The slope of the line is the ratio of the "rise" – how much the line goes up vertically – over the "run" – how much the line moves along horizontally. For example, a line with a slope of 1 goes up 1 unit and over 1 unit each time. The line has a 45-degree angle. (The whole quadrant has a 90-degree angle.)

Notice that for supply, the slope of the line is positive: as price goes up (+), quantity supplied goes up (+). Notice that for demand, the slope of the line is negative: as price goes up (+), quantity demanded goes down (−).

The slope indicates whether the line points up (positive slope) or downward (negative slope) and also whether the line is steep or flat. (In Chapter 3 [and Appendix C], the concept of price elasticity of demand connects strongly to the slope of the line.) You can practice redrawing the line above with the slope m equal to 2 or to ½ and with the y-intercept equal to 0 or 1.

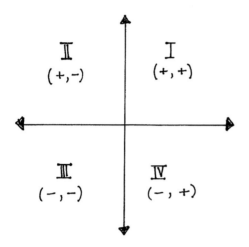

FIGURE A.1 The four quadrants.

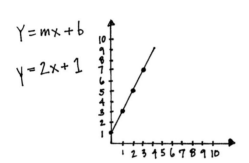

FIGURE A.2 The equation for a line.

I maintain my conviction, honed over many years of teaching, that most people who think they are bad at math are not bad at math; they are "derive the equation" people who need to understand the whole of how something works and get the "why," but they were taught math in a rules-bound way.

Notice that the relationship, here between price and quantity, holds true even when they are drawn with differently assigned axes. By convention, the diagram of supply and demand is drawn with price on the y-axis (the vertical one) and quantity on the x-axis (the horizontal one). If you find yourself mentally flipping the lines or axes, some people remember the position heuristically (e.g., demand goes "down"/"D" for demand and "D" down and supply goes up, like the abbreviation of "what's up" (s'up)). I encourage you to develop your own heuristic if helpful to you, and if you flip the axes or lines I encourage you to celebrate your visual and spatial acuity in being confusable.

Appendix B
Indifference Curves

An **indifference curve** is a tool in economics to think systematically about a trade-off between two options. Imagine a collector choosing between prints by two different artists, or a gallerist deciding the mix of local and international art fairs to attend. We could create indifference curves for either of these examples. Indifference curves are most easily used for goods that are at least relatively uniform and are purchased in a quantity greater than one.

Consider for example an artist deciding about how many tubes of paint to purchase at $15 each or how many canvases to purchase for $30 each. The artist has a budget of $120. If she spent all of her money on paint, she could purchase eight tubes, and if she spent all of her money on canvases she could purchase four canvases (see Table B.1). We can use this information to draw her **budget line**, which is the frontier of the maximum she can purchase as combinations of these goods given the amount of money she has to spend (see Figure B.1).

Regarding the budget line, notice that you can infer the equation of the line from the information given. The y-intercept (b) – where the line crosses the Y-axis – is 8. We know the slope is negative because the line is downward sloping. If we look for the slope – the rise over the run – we can see that for every 2 units the line rises (falls), it moves horizontally 1 unit, making the slope $-2/1$ or -2. Thus, the equation of the line (y = mx + b) would be $y = -2x + 8$, which we could also write as $y = 8 - 2x$.

Now we can add indifference curves. What the indifference curve shows is the optimal combinations of goods for the person who is budget-limited and utility-maximizing. Within the economic world of trading off costs and benefits, this line shows what

Table B.1 *Purchase of paint tubes and canvases with $120 budget*

Number of canvases (at $30 each)	Money spent on canvases (US dollars)	Remaining money (US dollars)	Number of tubes of paint (at $15 each)
0	$0	$120	8
1	$30	$90	6
2	$60	$60	4
3	$90	$30	2
4	$120	$0	0

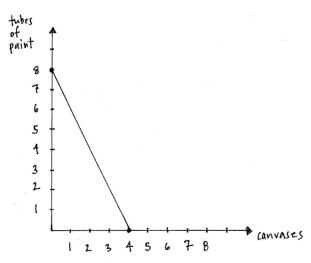

FIGURE B.I Budget line.

a consumer prefers. All of the points on the indifference curve are equally desirable to the consumer. The consumer will choose the combination for which the point on the budget line runs tangent to the greatest indifference curve (see Figure B.2).

This conceptual tool maps trade-offs. In the case of paint and canvas, the goods are often complements, and thus the artist might need at least some paint or at least some canvas. The tool of indifference curves works most simply for goods that are substitutes.

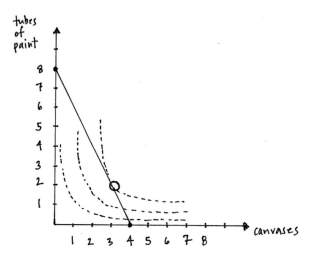

FIGURE B.2 Indifference curve with budget line.

See if you can devise an indifference curve for a different scenario in the arts, for instance, a museum managing a portfolio of exhibitions for which there are different types (e.g., blockbuster, emerging artist, design, or traveling, loan, or collections show) or a collector deciding which works to purchase.

Appendix C
Price Elasticity of Demand

Price elasticity of demand (PED) describes the relationship between a change in price and a corresponding change in the quantity demanded. The equation is:

Price elasticity = Percentage change in quantity/percentage change in price

("Change in" is notated formally by a triangle, "delta.")

The equation we use for price elasticity of demand is the arc or midpoint formula. We use it so that we will get the same answer when a price is raised or lowered. Notice that mathematically, using the simple equation above, we will arrive at a different number for PED if the price is lowered or if the price is raised. For example, if we raise the price of a cup of coffee from $3 to $4, we measure the $1 change over the $3 starting point. If we lower the price of a cup of coffee from $4 to $3, we measure the $1 over the $4 starting point. In using the midpoint formula, we rely on the average – in this case, $3.50 – as the denominator so that we get the same answer in both directions.

To solve for price elasticity of demand, we isolate four numbers: the starting price (P1), the ending price (P2), the starting quantity (Q1), and the ending quantity (Q2). If we return to the example from Chapter 3 of the admissions prices from the Indianapolis Museum of Art, at a starting price (P1) of $7.00 for a museum ticket we have a starting quantity (Q1) of 185,000 visitors. At the later price (P2) of $0 for the free admission, we have a corresponding quantity of 462,000 visitors:

P1 = $7.00
P2 = $0.00
Q1 = 185,000
Q2 = 462,000

If we use the arc or midpoint formula for price elasticity, we get PED = −0.4281. We drop the sign, round to two decimal places, and find PED of 0.42. What does this number mean?

First, notice that the number we calculate is negative and we, by convention, express it as a positive number. The PED of 0.42 is less than one. This tells us that customers are insensitive. We can think of price elasticity as tracking the slope of the demand curve. Here, for each percentage point the price is decreased, there is less than one percent (0.42%) increase in quantity demanded. Thus, consumers are inelastic or insensitive.

Notice that it does not matter whether you use Q1 − Q2 or Q2 − Q1. You get the same answer either way. Notice that the units – dollars and museum visitors – cancel out in the equation, so we are left with just a number. That number represents the *ratio* of the percentage change in quantity relative to a percentage change in price.

In this case, we have a tricky data problem. The numbers may not be *ceteris paribus* because of a closure that affected attendance and a change in measurement of the turnstile that possibly started counting museum employees. We therefore could rerun this calculation a number of different ways. If we assumed, for example, that attendance had been dampened by the building renovations and that it would have been closer to 350,000 than 185,000, if we reran the calculation with 350,000 as Q1, we would see price elasticity of 0.14, which is even more strongly price inelastic. We could run many different scenarios. In likely all cases though, we would see that museum admission is broadly price inelastic. Changing the ticket price slightly does not have a huge impact on people's decisions to visit the museum because people are very insensitive to a change in price. This information can help to guide pricing strategy, which might also be set by larger institutional values such as the museum's role as "a charitable, educational, and civic organization" accessible to all.[1]

Appendix D
Auction Theory

Because auctions account for roughly half of worldwide art sales, it is important to consider them more closely. In the economic literature, auctions are described as an efficient clearing mechanism – a means of discovering and revealing the highest prices. In the sociological literature, auctions are described as performative, as specific social networks and interactions. For game theorists, auctions are complex negotiations both of one's own position in a vacuum and of one's assessment of the best strategy given other actors' potential behavior. Auctions themselves date back at least as far as ancient Babylonia. They have concerned sales as problematic as slaves and wives and as unusually large as the entire Roman Empire. Today, outside the arts, auctions are commonly used for everything from Dutch tulips to airwaves rights to eBay finds.[2]

Theoretically, there are four main types of auctions:

1. **Ascending bid** (also called an English auction): Bidders offer increasingly large prices until a single bidder is left. Bidders are aware of each other's bids.
2. **Descending bid** (also called a Dutch auction): Bidders watch an auctioneer reduce the offered price until someone bids. The first bidder wins. (Or if there are multiple sets of goods, the first set of bidders wins.) Bidders can see each other's bids.
3. **First-price sealed bid**: Bidders submit their bids privately. The highest bid wins.
4. **Second-price sealed bid** (also called a Vickrey auction): Bidders submit their bids privately. The highest bidder wins but pays the price put forward by the second-highest bidder.[3]

In theory, the four types of auctions form two pairs that share pricing outcomes with each other. An open ascending auction and a second-price sealed-bid auction will yield the same price: the price of the underbidder. And a descending auction or a first-price sealed-bid auction will yield the same price: that of the top bidder. In the arts, as we will see, these types are not exactly equivalent because the pricing is not continuous but structured in bid increments. In this case, the English auction and the second-price sealed-bid auction yield the same price, within one bid increment, a topic we explore momentarily.

As a slightly confusing overlap in nomenclature, the minimum price that a consignor will accept and therefore the minimum price at which an auction house is authorized to sell a work is called the **reserve price** or just the **reserve**. In economics, the maximum price that a bidder is willing to pay is called the **reservation price**, which is essentially synonymous with the bidder's **willingness to pay**. In order to avoid confusion, we will use the term **maximum price** to describe the bidder's maximum willingness to pay or reservation price.

The bidders determine their maximum price or willingness to pay. This decision is informed by the determinants of demand. It may also entail an investment calculation, for example, what the bidder expects to make in revenue from an auctioned asset (e.g., airwaves rights or an artwork that a dealer plans to resell). When bidders are valuing something that will be auctioned, objects can be said to have **private values** or **common values**, or a combination of both. A private value describes a subjective attachment, for instance to a house or a car, whereas a common value indicates the presence of information that all bidders could use to analyze the value of the asset, for instance data to assess something like geologic mining rights. One could argue that, as price databases such as Artnet continue to flourish, increasing the amount of data available to analyze art prices, common values in art auctions become more widespread. Still, art can easily have highly subjective value for various bidders, and bidders can have substantially different wealth and therefore ability to pay.

In addition, connoisseurship and art historical research can equip a bidder with special information. For example, in 2016 the Dutch art dealer Jan Six XI dropped his children at school, opened a Christie's London auction catalogue over coffee, and recognized an unattributed painting by Rembrandt. The painting had been placed in a day sale among lesser-valued works. Six was able to distinguish the work in part by the geometry of how the bobbin-lace collar had been painted. In addition, the catalogue attributed the work to "Circle of Rembrandt." However, the work dated to between 1633 and 1635. Six knew from the artist's life that Rembrandt was not yet well known at that time; there was no circle. Six had private knowledge that would give him a different appraisal estimate for the work.[4]

When Six bid on this work, he engaged in the most common structure of auction in the arts: the English auction or open ascending auction. Bidders in a room raise their paddles until only two bidders are left. At that stage, one bidder drops out, and the winner pays an amount within a bid increment of the underbidder's maximum price. For example, suppose that an artwork sells for $10,000. At some point in the auction, everyone else has dropped out besides the top two bidders. One bids $9,000 then the other bids $10,000. No further bid is made, and the winner pays $10,000. What are the maximum prices of the two bidders? We know that the underbidder is willing to pay at least $9,000 but not $10,000. The underbidder's maximum price falls somewhere between $9,000 and $9,999. We know the winner is willing to pay $10,000 and perhaps considerably more. The winner's maximum price is not revealed. We only know that it is at least equal to $10,000. The winner then pays the underbidder's maximum price. Or, in the case of art, the winner pays within one bid increment. The increment here is the $1,000 gap from $9,000 to $10,000 – of the underbidder's maximum price.[5]

Increments are mathematically important for two reasons. First, auctioneers must clear the reserve price – the price agreed between the auction house and the seller as the minimum price at which the work can be sold. Second, auctioneers have a fiduciary duty to the seller to obtain the highest possible price. Thus, auctioneers are constantly managing their **footing**, which is their ability to land on a price as intended. Footing matters for clearing the reserve and also for clearing any absentee bids that are left in the auctioneer's "book," the record of the sale that the auctioneer has on the podium. For example, under US and New York commercial law, auctioneers are allowed to take fake bids below the reserve price. The rationale is that these "fake" bids are bids on behalf of the seller to establish the momentum of the sale. As discussed in Chapter 3, they are often called **chandelier bids**, as if the auctioneer is taking a bid off of the chandelier – or the back wall or an imaginary person in the fourth row. However, it is illegal to take a fake bid at or above the reserve.

According to Barbara Strongin, a longtime Christie's auctioneer and then auctioneer trainer and teacher, auctioneers tend to use standard increments. Over $500, the increments move by $50, with bids taken at $550, $600, $650, and so on. If a bidder tried to offer $575, it would be at the auctioneer's discretion to *break* the increment. Over $1,000, the increments move by $100, with bids taken at $1,100, $1,200, and so on. In the $2,000 range, the footing is by 2's – meaning $2,200, $2,400, $2,600, $2,800 – but in the $3,000 and $4,000 range, the footing is 2, 5, 8 – meaning $3,200, $3,500, $3,800. In the $5,000 range, the increments shift to $500s. In the larger numbers, the auctioneer has some discretion – reading the room and pace of bidding. The price tends to move up by not more than 10% at a time.[6]

The increments become important for the auctioneer in establishing footing that lands on the reserve. For example, consider an artwork with a reserve of $3,500. Suppose the auctioneer opens the bidding at $2,400. In this example, while it may look like this first bid is coming from someone in the room, it is really generated by the auctioneer. Assuming there is interest in the room, then a real bidder counters at the next increment, $2,600. Suppose that person is the only bidder. The auctioneer can counter with a chandelier bid – $2,800 – then the bid is with the room at $3,000, then with the auctioneer at $3,200, and then with the bidder in the room at $3,500.

The auctioneer has landed her footing correctly so that she has a real bid at the reserve. As Strongin says, "Where you open the bidding determines where you end up. Miscalculate the bidding sequence and you'll land on the reserve without a real bidder." Had she started at $2,600, the bidding would have been with her at the reserve, and she would not have been able to bid legally – or if she had she would have bought the work for the auction house.[7]

The consequence of getting the footing wrong is risking that the work fails to sell, that is, is **bought in**. Auctioneers are thus doing complicated math to manage footing, especially if other bidders in the room enter and then leave the bidding below the reserve or if someone tries to split an increment below the reserve. In tracking footing, bids are "even" or "odd," meaning the footing is with the auctioneer or with the room. Theoretically, an auctioneer could take chandelier bids all the way to the threshold of the reserve. However, if it appears that no one is going to bid, an auctioneer might declare the work bought in below the reserve; otherwise, the larger price, even if based on chandelier bids, negatively affects the statistics of the sale. Auctioneers may need to make judgment calls, particularly because some bidders will wait to join later, not wanting to reveal their interest in the work early or simply waiting for the determinative part of the bidding.[8]

The auctioneer has a substantial responsibility but also discretion. The auctioneer must preserve fairness – and the appearance of fairness – in the room. If she takes a broken increment from someone, she is likely to have to do it again. Art auctioneers are commonly consummate performers, in some cases famously so. Yet they are managing theatrical flourish, psychological energy, and serious word-problem math.

Appendix E
Net Present Value and Internal Rates of Return

To reason our way into computing net present value, we start with the equation for compounding interest, which takes the principal amount invested and multiplies it by one plus the rate of return, raised to the exponential power of the number of time periods. (In the equation, the percentage return is represented in its decimal form, as 0.10 rather than as 10%.) Consider an example in which 10% is the rate of return on $100 invested, with P defined as the value of the investment at the end of two years:

$$P = 100 \times (1 + 0.10)^2 = 100 \times 1.21 = 121$$

The equation would read, in words: the value of the investment at the end of two years is equal to the principal invested ($100) times one plus the interest rate raised to the power of two (for the two year-long time periods), which equals 100 multiplied by 1.21, or $121.

To apply the opportunity cost of capital, we essentially reverse the thought process of this equation. The tool of discounting cash flows allows us to apply opportunity cost to amounts of money received at different points in time. Intuitively, in the above example, at a 10% discount rate, $110 received in one year is mentally equivalent to $100 now, and $121 received in two years is mentally equivalent to $100 now. And if someone gave you $100 in two years, it would be worth less to you than $100 now because if you had the $100 now you could invest it at 10% interest and have $110 at the end of year one and $121 at the end of year two, and so on.

The equation for discounting cash flows is the inverse of the equation for compounding interest. Instead of multiplying by one plus the interest rate raised to the number of time frames, we divide by it. What we are solving for is the present value. **Present value** is the equivalent in today's dollars of an amount of money paid in the future, by adjusting that future payment to reflect the opportunity cost of the capital over the period of time. The equation is usually expressed as solved for present value (PV). The equation is generalized so that C = the future cash flow, r = the discount rate, and t = the time period. (We use annual interest rates, but you could have a daily or monthly interest rate too.)

$$PV = C \div (1+r)^t$$

The present value equals the cash flow received in time t divided by one plus the discount rate raised to the power of the number of time periods. In this case, the present value of $121 in two years at a discount rate of 10% is $100.

Imagine we were trying to evaluate a very simple investment decision. We might be asked whether to invest $100 in a venture that will repay us $150 in two years, or $110 in two years. We know intuitively from the fact that $121 is exactly $100 in present value that $150 is better than a 10% return and $110 is worse. We can solve for both more precisely. The present value of $150 is $150 ÷ 1.1² = $124, and the present value of $110 is $110 ÷ 1.1² = $91. These equations tell us, respectively, that if we invest $124 at a 10% rate of return we will have $150 in two years and if we invest $91 at a 10% rate of return we will have $110 in two years. **Net present value** is the difference between that present value and the amount of investment made to receive it. If we must invest $100 now to get these sums, then the *net* present value for the $150 is $124 − $100, or $24. The net present value for the $110 offering is $91 − $100, or −$9. The $150 offer outperforms our 10% discount rate, and the $110 does not.

Note that there are several related ways in which investors evaluate returns on investment. Discounting cash flows is the first-principle way of doing it, and so it is the way shown here. One can also solve for the annualized rate of return between two numbers. To use an internal rate of return (IRR) calculation in Excel, one needs to know the amount

Table E.1 *IRR for Tate Modern according to different investment assumptions*[3]

	Including Tate Modern's annual spend as part of investment[1]	Excluding Tate Modern's annual spend as per investment[1]
Return on total investment	252%	597%
Return on public investment[2]	435%	1,031%

[1] Includes or excludes ongoing annual operational spend as part of capital investment.
[2] Public investment weighted at 58% of total investment. Total benefit attributed to this investment.
[3] Other assumptions: Visitor figures decrease to 2.2 million in 2002 and remain with 0% growth, 6% discount factor used.
Source: Tate Modern; McKinsey analysis[9]

of money invested, the amount of money earned, and the time frame. (Excel will also compute present value, but solving for a rate of return is particularly difficult to do without a computer.) When McKinsey & Co. analyzed the plans for the opening of Tate Modern, they used an IRR for the project overall. (See Table E.1) Notice that this IRR for Tate Modern is extremely sensitive to investment assumptions and also that this document likely had some advocacy purpose.

We could apply this method of discounting cash flows to analyze an investment in a single work of art. For example, if you bought a work of art at auction for $1,000,000 and resold it at auction five years later for $2,000,000, what would be the net present value and the annualized return on investment? Here, the $1,000,000 would be the initial investment. The selling price $2,000,000 is the cash flow (C) that we receive for having made that investment. Suppose our opportunity cost of capital is 5% over the five years (t = 5). We would divide $2,000,000 by $(1 + 0.05)^5$.

$$2,000,000 \div 1.276 = \$1,567,052$$

Table E.2 *Calculating the buyer's premium to include transaction costs in investment return*[1]

Tranche of artwork price	Percentage of the hammer price	Amount of this purchase price in each tranche	Buyer's premium in this case
Up to $300,000	25%	$300,000	$75,000
From $300,000 to $4,000,000	20%	$700,000	$140,000
Above $4,000,000	13.5%	$0	$0
Total buyer's premium			$215,000

[1] Christie's Inc. (2019, February 1). Buying at Christie's: New Buyers Premium Schedule. www.christies.com/buying-services/buying-guide/financial-information.

The present value of the $2,000,000 sales price is $1,567,052.

The net present value (NPV) – that is, the present value of the future cash flow minus the original investment of $1,000,000 – is $567,052. By this calculation, the painting is a strongly NPV-positive investment. However, we have not included two main categories of cost: transaction cost and carrying costs. Supposing you purchased the work at auction, you would have paid a buyer's premium (see Table E.2).

The buyer's premium when you purchased the work for $1,000,000 would be $215,000. Thus, our initial investment is not $1,000,000 but, with transaction costs, $1,215,000. We may have further transaction costs, for instance, an art advisor or insurance or shipping. For this example, we will focus on the purchase costs. We are also likely to have transaction costs when we sell. If an auction house charges us a seller's commission of 10%, then our sales price is $2,000,000 less 10%, or $1,800,000. Now we are evaluating an investment of $1,215,000 that leads to a gain five years later of $1,800,000. Thus our math now becomes:

Table E.3 *Calculating IRR*
for an art investment

Investment	−1,215,000
Year 1	0
Year 2	0
Year 3	0
Year 4	0
Year 5	1,800,000
IRR	8%

$$PV = \$1,800,000 \div (1 + 0.05)^5$$

$$= \$1,800,000 \div 1.276 = \$1,410,347$$

The present value of the auction sale is now $1,410,347. The net present value is $1,410,347 minus $1,215,000, which equals $195,347. Our project is still NPV-positive, but our assumptions are much more sensitive, and we have not considered the expense of insuring and otherwise taking care of the work for those five years.

We could also solve for an implied annual rate of return – the IRR. First, we can solve for the rate of return of the work, finding an IRR or internal rate of return between a $1,215,000 investment, the passage of five years, and a $1,800,000 payment in five years. (In Excel, we need to reflect the years with no payment to communicate to the program the number of time frames.) Using the IRR function in Excel, we find that the internal rate of return is 8%.[10]

We could modify this calculation to apply an annual carrying cost of insurance or maintenance in years one through five. Supposing it costs $10,000 to maintain the work including storage, appraisal, maintenance, and insurance. To simplify, we pay these fees once annually (see Table E.4).

Our IRR has now dropped to 7%. We are still above our 5% threshold but closer to it. Note that the IRR gives us a nominal rate

Table E.4 *Calculating IRR for an art investment, including carrying costs*

Investment	−1,215,000
Year 1	−10,000
Year 2	−10,000
Year 3	−10,000
Year 4	−10,000
Year 5	1,790,000
IRR	7%

of return. The nominal rate does not account for inflation whereas a real rate of return does. The tool of present value uses nominal rates because the opportunity cost of capital can itself be set to reflect inflation.

Notes

PREFACE

1. Fourcade, Marion, Ollion, Étienne and Algan, Yann. (2015). The Superiority of Economists. *Journal of Economic Perspectives*, 29(1): 89–114, at p. 111.
2. Canonica, Finn. (2018). Preface. In Hans Ulrich Obrist, *Somewhere Totally Else*. Zurich: JRP Editions. See also documenta. (1982). *documenta 7*. Kassel, Germany: P. Dierichs.
3. Churchill, Winston S. (1947, November 11). Speech in the House of Commons. According to *Churchill By Himself*, a collection of Churchill quotations, Churchill is quoting an earlier speaker or an adage because he uses the phrase "it has been said." See Langworth, Richard, ed. (2008). *Churchill by Himself: The Definitive Collection of Quotations*. New York: Public Affairs, p. 574.
4. Although the argument here concerns the language of economics, for a comprehensive economic analysis of language more broadly, see Ginsburgh, Victor and Weber, Schlomo. (2020). The Economics of Language. *Journal of Economic Literature*, 58(2): 348–404.
5. Bayer, Thomas M. and Page, John R. (2014). *The Development of the Art Market in England: Money As Muse 1730–1900*. London: Pickering & Chatto, p. 3.

INTRODUCTION

1. La Berge, Leigh Claire. (2019). *Wages against Artwork: Decommodified Labor and the Claims of Socially Engaged Art*. Durham, NC: Duke University Press, p. 3. Mirroring this idea of bringing economics toward art is Michael Hutter's earlier work on the influence of cultural economics on economics, that is, the bringing of economics toward cultural economics (toward art). See Hutter, Michael. (1996). The Impact of Cultural Economics on Economic Theory. *Journal of Cultural Economics*, 20(4): 263–268.
2. Avildsen, John G. (1984). *The Karate Kid*. Columbia, USA. Mr. Miyagi was played by Pat Morita (1932–2005).

3. The idea of inventing point B comes from Whitaker, Amy. (2016a). *Art Thinking*. New York: Harper Business, pp. 7–8. The idea is adapted from Martin Heidegger's writing on the definition of art. See Heidegger, Martin. (1993 [1947]). The Origin of the Work of Art. In David Farrell Krell, ed., *Basic Writings*. New York: Harper Perennial, pp. 143–206. These ideas are also addressed generally in the field of creative industries and cultural economics, see, e.g., Walls, W. David and McKenzie, Jordi. (2020). Black Swan Models for the Entertainment Industry with an Application to the Movie Business. *Empirical Economics*, 59(6): 3019–3032. Caves, Richard E. (2000). *Creative Industries: Contracts between Art and Commerce*. Cambridge, MA: Harvard University Press.

4. "The firm" is a general hold-all term for any standalone economic unit, be that an artist or an art gallery. The terms "firm" and "organization" are used somewhat interchangeably in this book to be more inclusive of the ways nonprofit organizations are described. A museum would be a "firm" in the broad sense. The "theory of the firm" originated with economist Ronald Coase's (1937) The Nature of the Firm. *Economica*, 4(16): 386–405, and owes subsequent debt to Alfred Chandler's (1962) *Strategy and Structure*. Cambridge, MA: MIT Press. For an empirical study of the firm in the Coasean sense, see Chisholm, Darlene C. (2005). Empirical Contributions to the Theory of the Firm. *Global Business and Economics Review*, 4(1): 119–130.

5. Bagehot, Walter. (1881). Adam Smith As a Person. In Richard Holt Hutton, ed., *Biographical Studies*. London: Longmans, Green, and Co., pp. 247–281, at p. 247.

6. Smith, Adam. (2002 [1759]). *The Theory of Moral Sentiments*. In Knud Haakonssen, ed., *Adam Smith: The Theory of Moral Sentiments*. Cambridge, UK: Cambridge University Press. See also Haakonssen, Knud. (2006). *The Cambridge Companion to Adam Smith*. Cambridge, UK: Cambridge University Press.

7. John Maynard Keynes, the British economist whose 1936 book *The General Theory of Employment, Interest, and Money* is foundational to macroeconomics, was also the first chairman of the Arts Council of England. For further reference on Keynes and his art collection, see Chambers, David, Dimson, Elroy, and Spaenjers, Christophe. (2020) Art As an Asset: Evidence from Keynes the Collector. *Review of Asset Pricing Studies*, 10(3): 490–520.

8. In the Keynes papers at King's College Cambridge, one can read the initial feedback on Keynes's 1908 dissertation, for instance, "Some of the exposition of conflicting views and of the critical discussion in it appears to me to be excellent. But as a contribution of fresh knowledge to the philosophy of the subject, I think it muddled and of very mediocre value . . .. As a consequence of Keynes's uncritical assumption of [various thinkers's] statements, his own theory of probability seems to me to be involved in a hopeless fog." See Whitehead, A. N. and Johnson W. E. (1908). Dr. A. N. Whitehead's and Mr. W. E. Johnson's Reports on Mr. Keynes's Dissertation, 1908: The Principles of Probability, pp. 2–4. John Maynard Keynes Papers, King's College Archives, Cambridge University. With gratitude to David Chambers, fellow of Clare College Cambridge and Reader in Finance at the Judge Business School, who shared these papers as part of his own ongoing research.

9. Especially in Jevons's work, one can hear how much the ideas were still in formation. Jevons spends pages of his preface to the first edition of *The Theory of Political Economy*, published in 1871, trying to convince his peers that they should start calling "political economy" just "economics." He poetically describes economics not as a cost–benefit analysis but as "a Calculus of Pleasure and Pain." Jevons, W. Stanley. (1965 [1871]). Preface to the First Edition. In *The Theory of Political Economy*, 5th ed. New York: Augustus M. Kelly, p. vi. In the preface to the second edition (1879), Jevons calls economists bad mathematicians, insulting his reader with real flair: "economists have long been mathematicians without being aware of the fact. The unfortunate result is that they have generally been bad mathematicians, and their works must fall . . .. Ordinary language can usually express the first axioms of a science, and often also the matured results; but only in the most lame, obscure, and tedious way can it lead us through the mazes of inference." Jevons, W. Stanley. (1965 [1879]). Preface to the Second Edition. In *The Theory of Political Economy*, 5th ed. New York: Augustus M. Kelly, pp. xxiii–xxiv.

10. For a history of economic thought around culture, see especially Goodwin, Craufurd. (2006). Art and Culture in the History of Economic Thought. In Victor A. Ginsburgh and David Throsby, eds., *Handbook of the Economics of Art and Culture*, vol. 1. Amsterdam: Elsevier North Holland, pp. 25–68. See also Ginsburgh, Victor A. and Throsby, David (Eds.) (2006). *Handbook of the Economics of Art and Culture*. Vol. 1.

Boston, MA: North Holland (Elsevier). Ginsburgh, Victor A. and Throsby David (Eds.) (2013). *Handbook of the Economics of Art and Culture*. Vol. 2. Boston, MA: North Holland (Elsevier). Towse, Ruth (Ed.) (2020). *Handbook of Cultural Economics*. 3rd ed. Cheltenham, UK: Edward Elgar. Heilbrun, James and Gray, Charles M. (2001). *The Economics of Art and Culture*, 2nd ed. Cambridge, UK: Cambridge University Press. Frey, Bruno S. and Pommerehne, Werner W. (1989). *Muses and Markets: Explorations in the Economics of the Arts*. Oxford, UK: Blackwells. Klamer, Arjo. (2009). The Lives of Cultural Goods. In Jack Amariglio and Joseph W. Childers, eds., *Sublime Economy: On the Intersection of Art and Economics*. London: Routledge. Nathalie Moureau also applies classical economic theory to art (in French): Moureau, Nathalie. (2000). *Analyse économique de la valeur des biens d'art: La peinture contemporaine*. Paris: Economica, pp. 1–18 and 11–96. For the insularity of economics as discipline, see Fourcade, et al., 2015, pp. 92–95.

11. Fraser, Andrea. (2018). Artist Writes No. 2 toward a Reflexive Resistance. *X-Tra*, 20(2). www.x-traonline.org/article/artist-writes-no-2-toward-a-reflexive-resistance.

12. Johnson, Randal. (1993). Introduction. In Randal Johnson, ed., *The Field of Cultural Production*. New York: Polity, pp. 1–28, at p. 3.

13. Bourdieu, Pierre. (1993). The Field of Cultural Production, or: The Economic World Reversed. In Randal Johnson, ed., *The Field of Cultural Production*. New York: Polity, pp. 29–73, at p. 50. The fuller passage reads, "Thus, the relationship of mutual exclusion between material gratification and the sole legitimate profit (i.e., recognition by one's peers) is increasingly asserted as the exclusive principle of evaluation as one moves down the hierarchy of economic gratifications. Successful authors will not fail to see this as the logic of resentment, which makes a virtue of necessity; and they are not necessarily wrong, since the absence of audience, and of profit, may be the effect of privation as much as a refusal, or a privation converted into a refusal."

14. Zelizer, Viviana. (2001). How and Why Do We Care about Circuits? *Accounts Newsletter of the Economic Sociology Section of the American Sociological Association*, 1 (2000): 3–5.

15. Velthuis, Olav. (2005). *Talking Prices: Symbolic Meanings of Prices on the Market for Contemporary Art*. Princeton, NJ: Princeton University Press.

16. Velthuis, 2005, p. 28.
17. Grampp, William D. (1989). *Pricing the Priceless.* New York: Basic Books, pp. 15–16. For a meditation on value that considers Grampp in a broader context of debates in the field of cultural economics, see Hutter, Michael and Throsby, David (Eds). (2008). *Beyond Price: Value in Culture, Economics, and the Arts.* Cambridge, UK: Cambridge University Press.
18. Gerber, Alison. (2017). *The Work of Art: Value in Creative Careers.* Stanford, CA: Stanford University Press, p. 32.
19. Hyde, Lewis. (1983). *The Gift: Imagination and the Erotic Life of Property.* New York: Vintage, p. xiii.
20. Baumol, William J. (1986). Unnatural Value: Or Art Investment As Floating Crap Game. *American Economic Review,* 76(2): 10–14.
21. William Baumol dustjacket endorsement for *Pricing the Priceless* (Grampp, 1989). On the economics side, David Throsby has made the case for "cultural capital," as described by sociologists, especially Bourdieu, as something distinct from, if complementary to, economic value. See Throsby, David. (1999). Cultural Capital. *Journal of Cultural Economics,* 23(1): 3–12.
22. Bingham, Juliet. (Ed.) (2010). *Ai Weiwei: Sunflower Seeds.* London: Tate Gallery Publishing, pp. 101 and 119.
23. Smith, Roberta. (2010, October 18). At Tate Modern, Seeds of Discontent by the Ton. *New York Times.* www.nytimes.com/2010/10/19/arts/design/19sunflower.html.
24. Author interview with Scott Briscoe, manager at Sikkema Jenkins & Co., September 26, 2019, and email correspondence June 25, 2020. The full title of the work is *Slavery! Slavery! Presenting a GRAND and LIFELIKE Panoramic Journey into Picturesque Southern Slavery or 'Life at "ol' Virginny's Hole" (sketches from Plantation Life)' See the Peculiar Institution as never before! All cut from black paper by the able hand of Kara Elizabeth Walker, an Emancipated Negress and leader in her Cause.*
25. The full title reads *A Subtlety: Or ... the Marvelous Sugar Baby an Homage to the unpaid and overworked Artisans who have refined our Sweet tastes from the cane fields to the Kitchens of the New World on the Occasion of the demolition of the Domino Sugar Refining Plant.*
26. The installation contained other elements beyond the sphinx-like structure. See Reinhardt, Mark. (2017). Vision's Unseen: On Sovereignty, Race, and the Optical Unconscious. In Shawn Michelle Smith and Sharon

Sliwinski, eds., *Photography and the Optical Unconscious.* Durham, NC: Duke University Press, pp. 174–222. Adams, Tim. (2015, September 27). Kara Walker: "There Is a Moment in Life Where One Becomes Black." *The Guardian.* www.theguardian.com/artanddesign/2015/sep/27/kara-walker-interview-victoria-miro-gallery-atlanta.

27. Tate Modern. (2019). *Kara Walker's* Fons Americanus. www.tate.org.uk/art/artists/kara-walker-2674/kara-walkers-fons-americanus. The full title of the work reads, *It Is With an Overabundance of Good Cheer and Great Enthusiasm that We Present the Citizens of the OLD WORLD (Our Captors, Saviors and Intimate Family) A GIFT and TALISMAN Toward the Reconciliation of Our Respective Mother-lands. AFRIQUE and ALBION / WITNESS! the FONS AMERICANUS – THE DAUGHTER OF WATERS – An Allegorical Wonder / Behold! The Sworling Drama of the Merciless Seas, routes and Rivers,* upon which our dark fortunes were traded *and on whose frothy shores lay prostrate Captain, Slave and Starfish, alike. Come, One and All, to Marvel and Contemplate* The Monumental Misrememberings *Of Colonial Exploits Yon. Gasp Plaintively, Sigh Mournfully, Gaze Knowingly and REGARD the Immaterial Void of the Abyss etc. etc. in a Delightful Family Friendly Setting / Created by that Celebrated Negress of the New World Madame Kara E. Walker, NTY.*

28. Davies, William. (2014). *The Limits of Neoliberalism: Authority, Sovereignty and the Logic of Competition.* London: Sage.

I MARKETS

1. Ardito, Mary. (1982). Creativity: It's the Thought That Counts. *Bell Telephone Magazine,* 61(1): 32. Elliot, Jeffrey M. (Ed.). (1989). *Conversations with Maya Angelou.* Jackson, MS: University Press of Mississippi, pp. vii and x.

2. Roberts, Veronica. (2017). Seat Assignment, Art in Airplane Mode. In Veronica Roberts, ed., Veronica Roberts, ed., *Nina Katchadourian: Curiouser.* Austin, TX: University of Texas Press, p. 13.

3. Roberts, 2017, p. 13.

4. Roberts, 2017, p. 29.

5. Roberts, 2017, p. 32.

6. For *Lavatory Self-Portraits in the Flemish Style,* Katchadourian usually tacked up either her red shawl or her black scarf to use as the portrait backdrop. The informality of the cell phone was artistically important. As

Nina said, "Once you pull out a real camera, it screams, 'I'm making art!'" (Roberts, 2017, p. 34).

7. Katchadourian observed, "I am conscious that when you are in a lavatory, it's the only private moment you have" (Roberts, 2017, p. 30).

8. Roberts, 2017, p. 15.

9. Graeber, David. (2011, August 23). *David Graeber: The Barter Myth and the Origin of Money*. Bookspan [video]. www.youtube.com/watch?v=CZIINXhGDcs.

10. Haskell, John. (2015, July 8). Caroline Woolard by John Haskell, *BOMB*. https://bombmagazine.org/articles/caroline-woolard.

11. Haskell, 2015.

12. Whitaker, Amy. (2019c). Barter: What I Learned about Generosity and Reciprocity. In Caroline Woolard, ed., *Trade School: 2009–2019*. New York: Caroline Woolard, pp. 72–75. This passage is also based on being one of the first teachers and also an early student at Trade School.

13. See Espeland, Wendy N. and Stevens, Mitchell L. (1998). Commensuration as a Social Process. *Annual Review of Sociology*, 24(1): 313–343 (definition of commensuration at p. 315). For a discussion of unusual cases of commensuration, e.g., organs or rare animals, see Fourcade, Marion. (2011). Cents and Sensibility: Economic Valuation and the Nature of "Nature". *American Journal of Sociology*, 116(6): 1721–1777. For an overview of the sociology of valuation, see Lamont, Michele. (2012.) Toward a Comparative Sociology of Valuation and Evaluation. *Annual Review of Sociology*, 38(1): 201–221.

14. *Relative Values* wall label: Diana and the Stag automaton, Joachim Friess (ca. 1579–1620). German, Augsburg, ca. 1620. Partially gilded silver, enamel, jewelry (case); iron, wood (movement). Gift of J. Pierpont Morgan, 1917 (17.190.746). See also Cleland, Elizabeth. (2019, November 1). Counting Cows – Curating *Relative Values: The Cost of Art in the Northern Renaissance. Now at the Met* blog. www.metmuseum.org/blogs/now-at-the-met/2017/curating-relative-values-counting-cows.

15. *Relative Values* wall label: Chalice, probably Otto Meier (active 1604–21), German, Westphalia (probably Lichtenau), 1608, with later renovations. Gold, enamel, jewels. Gift of J. Pierpont Morgan, 1917 (17.190.371). Made originally for the dean of Speyer Cathedral.

16. See also Kline, Katy. (2002). *Pointed Pairings: The Valuing of Art*. Brunswick, ME: Bowdoin College Museum of Art. https://digitalcom

mons.bowdoin.edu/art-museum-exhibition-catalogs/77. The exhibition paired works of art to discuss why one was more valuable than the other, e.g., because of its frame.

17. The intersection of supply and demand is probably the most common diagram in microeconomics. For its origins, see Marshall, Alfred. ([1997] 1920). *Principles of Economics*, 8th ed. (Amherst, NY: Prometheus Books). See book III for an overview of demand (pp. 83–137) and book V for the general introduction to markets and the intersection of supply and demand (pp. 139–292). These topics are also widely covered in general microeconomics textbooks, of which there are many. See, e.g., McConnell, Campbell, Brue, Stanley, and Flynn, Sean. (2018). *Economics*, 21st ed. New York: McGraw-Hill. Case, Karl E., Fair, Ray C. and Oster, Sharon E. (2017). *Principles of Economics*, 12th ed. New York: Pearson. Krugman, Paul, Wells, Robin, and Graddy, Kathryn. (2013). *Essentials of Economics*, 3rd ed. New York: Worth. Graddy is the author of the auction and other art-market papers cited in this book.

18. I use the term money in a general way. One could have in-kind income. Money is used here to cover wage income and other sources, e.g., if someone received dividends or interest on investments.

19. Bourdieu, Pierre. (1984). *Distinction: A Social Critique of the Judgment of Taste* (trans. Richard Nice). Cambridge, MA: Harvard University Press.

20. Johnson, 1993, p. 7.

21. Adorno, Theodor W. (1991 [1938]). On the Fetish-Character in Music and the Regression of Listening. In J. M. Berstein, ed., *The Culture Industry*. London: Routledge, pp. 29–60.

22. See, e.g., Bürger, Peter. (1984). *Theory of the Avant-Garde.* (trans. Michael Shaw). Minneapolis: University of Minnesota Press. Cowen, Tyler and Tabarrok, Alexander. (2000). An Economic Theory of Avant-Garde and Popular Art, or High and Low Culture. *Southern Economic Journal*, 67(2): 232–253. For an economic treatment of taste in the arts, see Throsby, David. (1994). The Production and Consumption of the Arts: A View of Cultural Economics. *Journal of Economic Literature*, 32 (March): 1–29. Throsby, David. (2001). *Economics and Culture*. Cambridge, UK: Cambridge University Press.

23. Betty Parsons Gallery records and personal papers, circa 1920–91, bulk 1946–1983. Archives of American Art, Smithsonian Institution.

24. de Coppet, Laura, and Jones, Alan. (1984). *The Art Dealers*. New York: Clarkson N. Potter (Crown), p. 26.

25. de Coppet and Jones, 1984, p. 26. The fuller quotation reads, "Art critics still seem always to want to find historical associations instead of creativity. That remains my one great complaint. They are all historians, they know their art history backwards, and all are beautiful writers. But when looking at something new they immediately feel the need to put it in its place, to make a new page in the art books like reporters with an exclusive for the tabloids. But you can't put something that's just been done into history; you've got to talk about its creative impact for the moment. A new work by a new artist is not history, it's the present. Leave it alone, at least for a while, let it come to life fully before you put it into this or that category."

26. Nichols, Camila. (2019, May). *Immaterial and Ephemeral Art in the Commercial Gallery: An Artist–Dealer Relationship Analysis.* Thesis in completion of the MA in Visual Arts Administration, New York University.

27. For a parallel problem of language to describe education – students writing on an evaluation form that they liked or enjoyed Freud – see Edmundson, Mark (1997, September). On the Uses of a Liberal Education: As Lite Entertainment for Bored College Students, *Harper's Magazine*, pp. 39–49, at p. 40.

28. Christie's Inc. (2017). Salvator Mundi: The Rediscovery of a Masterpiece: Chronology, Conservation, and Authentication. www.christies.com/features/Salvator-Mundi-timeline-8644-3.aspx. For the bidding path, see Freeman, Nate. (2017, November 15). Leonardo da Vinci's "Salvator Mundi" Sells for $450.3 M at Christie's in New York, Shattering Market Records. *ARTnews*. www.artnews.com/art-news/news/leonardo-da-vincis-salvator-mundi-sells-450-3-m-christies-new-york-9334.

29. Maslow, Abraham. (1943). A Theory of Human Motivation. *Psychological Review*, 50(4): 370–396.

30. Some, by personality or experience, become martyrs to ideals, foregoing other categories of need. Maslow, 1943, p. 386 [reversals of need], p. 387 [underestimation of well-met needs, martyr tendency].

31. Fraser, Andrea. (2011, September). Le 1% C'est Moi. *Texte zur Kunst*, 83: 114–127.

32. Thompson, Don. (2017). *The Orange Balloon Dog*. Madeira Mark, BC: Douglas and McIntyre, p. 23.

33. Karpik, Lucien. (2010). *Valuing the Unique: The Economics of Singularities*. Princeton, NJ: Princeton University Press.

34. See, e.g., Bryce, Kristy. (2012). *Andy Warhol Flowers* [exhibition]. Eykyn Maclean Gallery, New York, November 1–December 8. Lobel, Michael. (2012). *Andy Warhol Flowers*. New York: Eykyn Maclean. Gopnik, Blake. (2020). *Warhol*. New York: HarperCollins. According to Gagosian Gallery, the series "Spot Paintings" (1986–2012) comprises more than one thousand works. See Gagosian Gallery. (2012). *Damien Hirst: The Complete Spot Paintings 1986–2011.* https://gagosian.com/exhibitions/2012/damien-hirst-the-complete-spot-paintings-1986-2011.

35. In addition to Karpik, 2010, see Kharchenkova, Svetlana and Velthuis, Olav. (2017). How to Become a Judgment Device: Valuation Practices and the Role of Auctions in the Emerging Chinese Art Market. *Socio-Economic Review*, 16(3): 459–477.

36. See, e.g., McNulty, Tom. (2013). *Art Market Research: A Guide to Methods and Sources*. Jefferson, NC: McFarland & Company.

37. McAndrew, Clare. (2007) *The Art Economy*. Dublin, Ireland: Liffey Press.

38. Mood, as approximated by weather, has been shown to affect auction prices. See De Silva, Dakshina G., Pownall, Rachel A. J. and Wolk, Leonard. (2012). Does the Sun "Shine" on Art Prices? *Journal of Economic Behavior & Organization*, 82(1): 167–178.

39. Veblen, Thorstein. (1953 [1899]). *The Theory of the Leisure Class: An Economic Study of Institutions*. New York: New America Library. See also Degen, Natasha (Ed.). (2013). *The Market*. London: Whitechapel Gallery and MIT Press.

40. Hirsch, Fred. (1976). *Social Limits to Growth*. Cambridge, MA: Harvard University Press. See also Pagano, Ugo (1999). Is Power an Economic Good? Notes on Social Scarcity and the Economics of Positional Goods. In Samuel Bowles, Maurizio Franzini and Ugo Pagano, eds., *The Politics and the Economics of Power*. London: Routledge, pp. 116–145. Schneider, Michael. (2007). The Nature, History and Significance of the Concept of Positional Goods. *History of Economics Review*, 45(1): 60–81.

41. Thompson, 2017, pp. 20–21.

42. Having sold for $58.4 million in 2013, Koons's *Balloon Dog (Orange)* held the record for most expensive work by a living artist until it was surpassed in 2018 by David Hockney's *Portrait of an Artist (Pool with Two Figures)*, which sold for $90.2 million, and then again in May 2019 by Koons's

Rabbit, which sold for $91.1 million, all prices including fees. Reyburn, Scott. (2019, May 15). Jeff Koons "Rabbit" Sets Auction Record for Most Expensive Work by Living Artist. *New York Times.* www.nytimes.com/2019/05/15/arts/jeff-koons-rabbit-auction.html.

43. Thompson, Don. (2008). *The $12 Million Stuffed Shark: The Curious Economics of Contemporary Art.* New York: St. Martin's Griffin, p. 69.

44. Grampp (1989, p. 15) quotes the Impressionist artist Pierre-Auguste Renoir, "Get this into your head, no one really knows anything about it. There's only one indicator for telling the value of paintings, and that is the sales room."

45. For a study of the price of copies in comparison to the price of original artworks, see Benhamou, Françoise and Ginsburgh, Victor A. (2006). Copies of Artworks: The Case of Paintings and Prints. In Victor A. Ginsburgh and David Throsby, eds., *Handbook of the Economics of Art and Culture*, vol. 1. Amsterdam: Elsevier North Holland, pp. 253–283.

46. Freeman, 2017.

47. Rosen, Sherwin. (1981). The Economics of Superstars. *American Economic Review*, 71(5): 845–858.

48. Haigney, Sophie. (2020, February 7). *The Scream* Is Fading: New Research Reveals Why. *New York Times.* www.nytimes.com/2020/02/07/arts/design/the-scream-edvard-munch-science.html.

49. Tan, Boon Hui. (2016). No Limits: Zao Wou-Ki. Asia Society website. https://asiasociety.org/new-york/exhibitions/no-limits-zao-wou-ki. See also the exhibition catalogue, Walt, Melissa J., Weitz, Ankeney and Yun, Michelle. (2016). *Zao Wou-Ki: No Limits.* New York: Asia Society Museum; Waterville, ME: Colby College Museum of Art.

50. For the market concentration, see McAndrew, Clare. (2019). *The Art Market 2019.* Basel, Switzerland: Art Basel and UBS. https://d2u3kfwd92fzu7.cloudfront.net/The_Art_Market_2019-5.pdf. (The 2019 report covers the art market in 2018.) If we look at Zao's biography and artistic formation, he shifted from figurative work to abstraction after immigrating to France. Following a 1957 trip to New York, Zao was offered representation by the Samuel Kootz Gallery, where Zao remained until the gallery closed in 1966. As a marker of the reception of Zao's work abroad, Jacques Chirac, the president of France, wrote the introduction to the catalogue for Zao's first retrospective in China in 1998, which took place during Chirac's presidency. See Christie's Inc. (2018). Ten Things to Know about Zao Wou-Ki. *Christies.com.* www.christies.com/features/Zao-Wou-Ki-8534-3.aspx.

2 COST

1. Herbert, Martin. (2016). *Tell Them I Said No*. Berlin, Germany: Sternberg Press, p. 65.

2. Boyd, Clark. (2014, November 18). Mine-Kafon: Wind-Blown Landmine Clearance. *BBC Future.* www.bbc.com/future/story/20120503-blowing-in-the-wind.

3. Landmine and Cluster Munitions Monitor. (2019, September 23). Afghanistan: Mine Action. www.the-monitor.org/en-gb/reports/2019/afghanistan/mine-action.aspx. This figure is from the Department of Mine Action Coordination. The Mine Action Program of Afghanistan is part of the Directorate of Mine Action, which is governed by the Afghan National Disaster Management Authority with some support from the United Nations Mine Action Service. As recently as 2001, Human Rights Watch estimated eighty-eight deaths per month (Human Rights Watch. [2001, October]. *Human Rights Watch Backgrounder: Landmine Use in Afghanistan.* www.hrw.org/legacy/backgrounder/arms/landmines-bck1011.pdf).

4. Landmine and Cluster Munitions Monitor, 2019. Some estimates range as high as 1,700 contaminated square kilometers. The United Nations estimates that over 110 million landmines have been used in conflict since the 1960s and that annually 15,000 to 20,000 people die from them (Boyd, 2014).

5. Hassani Design BV. (n.d.). About the Founders. http://ha55ani.com/about.

6. Swinkels, Ingrid. (2009). Interview with Massoud Hassani. *DAE (Design Academy Eindhoven) Magazine.* http://massoudhassani-aboutme.blogspot.com/2009/12/where-are-you-from-i-am-originally-from.html.

7. Museum of Modern Art. (2011). Massoud Hassani: Mind Kafon Wind-Powered Deminer. www.moma.org/collection/works/160434.

8. See entry for "factors of production" in Calhoun, Craig (Ed.). (2002). *Dictionary of the Social Sciences.* Oxford: Oxford University Press.

9. Gleeson-White, Jane. (2012). *Double Entry: How the Merchants of Venice Created Modern Finance.* New York: W. W. Norton, pp. 136–138, at p. 137.

10. White, Harrison C. and White, Cynthia A. (1993 [1965]). *Canvases and Careers: Institutional Change in the French Painting World.* Chicago, IL: Chicago University Press, p. 126.

11. White and White, 1993 [1965], pp. 132–133. The calculation of roughly $300,000 is highly approximate. It uses a more contemporary 5.85 franc-to-dollar conversion and a dollar inflation calculator from 1880 to 2020, finding that 75,000 francs is equivalent to $12,820 in 1880 or $322,000. (Inflation calculator, e.g., www.officialdata.org/us/inflation/1880?amount=12820.)

12. White and White, 1993 [1965], pp. 112–113 and 130–134.

13. For a more detailed discussion of transaction costs, see Williamson, Oliver E. (1985). *The Economic Institutions of Capitalism: Firms, Markets, Relational Contracting*. New York: Free Press, in particular chapter 1, "Transaction Cost Economics," pp. 15–42.

14. Coase, 1937.

15. There are so many examples to include; see, e.g., Jacobs, Luis. (Ed.) (2011). *Commerce by Artists*. Toronto, ON: Art Metropole. See also Louden, Sharon. (Ed.) (2013). *Living and Sustaining a Creative Life: Essays by 40 Living Artists*. Bristol, UK: Intellect Books.

16. Herbert, 2016, p. 39.

17. Herbert, 2016, pp. 42 and 47.

18. Herbert, 2016, pp. 38–41.

19. Savino, David M. (2016). Frederick Winslow Taylor and His Lasting Legacy of Functional Leadership Competence. *Journal of Leadership, Accountability and Ethics*, 13(1): 70–76. See also Gramsci's essay "Americanism and Fordism" in Gramsci, Antonio. (1971). *Prison Notebooks*. London: Lawrence and Wishart, p. 286. Taylor, Frederick Winslow. (1911). *The Principles of Scientific Management*. New York: Harper.

20. Herbert, 2016, p. 39.

21. Cascone, Sarah. (2019, March 11). Minimalist Sculptor Charlotte Posenenske Was on the Edge of Art-World Acclaim. She Walked Away in 1968. Now, Dia Is Bringing Her Back. *Artnet News*. www.news.artnet.com/exhibitions/charlotte-posenenske-retrospective-diabeacon-1484476.

22. Herbert, 2016, p. 39.

23. Herbert, 2016, p. 41.

24. Cascone, 2019, March. The Association of Art Museum Directors (AAMD), which wields some of the strictest deaccessioning rules, announced that it would not enforce them during the two years following the coronavirus pandemic. See Gold, Mark S. and Jandl, Stefanie S. (2020, May 18). Why the

Association of Art Museum Directors's Move on Deaccessioning Matters so Much. *The Art Newspaper.* www.theartnewspaper.com/comment/why-the-aamd-s-move-on-deaccessioning-matters-so-much.

25. Cascone, 2019, March. See also the exhibition catalogue: Lowry, Alexis and Morgan, Jessica (Eds.). (2019). *Charlotte Posenenske: Work in Progress*. Cologne, Germany: Walther König.

26. Clayton, Lenka. (2012–ongoing). Typewriter Drawings. www .lenkaclayton.com/work#/typewriter-drawings-4-1-1.

27. Donnachie, Ian. (n.d.). Thomas Bell. *Oxford Dictionary of National Biography.* https://doi.org/10.1093/ref:odnb/65053.

28. Chiappe, Paul. (n.d.). Drawings. http://paulchiappe.com. Artlyst. (2013, January 25). Paul Chiappe Exposes a Tissue of Lies in New London Exhibition. *Artlyst.* www.artlyst.com/news/paul-chiappe-exposes-a-tissue-of-lies-in-new-london-exhibition.

29. Rand, John. (1841). Improvement in the Construction of Vessels or Apparatus for Preserving Paint, US Patent 2252. https://patents .google.com/patent/US2252A/en.

30. Bailey, Jason. (2019, May 26). Mass Appropriation, Radical Remixing, and the Democratization of AI Art. *Artnome.* www.artnome.com/news/2019/ 5/13/mass-appropriation-radical-remixing-and-the-democratization-of-ai-art.

31. Valenzuela, Cristóbal. (2018, May 28). Machine Learning en Plein Air: Building Accessible Tools for Artists. *Medium.* https://medium.com/run wayml/machine-learning-en-plein-air-building-accessible-tools-for-artists-87bfc7f99f6b.

32. Dubois, R. Luke. (2016). Insightful Human Portraits Made from Data. *TED2016*, at 12:03. www.youtube.com/watch?v=9kBKQS7J7xI.

33. Although there are many textbooks in accounting, two clear introductory books are Buffett, Mary and Clark, David. (2008). *Warren Buffett and the Interpretation of Financial Statements: The Search for the Company with Durable Competitive Advantage*. New York: Scribner. Mullis, Darrell and Orloff, Judith. (2008). *The Accounting Game: Basic Accounting Fresh from the Lemonade Stand*. Naperville, IL: Sourcebooks.

34. White and White, 1993 [1965], p. 136.

35. White and White, 1993 [1965], p. 135.

36. White and White, 1993 [1965], pp. 129–130.

37. White and White, 1993 [1965], p. 136.

38. Greffe, Xavier. (2002). *Art and Artists from an Economic Perspective* (trans. Latika Saghal). Paris: UNESCO, p. 125.

39. Nichols, 2019.

40. Dover, Caitlin. (2018). Who Was Hilma af Klint?: At the Guggenheim, Paintings by an Artist ahead of Her Time. *Guggenheim.com*. www .guggenheim.org/blogs/checklist/who-was-hilma-af-klint-at-the-guggenheim-paintings-by-an-artist-ahead-of-her-time.

41. Stein, Judith E. (2016). *Eye of the Sixties: Richard Bellamy and the Transformation of Modern Art*. New York: Farrar, Straus and Giroux, p. 61.

42. Montias, John Michael. (1989). *Vermeer and His Milieu: A Web of Social History*. Princeton, NJ: Princeton University Press, p. 186.

43. Montias, 1989, p. 206.

44. Montias, 1989, p. 206.

45. Montias, 1989, pp. 217–218.

46. Montias, 1989, p. 218.

47. Montias, 1989, p. 255.

48. Trepasso, Erica. (2013, August 19). Johannes Vermeer: The 36th Painting. *Artnet News*. https://news.artnet.com/market/johannes-vermeer-the-36th-painting-30525. The precise metric conversion of 8 × 10 inches is 20.32 × 25.4 cm.

49. Chandler, Jr., Alfred D. (1994*). Scale and Scope: The Dynamics of Industrial Capitalism*. Cambridge, MA: Harvard University Press, p. 17.

50. This diagram is adapted from Whitaker, Amy. (2016b). *Business Structures and Planning: Performance Practice, Curriculum for Choreographers and Movement Artists*. New York: Lower Manhattan Cultural Council and the Actors Fund.

51. Kuzui, Fran. (2018, September 15). Japan's teamLab Transcends Borders of Art and Business. *Nikkei Asian Review*. https://asia.nikkei.com/Life-Arts /Arts/Japan-s-teamLab-transcends-borders-of-art-and-business. Founded by Toshiyuki Inoko, teamLab's 500 or so members engage in both corporate commissions and fine art installations, the latter represented by Pace Gallery. In 2018, teamLab's artwork *Ever Blossoming Life – Gold* sold for $225,000 at Christie's New York, over an estimate of $70,000 to $100,000.

52. Urstadt, Bryant. (2010, May 6). Uniqlones. *New York*. https://nymag.com /fashion/features/65898.

53. Glimcher, Marc. (2018, December 5). *The Art of Blockchains: Tech and the Art Market*. Panel with Emmanuel Aidoo, Credit Suisse, Head Distributed Ledger Strategy Nanne Dekking, TEFAF, Chairman of the Board; Artory, Founder & CEO Marc Glimcher, Pace Gallery, President & CEO Dan Long, ARTBLX, Co-Founder & CEO Andy Milenius, MakerDAO, Chief Technology Officer Moderated by Arthur Falls, DFINITY, Director of Communications, Faena Forum, Miami, Florida. www.youtube.com/watch?v=eeha-9JzkJ8, at 00:31:20.

54. Winkleman, Edward. (2015). *Selling Contemporary Art: How to Navigate the Evolving Market*. New York: Allworth Press, especially "The Rise of the Mega-Gallery," pp. 29–61.

55. Gagosian Gallery, 2012.

56. 1–54. (n.d.). About. www.1-54.com/about.

57. Art Basel. (n.d.). Our History. www.artbasel.com/about/history.

58. Shnayerson, Michael. (2019). *Boom: Mad Money, Mega Dealers, and the Rise of Contemporary Art*. New York: PublicAffairs, pp. 221–222.

59. Shnayerson, 2019, pp. 221–222.

60. Odell, Jenny. (2019). *How to Do Nothing: Resisting the Attention Economy*. New York: Melville House.

61. Clayton, Lenka. (2007). *Local Newspaper.* www.lenkaclayton.com/work#/local-newspaper. Clayton, Lenka. (2017). *Unanswered Letter.* www.lenkaclayton.com/work#/unanswered-letter. *Unanswered Letter* was made in collaboration with the Fabric Workshop and Museum, Philadelphia, PA. See also Clayton, Lenka. (2018). *Sculptures for the Blind.* Atlanta, GA: J&L Books.

62. Clayton, Lenka. (2012–15). *Artist Residency in Motherhood.* www.lenkaclayton.com/work#/man-boy-man-etc.

63. Phillips, Patricia C. (2016). Making Necessity Art: Collisions of Maintenance and Freedom. In Patricia C. Phillips, ed., *Mierle Laderman Ukeles: Maintenance Art*. New York: Prestel; New York: Queens Museum, pp. 23–193. Jacobs, 2011. See also Kee, Joan. (2019). *Models of Integrity: Art and Law in Post-Sixties America*. Oakland, CA: University of California Press, pp. 129–162.

64. *The Guardian.* (2017, September 1). The Parthenon of Books, Kassel, Germany – in Pictures. *The Guardian.* www.theguardian.com/travel/gallery/2017/sep/01/the-parthenon-of-books-kassel-germany-art-installation-nazi-book-burning-in-pictures. See also Laurinavičius,

Rokas. (2018). Artist Uses 100,000 Banned Books to Build a Full-Size Parthenon at Historic Nazi Book Burning Site. *Bored Panda.* www .boredpanda.com/parthenon-books-marta-minujin-germany/?utm_ source=google&utm_medium=organic&utm_campaign=organic.</int_i.

65. Weiner, Andrew Stefan. (2017, August 14). The Art of the Possible: With and against documenta 14. *Biennial Foundation.* www.biennialfoundation.org/ 2017/08/art-possible-documenta-14.

66. Mandiberg, Michael. (2016). *FDIC Insured by Michael Mandiberg.* http:// fdic.mandiberg.com/#/about.

67. Mandiberg, Michael. (2018). *Postmodern Times.* www.mandiberg.com/ postmodern-times.

3 PRICE

1. Bayer and Page, 2014, p. 2.
2. Bayer and Page, 2014, p. 198.
3. Velthuis, 2005, p. 1.
4. Velthuis, 2005, p. 2.
5. Velthuis, 2005, pp. 4 and 8.
6. Damodaran, Aswath. (2017). Executive Education Short Course: Valuation, Stern School of Business, New York University, August 14–16.
7. Anthony, Cara. (2014, December 13). Indianapolis Museum of Art to Charge Admission. *IndyStar.* https://eu.indystar.com/story/news/2014/ 12/12/indianapolis-museum-art-charge-admission/20306373. The related Virginia B. Fairbanks Art & Nature Park remained free. The 100-acre park and museum facilities were now bundled into a single ticket. Newfields is made up of the Indianapolis Museum of Art, the Garden, Lilly House, Miller House and Garden, and the Virginia B. Fairbanks Art & Nature Park: 100 Acres (referred to in short officially now as the Fairbanks Park).
8. Author correspondence with Anne Young and Jerry Wise, May–July 2020.
9. Russeth, Andrew. (2019, July 9). The Ringmaster: Is Charles Venable Democratizing a Great Art Museum in Indianapolis – or Destroying It? *ARTnews.* www.artnews.com/art-news/news/charles-venable-newfields-indianapolis-museum-12938. See also Bahr, Sarah. (2021, February 17). Charles Venable Resigns As Head of Indianapolis Museum of Art. *New York Times.* www.nytimes.com/2021/02/17/arts/design/charles-venable-resigning-indianapolis-museum.html.

10. Anthony, 2014. As Rushton has studied, museums cannot follow the economic edict to price where the price equals the marginal cost. The marginal cost for museum attendance is zero. Over a wide number of visitors, one more person can usually fit in without effect. Rushton advocates for museum membership as a pricing strategy in response. Rushton, Michael. (2017). Should Public and Nonprofit Museums Have Free Admission? A Defense of the Membership Model. *Museum Management and Curatorship*, 32(3): 200–209.

11. See, e.g., Pes, Javier. (2018, June 15). Artist Olafur Eliasson's Little Sun Is Teaming up with Ikea on a New Line of Solar Powered Products, *Artnet News.* https://news.artnet.com/art-world/olafur-eliasson-ikea-collaboration-1303436.

12. Musée du Louvre. (n.d.1). Free admission to the Musée du Louvre. www.louvre.fr/en/free-admission-musee-du-louvre. Musée du Louvre. (n.d.2). Hours, Admissions & Directions. www.louvre.fr/en/hours-admission-directions/admission#tabs.

13. Musée du Louvre. (n.d.4). Patron's Circle. www.louvre.fr/en/patrons-circle. See also Musée du Louvre. (n.d.3). Membership: Become a Friend of the Louvre! www.louvre.fr/en/membership-become-friend-louvre.

14. For a further overview of price discrimination, see Vohra, Rakesh and Krishmamurthi, Lakshman. (2012). *Principles of Pricing: An Analytic Approach.* Cambridge, UK: Cambridge University Press, pp. 106–158.

15. Pigou, Arthur Cecil. (2017 [1920]). *The Economics of Welfare.* London: Routledge, pp. 275–289.

16. Flux Theatre Ensemble. (n.d.). The Living Ticket. www.fluxtheatre.org/living-ticket.

17. See De Donno, Emanuele. (2019). Books as a System: The Artists' Books of Sol LeWitt [exhibition]. Printed Matter, New York, June 28–September 29. www.printedmatter.org/programs/events/877.

18. See Ginsburgh, Victor A. and Zang, Israel. (2007b). Bundling by Competitors and the Sharing of Profits. *Economics Bulletin*, 12(16): 1–9. Ginsburgh and Zang have also written about the peculiar pricing problem of revenue sharing across museums that offer a common ticket. One can approach this problem mentally as an issue of pricing – of assigning a value to each part of the bundle of the joint museum ticket.

19. Oi, Walter Y. (1971). A Disneyland Dilemma: Two-Part Tariffs for a Mickey Mouse Monopoly. *Quarterly Journal of Economics*, 85(1): 77–96.

20. Howard Becker pioneered the idea of "art worlds" in 1982 to describe these overlapping and often unacknowledged constellations of people who make up the art world, beyond the projection of the artist or other actors as atomized individuals. See Becker, Howard Saul. (1982). *Art Worlds*. Berkeley: University of California Press. John Zarobell has also written on the definition of the art market in an international context: "The two main problems with the idea of the art market as a singular entity are problems of circumscription. How does one determine what counts as art when it comes to the art market? How does one measure it? ... I argue that the writings on the so-called art market, be they academic analyses or journalism, do not only assume but in fact manufacture an art market. The art market is a result of discourse, a tacitly understood boundary of the art trade that is reinforced every time a writer types the words art market." Zarobell, John. (2017). *Art and the Global Economy*. Oakland: University of California Press, p. 170.

21. Author interview with Elisabeth Sunday, January 20, 2019.

22. Author interviews with Elisabeth Sunday, January 20, 2019, and May 15, 2020. Sunday, Elisabeth. (In press). *The Collector's Circle.*

23. Stein, 2016, p. 66.

24. Rushton, 2017. Frey, Bruno S., and Steiner, Lasse. (2012). Pay As You Go: A New Proposal for Museum Pricing. *Museum Management and Curatorship*, 27(3): 223–235. Baumol, William J. and Bradford, David F. (1970). Optimal Departures from Marginal Cost Pricing. *American Economic Review*, 60(3): 265–283.

25. David, Géraldine, Oosterlinck, Kim and Szafarz, Ariane. (2013). Art Market Inefficiency. *Economic Letters*, 121(1): 23–25.

26. Celarier, Michelle. (2015, March 13). The Huge Controversy behind Hedge Funder's $93.5 Million Art Sale." *New York Post.* https://nypost.com/2015/03/13/hedgie-steve-cohen-an-unwitting-player-in-art-sale-controversy.

27. Thompson, 2008, p. 3.

28. Johnston, Bob and Johnston, Nadine. (2012). *White Persian [Cat] in Pansy Patch.* https://fineartamerica.com/featured/white-persian-in-pansy-patch-original-forsale-bob-and-nadine-johnston.html.

4 FAILURE

1. Higgins, Charlotte. (2017, June 22). How Nicholas Serota's Tate Changed Britain. *The Guardian.* www.theguardian.com/artanddesign/2017/jun/22/how-nicholas-serota-tate-changed-britain.

2. The Tate Gallery, Millbank, was renamed Tate Britain, and the working project called "The Tate Gallery of Modern Art" became Tate Modern. The entire collection of Tate locations including Liverpool and St. Ives is called "Tate." Both the original Tate Gallery and the overall Tate federation are commonly referred to as "the Tate."

3. Muir, Gregor and Massey, Anne. (2014). *Institute of Contemporary Arts: 1946–1968.* Amsterdam: Roma Publications; London: ICA.

4. Stephenson, Andrew. (2018). A Failed Charm Offensive: Tate and the Peggy Guggenheim Collection. In Alex J. Taylor, ed., *Modern American Art at Tate 1945–1980.* www.tate.org.uk/research/publications/modern-american-art-at-tate/essays/tate-peggy-guggenheim.

5. Stephenson, 2018. Guggenheim, Peggy. (2005 [1979]). *Out of This Century: Confessions of an Art Addict.* Andre Deutsch: London, p. 369.

6. Lena, Jennifer C. (2019). *Entitled: Discriminating Tastes and the Expansion of the Arts.* Princeton, NJ: Princeton University Press, pp. 26–40. Operating from 1935 until 1943, the program resulted in the creation of "2,566 murals, 17,744 sculptures, 108,099 paintings, 250,000 prints from 11,285 images, 2 million posters from 35,000 designs, and more than 22,000 design plates." Lena, 2019, p. 27.

7. Burns, Charlotte (2019, February 13). Transcript of Sir Nicholas Serota: "We All Want to Know What It Means to Be Alive Today." *In Other Words.* www.artagencypartners.com/transcript-nicholas-serota.

8. Kettle's Yard. (n.d.). Timeline. www.kettlesyard.co.uk/collection/recollection/timeline.

9. The only exception is that visitors were strictly forbidden from dislodging displays of pebbles – say, the concentric circles of pebbles arranged in a side table. In today's Kettle's Yard, visitors are still encouraged to sit although the house is more museum than it was.

10. Salmon, Frances E. (1945, March 20). Letter to Mr. Harold Ede from American Red Cross. Kettle's Yard Archive.

11. At the time, Modern Art Oxford was called Museum of Modern Art Oxford. (Author correspondence with Sandy Nairne, September 14, 2020.)

12. Author interview with Nicholas Serota, December 4, 2019. See also Burns, 2019.

13. Whitechapel Gallery. (n.d.). Exhibitions 1950–Present. www .whitechapelgallery.org/about/history/exhibitions-1950-present.

14. Serota, Nicholas. (1987). Grasping the Nettle. Tate Archives. The document is in a section of the archives requiring permissions.

15. Tomkins, Calvin. (2012, July 2). The Modern Man. *The New Yorker.* www .newyorker.com/magazine/2012/07/02/the-modern-man.

16. Author interview with Nicholas Serota, December 4, 2019.

17. Author interview with Nicholas Serota, December 4, 2019.

18. Tomkins, 2012, p. 55.

19. Author interview with Nicholas Serota, December 4, 2019.

20. Tomkins, 2012.

21. The Millennium Bridge was designed by the architect Norman Foster's practice, Foster + Partners. See Foster + Partners. (n.d.). Millennium Bridge. www.fosterandpartners.com/projects/millennium-bridge.

22. I gratefully acknowledge comments and advice from Dennis Stevenson, Alex Beard, and Nicholas Serota. Email correspondence with Dennis Stevenson, March 10, 2020. Author interview with Alex Beard, December 2, 2020. Author interview with Nicholas Serota, December 4, 2019.

23. Author interview with Alex Beard, December 2, 2019.

24. Tate. (1999, October 6). New Millennium Sees Major Expansion of Tate Gallery. www.tate.org.uk/press/press-releases/new-millennium-sees-major-expansion-tate-gallery.

25. Author interview with Alex Beard, December 2, 2019.

26. The Tate is part of a longstanding arrangement by which the government funds British national museums, and this funding is tied to free entry to the collections. (Sandy Nairne, author correspondence, September 14, 2020.) The arrangement came about from a 2001 government initiative to make flagship national museums free in order to increase access. See Youngs, Ian. (2011, December 1). Museums Enjoy 10 Years of Freedom. *BBC.* www.bbc.com/news/entertainment-arts-15927593.

27. See, e.g., Hutter and Throsby, 2008.

28. Meade, James E. (1952). External Economies and Diseconomies in a Competitive Situation. *Economic Journal,* 62(245): 54–67. Cheung, Steven N. S. (1973). The Fable of the Bees: An Economic Investigation. *Journal of Law & Economics,* 16(1): 11–33. The theory of externalities is usually

dated back to Arthur C. Pigou's *The Economics of Welfare* and to Henry
Sidgwick's analysis of lighthouses as public goods. Pigou, 2017 [1920].
Sidgwick, Henry. (1883). *The Principles of Political Economy*. New York:
MacMillan and Company.) For a summary article (written by a political
scientist) see Munger, Michael. (2008, May 5). Orange Blossom Special:
Externalities and the Coase Theorem. *The Library of Economics and
Liberty*. www.econlib.org/library/Columns/y2008/Mungerbees.html.

29. Hardin, Garrett. (1968, December 13). The Tragedy of the Commons.
    Science, 162 (3859): 1243–1248.

30. Akerlof, George A. (1970). The Market for "Lemons": Quality Uncertainty
    and the Market Mechanism. *Quarterly Journal of Economics*, 84(3):
    488–500.

31. Bayer and Page, 2014.

32. The US and other governments run indemnity programs to help defray
    the cost of insuring artworks especially internationally. Making use of
    the program is not a moral hazard but an intended subsidy. See:
    National Endowment for the Arts. (n.d.). Art and Artifacts Indemnity
    Program: International Indemnity. www.arts.gov/artistic-fields/museums/
    arts-and-artifacts-indemnity-program-international-indemnity.

33. Contingent valuation methods were not generally accepted in economics
    for some time, while some practitioners of CVM consider economic
    development to be entirely separate from economic analysis – the purview
    of arts advocates with a specific agenda of championing the importance of
    the arts more than any "neutral" research interest in economic value.
    These tools are presented here as useful where they can be applied. For
    a helpful overview of research on economic development, see
    Seaman, Bruce A. (2011). Economic Impact of the Arts. In Ruth Towse, ed.,
    A Handbook of Cultural Economics, 2nd ed. Cheltenham, UK: Edward
    Elgar. For academic methodologies in economic development, see also
    Johnson, Peter and Thomas, Barry. (1998). The Economics of Museums:
    A Research Perspective. *Journal of Cultural Economics*, 22(2–3): 75–85.
    Greffe, Xavier. (2011). The Economic Impact of the Louvre. *Journal of Arts
    Management, Law, and Society*, 41(2): 121–137.

34. Johnson, Peter and Thomas, Barry. (1998). The Economics of Museums:
    A Research Perspective. *Journal of Cultural Economics*, 22(2–3): 75–85;
    and Greffe, 2011.

35. Johnson and Thomas, 1998, pp. 80 and 82.

36. McKinsey & Co. (2001, May 10). Assessing the Economic Impact of Tate Modern. Tate Gallery Archives, TG 12/1/3/11. (The 2001 report includes the summary date of the 1994 report which is also available in the Tate Gallery Archives, TG 12/1/3/5.)

37. Sterngold, Arthur H. (2004). Do Economic Impact Studies Misrepresent the Benefits of Arts and Cultural Organizations? *Journal of Arts Management, Law, and Society*, 34(3): 166–187.

38. Author correspondence with Dennis Stevenson, March 10, 2020.

39. Noonan, Douglas S. (2003). Contingent Valuation and Cultural Resources: A Meta-Analytic Review of the Literature. *Journal of Cultural Economics*, 27(3–4): 159–176. Epstein, Richard A. (2003). The Regrettable Necessity of Contingent Valuation. *Journal of Cultural Economics*, 27(3–4): 259–274. Epstein writes, "We must learn to make peace with the irreducible uncertainty associated with private valuations of ordinary goods and services" (p. 262). To consider these themes within the management of arts organizations, see Woronkowicz, Joanna, Joynes, D. Carroll and Bradburn, Norman. (2014). *Building Better Arts Facilities: Lessons from a US National Study*. London: Routledge.

40. O'Brien, D. (2010). *Measuring the Value of Culture: A Report to the Department for Culture Media and Sport*. London: Department for Culture, Media and Sport. www.gov.uk/government/uploads/system/uploads/attach ment_data/file/77933/measuring-the-value-culture-report.pdf.

41. Pung, Caroline, Clarke, Ann and Patten, Laurie. (2004). Measuring the Economic Impact of the British Library. *New Review of Academic Librarianship*, 10(1): 79–102. The researchers used the WTA method as well as a direct WTP study of both users and nonusers to arrive at their Total Economic Value. The present-day values are updated from the AHRC report using a Bank of England inflation calculator (Bakhshi, Hasan, Fujiwara, Daniel, Lawton, Ricky, Mourato, Susana and Dolan, Paul. (2015). *Measuring Economic Value in Cultural Institutions: A Report Commissioned by the Arts and Humanities Research Council's Cultural Value Project*. https://ahrc.ukri.org/documents/project-reports-and-reviews/measuringeconomicvalue).

42. Plaza, Beatriz, González-Casimiro, Pilar, Moral-Zuaco, Paz and Waldron, Courtney. (2015). Culture-Led City Brands As Economic Engines: Theory and Empirics. *Annals of Regional Science*, 54(1): 179–196.

43. Bakhshi et al., 2015, p. 3. See also, in particular, the underlying source: Pearce, David, Atkinson, Giles and Mourato, Susana. (2006). *Cost–Benefit Analysis and the Environment: Recent Developments*. Paris: OECD.

44. Bakhshi et al., 2015.

45. Bakhshi et al., 2015, p. 7.

46. Bakhshi et al., 2015, p. 12.

47. Bakhshi et al., 2015, pp. 25 and 69.

48. Bakhshi et al., 2015, p. 38.

49. The AHRC report and Doug Noonan's 2003 literature review are both resources to readers wishing to build CVM surveys in more detail (Bakhshi et al., 2015; and Noonan, 2003).

50. The Equal Justice Initiative. (n.d.). The National Memorial for Peace and Justice. https://museumandmemorial.eji.org/memorial.

51. Battaglia, Andy. (2019, July 2). The ARTnews Accord: Kaywin Feldman and Bryan Stevenson on Embracing Empathy and Confronting American Racism in Museums. *ARTnews.* www.artnews.com/artnews/news/ national-gallery-kaywin-feldman-bryan-equal-justice-initiative-stevenson-conversation-12896.

52. Sandy Nairne, author correspondence, September 14, 2020.

53. Wyma, Chloe. (2014). 1% Museum: The Guggenheim Goes Global. *Dissent* (summer), pp. 5–10, at p. 7.

54. Wyma, 2014, pp. 7–8.

55. Zhang, Amy Y. (2019). Placing Arts Districts within Markets: A Case Study of 798 Arts District in Beijing. *International Journal of Urban and Regional Research*, 43(6): 1028–1045.

56. UCCA (Ullens Center for Contemporary Art). (n.d.). History. https://ucca .org.cn/en/about/#:about_1.

57. Zhang, 2019, p. 1036.

58. Wu, Kejia. (2019). Executive Summary TEFAF Art Market Report 2019. www.amr.tefaf.com/chapter/introduction?printMode=true.

59. West Bund. (n.d.). West Bund History. www.westbund.com/en/index/ ABOUT-WEST-BUND/History/West-Bund-History.html. See also Diaz, Jesus. (2019, April 30). This Gorgeous Museum Is Made from Old Jet Fuel Tanks. *Fast Company.* www.fastcompany.com/90341401/this-gorgeous-museum-is-made-from-old-jet-fuel-tanks.

60. In the United States, the Association of Art Museum Directors (AAMD) allows member institutions to deaccession artworks if certain standards

are met, including the usage of the proceeds from the sale only for acquisition of other artworks. In the past, collectors such as Charles Saatchi and Dakis Joannou have been criticized for using public exhibition strategy to anchor private art collection value.

61. Wyma, 2014, p. 5.
62. Wyma, 2014, pp. 5–6.
63. Wyma, 2014, p. 9.
64. Callanan, Laura, Wei-Skillern, Jane and Onayemi, Prentice. (2014). *Theaster Gates: Artist As Catalyst for Community Development.* Berkeley-Haas Case Series. Berkeley: University of California. Finkelpearl, Tom. (2013). *What We Made: Conversations on Art and Social Cooperation.* Durham, NC: Duke University Press.
65. Associated Press. (2019, October 4). Jeff Koons' "Bouquet of Tulips" Honors Victims of Paris Terror Attacks. *The Guardian.* www .theguardian.com/artanddesign/2019/oct/04/jeff-koons-bouquet-of-tulips-honours-victims-of-paris-terror-attacks.
66. BBC News. (2019, October 8). Jeff Koons' Paris Bataclan Sculpture Mocked As "Pornographic." www.bbc.co.uk/news/world-europe-49958897. The sculpture is 12.6 meters tall and made of polychrome bronze, stainless steel, and aluminum. In addition to the 130 people killed, 416 people were injured, 100 of them very seriously.
67. Kaufman, Jason Edward. (2008). Why the Guggenheim Won't Open a Branch in Guadalajara. *The Art Newspaper*, 17(June): 27. Author interview with Thomas Krens, July 2014.
68. Collier, Caroline and Serota, Nicholas. (2015). *Plus Tate: Connecting Art to People and Places.* London: Tate. www.tate.org.uk/about-us/national-international-local/plus-tate.
69. Collier and Serota, 2015, pp. 92–93.
70. Collier and Serota, 2015, pp. 16, 20, 25, 27, 33, 36, 40, 44, 48, 55, 61, 64, 79, 86, and 91.
71. Higgins, 2017.
72. Higgins, 2017.
73. Salisbury, Josh. (2018, October 1). Southbank Single Mum Has Tate Modern Building Named after Her in Recognition of Good Deeds. *Southwark News.* www.southwarknews.co.uk/news/southbank-tate-modern-coin-street-natalie-bell.
74. Tate. (1991). *The Tate Gallery Biennial Report 1988–1990.* London: Tate Gallery Publications, p. 16. See also Donnellan, Caroline. (2018). *Towards*

Tate Modern: Public Policy, Private Vision. London: Routledge. Sabbagh, Karl. (2001). *Power into Art: The Making of Tate Modern.* London: Penguin.

75. Hickley, Catherine. (2017, September 12). documenta Faces Yawning Euro 7m Deficit, Seeks Financial Help. *The Art Newspaper.* www .theartnewspaper.com/news/documenta-faces-yawning-euro7m-deficit-seeks-financial-help.

76. Kulenkampff, Annette, Szymczyk, Adam, et al. (2017, December 1). Open Letter Defending Exhibition. *Artforum.* www.artforum.com/news/ documenta-14-artists-pen-second-open-letter-defending-exhibition-72702.

77. Hickley, 2017.

78. For a discussion of public choice theory and art, see Potts, Jason. (2015, August 3). The Economics of the Politics of the Arts. *The Conversation.* https://theconversation.com/the-economics-of-the-politics-of-the-arts-40555. For a discussion of foundational ideas and texts in public choice theory, see Shughart, II, William F. (n.d.) Public Choice. *The Library of Economics and Liberty.* www.econlib.org/library/Enc/PublicChoice.html.

79. Glueck, Grace. (1985, February 3). What Part Should the Public Play in Choosing Public Art? *New York Times.* www.nytimes.com/1985/02/03/ arts/what-part-should-the-public-play-in-choosing-public-art.html. Numerous academic and journalistic sources have covered *Tilted Arc.* See, e.g., Senie, Harriet. (1989). Richard Serra's *Tilted Arc*: Art and Non-Art Issues. *Art Journal*, 48(4): 298–302.

80. Bishop, Claire and Columbus, Nikki. (2020, January 7). Free Your Mind: A Speculative Review of #NewMoMA. *n+1 Magazine.* https://nplusone mag.com/online-only/paper-monument/free-your-mind.

5 STRUCTURE

1. Douglas Franz, Douglas, Vogel, Carol and Blumenthal, Ralph. (2000, October 8). Private Files Fuel an Art Auction Inquiry. *New York Times.* www.nytimes.com/2000/10/08/us/secret-partners-unraveling-conspiracy-private-files-fuel-art-auction-inquiry.html.

2. Ashenfelter, Orley and Graddy, Kathryn. (2005). Anatomy of the Rise and Fall of a Price-Fixing Conspiracy: Auctions at Sotheby's and Christie's. *Journal of Competition Law and Economics*, 1(1): 3–20.

3. Mason, Christopher. (2004). *The Art of the Steal: Inside the Sotheby's– Christie's Auction House Scandal.* New York: Berkley Books, p. 158.

I especially thank Mason for his definitive reporting on this case. I am also grateful to Stewart, whose 2001 *New Yorker* article offered early investigation, and to Ashenfelter and Graddy, whose 2005 article framed the case academically. Stewart, James B. (2001, October 15). Bidding War. *The New Yorker*, pp. 158–175.

4. Ashenfelter and Graddy, 2005.
5. McAndrew, Clare. (2010). An Introduction to Art and Finance. In Clare McAndrew, ed., *Fine Art and High Finance: Expert Advice on the Economics of Ownership*. New York: Bloomsbury, pp. 1–30, at p. 12.
6. Mason, 2004, pp. 75–76.
7. Stewart, 2001. Sotheby's and Christie's competed for major consignments by offering financial and general benefits. They offered no-interest loans that functioned as guarantees. For instance, a collector could contact the auction house in June to sell a collection of works, and although the auction house would not sell the works until the twice-yearly sales in May and November, they would front the collector a certain amount of money, interest-free, that the collector could keep if the works failed to sell, effectively promising for the auction house to purchase the works. The houses also offered softer perks such as tours of major works internationally before a sale, formidably printed catalogues, and donations to consignors' charities of choice. (Some of the donations were to family foundations, making the last perk a sometimes more direct benefit.) Ashenfelter and Graddy, 2005, p. 5.
8. Ashenfelter and Graddy, 2005, p. 6.
9. Mason, 2004, pp. 62–73.
10. See United Kingdom Competition Act 1998 (Competition Act) § 36. The UK law was amended in 2002 by the Enterprise Act to create criminal penalties for violation of UK competition law. For a law firm memo citing the Christie's–Sotheby's scandal as impetus, see Crowell & Moring. (2002). *The United Kingdom's Criminalization of Price-Fixing and Other Collusive Conduct.* www.crowell.com/pdf/UK.pdf.
11. Mason, 2004.
12. Mason, 2004, p. 13.
13. Mason, 2004, pp. 8, 10, and 23.
14. Mason, 2004, pp. 30–31.
15. Mason, 2004, p. 32.
16. Mason, 2004, pp. 32–33.

17. Mason, 2004, pp. 79 and 133.
18. Mason, 2004, p. 361.
19. The Daily Telegraph. (2011, August 8). Sir Anthony Tennant [obituary]. *The Daily Telegraph.* p. 25. www.telegraph.co.uk/news/obituaries/finance-obituaries/8687415/Sir-Anthony-Tennant.html. Mason, 2004, p. 95.
20. The Daily Telegraph, 2011.
21. Mason, 2004, p. 98.
22. Mason, 2004, pp. 62–65.
23. Mason, 2004, pp. 61–62.
24. Mason, 2004, p. 64.
25. Mason, 2004, p. 66.
26. Mason, 2004, p. 60.
27. Mason, 2004, p. 68.
28. Mason 2004, p. 249.
29. Mason, 2004, p. 98.
30. Mason, 2004, p. 133.
31. Mason, 2004, pp. 139–140.
32. Mason, 2004, p. 155.
33. Mason, 2004, p. 168.
34. Mason, 2004, pp. 169 and 170.
35. Mason, 2004, p. 192.
36. Ashenfelter and Graddy, 2005, p. 7. The UK Office of Fair Trading operated from 1973 until 2014 and was merged into the Competition and Markets Authority by the Enterprise and Regulatory Reform Act of 2013.
37. Mason, 2004, p. 205.
38. Mason, 2004, p. 208.
39. Stewart, 2001, pp. 160–161.
40. Stewart, 2001, pp. 163–164; Mason, 2004, p. 237.
41. Mason, 2004, pp. 238–239.
42. Mason, 2004, p. 251.
43. Mason, 2004, p. 244.
44. Mason, 2004, p. 245.
45. Mason, 2004, p. 246.
46. Mason, 2004, p. 249.
47. Mason, 2004, p. 250.
48. Mason, 2004, pp. 252–256.
49. Mason, 2004, pp. 360–364.

50. Ashenfelter and Graddy, 2005, p. 4.

51. Mason, 2004, p. 296.

52. Mason, 2004, p. 281.

53. Mason, 2004, pp. 297–298.

54. Given that when Sotheby's was a publicly traded company its annual profits were on the order of just over $100 million, it is hard to imagine that the increase in revenue through collusion in any way compared to the punitive damages.

55. Coase, 1937, p. 338. Alfred Marshall also opined on the question of competition in his 1890 *Principles of Economics* when he wrote: "The term 'competition' has gathered about it evil savour, and has come to imply a certain selfishness and indifference to the wellbeing of others. Now it is true that there is less deliberate selfishness in early than in modern forms of industry; but there is also less deliberate unselfishness. It is the deliberateness, and not selfishness, that is the characteristic of the modern age." Marshall, 1920 [1890], p. 6.

56. Leyrer, Jonas. (2017, December 26). The Brannock Device: A 90-Year Monopoly. *JML Blog.* www.jonasleyrer.com/2017/12/26/the-brannock-device-a-90-year-monopoly.

57. Organization of the Petroleum Exporting Countries (OPEC). (n.d.). Brief History. www.opec.org/opec_web/en/about_us/24.htm.

58. See Williamson, Oliver E. (1987). *Antitrust Economics: Mergers, Contracting, and Strategic Behavior.* Oxford, UK: Basil Blackwell, p. 56. Oster, Sharon M. (1999). *Modern Competitive Analysis*, 3rd ed. New York: Oxford University Press, p. 36.

59. According to Sotheby's Inc.'s 2015 10-K annual filing with the US Securities and Exchange Commission, its net income was $130 million in 2013, $117,992 in 2014, and $43.5 million in 2015. The last year was unusual with regard to governance, early retirements, and hostile interest from the hedge-fund investor Daniel Loeb. The company lists double its usual income tax expense ($131 million) in 2015. Earnings before tax are more consistent across years ($169–$193 million). Sotheby's Inc. (2016). Form 10-K: 2015, p. 63. www.sec.gov/Archives/edgar/data/823094/000082309416000080 /bid1231201510k_xbrl2015.htm. See also Kinsella, Eileen and Genocchio, Benjamin. (2015, March 23). Will Sotheby's Again Fall Victim to Corporate Hubris with Dan Loeb, Tad Smith Takeover?

Artnet News. https://news.artnet.com/art-world/sothebys-takeover-dan-loeb-tad-smith-278897.

60. McAndrew, 2019, pp. 144–147.

61. McAndrew, 2019, p. 144.

62. Greenberger, Alex. (2018, October 19). Signal Gallery, Hotbed for Vanguard Art in Brooklyn, Will Close. *ARTnews.* www.artnews.com/art-news/market/signal-gallery-hotbed-vanguard-art-brooklyn-will-close-11202.

63. Norte Maar was founded in 2004 outside of New York City and then began its Brooklyn living-room events in 2006. The gallery is incorporated as a 501(c)3 nonprofit. Norte Maar. (n.d.). Norte Maar for Collaborative Projects in the Arts. www.nortemaar.org/history.

64. Kinsella, Eileen. (2020, February 19). The $450 Marron Collection Is the Art Market's Ultimate Prize. Now, Three of the World's Top Rival Galleries Are Joining Forces to Sell It. *Artnet News.* https://news.artnet.com/market/donald-marron-collection-pace-acquavella-gagosian-1781181.

65. Crow, Kelly. (2020, February 19). Three New York Galleries to Sell Financier's Collection. *Wall Street Journal.* www.wsj.com/articles/three-new-york-galleries-to-sell-financiers-art-collection-11582142146.

66. Reyburn, Scott. (2018, October 6). Banksy Painting Self-Destructs after Fetching $1.4 Million at Sotheby's. *New York Times.* www.nytimes.com/2018/10/06/arts/design/uk-banksy-painting-sothebys.html.

67. See, e.g., Ostrom, Elinor. (1990). *Governing the Commons: The Evolution of Institutions for Collective Action.* Cambridge, UK: Cambridge University Press, pp. 3–5. The game was originally conceived by the mathematician Albert W. Tucker.

68. Barbara Strongin, author interview, August 30, 2020. See also Watson, Peter. *From Manet to Manhattan: The Rise of the Modern Art Market.* New York: Random House, pp. 11–12.

69. Ashenfelter, Orley, Ginsburgh, Victor, Graddy, Kathryn, Legros, Patrick and Sahuguet, Nicholas. (2003, November). Auction House Settlement: Winning Twice? *The Art Newspaper,* 141(11): 42.

70. Pogrebin, Robin. (2016, January 11). Sotheby's, in a Gamble, Acquires Boutique Art Advisory Firm. *New York Times.* www.nytimes.com/2016/01/12/arts/sothebys-in-a-gamble-acquires-boutique-art-advisory-firm.html.

71. For Mei Moses, see Freeman, Nate. (2016, October 27). Sotheby's Acquires Mei Moses Art Indices, an Analytic Tool That Evaluates Market Strength on Basis of Repeat Sales. *ARTnews*. www.artnews.com/art-news/market/ sothebys-acquires-mei-moses-art-indices-an-analytic-tool-that-evaluates-market-strength-on-basis-of-repeat-sales-7208. For Orion Analytical, see Rivetti, Ermanno. (2016, December 6). Sotheby's Buys Orion Analytical Lab in Fight against Art Fraud. *The Art Newspaper*. www.theartnewspaper .com/news/sotheby-s-buys-orion-analytical-lab-in-fight-against-art-fraud. For Art Agency, Partners, see Pogrebin, 2016.

72. Maneker, Marion. (2020, May 4). Should We Be Worried about Sotheby's Ability to Meet Its Obligations? *Art Market Monitor*. www.artmarket monitor.com/2020/05/04/should-we-be-worried-about-sothebys-ability -to-meet-its-obligations/.

73. Barbara Strongin, author interview September 19, 2020.

74. Abbing, Hans. (2002). *Why Are Artists Poor? The Exceptional Economy of the Arts*. Amsterdam: Amsterdam University Press, pp. 259–279. Winkleman, 2015, pp. 29–61.

6 POWER

1. The day sale on September 16 contained 167 lots and brought £40.92 million. The evening sale on September 15 contained 56 lots and brought £70.55 million. Sotheby's Inc. (2008, September 15–16). Beautiful Inside My Head Forever. www.sothebys.com/en/search-results.html? query=Damien%20Hirst%20beautiful%20inside%20my%20head% 20forever.

2. Tate. (n.d.3). Young British Artists. www.tate.org.uk/art/art-terms/y/ young-british-artists-ybas. Freeman, Nate. (2018, August 24). How Damien Hirst's $200 Million Auction Became a Symbol of Pre-Recession Decadence. *Artsy*. www.artsy.net/article/artsy-editorial-damien-hirsts-200-million-auction-symbol-pre-recession-decadence. Hirst's contribution to *Freeze* was an arrangement of cardboard boxes covered in latex paint. After graduation, he hosted another exhibition, *Gambler*, cocurated with Carl Freedman and organized in the Bermondsey neighborhood of southeast London. Hirst created a work, *A Thousand Years*, consisting of a dead cow's head inside a vitrine, separated from a group of flies by a glass partition and an electric bug zapper. Saatchi bought the work and commissioned Hirst's next piece, which became *The*

Physical Impossibility of Death in the Mind of Someone Living, or shark in formaldehyde tank. Thompson, 2008, pp. 62–63.

3. Bostaph, Samuel. (2015). *Andrew Carnegie: An Economic Biography.* Lanham, MD: Lexington Books, pp. 67 and 99–104. Wall, Joseph Frazier. (1970). *Andrew Carnegie.* Pittsburgh, PA: University of Pittsburgh Press, pp. 485–486 and 586.

4. Abboud, Lela. (2020, March 19). Inside the Factory: How LVMH Met France's Call for Hand Sanitizer in 72 Hours. *Financial Times.* www .ft.com/content/e9c2bae4-6909-11ea-800d-da70cff6e4d3. The output quantity was 12 metric tons or 12,000 kilograms.

5. Schneider, Tim. (2018, September 12). A Decade After Damien Hirst's Historic "Beautiful Inside My Head Forever" Auction, Resale Prices Are Looking Ugly. *Artnet News.* https://news.artnet.com/market/damien-hirst-beautiful-resales-1346528.

6. Alpers, Svetlana. (1988). *Rembrandt's Enterprise: The Studio and the Market.* Chicago, IL: University of Chicago Press, p. 71 (separation of painting, drawing, and etching), p. 99 (nearly finished work), and p. 100 (small changes to etchings). For a more contemporary study of "supply chain" trajectories of successful artists, see Fraiberger, Samuel P., Sinatra, Roberta, Resch, Magnus, Riedl, Christoph and Barabási, Albert-László. (2018). Quantifying Reputation and Success in Art. *Science,* 362 (6416): 825–829. For further study of the connection of Dutch painting and the market, see Vermeylen, Filip. (2003). *Painting for the Market: Commercialization of Art in Antwerp's Golden Age.* Turnhout, Belgium: Brepols.

7. Winkleman, Edward and Hindle, Patton. (2018). *How to Start and Run a Commercial Gallery*, 2nd ed. New York: Allworth.

8. Lovo, Stefano and Spaenjers, Christophe. (2018). A Model of Trading in the Art Market. *American Economic Review,* 108(3): 744–774. https://doi.org/10.1257/aer.20160522.

9. For an overview of the structure of the art market, see also Robertson, Iain. (2016). *Understanding Art Markets: Inside the World of Art and Business.* London: Routledge, pp. 3–35. For a provocative but data-driven approach to the precarity of the industry, see Resch, Magnus. (2016). *Management of Art Galleries*, 2nd ed. London: Phaidon Press.

10. See, e.g., Williamson, Oliver E. (1971). The Vertical Integration of Production. *The American Economic Review: Papers and Proceedings of*

306 notes to pages 162–166

the *Eighty-Third Annual Meeting of the American Economic Association,* 61(2): pp. 112–123.

11. Keefe, Patrick Radden. (2012, June 15). Cocaine Incorporated. *New York Times Magazine.* www.nytimes.com/2012/06/17/magazine/how-a-mexi can-drug-cartel-makes-its-billions.html.

12. Hirst's ability to conceive of the work may also have depended on his work placement in a mortuary during his student years at Goldsmiths. Thompson, 2008, pp. 2–3 (shark) and p. 62 (mortuary).

13. Freeman, 2018.

14. Freeman, 2018. In 2017, the artist tried to disintermediate art world systems again by investing his own money for a project in François Pinault's contemporary art spaces in the Palazzo Grassi and the Punta della Dogana in Venice, therefore alongside but not through the curatorial channels of the Venice Biennale. Although Hirst's show, *Treasures from the Wreck of the Unbelievable,* was organized by the independent curator Elena Geuna, Nate Freeman of *Artsy* argues that Hirst was circumventing the dealer–critic system again in this instance. For Hirst and Jeff Koons in context of kitsch and fashion, see also Kim, Kibum and Degen, Natasha. (2017, July 2). The Kitsch Gazes Back: Jeff Koons and Damien Hirst Return. *Los Angeles Review of Books.* https://lareviewofbooks.org/ article/the-kitsch-gazes-back-jeff-koons-and-damien-hirst-return.

15. Williamson, 1971. Williamson's argument draws strongly on Coase's 1937 article on the nature of the firm.

16. Urstadt, 2010.

17. Goetzmann, Zoe. (2017). *Artists on Instagram: The Art World of Instagram.* Thesis in completion of the MA in Art Business, Sotheby's Institute of Art, London.

18. Stuckey, John and White, David. (1993). When and When Not to Vertically Integrate. *Sloan Management Review,* 34(3): 71–83.

19. Gleadell, Colin. (2017, July 28). Artist Pension Trust Faces Yet Another Crisis As Artists Fume over New Storage Fees. *Artnet News.* https://news .artnet.com/market/artist-pension-trust-storage-fee-1035569.

20. Williamson, 1985, p. 47.

21. For example, the artist Sol LeWitt worked with a group of draftspersons who have for a very long time created his wall drawings. See Garrels, Gary. (2000). A Conversation with Sol LeWitt. *Open: Member's Magazine of the San Francisco Museum of Modern Art.* Reprinted in the Sol LeWitt Wall

Drawings Catalogue Raisonné, www.artifexpress.com/catalogues/sol-lewitt-wall-drawings. See also Roberts, Veronica (2014). *Converging Lines: Eva Hesse and Sol LeWitt.* New Haven, CT: Blanton Museum of Art in association with Yale University Press.

22. Museum of Modern Art. (n.d.). UNIQLO Free Friday Nights. *MoMA.org.* www.moma.org/calendar/events/5601. Uniqlo. (n.d.). New York Museum of Modern Art (MoMA) Partnership (US) UNIQLO. www .uniqlo.com/en/sustainability/culture/artmuseum.

23. Didion, Joan. (2014). *Where I Was From.* New York: Vintage.

24. Campbell, Duncan, (2002, July 8). Land of the Twee. *The Guardian.* www .theguardian.com/culture/2002/jul/08/artsfeatures1.

25. It is interesting to compare and contrast Kinkade's process and that of Rembrandt, structurally if not artistically. Kinkade's strategy of adding small touches of paint – the hand of the artist – to distinguish one image from the next, calls to mind Rembrandt's strategy of leaving a nearly finished canvas to complete to a collector's specifications or his practice of refashioning etching plates to create new work.

26. Khaire, Mukti. (2017). *Culture and Commerce: The Value of Entrepreneurship in Creative Industries.* Stanford, CA: Stanford University Press, p. 50.

27. Khaire, 2017, p. 55.

28. Khaire, 2017, pp. 57, 77–78, 87, and 99.

29. Velthuis, Olav. (2011). The Venice Effect. *The Art Newspaper*, 20(225): 21–24. Hans Abbing also frames this observation when he writes: "It is commercial to be anti-commercial." Abbing, 2002, p. 12.

30. White and White, 1993 [1965].

31. Winkleman, 2015, pp. 29–61. Fite-Wassilak, Chris. (2019, December 20). How Hauser & Wirth Took Over the World. *Frieze.* https://frieze.com/ article/how-hauser-wirth-took-over-world. Hauser & Wirth is also in the process of opening a residency and art center in Spain, in an old naval hospital in Menorca. Duron, Maximiliano. (2019, June 13). Hauser & Wirth Will Open Exhibition Space, Residency Program on Menorca's Isla del Rey. *ARTnews.* www.artnews.com/art-news/news/hauser-wirth-menorca-exhibition-space-12783.

32. Hauser & Wirth. (n.d.). Publishers. www.hauserwirth.com/publishers.

33. Project Row Houses. (n.d.). Mission and History. https://projectrowhouses .org/about/mission-history. Theaster Gates's work in Chicago's South Side is also pioneering in this transformation via creative placemaking.

Gates, Theaster. (n.d.). Rebuild Foundation. www.theastergates.com/
project-items/rebuild-foundation.

34. Valentine, Victoria L. (2015, September 20). Mark Bradford's Art + Practice
Is on a Mission to Change Lives. *Culture Type.* www.culturetype.com/
2015/09/20/mark-bradfords-art-practice-is-on-a-mission-to-change-lives.

35. Valentine, 2015. Art + Practice. (n.d.). About. www.artandpractice.org
/about.

36. Bradford, Mark and Golden, Thelma. (2015). *Mark Bradford in
Conversation with Thelma Golden.* Hauser & Wirth, New York, at 10:20.
www.hauserwirth.com/resources/18701-mark-bradford-conversation-
thelma-golden.

37. Bradford and Golden, 2015, at 41:55.

38. Oster, 1999, p. 4.

39. Porter, Michael E. (2008). The Five Competitive Forces That Shape
Strategy. *Harvard Business Review.* https://hbr.org/2008/01/the-five-
competitive-forces-that-shape-strategy. The article revisits Porter's
original 1979 article "How Competitive Forces Shape Strategy." See also
Oster, 1999, p. 51 and the entirety of chapter 4, "Understanding the
Impediments to Entry."

40. Oster, Sharon M. (1995). *Strategic Management for Nonprofit
Organizations.* New York: Oxford University Press.

41. Brandenburger, Adam M. and Nalebuff, Barry J. (1996). *Co-opetition.*
New York: Doubleday.

42. Brandenburger and Nalebuff, 1996, p. 13.

43. Brandenburger and Nalebuff, 1996, p. 46.

44. Jackson, Brian Keith. (2019, April 14). Kehinde Wiley's Art Annex.
New York. www.thecut.com/2019/04/tour-kehinde-wiley-art-annex-in-
dakar-senegal.html.

45. Black Rock. (n.d.). The Residency. https://blackrocksenegal.org/the-
residency.

46. Nkontchou, Bimpe. (2020). Philanthropy in African Art. In Anders
Petterson, ed., *Art Patronage in the 21st Century: The TEFAF Art Market
Report*, pp. 87–89.

47. Kinsella, Eileen. (2016, January 11). Sotheby's Acquires Amy
Cappellazzo's Art Agency Partners for $50 Million. *Artnet News.* https://
news.artnet.com/market/sothebys-pays-50m-art-agency-partners-
404951.

48. International Council of Museums (ICOM). (n.d.). Guidelines on Deaccessioning of the International Council of Museums. https://icom .museum/wp-content/uploads/2019/08/20170503_ICOM_standards_deac cessioning_final_EN-v2.pdf. Association of Art Museum Directors (AAMD). (2015, September). AAMD Policy on Deaccessioning. https:// aamd.org/sites/default/files/document/AAMD%20Policy%20on%20Deacc essioning%20website_0.pdf. See also Oster, 1995, pp. 29–42 and 289–291.

7 LABOR

1. Wagenknecht, Addie. (2019, December 22). Something Weird about the Art World . . .. @wheresaddie. https://twitter.com/wheresaddie/status/ 1208677391683469312?s=20.
2. Rachleff, Melissa. (2017). *Inventing Downtown: Artist-Run Galleries in New York City, 1952–1965*. New York: Grey Art Gallery, New York University; New York: DelMonico Books, pp. 53–55.
3. In her biography of Richard Bellamy, *Eye of the Sixties*, Judith Stein reports that the co-op received a loan of $1,000 from Allan Kaprow, the artist best known for Happenings, the planned, participatory art events he organized. Stein, Judith E. (2016). *Eye of the Sixties: Richard Bellamy and the Transformation of Modern Art*. New York: Farrar, Straus and Giroux, p. 59. See also Beaven, Kirstie. Performance Art: The Happening. *Tate.org. uk*. www.tate.org.uk/art/art-terms/h/happening/happening.
4. Stein notes that some of the artists' girlfriends volunteered shifts as well (Stein, 2016, p. 60). The US federal poverty threshold in 2017 was $12,060 for a family of one and $24,600 for a family of four, bringing this salary out of contention for meeting standalone economic necessity. US Department of Health and Human Services. (2017). Poverty Guidelines. https://aspe.hhs.gov/2017-poverty-guidelines#threshholds. Rachleff notes that the cost of living was much lower even in inflation-adjusted terms, in large part because real estate was much cheaper at the time (email correspondence with the author, June 3, 2020). The calculation from 1952 to 2019 dollars comes from the US Consumer Price Index (CPI) calculator accessed at www.in2013dollars.com/us/inflation/1952.
5. Rachleff, 2017, p. 57.
6. Rachleff, email correspondence with the author June 3, 2020.
7. Stein, 2016, p. 61; Rachleff, 2017, p. 58.

8. Stein, 2016, p. 62. Stein mentions the two marriages. Rachleff identifies them as nephews (email correspondence with the author, June 3, 2020).

9. *Essentials of Astronomy* was based on the introductory astronomy course taught at Columbia University. With the inclusion of lucid drawings and substantial archival materials (e.g., the 1066 depiction of Haley's Comet in the Bayeux tapestry, p. 9), one feels a hand of her artistry in the book. Motz, Lloyd and Duveen, Anneta. (1966). *Essentials of Astronomy*. Belmont, CA: Wadsworth.

10. Rachleff. 2017, p. 58. See also Stein, 2016, p. 81.

11. Stein, 2016, p. 62. Rachleff, 2017, p. 58. The $40 per month was in Bellamy's recollection.

12. Stein, 2016, pp. 62–64.

13. Stein, 2016, p. 66.

14. *The Village Voice* was founded by Dan Wolf, Ed Fancher, and Norman Mailer in 1955. Village Voice (n.d.). *About the Village Voice.* www .villagevoice.com/about. That Karp was the art critic: Rachleff, 2017, p. 59. Rachleff, email correspondence with the author, June 3, 2020.

15. Stein, 2016, pp. 65–66.

16. Rachleff, 2017, pp. 56 and 58.

17. Rachleff, 2017, p. 70, and email correspondence with the author, June 3, 2020.

18. Rachleff, 2017, p. 57.

19. Rachleff, 2017, p. 57 (see also footnote 67).

20. Rachleff, 2017, p. 56.

21. Rachleff, 2017, p. 70.

22. Rachleff, 2017, p. 59.

23. Whitaker, Amy. (2009). *Museum Legs: Fatigue and Hope in the Face of Art*. Tucson, AZ: Hol Art Books.

24. See, e.g., Mabuchi, Jun. (2019). *Decentralizing the Whiteness in the Museum: Sustainable Framework of DEI*. Thesis in completion of the MA in Visual Arts Administration, New York University.

25. Britten, Mathew and Grist, Kerry. (2019). Tough Love: Museum Salaries and the Working Class. In Dawn E. Salerno, Mark S. Gold, and Kristina L. Durocher, eds., *For Love or Money: Confronting the State of Museum Salaries*. Edinburgh: MuseumsEtc, pp. 90–95.

26. Nie, Taryn R. (2019). Far Too Female: Museums on the Edge of a Pink Collar Profession. In Dawn E. Salerno, Mark S. Gold, and Kristina

L. Durocher, eds., *For Love or Money: Confronting the State of Museum Salaries*. Edinburgh: MuseumsEtc, pp. 120–163, at p. 144. See also, e.g., Kendi, Ibram X. (2019). *How to Be an Antiracist.* New York: Random House.

27. The percentage spend on compensation ranged as high as 65.1% of operating budget (Nie, 2019, p. 124).

28. Based on internal New Museum memos at the time of formation of the New Museum Union (UAW Local 2110) in New York, union-eligible workers received median pay of $52,000. Jandl, Stefanie. (2019). OMG We Won! The New Museum Union. In Dawn E. Salerno, Mark S. Gold, and Kristina L. Durocher, eds., *For Love or Money: Confronting the State of Museum Salaries.* Edinburgh: MuseumsEtc, pp. 306–325. While the findings of the Art + Museum Transparency working group are still being processed, preliminarily, the median pay appears to be $48,000 (converted to US dollars from a variety of countries). However, the standard deviation is $30,743 because those salaries range from $14,000 to $601,000 with over seventy salaries above $100,000 including a number of chief curator roles with salaries over $200,000. The salaries reflect the increasingly contingent nature of museum work, with 27% of respondents in hourly positions and 9% in contingent contract work. Art + Museum Transparency. (2019, December 9). A 20/20 Vision for Art + Museum Transparency for 2020: Sharing, Analyzing, Moving Forward. *Medium.* https://medium.com/@artandmuseumtransparency/a-20-20-vision-for-art-museum-transparency-for-2020-sharing-analyzing-moving-forward-3eef299cdea0. Dataset available at https://medium.com/@artandmuseumtransparency/links-to-our-crowdsourced-spreadsheets-f7130e7771f.

29. Martin, Charlotte, Maldonado, Sarah and Song, Anthea. (2019). A Case for Salary Transparency in Job Postings. In Dawn E. Salerno, Mark S. Gold, and Kristina L. Durocher, eds., *For Love or Money: Confronting the State of Museum Salaries.* Edinburgh: MuseumsEtc, pp. 306–325. City of New York. (2019). *Diversity & Equity in New York City's Cultural Workforce.* www1.nyc.gov/site/diversity/index.page.

30. Strategic National Arts Alumni Project (SNAAP). (2018). *2015, 2016 & 2017 Aggregate Frequency Report.* http://snaap.indiana.edu/pdf/2017/SNAAP15_16_17_Aggregate_Report.pdf.

31. Alper, Neal, et al. (1996). *Artists in the Workforce: Employment and Earnings, 1970, 1980, and 1990.* Washington, DC: Seven Locks Press. See

also National Endowment for the Arts (1976, April). *Employment and Unemployment of Artists 1970–1975, 1976. Research Division Report #1.* https://credo.library.umass.edu/view/full/mums686-b002-i028. National Endowment for the Arts. (1978, January). *Minorities and Women in the Arts: 1970. Research Division Report #7.* https://credo .library.umass.edu/cgi-bin/pdf.cgi?id=scua:mums686-b002-i030. Gender nonbinary was not tracked in the Alliance of American Museums or in the historical reports. Terminology for racial categories has also evolved and was changed where the terminology represented the category (e.g., Native American) and not where there might be definitional differences (e.g., Spanish instead of Latinx).

32. Creative Independent. (2018). *A Study on the Financial State of Visual Artists Today.* https://thecreativeindependent.com/artist-survey.

33. TBR Creative and Cultural Team. (2018, December 14). *Livelihoods of Visual Artists: 2016 Data Report.* London: Arts Council England. www .artscouncil.org.uk/sites/default/files/download-file/Livelihoods%20of %20Visual%20Artists%202016%20Data%20Report.pdf.

34. Wagley, Catherine. (2020, March 2). Museum Unions Aren't Just Demanding Higher Pay. They're Also Fundamentally Questioning the Way Their Institutions Work. *Artnet News.*

35. Wagley, Catherine. (2019, November 25). Museum Workers across the Country Are Unionizing. Here's What's Driving a Movement That's Been Years in the Making. *Artnet News.*

36. Luciano-Adams, Beige. (2020, January 31). The Art of Organizing. *The American Prospect.* https://prospect.org/labor/the-art-of-organizing.

37. Flanagan, Robert. J. (1990). The Economics of Unions and Collective Bargaining. *Industrial Relations: A Journal of Economy and Society,* 29(2): pp. 300–315.

38. Soskolne, Lise. (2015, February 22). On Merit. *The Artist as Debtor: The Work of Artists in the Age of Speculative Capitalism.* https://artanddebt .org/artist-as-debtor.

39. Soskolne, 2015.

40. Velthuis, 2011.

41. Author interview with Angie Kim, May 11, 2020.

42. Phillips, 2016. See also Queens Museum of Art. (2016). Mierle Laderman Ukeles: Maintenance Art, September 18, 2016–February 19, 2017 [exhibition brochure]. https://queensmuseum.org/wp-content/uploads/2016/12/Mierle %20Laderman%20Ukeles_Maintenance%20Art_Brochure.pdf.

43. Ukeles, Mierle Laderman. (1969). Manifesto! For Maintenance Art. Proposal for an Exhibition "Care." https://queensmuseum.org/wp-content/uploads/2016/04/Ukeles-Manifesto-for-Maintenance-Art-1969 .pdf. See also Phillips, 2016, p. 24.

44. Steinhauer, Jillian. (2017, February 10). How Mierle Laderman Ukeles Turned Maintenance Work into Art. *Hyperallergic.* https://hyperallergic .com/355255/how-mierle-laderman-ukeles-turned-maintenance-work-into-art.

45. Phillips, 2016, p. 60.

46. Steinhauer, 2017.

47. Lippard, Lucy. (2016). Never Done: Women's Work by Mierle Laderman Ukeles. In Patricia C. Phillips, ed., *Mierle Laderman Ukeles: Maintenance Art.* New York: Prestel; New York: Queens Museum, pp. 14–20, at p. 16. See also Ukeles, Mierle Laderman. (2019, May 15). Mierle Laderman Ukeles. In Paola Antonelli, curator, *MoMA R&D Salon #31: Workspheres.* http://momarnd.moma.org/salons/salon-31-workspheres-1.

48. Phillips, 2016, p. 25. Ukeles enacted other performances of maintenance, for example, *The Keeping of the Keys* (1973), in which she locked and unlocked museum gallery spaces, and *Washing / Tracks / Maintenance: Outside* (1973) in which she scrubbed the steps of the Wadsworth Atheneum in Hartford, Connecticut as part of her exhibition there. Phillips, 2016, p. 58 (keys) and p. 60 (washing).

49. Antonelli, Paola. (2019, May 15). Introduction. *MoMA R&D Salon #31: Workspheres.* http://momarnd.moma.org/salons/salon-31-work spheres-1.

50. Shah, Palak. (2019, May 15). Palak Shah. In Paola Antonelli, curator, *MoMA R&D Salon #31: Workspheres.* http://momarnd.moma.org/salons/ salon-31-workspheres-1. Shah is quoted both from her talk and from the Q&A period.

51. Shah, 2019.

52. Shah, 2019.

53. Thurow, Lester C. (1978). Psychic Income: Useful or Useless? *American Economic Review*, 68(2): 142–145.

54. Pink, Daniel H. (2009). *Drive: The Surprising Truth about What Motivates Us*. New York: Riverhead Books. See also the related animation: Pink, Daniel H. and RSA Animate. (2010). Drive: The Surprising Truth about What Motivates Us. www.youtube.com/watch?v=u6XAPnuFjJc.

55. Dweck, Carol. (2008). *Mindset: The New Psychology of Success.* New York: Ballantine Books.

56. Staple, Polly. (2016). Preface. In Chisenhale Gallery, *Maria Eichhorn: 5 Weeks, 25 Days, 175 Hours.* London: Chisenhale, pp. 3–7, at p. 4. https:// chisenhale.org.uk/wp-content/uploads/Maria-Eichhorn_5-weeks-25-days- 175-hours_Chisenhale-Gallery_2016.pdf.

57. Staple, 2016, p. 6.

58. Staple, 2016, p. 6.

59. Halperin, Julia. (2017, December 22). How the High Museum in Atlanta Tripled Its Nonwhite Audience in Two Years. *Artnet News.* https://news .artnet.com/art-world/high-museum-atlanta-tripled-nonwhite-audience- two-years-1187954.

60. Ukeles, 2019.

61. Ukeles, 2019.

62. Steinhauer, Jillian. (2015, August 12). Are You a Commuting Adjunct? There's a Magazine for You (Sort of). *Hyperallergic.* https://hyperallergic .com/229383/are-you-a-commuting-adjunct-theres-a-magazine-for-you- sort-of/.

8 PROPERTY

1. van Haaften-Schick, Lauren. (2018). Conceptualizing Artists' Rights: Circulations of the Siegelaub–Projansky Agreement through Art and Law. *Oxford Handbooks Online.* https://doi.org/10.1093/oxfordhb/ 9780199935352.013.27, p. 2.

2. Tate. (n.d.1). Biography: Panayiotis Vassilakis. www.tate.org.uk/art/art ists/takis-2019. See also van Haaften-Schick, 2018, p. 10.

3. Kamps, Toby. (2015). *Takis: The Fourth Dimension,* January 24–July 26, 2015. [exhibition]. The Menil Collection, Houston, TX. www.menil.org /exhibitions/37-takis-the-fourth-dimension. The "instinctive scientist" quotation comes from the exhibition overview, confirmed in author correspondence with Toby Kamps, November 25, 2019.

4. Tate. (n.d.2). Wall label for *Magnetic Fields,* 1969. See also Tate. (n.d.4). Takis: 3 July–27 October 2019 [Large Print Guide], p. 5. www.tate.org.uk /whats-on/tate-modern/exhibition/takis/exhibition-guide.

5. Basciano, Oliver. (2019, August 16). Takis Obituary. *The Guardian.* www.theguardian.com/artanddesign/2019/aug/16/takis-obituary.

6. Author correspondence with Toby Kamps, November 25, 2019. MoMA listing for the artwork: Museum of Modern Art. (1962). Takis: Tele-Sculpture, Paris 1960 (Cork Added 1962). www.moma.org/collection/works/81217.

7. Hultén, K. G. Pontus. (1968). *The Machine, As Seen at the End of the Mechanical Age*. New York: Museum of Modern Art. (Out of print and available via the MoMA website: https://assets.moma.org/documents/moma_catalogue_2776_300292931.pdf?_ga=2.45998050.793891684 .1593464817-528654.1593362002.)

8. Lippard, Lucy. (1970, November). The Art Workers' Coalition: Not a History. *Studio International*. http://artsandlabor.org/wp-content/uploads/2011/12/Lippard_AWC.pdf.

9. Ault, Julie. (2002). *Alternative Art New York, 1965–1985*. New York: The Drawing Center; Minneapolis: University of Minnesota Press. See also Art Workers' Coalition (1969). *Artworkers Coalition: Documents*. Primary Information. www.primaryinformation.org/art-workers-coalition.

10. Regarding data sovereignty, see Hudson, Māui, Farrar, Dickie and McLean, Lesley. (2016). Tribal Data Sovereignty: Whakatōhea Rights and Interests. In Tahu Kukutai and John Taylor, eds., *Indigenous Data Sovereignty: Toward an Agenda*. Canberra: Australian National University Press, pp. 157–178. Regarding authorship, see Anderson, Jane and Christen, Kim. (2013). Chuck a Copyright on It: Dilemmas of Digital Return and the Possibilities for Traditional Knowledge Licenses and Labels. *Museum Anthropology Review*, 7 (1–2): 105–126. Anderson, Jane and Christen, Kim. (2019). Decolonizing Attribution: Traditions of Exclusion. *Journal of Radical Librarianship*, 5: 113–152.

11. The "unusual form of property" quotation comes from van Haaften-Schick, 2018, p. 3. And from Colonna, Carl M. and Colonna, Carol G. (1982). An Economic and Legal Assessment of Recent Visual Artists' Reversion Rights Agreements in the United States. *Journal of Cultural Economics*, 6(2): 77–85, at p. 77. See also Alexander, Gregory. S. (2017). Objects of Art; Objects of Property. *Cornell Journal of Law and Public Policy*, 26(3): 461–468, at p. 466. Nickson, Jr., Jack W. and Colonna, Carl M. (1977). The Economic Exploitation of the Visual Artist. *Journal of Cultural Economics*, 1(1): 75–79.

12. Honoré, Tony. (1987). *Making Law Bind: Essays Legal and Philosophical*. Oxford: Oxford University Press.

13. Siegelaub, Seth and Projansky, Robert (1971). *The Artist's Reserved Rights Transfer and Sale Agreement*. New York: School of Visual Arts. https://primaryinformation.org/product/siegelaub-the-artists-reserved-rights-transfer-and-sale-agreement.

14. van Haaften-Schick, 2018, p. 2. The formal title is The Artist's Reserved Rights Transfer and Sale Agreement (ARRTSA). Some call it the Siegelaub–Projansky Agreement. Lawyers tend to call it the Projansky Agreement, foregrounding the lawyer. I have chosen the Artist's Contract both to foreground the role of artists and because it is simplest and most fundamental. A contract originating with an artist as opposed to an organization is also novel and somewhat revolutionary in and of itself. For a history of artists' uses of the contract, see Eichhorn, Maria. (2009). *The Artist's Contract*, edited by Gerti Fietzek. Cologne, Germany: Verlag der Buchhandlung Walther König.

15. Author interview with Lauren van Haaften-Schick, May 3, 2020.

16. Eichhorn, Maria. (2009). Interview with Adrian Piper. In Gerti Fietzek, ed., *The Artist's Contract*. Cologne, Germany: Walther König, pp. 193–215, at p. 196.

17. van Haaften-Schick, 2018, p. 9.

18. Shipley, David. E. (2017). Droit de Suite, Copyright's First Sale Doctrine and Preemption of State Law. *Hastings Communications and Entertainment Law Journal*, 39(1): 1–42.

19. US Constitution. Article I, § 8, cl. 8.

20. Although patents are outside the scope of this book, one very interesting and influential study of patents sheds light on the ways in which structural discrimination and race-based violence hampers innovation. In studying historical data on patent filings in the United States, the economist Lisa D. Cook found that patent applications from Black Americans decreased 15% per year from 1882 to 1940, especially tracking episodes of racial violence. See Cook, Lisa. (2014). Violence and Economic Activity: Evidence from African American Patents, 1870–1940. *Journal of Economic Growth*, 19(2): 221–257, especially at pp. 222–225.

21. For works made for hire, see US Copyright Office. (2012). Works Made for Hire, Circular 9. www.copyright.gov/circs/circ09.pdf. The details of US copyright law are complex and subject to legislative change or substantial

judicial reinterpretation. For further detail see, for instance, Stim, Richard.
(2016). Copyright Basics FAQ, Stanford University Libraries. https://fair
use.stanford.edu/overview/faqs/copyright-basics/. This overview is
adapted from the book: Stim, Richard. (2019). *Getting Permission: How to
License and Clear Copyrighted Materials Online and Off*, 7th ed.
Berkeley, CA: Nolo. The US government also offers copyright resources,
e.g., US Copyright Office. (2011). Duration of Copyright, Circular 15a.
www.copyright.gov/circs/circ15a.pdf. In 2015, the College Art
Association published a guide to fair use in the arts: College Art
Association. (2015). *Code of Best Practices in Fair Use for the Visual Arts.*
www.collegeart.org/pdf/fair-use/best-practices-fair-use-visual-arts.pdf.

22. 17 U.S.C. § 107 (1992).
23. Leval, Pierre N. (1990). Toward a Fair Use Standard. *Harvard Law
    Review*, 103(5): pp. 1105–1136, at p. 1110.
24. Leval, 1990, p. 1111.
25. Leval, 1990, p. 1111.
26. Leval, 1990, pp. 1120–1121.
27. Leval, 1990, p. 1122.
28. Leval. 1990, p. 1123. Note also the inclusion of "potential" so as to
    consider not the already demonstrated market but the "market
    potential."
29. Leval, 1990, p. 1124.
30. Leval, 1990, p. 1125.
31. Leval, 1990, p. 1126.
32. Adler, Amy. (2016). Fair Use and the Future of Art. *NYU Law Review*, 91
    (3): 559–626.
33. Gilbert, Laura. (2018, October 10). Richard Prince Defends Reuse of
    Others' Photographs. *The Art Newspaper.* www.theartnewspaper.com/
    news/richard-prince-defends-re-use-of-others-photographs. I have served
    as an expert, *pro bono,* on the Eric McNatt and Donald Graham side of
    the case.
34. Munro, Cait. (2015, May 27). Who Are the Suicide Girls? Inside the Nude
    Pin-Up Community That Trolled Richard Prince. *Artnet News.* www
    .news.artnet.com/art-world/suicide-girls-inside-pin-community-
    challenged-richard-prince-302760.
35. Deedham, Alex. (2015, May 27). Richard Prince v. Suicide Girls in an
    Instagram Price War. *The Guardian.* www.theguardian.com/artandde
    sign/2015/may/27/suicide-girls-richard-prince-copying-instagram.

36. Deedham, 2015.
37. Davis, Ben. (2015, August 13). Art Flippers Attempt to Unload Suicide Girls' Version of Richard Prince Artwork. *Artnet News*. www.news.art net.com/market/art-flippers-suicide-girls-richard-prince-prints-324580.
38. Davis, 2015.
39. Davis, 2015. For a discussion of the ways in which the fair-use factors place judges in the position of making aesthetic determinations, see Sarmiento, Sergio Muñoz and van Haaften-Schick, Lauren. (2014). *Cariou v. Prince*: Toward a Theory of Aesthetic-Judicial Judgments. *Texas A&M Law Review*, 1(4): 941–958.
40. Brandenburger, Adam M. and Nalebuff, Barry J. (1997). The Added-Value Theory of Business. *Strategy + Business*. www.strategy-business.com/article/12669?gko=5c72a.
41. Fisher, William W. III, Cost, Frank, Fairey, Shepard, Feder, Meir, Fountain, Edwin, Stewart, Geoffrey and Sturken, Marita. (2012). Reflections on the Hope Poster Case. *Harvard Journal of Law and Technology*, 25(2): 244–338. See also Whitaker, Amy. (2019a). Shared Value over Fair Use: Technology, Added Value, and the Reinvention of Copyright. *Cardozo Arts and Entertainment Law Journal*, 37(3): 635–657.
42. Fisher et al., 2012, p. 247.
43. For a description of Fairey's artistic process, see Fisher et al., 2012, pp. 249–252.
44. Fisher et al., 2012, p. 254. See also Hillel Italie and Associated Press. (2009, February 4). AP Alleges Copyright Infringement of Obama Image. *San Diego Union Tribune*. www.sandiegouniontribune.com/sdut-obama-poster-020409-2009feb04-story.html.
45. Fisher et al., 2012, p. 269.
46. I have made this argument for emphasizing the "value" part of the market test and developing economic complements to copyright in Whitaker, 2019a. For some of the pioneering work on technological complements to copyright, see Zittrain, Jonathan L. (2005). *Technological Complements to Copyright*. St. Paul, MN: Foundation Press.
47. At the same time, academic organizations have been advocating for broader understanding of fair use. The College Art Association, a US trade body of academic artists and art historians, has published a guide to

fair use that has had the effect of normalizing the use of images in scholarship. And museums and other organizations have increasingly placed images in the public domain, or under open access licenses, as part of initiatives in the digital humanities. These developments are intertwined with technology itself, whether command-and-control systems of digital rights management, decentralized registries using blockchain, or evolving regulatory structures, such as the DACS rights collections agency in the United Kingdom, which successfully distributes copyright and resale royalty payments at a scale rivaling public-sector support for individual artists. See College Art Association, 2015.

48 Pettit, Clare. (2007). A Dark Exhibition: The Crystal Palace, Bleak House, and Intellectual Property. In Jim Buzard, Joseph Childers, and Eileen Gillooly, eds., *Victorian Prism: Refractions of the Crystal Palace.* Charlottesville: University of Virginia, pp. 250–269, at p. 215.

49. US Copyright Office. (2021). International Copyright Relations of the US Copyright Office, Circular 38A (revised February 2021). www .copyright.gov/circs/circ38a.pdf.

50. World Intellectual Property Organization (n.d.1). What Is WIPO? www .wipo.int/about-wipo/en. See also World Intellectual Property Organization. (1967, July 14). Convention Establishing the World Intellectual Property Organization. www.wipo.int/treaties/en/text.jsp? file_id=283854.

51. World Intellectual Property Organization. (n.d.2). Summary of the Berne Convention for the Protection of Literary and Artistic Works (1886). www.wipo.int/treaties/en/ip/berne/summary_berne.html. The Berne Convention was revised in 1896 (Paris), 1908 (Berlin), 1914 (Berne), 1928 (Rome), 1948 (Brussels), 1967 (Stockholm), 1971 (Paris), and 1979 (Paris).

52. World Intellectual Property Organization, n.d.2.

53. US Copyright Office, 2021, p. 2.

54. US Copyright Office, 2021, p. 1.

55. 17. US Code § 106 (a).

56. van Haaften-Schick, 2018, p. 52 (note 81).

57. Smith, Roberta. (2007, September 16). Is It Art Yet? And Who Decides? *New York Times.* www.nytimes.com/2007/09/16/arts/design/16robe.html.

58. Smith, 2007; author site visit. See also Buskirk, Martha. (2012). *Creative Enterprise: Contemporary Art between Museum and Marketplace.* London: Bloomsbury, p. 192.

59. Smith, 2007.

60. Smith, 2007.

61. According to Mass MoCA's 2005 Form 990 annual tax filing, the museum took in $9.329 million in 2005 and spent $6.433 million on expenses. In 2006, Mass MoCA took in $13.602 million in revenue and spent $6.8 million. The museum's fiscal year goes through August, placing the Büchel exhibition largely on the 2006 Form 990, though splitting Büchel's planning expenses over multiple years. Massachusetts Museum of Contemporary Art Foundation, Inc. (Mass MoCA). (2005). Form 990 Return of Organization Exempt from Income Tax, 2005. Mass MoCA. (2006). Form 990 Return of Organization Exempt from Income Tax, 2006. Both accessed from Propublica, https://projects.propublica.org/nonprofits/organizations/43113688.

62. Mass MoCA, 2006, Statement 6, p. 46.

63. Kennedy, Randy. (2010, January 28). Artists Rights Act Applies in Dispute, Court Rules. *New York Times.* www.nytimes.com/2010/01/29/arts/design/29artist.html. See also Massachusetts Museum of Contemporary Art Foundation v. Büchel, No. 08-2199 (1st Cir. Jan. 27, 2010). VARA is considered the closest protection that the United States has for moral rights. Moral rights, as originate in France, are inalienable from the person and derive from an idea that the innate dignity of artists' work is an extension of themselves. A technicality of the case had been whether VARA applies only to finished works or not. Mass MoCA had argued their right to show the work because it was unfinished, and the court disagreed. The panel of three judges concluded, "Moral rights protect the personality and creative energy that an artist contributes to his or her work . . .. That convergence between artist and artwork does not await the final brushstroke or the placement of the last element in a complex installation." Dowd, Ray. (2010, January 30). Visual Artists Rights Act: Artist moral rights in unfinished sculptural works. *Copyright Litigation Blog.* https://copyrightlitigation.blogspot.com/2010/01/visual-artists-rights-act-artist-moral.html. See also Rosenbaum, Debbie and Del Riego, Alissa (Eds.). (2010, February 2). Massachusetts Museum of Contemporary Art v. Büchel: First Circuit Holds That Artists Have Moral Rights in Unfinished Works. *JOLT (Harvard Journal of Law & Technology) Digest.* http://jolt.law.harvard.edu/digest/massachusetts-museum-of-contemporary-art-foundation-v-buchel.

64. Velthuis, 2011.

65. Noh, Megan E. (2020). US Law's Artificial Cabining of Moral Rights: The Copyrightability Prerequisite and Cady Noland's Log Cabin. *Columbia Journal of Law and the Arts*, 43(3): 353–365.

66. Halperin, Julia and Kinsella, Eileen. (2017, July 21). Cady Noland Sues Three Galleries for Copyright Infringement over Disavowed Log Cabin Structure. *Artnet News.* https://news.artnet.com/art-world/cady-noland-copyright-infringement-log-cabin-1030649. Cascone, Sarah. (2019, July 15). Artist Cady Noland Refuses to Give Up Her Legal Fight over the Restoration of Her Disavowed Log Cabin Structure. *Artnet News.* https://news.artnet.com/art-world/cady-noland-log-cabin-lawsuit-refiled-1594249.

67. Kinsella, Eileen. (2015, June 25). Cady Noland Disowns $1.4 Million "Log Cabin" Artwork Sparking Collector Lawsuit. *Artnet News.* https://news.artnet.com/market/cady-noland-log-cabin-lawsuit-311283. The work is called "Log Cabin," sometimes with the word "Façade" (legal documents) and sometimes (Kinsella) *Log Cabin Blank With Screw Eyes and Cafe Door.*

68. Zaretsky, Donn. (2019, July 5). Cady Noland's Lawsuit Was Dismissed in March. *The Art Law Blog.* http://theartlawblog.blogspot.com/2019/07/cady-nolands-lawsuit-was-dismised-in.html. See also Cady Noland v. Galerie Michael Janssen et al. United States District Court Southern District New York (No. 17-CV-5452 (JPO)). In 2012, Noland disavowed a work *Cowboys Milking*, requiring Sotheby's to pull the artwork from a scheduled sale. See Adler, Amy. (2016, March 4). *Cowboys Milking*: Formerly Attributed to Cady Noland. *Brooklyn Rail.* www.brooklynrail.org/2016/03/criticspage/cowboys-milking-formerlyattributed-to-cady-noland.

69. Noh, 2020.

70. US Copyright Office. (2013). *Resale Royalties: An Updated Analysis*, pp. 4–6. www.copyright.gov/docs/resaleroyalty/usco-resaleroyalty.pdf. See also Frye, Brian. (2017). Equitable Resale Royalties. *Journal of Intellectual Property Law*, 24(2): 237–276.

71. Marber, Sinclaire D. (2019). Will the Art Market Really Soar? Revisiting Resale Rights after BREXIT. *Art, Antiquity and Law*, 24(2): 137–150, at p. 145. See also DACS. (2016). *Ten Years of the Artist's Resale Right: Giving Artists Their Fair Share.* www.dacs.org.uk/DACSO/media/DAC

SDocs/reports-and-submissions/Ten-Years-of-the-Artist-s-Resale-Right-Giving-artists-their-fair-share-DACS-Feb-16.pdf. Bradley, Christopher G. and Frye, Brian L. (2018–19). Art in the Age of Contractual Negotiation *Kentucky Law Journal*, 107(4): 547–592.

72. Marber, 2019, pp. 143–145. See also DACS (2019). *Annual Review 2018*, p. 11. www.dacs.org.uk/DACSO/media/DACSDocs/DACS-Annual-Review-2018.pdf.

73. A cost basis is the amount one paid to purchase an asset. Without a cost basis, the royalty is charged on the entire purchase price, not the increase over the cost basis. See Whitaker, Amy. (2018). Artist As Owner Not Guarantor: The Art Market from the Artist's Point of View. *Visual Resources*, 34(1–2): 48–64, at p. 53.

74. In contrast, in the Siegelaub–Projansky Artist's Contract that resulted from the Art Workers' Coalition work mentioned at the start of the chapter, the 15% is charged on the "accrued value," meaning the amount above the cost basis. Thus, private contracts like the Siegelaub–Projansky Agreement can be used to enact resale royalties in the United States. See van Haaften-Schick, 2018; Bradley and Frye, 2018–19.

75. US Copyright Office, 2013, p. 1.

76. Rub, Guy A. (2014). The Unconvincing Case for Resale Royalties. *Yale Law Journal Forum*. www.yalelawjournal.org/forum/the-unconvincing-case-for-resale-royalties.

77. Sprigman, Chris and Rub, Guy A. (2018, August 8). Resale Royalties Would Hurt Emerging Artists. *Artsy*. www.artsy.net/article/artsy-editorial-resale-royalties-hurt-emerging-artists.

78. Banternghansa, Chanont and Graddy, Kathryn. (2011). The Impact of the "Droit de Suite" in the UK: An Empirical Analysis. *Journal of Cultural Economics*, 35(2): pp. 81–100.

79. Petty, M. Elizabeth. (2014). Rauschenberg, Royalties, and Artists' Rights: Potential Droit de Suite Legislation in the United States. *William and Mary Bill of Rights Journal*, 22(3): 977–1009. Shipley, David. E. (2017). Droit de Suite, Copyright's First Sale Doctrine and Preemption of State Law. *Hastings Communications and Entertainment Law Journal*, 39(1): 1–42. See also Prowda, Judith B. (2013). *Visual Arts and the Law: A Handbook for Professionals*. London: Lund Humphries. Colonna and Colonna, 1982, p. 84. The Sculls would have also paid "carrying costs," that is, the continual maintenance costs of caring for, insuring, and

storing the art. We will cover these costs as part of art investment in the next chapter. For an overview of costs of collections management, see Rozell, Mary. (2020). *The Art Collector's Handbook: A Guide to Collection Management and Care*, 2nd ed. London: Lund Humphries.

80. Petty, 2014, pp. 977–978.

81. Glueck, Grace. (1989, May 10). Castelli Donates Major Work to the Modern. *New York Times.* www.nytimes.com/1989/05/10/arts/castelli-gives-major-work-to-the-modern.html. See also Cohen-Solal, Annie. (2010). *Leo and His Circle: The Life of Leo Castelli.* New York: Knopf.

82. The artist William Powhida recently constructed a contract to allow friends to store-to-own his art as a decision to manage his storage costs and studio space. Dafoe, Taylor. (2020, February 28). Artist William Powhida Doesn't Have Room to Store All His Work – So He Wants You to Borrow It, for Free. *Artnet News.* https://news.artnet.com/market/william-powhida-store-to-own-1790187. See also Whitaker, Amy and Kräussl, Roman. (2020). Fractional Equity, Blockchain, and the Future of Creative Work. *Management Science*, 66(10): 4594–4611.

83. That number exceeded the entire projects grants budget category for visual art, as administered by the Arts Council England. Whitaker, Amy and Grannemann, Hannah. (2019). Artists' Royalties and Performers' Equity: A Ground-Up Approach to Social Impact Investment in Creative Fields. *Cultural Management*, 3(2): 33–51. See also DACS, 2019; DACS, 2016.

84. Coase, Ronald H. (1960). The Problem of Social Cost. *Journal of Law and Economics*, 3(October): 1–44. The paper was popularized by George Stigler, Coase's colleague at the University of Chicago. See Stigler, George J. (1989). Two Notes on the Coase Theorem. *Yale Law Journal*, 99(3): 631–633.

85. Whitaker, 2018, pp. 55–56.

86. Many different forms of contract could be designed so that the right carried on in perpetuity or dissolved at a specified point of sale, e.g., first auction. See Hansmann, Henry and Kraakman, Reinier. (2002). Property, Contract, and Verification: The Numerus Clausus Problem and the Divisibility of Rights. *Journal of Legal Studies*, 31(S2): 373–420.

87. Whitaker and Kräussl, 2020. See also Whitaker, Amy. (2014). Ownership for Artists. In Pablo Helguera, Michael Mandiberg, William Powhida, Amy Whitaker, and Caroline Woolard, eds., *The Social Life of Artistic Property*. Hudson: Publication Studio, pp. 70–84.

88. Merryman, John Henry. (1985). Thinking about the Elgin Marbles. *Michigan Law Review*, 83(8): 1880–1923. http://blogs.bu.edu/aberlin/files/ 2011/09/Merryman-1985.pdf. For a classical economic treatment of property see Mill, John Stuart. (2005 [1871]). *The Principles of Political Economy*, 7th ed., edited by Jonathan Riley. Oxford, UK: Oxford University Press, pp. 7–10.

89. Sarr, Felwine and Savoy, Bénédicte. (2018). *The Restitution of African Cultural Heritage: Toward a New Relational Ethics* (trans. Drue S. Burk). www.about-africa.de/images/sonstiges/2018/sarr_savoy_en.pdf.

90. Whitaker, Amy, Bracegirdle, Anne, De Menil, Susan, Gitlitz, Michelle Ann and Saltos, Lena (2020). Art, Antiquities, and Blockchain: New Approaches to the Restitution of Cultural Heritage. *International Journal of Cultural Policy*. DOI: 10.1080/10286632.2020.1765163.

91. Regarding data sovereignty, see Hudson, Farrar and McLean, 2016; Anderson and Christen, 2013; Anderson and Christen, 2019.

92. Anderson and Christen, 2013; Anderson and Christen, 2019.

93. Lippard, 1970, p. 15.

94. As noted by Steve Schindler, having museum workers take political positions would complicate their nonprofit status and their board members's fiduciary duties. Most museums are 501(c)3 charities, which are not allowed to engage in lobbying activities. Author correspondence with Steve Schindler, May 23, 2020.

95. Lippard, 1970, pp. 12–13.

96. Buchloh, Benhamin H. D. (1990). Conceptual Art 1962–1969: From the Aesthetic of Administration to the Critique of Institutions. *October*, 55 (Winter): 105–43.

97. Alberro, Alexander. (2003). *Conceptual Art and the Politics of Publicity*. Cambridge, MA: MIT Press.

98. van Haaften-Schick, 2018, p. 7.

99. You may also wish to consult Kee, 2019; van Haaften-Schick, 2018; Bradley and Frye (2018–19).

100. See, e.g., College Art Association, 2015; Adler, 2016; Whitaker, 2019a.

101. Brankov, Amelia. (2020, March 27). 5Pointz Developer Aiming for Supreme Court Review of $6.75 Million Damages Award. *IP & Media Law Updates*. Frankfurt Kurnit Klein + Selz. https://ipandmedialaw .fkks.com/post/102g2z9/5pointz-developer-aiming-for-supreme-court- review-of-6-75-million-damages-award.

102. Durkee, Musetta. (2019, March 21). International Perspectives on Street Art. *Center for Art Law Blog.* https://itsartlaw.org/2019/03/21/wywh-international-perspectives-on-street-art. And author conversation with Meres One, February 6, 2019, at the "International Perspectives on Street Art" panel, Fordham Law School, New York.

103. Price, Sally. (2020, January 6). Has the Sarr–Savoy Report Had Any Effect Since It Was First Published? *Apollo Magazine.* www.apollo-magazine .com/sarr-savoy-report-sally-price-dan-hicks. See also Sarr and Savoy, 2018.

104. Anderson and Christen, 2013. See also Whitaker et al., 2020.

105. Whitaker, Amy (2019d). Art and Blockchain: A Primer, History, and Taxonomy of Blockchain Use Cases in the Arts. *Artivate: A Journal of Entrepreneurship in the Arts*, 8(2): 21–46. See also Bailey, Jason. (2018, July 21). Art World, Meet Blockchain. *Artnome.* www.artnome.com/news/ 2018/7/21/artworld-meet-blockchain. Brekke, Jaya Klara. (2019). The White Paper Guide. In Jaya Klara Brekke and Ben Vickers, eds., *The White Paper by Satoshi Nakamoto.* London: Ignota, pp. 19–63. Catlow, Ruth, Garrett, Marc, Jones, Nathan and Skinner, Sam (Eds.). (2017). *Artists Re: Thinking the Blockchain.* Liverpool, UK: Torque Editions, Furtherfield and Liverpool University Press. Alt, Casey, Moss-Pultz, Sean, Whitaker, Amy, and Chen, Timothy. (2016). Defining Property in the Digital Environment. *DCG Insights Report.* https://insights.dcg.co/defining-property-in-the-digital-environment-4ec3b9b79403.

106. For 1–54, see e.g., Wrathall, Claire. (2018, July 12). Touria El Glaoui: Putting Contemporary African Art on the Map. *Christie's Inc.* www .christies.com/features/Touria-El-Glaoui-on-Africas-new-wave-9311-1 .aspx. For TEFAF vetting see, for example: TEFAF. (n.d.). Stringent and Transparent Vetting Standards and Procedures. www.tefaf.com/about/ vetting. For Artory and the Ebsworth sale see, e.g., Neuendorf, Henri. (2018, October 12). Christie's Will Become the First Major Auction House to Use Blockchain in a Sale. *Artnet News.* https://news .artnet.com/market/christies-artory-blockchain-pilot-1370788.

9 INVESTMENT

1. Salmon, Felix. (2019, November 5). What Is Art Really Worth?, with Julia Halperin. *Slate Money*, at 3:20. https://slate.com/podcasts/slate-money/ 2019/11/julia-halperin-artnet-art-good-investment.

2. Kramarsky's character as a person was in evidence well before his reputation as a collector of art. After an early career in banking, Kramarsky served from 1975 until 1982 as the commissioner of the New York State Division of Human Rights. During that time Kramarsky helped a wide array of people. On his watch, the New York City Marathon was required to allow wheelchair competitors, the state prison system could no longer discriminate against guards on the basis of their height, job seekers could no longer be excluded merely on the basis of obesity, and tennis clubs could no longer discount memberships for married couples to the disadvantage of the single. Roberts, Sam. (2019, August 25). Werner Kramarsky, Rights Official and Arts Patron, Dies at 93. *New York Times*. www.nytimes.com/2019/08/23/nyregion/werner-kramarsky-dies.html. One indication of Kramarsky's personal generosity is that the first two folders of his correspondence files in his papers, which are held at the Museum of Modern Art, are called "Requests and Favors" (1989–2005 and 1986–8). Werner H. Kramarsky Papers, [VII.1–2]. Museum of Modern Art Archives, New York. www.moma.org/research-and-learning/archives/finding-aids/Kramarskyb.html.

3. Russeth, Andrew. (2019, August 23). Wynn Kramarsky, Venturesome Drawings Collector and Arts Patron, Is Dead at 93. *ARTnews*. www.artnews.com/art-news/news/wynn-kramarsky-dead-13143.

4. Corbett, William. (2008, June). Wynn Kramarsky in Conversation with William Corbett. *Brooklyn Rail*. https://brooklynrail.org/2008/06/art/wynn-kramarsky-with-william-corbett. Wynn on his training in art and in general: "I was a multiple dropout, long before that was fashionable, and that's what he wants to hear. I dropped out of elementary school because I ran away from home. I dropped out of high school because I wanted to work. I dropped out of college because I wanted to do some other work, and currently, I'm a law school dropout." Corbett, 2008.

5. Russeth, 2019. That year, 1959, was when Leo Castelli hosted Jasper Johns's breakout first exhibition, from which the Museum of Modern Art famously bought three works directly. The notebook of Castelli's sales does not immediately show the Kramarsky work but does show those works sold to the Museum of Modern Art ("MAM" or presumably *museo di arte moderna* in Castelli's native Italian). Leo Castelli Gallery records, circa 1880–2000, bulk 1957–99. Archives of American Art, Smithsonian Institution.

6. Kramarsky: "I've done a lot of crazy things in my life. I worked in a machine shop for a while and learned about forging metal, which has put me on good terms with the artists I've known, because I've been able to help them with stuff that *they* didn't know. I worked in the securities business for many, many years – hated all of it – and then I ended up, for my sins, in politics and government." Corbett, 2008.

7. Corbett, 2008; Russeth, 2019. The works given to MoMA represented seventy artists, twenty-four of whom were entering the MoMA collection for the first time (Russeth, 2019).

8. Watson, 1992, p. 5. Siegfried Kramarsky bought *Portrait of Dr. Gachet* from Städtische Galerie in Frankfurt in the 1930s. The family arrived in Canada in 1940 and into the United States in 1942. Wynn Kramarsky's father was a currency trader and his mother a schoolteacher (Watson, 1992, p. 5).

9. Watson, 1992, p. 3.

10. The work in the Musée d'Orsay is referred to as "Le Docteur Paul Gachet [Dr. Paul Gachet]." Musée d'Orsay. (n.d.). Vincent Van Gogh: Dr. Paul Gachet. *Musee-Orsay.fr*. www.musee-orsay.fr/en/collections/works-in-focus/search/commentaire/commentaire_id/dr-paul-gachet-2988.html.

11. The auction could only take place after a years-long legal process given that Kramarsky's mother's signature was required but she was then in an invalid state (Watson, 1992, pp. 5–7). The original sale date for *Portrait of Dr. Gachet* had been May 10, 1990, which was the fiftieth anniversary of the May 10, 1040, Nazi invasion of the Netherlands. The sale had been moved at the Kramarsky family's request and took place on May 15, 1990 (Watson, 1992, p. 7). For more information see, e.g., Rijksmuseum. (n.d.). Timeline of Dutch History: 1940 Invasion. www.rijksmuseum.nl/en/rijksstudio/timeline-dutch-history/1940-invasion.

12. Watson, 1992, pp. 3 and 9. The reserve price, meaning the lowest price at which the consignor agrees to sell, was higher than usual. Typically, the reserve is close to 75% of the low estimate. In this case the reserve – only agreed by the family the day of the sale – was $35 million or 87.5% of the low estimate (Watson, 1992, p. 18).

13. In 1990, the prevailing auction record for a work by van Gogh was the 1987 sale of *Irises*, which had sold for $52.9 million at Sotheby's (Watson, 1992, pp. 3–4). The outcome of the Kramarsky auction seemed uncertain at the time. On the one hand, markets for Impressionist and post-Impressionist

works had been buoyant in the 1980s. According to Peter Watson's definitive and sweeping history of the art market, *From Manet to Manhattan*, the prices for Impressionist works had risen 940% over the decade beginning in 1980. Yet while the art market had been ascendant, the 1987 stock market crash still felt fresh. In the lead-up to the *Dr. Gachet* sale, even in the days just before, other auction sales had wobbled (Watson, 1992, p. 4). Kramarsky had in some ways anticipated this market risk. Perhaps owing to the delay in the sale caused by the legal process, Kramarsky negotiated a highly unusual contractual term with Christie's: The contract included a formula that essentially removed the painting from the sale automatically if any two-out-of-three combination of stock indices in London, New York, and Tokyo fell by more than 25% in the days leading to the sale. Although there was no seller's commission on the sale, Kramarsky insisted on paying the auction house a commission of 3%. The Kramarskys were Sunday-supper friends with the family of Stephen Lash, the executive vice president handling the sale (Watson, 1992, p. 8).

14. In a sale at that level, the likely bidders would have not only been known to the auction house but would have been actively courted. Watson relays the detailed politics of gift-giving and auction-room seat-getting. Kobayashi had simply registered for a bidding paddle without fanfare by normal processes (Watson, 1992, pp. 24–25).

15. Watson, 1992, p. 75.

16. Ashenfelter, Orley and Graddy, Kathryn. (2003). Auctions and the Price of Art. *Journal of Economic Literature*, 41(3): 763–786. Ashenfelter, Orley and Graddy, Kathryn. (2011). Sale Rates and Price Movements in Art Auctions. *American Economic Review*, 101(3): 212–216. Beggs and Graddy have shown that auction prices and auction-house estimates are anchored to prior auction prices. See Beggs, Alan and Graddy, Kathryn. (2009). Anchoring Effects: Evidence from Art Auctions. *American Economic Review*, 99(3): 1027–1039. Beckmann has studied the noisy auction-room signal of sellers who bid on their own items. See Beckmann, Michael. (2004). Why Do Sellers at Auctions Bid for Their Own Items? Theory and Evidence. *Schmalenbach Business Review*, 56(4): 312–337.

17. On some occasions the artist has a commission or the artist's gallery helps to front the cost of a work. Historically, some dealers, exemplified by Leo

Castelli, paid artists monthly stipends. Whitaker, Amy. (2019b). Economic Provenance: The Financial Analysis of Art Historical Records. *Journal of Contemporary Archival Studies*, 6(27): 1–17. https://elischolar .library.yale.edu/jcas/vol6/iss1/27.

18. Baumol is also the co-author, with William Bowen, of the influential 1968 book on performing-arts management in which they coined the term "cost disease" to describe the difficulty of performing-arts organizations that they cannot access economies of scale and never become cheaper to produce over time. Kreuger, Alan B. (2001). An Interview with William J. Baumol. *Journal Economic Perspectives*, 15(3): 211–231. Baumol, William J. and Bowen, William G. (1968). *Performing Arts: The Economic Dilemma*. Cambridge, MA: MIT Press.

19. The full title is *The Economics of Taste: The Rise and Fall of the Picture Market, 1760–1960*. Reitlinger, Gerald. (1961–70). *The Economics of Taste*. 3 vols. London: Barrie and Rockliffe.

20. The nominal rate of return on bonds was 3.25%, which, adjusted for a 0.7% rate of inflation, gave the bonds in Baumol's study a 2.5% real rate of return. Later scholars have revisited Baumol's work directly. Renneboog and Spaenjers found similar returns for art and corporate bonds but with much higher risk or volatility for art. Buelens and Ginsburgh found slightly more optimistic returns for art. See Renneboog, Luc and Spaenjers, Christophe. (2013). Buying Beauty: On Prices and Returns in the Art Market. *Management Science*, 59: 36–53. Buelens, Nathalie and Ginsburgh, Victor A. (1993). Revisiting Baumol's "Art As Floating Crap Game." *European Economic Review*, 37(7): 1351–1371.

21. This theory of efficient markets dates to the nineteenth century and an 1863 work by Jules Regnault, according to William Goetzmann, author of several studies on historical returns to art investment, some covered later in this chapter. More contemporary studies typically cite works on the Efficient Market Hypothesis (EMH) by scholars such as Eugene Fama. See Regnault, Jules. (1863). *Calcul des chances et philosophie de la bourse*. Paris: Mallet-Bachelier et Castel. Fama, Eugene. (1965). The Behavior of Stock Market Prices. *Journal of Business*, 38(1): 34–105.

22. For example, Roger Ibbotson and William Goetzmann have estimated long-term returns to the stock market and the equity risk premium, meaning the outsize return to equities over what we will explore as the risk-free rate. See, e.g., Ibbotson, Roger G. and Sinquefield, Rex A. (1989).

Stocks, Bonds, Bills, and Inflation: Historical Returns. New York: Richard D. Irwin. Ibbotson, Roger G. and Goetzmann, William N. (2005). History and the Equity Risk Premium. *Yale ICF Working Paper No. 05–04.* https://ssrn.com/abstract=702341. Goetzmann, William N. and Ibbotson, Roger G. (1994). Do Winners Repeat? *Journal of Portfolio Management,* 20(2) 9–18. The firm Ibbotson Associates was well known for tracking historic returns to stocks, bonds, and US Treasuries. Ibbotson founded the firm in 1977 when he was a professor at the University of Chicago. The firm was acquired by Morningstar in 2006. Morningstar. (2015, July 2). Morningstar Acquires Remaining Ownership Interest in Ibbotson Associates Japan Inc. https://newsroom.morningstar.com/news room/news-archive/press-release-details/2015/Morningstar-Acquires-Remaining-Ownership-Interest-in-Ibbotson-Associates-Japan-Inc/default .aspx. Siegel, Laurence. (2019, July 25). History of Ibbotson Associates. *American Business History Center.* https://americanbusinesshistory.org /history-of-ibbotson-associates.With regard to historical rates, notice that technically one would say that opportunity cost of capital cannot technically be known *ex ante* – ahead of time – but that it can be analyzed *ex post* – after the fact – well enough to have predictive usefulness toward the future.

23. Frey, Bruno S. and Eichenberger, Reiner. (1995a). On the Rate of Return in the Art Market: Survey and Evaluation. *European Economic Review,* 39 (3–4): 528–537.

24. See Frey and Eichenberger, 1995a. Frey, Bruno S. and Eichenberger, Reiner. (1995b). On the Return of Art Investment Return Analyses. *Journal of Cultural Economics,* 19(3): 207–220. For a more journalistic overview of free ports through the lens of lawsuits concerning free-port owner Yves Bouvier, see Knight, Sam. (2016, February 8 and 15). The Bouvier Affair. *The New Yorker,* pp. 62–71. Adam, Georgina. (2017). *Dark Side of the Boom: Excesses of the Art Market in the 21st Century.* London: Lund Humphries. Of course, this idea of psychic returns applies most in cases in which the art is held and enjoyed as opposed to stored tax-free in a free port, unless the satisfaction is in owning the art more than satisfaction in the art itself.

25. The investor can lose a maximum of $45, unless the investor has engaged in complicated extra investment steps such as using leverage, of which more momentarily.

26. As Donald MacKenzie wrote in a 2008 *London Review of Books* essay, LIBOR was a reference point for interest rates in $300 trillion worth of contracts worldwide. See MacKenzie, Donald. (2008, September 25). What's in a Number? *London Review of Books*, 30(18). www.lrb.co.uk/the-paper/v30/n18/donald-mackenzie/what-s-in-a-number. LIBOR was subject of a vast rate-fixing scandal from 2005 to 2010. See Enrich, David. (2017). *The Spider Network*. New York: HarperCollins.

27. A call option is a right to buy at a certain price at, or over, a certain period of time. A put option is a right to sell at a certain price at, or over, a certain period of time. American options can be exercised before the expiration date while European options can be exercised only on the expiration date. To hold an option is to possess a *right* to buy or to sell. To issue an option is to have an *obligation* or promise to sell or buy according to those terms.

28. We could tell many stories here about whether the weather creates a shortage which drives the prices up so much she makes more. We assume relatively elastic demand so that when there are fewer oranges the price cannot be raised enough to protect total revenue.

29. I use the term futures contract in a general way. In a more specific finance usage, a futures contract is an agreement to buy or sell a set quantity of a defined good to be delivered at a specified date in the future. These contracts are commonly traded secondarily by people who are not interested in the underlying goods, as such; by uncorroborated story, occasionally crates of coffee or other commodities are physically delivered to the proprietary trading desks of investment firms if someone neglects to close out a futures position before the delivery date. A forward contract is similar to a futures contract but more likely to be used by parties who are intending to buy and sell the underlying asset not just trade on the potential movement in price of the underlying asset. An option is, as in the note above, a general derivative that grants a right to buy (call option) or a right to sell (put option), while creating the parallel obligation to buy or sell for the issuer of the option.

30. An auction house might give her an advance, meaning they would front an amount of money to her now in exchange for the promise of selling the work at their future auction. They might also grant her a guarantee, meaning a price they promise to pay her regardless of whether the work sells successfully at the auction. The auction house could guarantee the sale itself or find a third-party guarantor who would essentially agree to

buy the work at the guarantee price. She might forfeit some of the upside in exchange for the certainty. For instance, if the guarantee were for $5 million and the work went on to sell for $9 million, she would typically split the amount above $5 million with the auction house. Although the advance would help her most with a pressing debt, the guarantee would also give her collateral against which to seek a loan. A bank, seeing her guaranteed future income, might loan her money now to bridge the time before the sale.

31. Markowitz, Harry M. (1952). Portfolio Selection. *Journal of Finance*, 7(1): 77–91. In fact, there are three different pieces of financial research from the 1950s to the 1970s that one can see as art projects – that is, as open-ended acts of invention that reshape the world and in this case reshaped financial markets. The authors of all three efforts were recognized with Nobel Prizes. The first is Markowitz's 1952 work. The second is a 1964 paper by William Sharpe, "Capital Asset Prices: A Theory of Market Equilibrium under Conditions of Risk," in which Sharpe proposes the Capital Asset Pricing Model, which generalizes Markowitz's work as a method of pricing individual stocks based on market risk and idiosyncratic risk. Like Alfred Marshall's early drawings of supply and demand, Sharpe's work is so intellectually new, that the author actually presents it with the X- and Y-axis reversed from the later, standardized presentation of his model. Sharpe, William, F. (1964, September). Capital Asset Prices: A Theory of Market Equilibrium under Conditions of Risk. *Journal of Finance*, 19(3): 425–442. The third paper is the Black–Scholes options pricing model, published in 1973. Black, Fischer and Scholes, Myron. (1973). The Pricing of Options and Corporate Liabilities. *Journal of Political Economy*, 81(3): 637–654.Myron Scholes and Robert C. Merton were awarded the Nobel Prize in 1997. Fischer Black had died in 1995, thus becoming ineligible for the Nobel, which was not awarded posthumously. However, in Black's obituary in the *New York Times* in 1995, Miller recounts that any time Black and Scholes wandered onto the floor of the Chicago Board Options Exchange (CBOE), the traders – who one imagines did not stop for much – stopped what they were doing to give them a standing ovation. Henriques, Diana B. (1995, August 31). Fischer Black, 57, Wall Street Theorist, Dies. *New York Times*, p. B15.

32. The club had thirteen individual members, but two of the voting member roles were shared, thus leaving eleven voting members who contributed

250 francs for each slot. Press, Clayton. (2017, October 24). Artful Art Investment: "The Skin of the Bear." *Forbes*. www.forbes.com/sites/ claytonpress/2017/10/24/artful-art-investment-the-skin-of-the-bear/ #55e2935d6988.

33. FitzGerald, Michael C. (1996). *Making Modernism: Picasso and the Creation of the Market for Twentieth Century Art*. Berkeley: University of California Press. Horowitz, Noah. (2014). *Art of the Deal: Contemporary Art in a Global Financial Market*. Princeton, NJ: Princeton University Press.

34. FitzGerald, 1996, p. 16 (resale royalties), p. 18 (Level's background in shipping), and p. 30 (1906 collecting Picasso).

35. Peers, Alexandra. (1996, July 5). British Pension Fund's Bet on Art Pays Off Respectably. *Wall Street Journal*. www.wsj.com/articles/SB8365297203 95795000. See also Horowitz, 2014, pp. 154–156.

36. Damodaran, 2017.

37. Bowley, Graham and Cohen, Patricia. (2014, April 12). Buyers Find Tax Breaks on Art: Let It Hang Awhile in Oregon. *New York Times*. www .nytimes.com/2014/04/13/business/buyers-find-tax-break-on-art-let-it-hang-awhile-in-portland.html.

38. Baumol, 1986, p. 11.

39. The nominal rate of return on bonds was 3.25%, which adjusted for a 0.7% rate of inflation gave the bonds in Baumol's study a 2.5% real rate of return. Later scholars have revisited Baumol's work directly. Renneboog and Spaenjers (2013) found similar returns for art and corporate bonds but with much higher risk or volatility for art. Buelens and Ginsburgh (1993) found slightly more optimistic returns for art.

40. Anderson, Robert C. (1974). Paintings As an Investment. *Economic Inquiry*, 12(1): 13–26. Baumol, 1986. Goetzmann, William N. (1993). Accounting for Taste: Art and the Financial Markets over Three Centuries. *American Economic Review*, 83(5): 1370–1376. Mei, Jianping and Moses, Michael. (2002). Art As an Investment and the Underperformance of Masterpieces. *American Economic Review*, 92(5): 1656–1668. Mei, Jianping and Moses, Michael. (2005). Vested Interest and Biased Price Estimates: Evidence from an Auction Market. *Journal of Finance*, 60(5): 2409–2435. These studies of art investment exist in a broader context of "collectibles" such as stamps or wine. See, e.g., Dimson, Elroy, Rousseau, Peter L. and Spaenjers, Christophe. (2015). The

Price of Wine. *Journal of Financial Economics*, 118(2): 431–449.
Ashenfelter, O. (1989). How Auctions Work for Wine and Art. *Journal of Economic Perspectives*, 3(3): 23–36. Burton, Benjamin T. and Jacobsen, Joyce P. (1999). Measuring Returns on Investments in Collectibles. *Journal of Economic Perspectives*, 13(4): 193–212. Collectibles share characteristics of illiquidity which complicate their inclusion in portfolios. See Ang, Andrew, Papanikolaou, Dimitris and Westerfield, Mark M. (2014). Portfolio Choice with Illiquid Assets. *Management Science*, 60(11): 2737–2761.

41. See de la Barre, Madeleine, Docclo, Sophie and Ginsburgh, Victor A. (1994). Returns of Impressionist, Modern and Contemporary European Paintings 1962–1991. *Annales d'économie et de statistique*, 35(35): 143–181. Chanel, Olivier, Gérard-Varet, Louis-André and Ginsburgh Victor. (1996). The Relevance of Hedonic Price Indices. *Journal of Cultural Economics*, 20(1): 1–24. Renneboog and Spaenjers, 2013. Korteweg, Kräussl, and Verwijmeren developed a hybrid method to correct for selection bias in repeat sales. See Korteweg, Arthur, Kräussl, Roman and Verwijmeren, Patrick. (2016). Does It Pay to Invest in Art? A Selection-Corrected Returns Perspective. *Review of Financial Studies*, 29 (4): 1007–1038.

42. Whitaker and Kräussl, 2020. See also Whitaker, 2019b.

43. For selection bias see Burton and Jacobsen, 1999. For heterogeneity within the data, see Spaenjers, Christophe, Goetzmann, William. N. and Mamonova, Elena. (2015). The Economics of Aesthetics and Record Prices for Art since 1701. *Explorations in Economic History*, 57: 79–94. Although based on a smaller data set, Whitaker and Kräussl (2020) have shown large differences in return from primary sale to first or second auction, as compared to the repeat-sales interval from first to second auction.

44. McAndrew, Clare. (2020). *The Art Market 2020.* Basel, Switzerland: Art Basel and UBS, p. 17. www.artbasel.com/about/initiatives/the-art-market. Each report covers the year prior, e.g., the 2020 report covers 2019 figures. The 2020 report estimates the 2019 market at $64.1 billion which was down 5% from the 2018 estimate.

45. In 2017, Rachel Pownall estimated the 2016 art market at $45 billion relative to McAndrew's estimate at $56.6 billion. For the TEFAF report by Pownall, see Pownall, Rachel A. J. (2017). TEFAF Art Market Report 2017. Maastricht, the Netherlands: European Fine Art Foundation. http://1uyx

qn3lzdsa2ytyzj1asxmmmpt.wpengine.netdna-cdn.com/wp-content/uplo
ads/2017/03/TEFAF-Art-Market-Report-20173.pdf. For the Basel report by
McAndrew, see McAndrew, Clare. (2017). *The Art Market 2017*. Basel,
Switzerland: Art Basel and UBS. https://d33ipftjqrd91.cloudfront.net/ass
et/cms/Art_Basel_and_UBS_The_Art_Market_2017.pdf. See also Shaw,
Anny and Hanson, Sarah P. (2017, April 30). Did the Art Market Grow or
Shrink in 2016? Depends Who You Ask. *The Art Newspaper*. www
.theartnewspaper.com/news/did-the-art-market-grow-or-shrink-in-2016-
depends-who-you-ask.

46. McAndrew, 2019, p. 28.
47. Spaenjers, Goetzmann, and Mamonova, 2015.
48. For studies of gender see Cameron, Laurie, Goetzmann, William N. and
    Nozari, Milad. (2019). Art and Gender: Market Bias or Selection Bias?
    Journal of Cultural Economics, 43(2): 279–307. Adams, Renée, Kräussl,
    Roman, Navone, Marco and Verwijmeren, Patrick. (2021). Gendered
    Prices. *Review of Financial Studies*. https://doi.org/10.1093/rfs/hhab046.
    Bocart, Fabian, Gertsberg, Marina and Pownall, Rachel Ann Jane (2021).
    An empirical analysis of price differences for male and female artists in the
    global art market. *Journal of Cultural Economic.*, https://doi-org/10.1007/
    s10824-020-09403-2. For studies of racial inclusion, see Boucher, Brian.
    (2016, October 11). Is the Art Market Racially Biased? *Artnet News.* http
    s://news.artnet.com/market/racial-bias-art-auction-market-672518.
    Case-Leal, James. (2017). Art Statistics [Artists by Age, Race, Nationality,
    Gender, and Education], produced with students in the Arts in NYC
    course at CUNY Guttman College. http://jamescaseleal.com/ArtStatisti
    cs2016.php.
49. Velthuis, 2011.
50. For example, in 2009, Gagosian Gallery organized a retrospective for the
    artist Piero Manzoni, who in 1961 created the work *Artist's Shit (Merda
    d'artista)*, which presented ninety sealed cans labeled "Artist's Shit" in
    Italian, English, French, and German and numbered 001 to 090. (Tate
    owns number 004.) The artist priced the work on par with the equivalent
    weight of gold. Howarth, Sophie. (2000). Piero Manzoni: *Artist's Shit* 1961,
    Summary. Tate. www.tate.org.uk/art/artworks/manzoni-artists-shit-
    t07667. See also Celant, Germano. (2009). *Piero Manzoni 1933–1963*.
    Milan: Skira; New York: Gagosian Gallery.

51. For fractional equity, see Whitaker and Kräussl, 2020; Whitaker, 2018; Whitaker, 2014.

52. Whitaker and Kräussl, 2020.

53. McAndrew, Clare. (2018). *The Art Market 2018*. Basel, Switzerland: Art Basel and UBS, p. 151 (table 3.8). https://d2u3kfwd92fzu7 .cloudfront.net/Art%20Basel%20and%20UBS_The%20Art%20Market _2018–1.pdf.

54. The sociologist Alison Gerber interviews artists about their ideas of investment in her book *The Work of Art*. Gerber notes many other forms of investment, for instance, in choosing work that allows flexibility to make art or in family decisions (Gerber, 2017, p. 34). See also Pierre-Michel Menger on the uncertainty of creative labor: Menger, Pierre-Michel. (2014). *The Economics of Creativity: Art and Achievement under Uncertainty*. Cambridge, MA: Harvard University Press.

55. Van Gogh Museum. (n.d.1). Was Van Gogh Poor? www.vangoghmuseum .nl/en/art-and-stories/vincent-van-gogh-faq/was-van-gogh-poor.

56. See, e.g., Nickson and Colonna, 1977.

57. van Gogh, Theo. (1890, January 31). Letter to Vincent van Gogh, Paris. www.vangoghletters.org/vg/letters/let847/letter.html.

58. Van Gogh Museum. (n.d.2). Vincent van Gogh: *Almond Blossom*, February 1890. www.vangoghmuseum.nl/en/collection/s0176V1962.

59. Pikkety, Thomas. (2013). *Capital in the Twenty-First Century* (trans Arthur Goldhammer). Cambridge, MA: Belknap Press.

60. McAndrew, 2018, p. 116.

61. Griffin, Nora. (2007–8, December–January). Werner Kramarsky and the Art of Collecting. *The Brooklyn Rail.* www.brooklynrail.org/2007/12/art/ werner.

62. Baumol, 1986; Lovo and Spaenjers, 2018.

63. Puglise, Nicole. (2016, August 24). Artist Peter Doig Victorious As Court Agrees "$10m" Painting Is Not His Work. *The Guardian.* www .theguardian.com/artanddesign/2016/aug/24/artist-peter-doig-landscape-painting-lawsuit. See also Whitaker, 2018.

10 SYSTEMS

1. Davis, Ben. (2013). *9.5 Theses on Art and Class*. Chicago, IL: Haymarket, p. 171.

2. At the time of donation, in 1989, Castelli could have sold the work for an estimated $7–$10 million. He did not, under then US tax policy, particularly benefit from the donation. Glueck, 1989; Cohen-Solal, 2010.

3. Author visit to Ugo Rondinone, *Human Nature*, and Gladstone Gallery, 2013.

4. Katchadourian, Nina. (2020, March 16). Welcome to Stickies's Art School for Kids. www.facebook.com/nina.katchadourian/posts/ 10156917541462091.

5. Katchadourian, Nina. (2020, March 19). Aaaannnnddddd…..Stickies Has FEEDBACK for You …. www.facebook.com/nina.katchadourian/posts/ 10156928658422091.

6. Brodeur, Michael Andrew. (2020, April 9). Artists Are Struggling to Find Inspiration in Isolation. *The Washington Post.* www.washingtonpost.com/ entertainment/music/artists-are-struggling-to-find-inspiration-in-isolation/ 2020/04/09/ee5e314c-7222-11ea-a9bd-9f8b593300d0_story.html.

7. Benanti, Laura. (2020, March 13). Dark Times for All …. https://twitter .com/LauraBenanti/status/1238540113795309569. Metropolitan Opera. (2020, March 21). Met Launches "Nightly Met Opera Streams." www .metopera.org/about/press-releases/met-launches-nightly-met-opera- streams-a-free-series-of-encore-live-in-hd-presentations-streamed-on-the- company-website-during-the-coronavirus-closure. Ma, Yo-Yo. (2020, March 13). In These Days of Anxiety …. https://twitter.com/YoYo_Ma/ status/1238572657278431234.

8. For stove DJ, see Cavazzini, Massimo. (2020, March 14). Italians after a Week in Lock Down [@Zizigno on TikTok]. https://twitter.com/maxkava/status/ 1238895581193547778. For German government support, see Brown, Kate. (2020, March 25). Germany Has Rolled Out a Staggering €50 Billion Aid Package for Small Business That Boosts Artists and Galleries – and Puts Other Countries to Shame. *Artnet News.* https://news.artnet.com/art-world/ german-bailout-50-billion-1815396. For Arts Council England, see Brown, Mark. (2020, March 24). Arts Council England Promises £160 Million to "Buoy Public" During Lockdown. *The Guardian.* www.theguardian.com/ world/2020/mar/24/arts-council-england-promises-160m-to-buoy-public- during-lockdown. For giving cash directly, see Ali, Yashar. (2020, April 3). Giving Away Some Cash Right Now …. https://twitter.com/yashar/status/ 1246266784556044288?s=20. Gay, Roxane. (2020, March 13). If You Are

Broke . . . . https://twitter.com/rgay/status/1238682576669118464?s=20. For design of flattening the curve charts, see Stevens, Harry. (2020, March 14). Why Outbreaks Like Coronavirus Spread Exponentially and How to "Flatten the Curve." *The Washington Post.* www.washingtonpost.com/graphics/2020/world/corona-simulator.

9. The museum is a partnership among the International Table Tennis Federation, the Chinese Table Tennis Association, and the Shanghai Municipal Education Commission. The museum itself is managed by the Shanghai University of Sport. ITTF Museum/CTT Museum, (n.d.). Visitor Guide. Hoey, Chuck. (2018). Museum Opening in Shanghai. *Table Tennis History Journal.* www.ittf.com/wp-content/uploads/2018/04/Museum OpeningSpecialEdition.pdf.

10. For an overview of sociological approaches to defining art, see Alexander, Victoria. D. (2003). *Sociology of the Arts: Exploring Fine and Popular Forms.* Hoboken, NJ: Wiley-Blackwell, pp. 1–18.

11. Lena, 2019, pp. 26–28.

12. Jones, Jonathan. (2012, November 30). Sorry MoMA, Video Games Are Not Art. *The Guardian.* www.theguardian.com/artanddesign/jonathanjo nesblog/2012/nov/30/moma-video-games-art. For a defining paper on classification of artistic genres and types, see DiMaggio, Paul. (1987). Classification in Art. *American Sociological Review*, 52(4): 440–455. We saw a shadow side of legitimation when the artist Maurizio Cattelan exhibited a banana duct-taped to a wall at the 2019 edition of Art Basel Miami Beach. The work, *Comedian*, was reportedly priced at $120,000. Of an edition of three, two were sold. A self-described performance artist took the banana off the wall and ate it. Police in Tampa, Florida, created their own tribute work called "Sgt. Donut," a donut duct-taped to a wall, priced at a starting bid of $10. Fruit sellers in New York posted signs next to duct-taped bananas. The joke was on the art market. Cattelan's dealer, Perrotin, described the work as "stimulating debates and discussions among audiences of all types around the world about the nature and the value of art." See Musumeci, Natalie (2019, December 10). Tampa Police Spoof Art Basel $120k Banana with $200k "Sgt. Donut." *New York Post.* https://nypost.com/2019/12/10/tampa-police-spoof-art-basel-120k-banana-with-200k-sgt-donut/. Perrotin. (n.d.). Maurizio Cattelan: Biography. www.perrotin.com/artists/Maurizio_Cattelan/2#biography.

13. Roy SeGuine (himself described as a friend of Chuck Hoey and also as the website manager for USA Table Tennis) describes Hoey as "a very gifted chess player, whose games were sometimes published in *Chess Life* magazine, and who once beat Bobby Fischer in an exhibition." USA Table Tennis. (n.d.) Hall of Fame Profiles: Chuck Hoey. www.teamusa.org/USA-Table-Tennis/History/Hall-of-Fame/Profiles/Chuck-Hoey.

14. USA Table Tennis, n.d.

15. WeRateDogs. (2020, May 29). Our Account Usually Acts . . . . https://twitter.com/artdecider/status/1266584418006847488?s=11.

16. Hybenova, Katarina. (2012, June 26). Three Bushwick Galleries Came to Their End. *Bushwick Daily.* https://bushwickdaily.com/bushwick/categories/arts-and-culture/581-3-bushwick-galleries-closed. And author visit to the gallery in 2012.

17. Karpik, 2010; Kharchenkova and Velthuis, 2018.

18. ARRAY. (n.d.). Our Story: About ARRAY. www.arraynow.com/our-story.

19. Goldberg, Emma. (2020, July 8). Ava DuVernay's Fight for Change Onscreen and Off. *New York Times.* www.nytimes.com/2020/07/08/movies/director-ava-duvernay-movies-police-protests.html.

20. Akerlof, George A. (2020). Sins of Omission and the Practice of Economics. *Journal of Economic Literature,* 58(2): 405–418.

21. Akerlof, 2020, p. 416.

22. Becker, Gary. (1996). *Accounting for Taste.* Cambridge, MA: Harvard University Press, p. 139. Also Becker, Gary. (1993). The Economic Way of Looking at Life. *Journal of Political Economy,* 101(3): 385–409.

23. The quotation borrows from Kennedy's 1961 inaugural address. See Kennedy, John F., Jr. (1961, January 20). *Ask Not What Your Country Can Do for You . . .*. 1961 Presidential Inaugural Address. www.jfklibrary.org/learn/about-jfk/historic-speeches/inaugural-address.

24. Potts, Maff. (2019, November 27). The Power of Friends and Purpose. Meaning Conference, Brighton, England. www.youtube.com/watch?v=_72KGzeP204.

25. La Berge, 2019, p. 3.

26. Harrison, Nate. (2020, March 8). Presentation on the panel Artists Modeling Legal Futures (Lauren van Haaften-Schick, Nate Harrison, Kenneth Pietrobono, Amy Whitaker) Roundtable. Law, Culture, and the Humanities Conference, Quinnapiac University, Hamden, CT. Hayes, Rob. (2018, January 22). LA's Notoriously Stealthy Freeway Sign. *ABC7.*

https://abc7.com/society/las-stealthy-freeway-sign-artist-still-up-to-his-old-tricks/2978744.

APPENDICES

1. Anderson, Maxwell L. (2021, February 23). I Led the Indianapolis Museum of Art for Five Years. Here's How Charles Venable, Its Recently Ousted President, Failed the Institution. *Artnet News.* https://news.artnet.com/opinion/indianapolis-museum-of-art-maxwell-anderson-1945878.
2. For an introduction to the economics of auctions, see Klemperer, Paul. (2004). *Auctions: Theory and Practice.* Princeton, NJ: Princeton University Press. For a sociological analysis of auctions, see Heath, Christian. (2012). *The Dynamics of Auctions: Social Interaction and the Sale.* Cambridge, UK: Cambridge University Press. For a short game-theory treatment, see Dixit, Avinash K. and Nalebuff, Barry J. (1991). *Thinking Strategically: The Competitive Edge in Business, Politics, and Everyday Life.* New York: W. W. Norton. pp. 319–323. For the history of auctions see both Klemperer (2004) and Heath (2012). Heath's view of auctions as part of social interactions can be read in the context of Granovetter's concept of "embeddedness." See Granovetter, Mark. (1985). Economic Actions and Social Structure: The Problem of Embeddedness. *American Journal of Sociology,* 91(3): 481–510.
3. See Klemperer, 2004. The Vickrey auction takes its name from the 1961 paper: Vickrey, William. (1961). Counterspeculation, Auctions, and Competitive Sealed Tenders. *Journal of Finance,* 16(1): 8–37.
4. Six, described by Russell Shorto in the *New York Times Magazine* as an "almost apologetically dapper man," also had a family history that lent him an uncommon amount of time around Rembrandt paintings growing up. See Shorto, Russell. (2019, February 27). Rembrandt in the Blood: An Obsessive Aristocrat, Rediscovered Paintings, and an Art-World Feud. *New York Times Magazine.* www.nytimes.com/2019/02/27/magazine/rembrandt-jan-six.html
5. Note that we are making a simplifying assumption by ignoring the buyer's premium in this example. In actuality, the winner would pay the hammer price plus the buyer's premium. Thus, their willingness to pay is not technically between $9,000 and $9,999 but the full price that corresponds to the hammer price plus premium.

6. Barbara Strongin author interview, August 23, 2020. See also Heath, 2012, p. 31.
7. Barbara Strongin author interview, September 18, 2020.
8. Barbara Strongin author interview, September 18, 2020.
9. McKinsey & Co. (2001). Tate Study, presentation 080501LNZXW293CJDK-P1, p. 39. Tate Gallery Archives, TG 12/1/3/5.
10. The IRR function asks for a range of values, which allows Excel to see how many time periods – in this case five – have passed. The equation is =IRR (range of cells, [guess of rate]). If these figures were in the top-left corner of a spreadsheet and thus in columns A and B and rows 1 to 7, then the equation would read: =IRR(B1:B6). One does not have to supply a guess as to a rate, but if one were looking at an equation with many orders of magnitude difference, an anchor starting rate helps the computer to arrive at the answer.

References

1-54. (n.d.). About. www.1-54.com/about.

Abbing, Hans. (2002). *Why Are Artists Poor? The Exceptional Economy of the Arts.* Amsterdam: Amsterdam University Press.

Abboud, Lela. (2020, March 19). Inside the Factory: How LVMH Met France's Call for Hand Sanitizer in 72 Hours. *Financial Times.* www.ft.com/content/e9c2ba e4-6909-11ea-800d-da70cff6e4d3.

Adam, Georgina. (2017). *Dark Side of the Boom: Excesses of the Art Market in the 21st Century.* London: Lund Humphries.

Adams, Renée, Kräussl, Roman, Navone, Marco and Verwijmeren, Patrick. (2021). Gendered Prices. *Review of Financial Studies.* https://doi.org/10.1093/rfs/ hhab046.

Adams, Tim. (2015, September 27). Kara Walker: "There Is a Moment in Life Where One Becomes Black." *The Guardian.* www.theguardian.com/artanddesign/2015/ sep/27/kara-walker-interview-victoria-miro-gallery-atlanta.

Adler, Amy. (2016). Fair Use and the Future of Art. *NYU Law Review*, 91(3): 559–626.

Adler, Amy. (2016, March 4). *Cowboys Milking*: Formerly Attributed to Cady Noland. *Brooklyn Rail* www.brooklynrail.org/2016/03/criticspage/cowboys-milking-formerly-attributed-to-cady-noland.

Adorno, Theodor W. (1991 [1938]). On the Fetish-Character in Music and the Regression of Listening. In J. M. Berstein, ed., *The Culture Industry.* London: Routledge, pp. 29–60.

Akerlof, George A. (1970). The Market for "Lemons": Quality Uncertainty and the Market Mechanism. *Quarterly Journal of Economics*, 84(3): 488–500.

Akerlof, George A. (2020). Sins of Omission and the Practice of Economics. *Journal of Economic Literature*, 58(2): 405–418.

Alberro, Alexander. (2003). *Conceptual Art and the Politics of Publicity.* Cambridge, MA: MIT Press.

Alexander, Gregory. S. (2017). Objects of Art; Objects of Property. *Cornell Journal of Law and Public Policy*, 26(3): 461–468.

Alexander, Victoria. D. (2003). *Sociology of the Arts: Exploring Fine and Popular Forms.* Hoboken, NJ: Wiley-Blackwell.

Ali, Yashar. (2020, April 3). Giving Away Some Cash Right Now . . .. https://twitter .com/yashar/status/1246266784556044288?s=20.

Alper, Neal et al. (1996). *Artists in the Work Force: Employment and Earnings, 1970 to 1990*. Washington, DC: Seven Locks Press. https://credo.library.umass .edu/view/full/mums686-b001-i044.

Alpers, Svetlana. (1988). *Rembrandt's Enterprise: The Studio and the Market*. Chicago, IL: University of Chicago Press.

Alt, Casey, Moss-Pultz, Sean, Whitaker, Amy and Chen, Timothy. (2016). Defining Property in the Digital Environment. *DCG Insights Report*. https://insights .dcg.co/defining-property-in-the-digital-environment-4ec3b9b79403.

Anderson, Jane and Christen, Kim. (2013). Chuck a Copyright on It: Dilemmas of Digital Return and the Possibilities for Traditional Knowledge Licenses and Labels. *Museum Anthropology Review*, 7 (1–2): 105–126.

Anderson, Jane and Christen, Kim. (2019). Decolonizing Attribution: Traditions of Exclusion. *Journal of Radical Librarianship*, 5: 113–152.

Anderson, Maxwell L. (2021, February 23). I Led the Indianapolis Museum of Art for Five Years. Here's How Charles Venable, Its Recently Ousted President, Failed the Institution. *Artnet News.* https://news.artnet.com/opinion/indianapolis-museum-of-art-maxwell-anderson-1945878.

Anderson, Robert C. (1974). Paintings As an Investment. *Economic Inquiry*, 12(1): 13–26.

Ang, Andrew, Papanikolaou, Dimitris and Westerfield, Mark M. (2014). Portfolio Choice with Illiquid Assets. *Management Science*, 60(11): 2737–2761.

Anthony, Cara. (2014, December 13). Indianapolis Museum of Art to Charge Admission. *IndyStar*. https://eu.indystar.com/story/news/2014/12/12/indian apolis-museum-art-charge-admission/20306373.

Antonelli, Paola. (2019, May 15). Introduction. *MoMA R&D Salon #31: Workspheres*. http://momarnd.moma.org/salons/salon-31-workspheres-1.

Ardito, Mary. (1982). Creativity: It's the Thought That Counts. *Bell Telephone Magazine*, 61(1): 32.

ARRAY. (n.d.). Our Story: About ARRAY. www.arraynow.com/our-story.

Art + Museum Transparency. (2019, December 9). A 20/20 Vision for Art + Museum Transparency for 2020: Sharing, Analyzing, Moving Forward. *Medium*. https:// medium.com/@artandmuseumtransparency/a-20-20-vision-for-art-museum-transparency-for-2020-sharing-analyzing-moving-forward-3eef299cdea0

Art + Practice. (n.d.). About. www.artandpractice.org/about.

Art Basel. (n.d.). Our History. www.artbasel.com/about/history.

Art Workers' Coalition. (1969). Artworkers Coalition: Documents. *Primary Information*. www.primaryinformation.org/art-workers-coalition.

Artlyst. (2013, January 25). Paul Chiappe Exposes a Tissue of Lies in New London Exhibition. *Artlyst*. www.artlyst.com/news/paul-chiappe-exposes-a-tissue-of-lies-in-new-london-exhibition.

Ashenfelter, Orley. (1989). How Auctions Work for Wine and Art. *Journal of Economic Perspectives*, 3(3): 23–36.

Ashenfelter, Orley and Graddy, Kathryn. (2003). Auctions and the Price of Art. *Journal of Economic Literature*, 41(3): 763–786.

Ashenfelter, Orley and Graddy, Kathryn. (2005). Anatomy of the Rise and Fall of a Price-Fixing Conspiracy: Auctions at Sotheby's and Christie's. *Journal of Competition Law and Economics*, 1(1): 3–20.

Ashenfelter, Orley and Graddy, Kathryn. (2011). Sale Rates and Price Movements in Art Auctions. *American Economic Review*, 101(3): 212–216.

Ashenfelter, Orley, Ginsburgh, Victor, Graddy, Kathryn, Legros, Patrick and Sahuguet, Nicholas. (2003, November). Auction House Settlement: Winning Twice? *The Art Newspaper*, 141(11): 42.

Associated Press. (2019, October 4). Jeff Koons' "Bouquet of Tulips" Honors Victims of Paris Terror Attacks. *The Guardian*. www.theguardian.com/artanddesign/2019/oct/04/jeff-koons-bouquet-of-tulips-honours-victims-of-paris-terror-attacks.

Association of Art Museum Directors (AAMD). (2015, September). AAMD Policy on Deaccessioning. https://aamd.org/sites/default/files/document/AAMD%20Policy%20on%20Deaccessioning%20website_0.pdf.

Ault, Julie. (2002). *Alternative Art New York, 1965–1985*. New York: The Drawing Center ; Minneapolis: University of Minnesota Press.

Avildsen, John G. (1984). *The Karate Kid*. Columbia Pictures, USA.

Bagehot, Walter. (1881). Adam Smith As a Person. In Richard Holt Hutton, ed., *Biographical Studies*. London: Longmans, Green, and Co., pp. 247–281.

Bahr, Sarah. (2021, February 17). Charles Venable Resigns As Head of Indianapolis Museum of Art. *New York Times*. www.nytimes.com/2021/02/17/arts/design/charles-venable-resigning-indianapolis-museum.html.

Bailey, Jason. (2018, July 21). Art World, Meet Blockchain. *Artnome*. www.artnome.com/news/2018/7/21/artworld-meet-blockchain.

Bailey, Jason. (2019, May 26). Mass Appropriation, Radical Remixing, and the Democratization of AI Art. *Artnome*. www.artnome.com/news/2019/5/13/mass-appropriation-radical-remixing-and-the-democratization-of-ai-art.

Bakhshi, Hasan, Fujiwara, Daniel, Lawton, Ricky, Mourato, Susana and Dolan, Paul. (2015). *Measuring Economic Value in Cultural Institutions: A Report Commissioned by the Arts and Humanities Research Council's Cultural*

Value Project. https://ahrc.ukri.org/documents/project-reports-and-reviews/measuringeconomicvalue.

Banternghansa, Chanont and Graddy, Kathryn. (2011). The Impact of the "Droit de Suite" in the UK: An Empirical Analysis. *Journal of Cultural Economics*, 35(2): 81–100.

Basciano, Oliver. (2019, August 16). Takis Obituary. *The Guardian*. www.theguardian.com/artanddesign/2019/aug/16/takis-obituary.

Battaglia, Andy. (2019, July 2). The ARTnews Accord: Kaywin Feldman and Bryan Stevenson on Embracing Empathy and Confronting American Racism in Museums. *ARTnews*. www.artnews.com/artnews/news/national-gallery-kaywin-feldman-bryan-equal-justice-initiative-stevenson-conversation-12896.

Baumol, William J. (1986). Unnatural Value: Or Art Investment As Floating Crap Game. *American Economic Review*, 76(2): 10–14.

Baumol, William J. (1989). *Pricing the Priceless*. New York: Basic Books.

Baumol, William J. and Bowen, William G. (1968). *Performing Arts: The Economic Dilemma*. Cambridge, MA: MIT Press.

Baumol, William J. and Bradford, David F. (1970). Optimal Departures from Marginal Cost Pricing. *American Economic Review*, 60(3): 265–283.

Bayer, Thomas M. and Page, John R. (2014). *The Development of the Art Market in England: Money As Muse 1730–1900*. London: Pickering & Chatto.

BBC News (2019, October 8). Jeff Koons' Paris Bataclan Sculpture Mocked As "Pornographic." www.bbc.co.uk/news/world-europe-49958897.

Beaven, Kirstie. (2012). Performance Art: The Happening. *Tate.org.uk*. www.tate.org.uk/art/art-terms/h/happening/happening.

Becker, Gary. (1993). The Economic Way of Looking at Life. *Journal of Political Economy*, 101(3): 385–409.

Becker, Gary. (1996). *Accounting for Taste*. Cambridge, MA: Harvard University Press.

Becker, Howard Saul. (1982). *Art Worlds*. Berkeley: University of California Press.

Beckmann, Michael. (2004). Why Do Sellers at Auctions Bid for Their Own Items? Theory and Evidence. *Schmalenbach Business Review*, 56(4): 312–337.

Beggs, Alan and Graddy, Kathryn. (2009). Anchoring Effects: Evidence from Art Auctions. *American Economic Review*, 99(3): 1027–1039.

Benanti, Laura. (2020, March 13). Dark Times for All …. https://twitter.com/LaurABenanti/status/1238540113795309569.

Benhamou, Françoise and Ginsburgh, Victor A. (2006). Copies of Artworks: The Case of Paintings and Prints. In Victor A. Ginsburgh and David Throsby, eds., *Handbook of the Economics of Art and Culture*, vol. 1. Amsterdam: Elsevier North Holland, pp. 253–283.

Betty Parsons Gallery. Records and personal papers, circa 1920–91, bulk 1946–83. Archives of American Art, Smithsonian Institution.

Bingham, Juliet (Ed.). (2010). *Ai Weiwei: Sunflower Seeds*. London: Tate Gallery Publishing.

Bishop, Claire and Columbus, Nikki. (2020, January 7). Free Your Mind: A Speculative Review of #NewMoMA. *n+1 Magazine*. https://nplusonemag.com/online-only/paper-monument/free-your-mind.

Black, Fischer and Scholes, Myron. (1973). The Pricing of Options and Corporate Liabilities. *Journal of Political Economy*, 81(3): 637–654.

Black Rock. (n.d.). The Residency. https://blackrocksenegal.org/the-residency.

Bocart, Fabian, Gertsberg, Marina and Pownall, Rachel Ann Jane (2021). An empirical analysis of price differences for male and female artists in the global art market. *Journal of Cultural Economic.*, https://doi-org/10.1007/s10824-020-09403-2.

Boltanski, Luc and Thevenot, Laurent. (2006). *On Justification: Economies of Worth*. Princeton, NJ: Princeton University Press.

Bostaph, Samuel. (2015). *Andrew Carnegie: An Economic Biography*. Lanham, MD: Lexington Books.

Boucher, Brian. (2016, September 6). Christie's Hikes Buyer's Fees for First Time in Three Years. *Artnet News*. https://news.artnet.com/market/christies-hikes-buyers-fees-636194.

Boucher, Brian. (2016, October 11). Is the Art Market Racially Biased? *Artnet News*. https://news.artnet.com/market/racial-bias-art-auction-market-672518.

Bourdieu, Pierre. (1984). *Distinction: A Social Critique of the Judgment of Taste* (trans. Richard Nice). Cambridge, MA: Harvard University Press.

Bourdieu, Pierre. (1985). The Market for Symbolic Goods. *Poetics*, 14 (1–2):13–44.

Bourdieu, Pierre. (1993). The Field of Cultural Production, or: The Economic World Reversed. In Randal Johnson, ed., *The Field of Cultural Production*. New York: Polity, pp. 29–73.

Bowley, Graham and Cohen, Patricia. (2014, April 12). Buyers Find Tax Breaks on Art: Let It Hang Awhile in Oregon. *New York Times*. www.nytimes.com/2014/04/13/business/buyers-find-tax-break-on-art-let-it-hang-awhile-in-portland.html.

Boyd, Clark. (2014, November 18). Mine-Kafon: Wind-Blown Landmine Clearance. *BBC Future*. www.bbc.com/future/story/20120503-blowing-in-the-wind.

Bradford, Mark and Golden, Thelma. (2015). *Mark Bradford in Conversation with Thelma Golden*. Hauser & Wirth, New York. www.hauserwirth.com/resources/18701-mark-bradford-conversation-thelma-golden.

Bradley, Christopher G. and Frye, Brian L. (2018–19). Art in the Age of Contractual Negotiation. *Kentucky Law Journal*, 107(4): 547–592.

Brandenburger, Adam M. and Nalebuff, Barry J. (1996). *Co-opetition*. New York: Doubleday.

Brandenburger, Adam M. and Nalebuff, Barry J. (1997). The Added-Value Theory of Business. *Strategy + Business*. www.strategy-business.com/article/12669? gko=5c72a.

Brankov, Amelia. (2020, March 27). 5Pointz Developer Aiming for Supreme Court Review of $6.75 Million Damages Award. *IP & Media Law Updates*. Frankfurt Kurnit Klein + Selz. https://ipandmedialaw.fkks.com/post/102g2z9/5pointz-developer-aiming-for-supreme-court-review-of-6-75-million-damages-award.

Brekke, Jaya Klara. (2019). The White Paper Guide. In Jaya Klara Brekke and Ben Vickers, eds., *The White Paper by Satoshi Nakamoto*. London: Ignota, pp. 19–63.

Britten, Mathew and Grist, Kerry. (2019). Tough Love: Museum Salaries and the Working Class. In Dawn E. Salerno, Mark S. Gold, and Kristina L. Durocher, eds., *For Love or Money: Confronting the State of Museum Salaries*. Edinburgh: MuseumsEtc, pp. 90–95.

Brodeur, Michael Andrew. (2020, April 9). Artists Are Struggling to Find Inspiration in Isolation. *The Washington Post*. www.washingtonpost.com/entertainment/music/artists-are-struggling-to-find-inspiration-in-isolation/2020/04/09/ee5e314c-7222-11ea-a9bd-9f8b593300d0_story.html.

Brown, Kate. (2020, March 25). Germany Has Rolled Out a Staggering €50 Billion Aid Package for Small Business That Boosts Artists and Galleries – and Puts Other Countries to Shame. *Artnet News*. https://news.artnet.com/art-world/german-bailout-50-billion-1815396.

Brown, Mark. (2020, March 24). Arts Council England Promises £160 Million to "Buoy Public" During Lockdown. *The Guardian*. www.theguardian.com/world/2020/mar/24/arts-council-england-promises-160m-to-buoy-public-during-lockdown.

Bryce, Kristy. (2012). *Andy Warhol Flowers* [exhibition]. Eykyn Maclean Gallery, New York, November 1–December 8, 2012.

Buelens, Nathalie and Ginsburgh, Victor A. (1993). Revisiting Baumol's "Art As Floating Crap Game." *European Economic Review*, 37(7): 1351–1371.

Buchloh, Benhamin H. D. (1990). Conceptual Art 1962–1969: From the Aesthetic of Administration to the Critique of Institutions. *October*, 55(Winter): 105–143.

Buffett, Mary and Clark, David. (2008). *Warren Buffett and the Interpretation of Financial Statements: The Search for the Company with Durable Competitive Advantage*. New York: Scribner.

Bürger, Peter. (1984). *Theory of the Avant-Garde* (trans. Michael Shaw). Minneapolis: University of Minnesota Press.

Burns, Charlotte (2019, February 13). Transcript of Sir Nicholas Serota: "We All Want to Know What It Means to Be Alive Today." *In Other Words*. www .artagencypartners.com/transcript-nicholas-serota.

Burton, Benjamin T. and Jacobsen, Joyce P. (1999). Measuring Returns on Investments in Collectibles. *Journal of Economic Perspectives*, 13(4): 193–212.

Buskirk, Martha. (2012). *Creative Enterprise: Contemporary Art between Museum and Marketplace*. London: Bloomsbury.

Calhoun, Craig (Ed.). (2002). *Dictionary of the Social Sciences*. Oxford, UK: Oxford University Press.

Callanan, Laura, Wei-Skillern, Jane and Onayemi, Prentice. (2014). *Theaster Gates: Artist As Catalyst for Community Development*. Berkeley-Haas Case Series. Berkeley: University of California.

Cameron, Laurie, Goetzmann, William N. and Nozari, Milad. (2019). Art and Gender: Market Bias or Selection Bias? *Journal of Cultural Economics*, 43(2): 279–307.

Campbell, Duncan. (2002, July 8). Land of the Twee. *The Guardian*. www .theguardian.com/culture/2002/jul/08/artsfeatures1.

Canonica, Finn. (2018). Preface. In Hans Ulrich Obrist, *Somewhere Totally Else*. Zurich: JRP Editions.

Cascone, Sarah. (2019, March 11). Minimalist Sculptor Charlotte Posenenske Was on the Edge of Art-World Acclaim. She Walked Away in 1968. Now, Dia Is Bringing Her Back. *Artnet News*. www.news.artnet.com/exhibitions/charlotte-posenenske-retrospective-diabeacon-1484476.

Cascone, Sarah. (2019, July 15). Artist Cady Noland Refuses to Give Up Her Legal Fight over the Restoration of Her Disavowed Log Cabin Structure. *Artnet News* https:// news.artnet.com/art-world/cady-noland-log-cabin-lawsuit-refiled-1594249.

Case, Karl E., Fair, Ray C. and Oster, Sharon E. (2017). *Principles of Economics*, 12th ed. New York: Pearson.

Case-Leal, James (2017). Art Statistics [Artists by Age, Race, Nationality, Gender, and Education], produced with students in the Arts in NYC course at CUNY Guttman College. http://jamescaseleal.com/ArtStatistics2016.php.

Catlow, Ruth, Garrett, Marc, Jones, Nathan and Skinner, Sam (Eds.). (2017). *Artists Re: Thinking the Blockchain*. Liverpool, UK: Torque Editions, Furtherfield and Liverpool University Press.

Cavazzini, Massimo. (2020, March 14). Italians after a Week in Lock Down [@Zizigno on TikTok]. https://twitter.com/maxkava/status/1238895581193547778.

Caves, Richard E. (2000). *Creative Industries: Contracts between Art and Commerce*. Cambridge, MA: Harvard University Press.

Celant, Germano. (2009). *Piero Manzoni 1933–1963*. Milan: Skira; New York: Gagosian Gallery.

Celarier, Michelle. (2015). The Huge Controversy behind Hedge Funder's $93.5 Million Art Sale. *New York Post*, March 13. https://nypost.com/2015/03/13/hedgie-steve-cohen-an-unwitting-player-in-art-sale-controversy.

Chambers, David, Dimson Elroy and Spaenjers, Christophe. (2020). Art As an Asset: Evidence from Keynes the Collector. *Review of Asset Pricing Studies*, 10(3): 490–520.

Chandler, Alfred D., Jr. (1962). *Strategy and Structure*. Cambridge, MA: MIT Press.

Chandler, Alfred D., Jr. (1994). *Scale and Scope: The Dynamics of Industrial Capitalism*. Cambridge, MA: Harvard University Press.

Chanel, Olivier, Gérard-Varet, Louis-André and Ginsburgh Victor. (1996). The Relevance of Hedonic Price Indices. *Journal of Cultural Economics*, 20(1): 1–24.

Cheung, Steven N. S. (1973). The Fable of the Bees: An Economic Investigation. *Journal of Law and Economics*, 16(1): 11–33.

Chiappe, Paul. (n.d.). Drawings. http://paulchiappe.com.

Chisholm, Darlene C. (2005). Empirical Contributions to the Theory of the Firm. *Global Business and Economics Review*, 4(1): 119–130.

Christie's Inc. (2017). Salvator Mundi: The Rediscovery of a Masterpiece: Chronology, Conservation, and Authentication. www.christies.com/features/Salvator-Mundi-timeline-8644-3.aspx.

Christie's Inc. (2018). Ten Things to Know about Zao Wou-Ki. *Christie's.com*. www.christies.com/features/Zao-Wou-Ki-8534-3.aspx.

Christie's Inc. (2019, February 1). Buying at Christie's: New Buyers Premium Schedule. www.christies.com/buying-services/buying-guide/financial-information.

City of New York. (2019). *Diversity & Equity in New York City's Cultural Workforce*. www1.nyc.gov/site/diversity/index.page.

Clayton, Lenka. (2007). *Local Newspaper*. www.lenkaclayton.com/work#/local-newspaper.

Clayton, Lenka. (2012–15). *Artist Residency in Motherhood*. www.lenkaclayton.com/work#/man-boy-man-etc.

Clayton, Lenka. (2012–ongoing). Typewriter Drawings. www.lenkaclayton.com/work#/typewriter-drawings-4-1-1.

Clayton, Lenka. (2017). *Unanswered Letter*. www.lenkaclayton.com/work#/unanswered-letter.

Clayton, Lenka. (2018). *Sculptures for the Blind*. Atlanta, GA: J&L Books.

Cleland, Elizabeth. (2019, November 1). Counting Cows – Curating *Relative Values: The Cost of Art in the Northern Renaissance*. *Now at the Met* blog.

www.metmuseum.org/blogs/now-at-the-met/2017/curating-relative-values-counting-cows.

Coase, Ronald H. (1937). The Nature of the Firm. *Economica*, 4(16): 386–405.

Coase, Ronald H. (1960). The Problem of Social Cost. *Journal of Law and Economics*, 3(October): 1–44.

Cohen-Solal, Annie. (2010). *Leo and His Circle: The Life of Leo Castelli*. New York: Knopf.

College Art Association. (2015). *Code of Best Practices in Fair Use for the Visual Arts*. www.collegeart.org/pdf/fair-use/best-practices-fair-use-visual-arts.pdf.

Collier, Caroline and Serota, Nicholas. (2015). *Plus Tate: Connecting Art to People and Places*. London: Tate. www.tate.org.uk/about-us/national-international-local/plus-tate.

Colonna, Carl M. and Colonna, Carol G. (1982). An Economic and Legal Assessment of Recent Visual Artists' Reversion Rights Agreements in the United States. *Journal of Cultural Economics*, 6(2): 77–85.

Cook, Lisa. (2014). Violence and Economic Activity: Evidence from African American Patents, 1870–1940. *Journal of Economic Growth*, 19(2): 221–257.

Corbett, William. (2008, June). Wynn Kramarsky in Conversation with William Corbett. *Brooklyn Rail*. www.brooklynrail.org/2008/06/art/wynn-kramarsky-with-william-corbett.

Cowen, Tyler and Tabarrok, Alexander. (2000). An Economic Theory of Avant-Garde and Popular Art, or High and Low Culture. *Southern Economic Journal*, 67(2): 232–253.

Creative Independent. (2018). *A Study on the Financial State of Visual Artists Today*. https://thecreativeindependent.com/artist-survey.

Crow, Kelly. (2020, February 19). Three New York Galleries to Sell Financier's Collection. *Wall Street Journal*. www.wsj.com/articles/three-new-york-galleries-to-sell-financiers-art-collection-11582142146.

Crowell & Moring. (2002). *The United Kingdom's Criminalization of Price-Fixing and Other Collusive Conduct*. www.crowell.com/pdf/UK.pdf.

DACS. (2016). *Ten Years of the Artist's Resale Right: Giving Artists Their Fair Share*. www.dacs.org.uk/DACSO/media/DACSDocs/reports-and-submissions/Ten-Years-of-the-Artist-s-Resale-Right-Giving-artists-their-fair-share-DACS-Feb-16.pdf.

DACS. (2019). *Annual Review 2018*. www.dacs.org.uk/about-us/corporate-resources/annual-reports.

Dafoe, Taylor. (2020, February 28). Artist William Powhida Doesn't Have Room to Store All His Work – So He Wants You to Borrow It, for Free. *Artnet News*. https://news.artnet.com/market/william-powhida-store-to-own-1790187.

The Daily Telegraph. (2011, August 8). Sir Anthony Tennant [obituary]. *The Daily Telegraph*, p. 25. www.telegraph.co.uk/news/obituaries/finance-obituaries/86 87415/Sir-Anthony-Tennant.html.

Damodaran, Aswath. (2017, August 14–16). Executive Education Short Course: Valuation, Stern School of Business, New York University.

David, Géraldine, Oosterlinck, Kim and Szafarz, Ariane. (2013). Art Market Inefficiency. *Economic Letters*, 121(1): 23–25.

Davies, William. (2014). *The Limits of Neoliberalism: Authority, Sovereignty and the Logic of Competition*. London: Sage.

Davis, Ben. (2013). *9.5 Theses on Art and Class*. Chicago, IL: Haymarket Books.

Davis, Ben. (2015, August 13). Art Flippers Attempt to Unload Suicide Girls' Version of Richard Prince Artwork. *Artnet News*. www.news.artnet.com/mar ket/art-flippers-suicide-girls-richard-prince-prints-324580.

de Coppet, Laura and Jones, Alan. (1984). *The Art Dealers*. New York: Clarkson N. Potter.

De Donno, Emanuele. (2019). Books as a System: The Artists' Books of Sol LeWitt [exhibition]. Printed Matter, New York, June 28–September 29. www .printedmatter.org/programs/events/877.

de la Barre, Madeleine, Docclo, Sophie and Ginsburgh, Victor A. (1994). Returns of Impressionist, Modern and Contemporary European Paintings 1962–1991. *Annales d'économie et de statistique*, 35(35): 143–181.

De Marchi, Neil and van Miegroet, Hans J. (Eds.). (2006). *Mapping Markets for Paintings in Europe, 1450–1750*. Turnhout, Belgium: Brepols.

De Silva, Dakshina G., Pownall, Rachel A. J. and Wolk, Leonard. (2012). Does the Sun "Shine" on Art Prices? *Journal of Economic Behavior and Organization*, 82 (1): 167–178.

Deedham, Alex. (2015, May 27). Richard Prince v. Suicide Girls in an Instagram Price War. *The Guardian*. www.theguardian.com/artanddesign/2015/may/27/ suicide-girls-richard-prince-copying-instagram.

Degen, Natasha (Ed.). (2013). *The Market*. London: Whitechapel Gallery and MIT Press.

Dempster, Anna M. (Ed.). (2014). *Risk and Uncertainty in the Art World*. London: Bloomsbury.

Diaz, Jesus. (2019, April 30). This Gorgeous Museum Is Made from Old Jet Fuel Tanks. *Fast Company*. www.fastcompany.com/90341401/this-gorgeous-museum-is-made-from-old-jet-fuel-tanks.

Didion, Joan. (2014). *Where I Was From*. New York: Vintage.

DiMaggio, Paul. (1987). Classification in Art. *American Sociological Review*, 52(4): 440–455.

Dimson, Elroy, Rousseau, Peter L. and Spaenjers, Christophe. (2015). The Price of Wine. *Journal of Financial Economics*, 118(2): 431–449.

Dixit, Avinash K. and Nalebuff, Barry J. (1991). *Thinking Strategically: The Competitive Edge in Business, Politics, and Everyday Life*. New York: W. W. Norton.

documenta. (1982). *documenta 7*. Kassel, Germany: P. Dierichs.

Donnachie, Ian. (n.d.). Thomas Bell. *Oxford Dictionary of National Biography*. https://doi.org/10.1093/ref:odnb/65053.

Donnellan, Caroline. (2018). *Towards Tate Modern: Public Policy, Private Vision*. London: Routledge.

Dover, Caitlin. (2018). Who Was Hilma af Klint? At the Guggenheim, Paintings by an Artist ahead of Her Time. *Guggenheim.com*. www.guggenheim.org/blogs/checklist/who-was-hilma-af-klint-at-the-guggenheim-paintings-by-an-artist-ahead-of-her-time.

Dowd, Ray. (2010, January 30). Visual Artists Rights Act: Artist Moral Rights in Unfinished Sculptural Works. *Copyright Litigation Blog*. https://copyrightlitigation.blogspot.com/2010/01/visual-artists-rights-act-artist-moral.html.

Dubois, R. Luke. (2016). Insightful Human Portraits Made from Data. *TED2016*. www.youtube.com/watch?v=9kBKQS7J7xI.

Durkee, Musetta. (2019, March 21). International Perspectives on Street Art. *Center for Art Law Blog*. https://itsartlaw.org/2019/03/21/wywh-international-perspectives-on-street-art.

Duron, Maximiliano (2019, June 13). Hauser & Wirth Will Open Exhibition Space, Residency Program on Menorca's Isla del Rey. *ARTnews*. www.artnews.com/art-news/news/hauser-wirth-menorca-exhibition-space-12783.

Dweck, Carol. (2008). *Mindset: The New Psychology of Success*. New York: Ballantine Books.

Edmundson, Mark (1997, September). On the Uses of a Liberal Education: As Lite Entertainment for Bored College Students. *Harper's Magazine*, pp. 39–49.

Eichhorn, Maria. (2009). *The Artist's Contract*, edited by Gerti Fietzek. Cologne, Germany: Verlag der Buchhandlung Walther König.

Eichhorn, Maria. (2009). Interview with Adrian Piper. In Gerti Fietzek, ed., *The Artist's Contract*, pp. 193–215. Cologne, Germany: Walther König.

Ekelund, Robert B., Jr., Jackson, John D. and Tollison, Robert D. (2017). *The Economics of American Art: Issues, Artists and Market Institutions*. New York: Oxford University Press.

Elliot, Jeffrey M. (Ed.). (1989). *Conversations with Maya Angelou*. Jackson, MS: University Press of Mississippi.

Enrich, David. (2017). *The Spider Network*. New York: HarperCollins.

Epstein, Richard A. (2003). The Regrettable Necessity of Contingent Valuation. *Journal of Cultural Economics*, 27(3–4): 259–274.

The Equal Justice Initiative. (n.d.). The National Memorial for Peace and Justice. https://museumandmemorial.eji.org/memorial.

Espeland, Wendy N. and Stevens, Mitchell L. (1998). Commensuration As a Social Process. *Annual Review of Sociology*, 24(1): 313–343.

Fama, Eugene. (1965). The Behavior of Stock Market Prices. *Journal of Business*, 38 (1): 34–105.

Finkelpearl, Tom. (2013). *What We Made: Conversations on Art and Social Cooperation*. Durham, NC: Duke University Press.

Fisher, William W. III, Cost, Frank, Fairey, Shepard, Feder, Meir, Fountain, Edwin, Stewart, Geoffrey and Sturken, Marita. (2012). Reflections on the Hope Poster Case. *Harvard Journal of Law and Technology*, 25(2): 244–338.

Fite-Wassilak, Chris. (2019, December 20). How Hauser & Wirth Took over the World. *Frieze*. https://frieze.com/article/how-hauser-wirth-took-over-world.

FitzGerald, Michael C. (1996). *Making Modernism: Picasso and the Creation of the Market for Twentieth Century Art*. Berkeley: University of California Press.

Flanagan, Robert. J. (1990). The Economics of Unions and Collective Bargaining. *Industrial Relations: A Journal of Economy and Society*, 29(2): 300–315.

Flux Theatre Ensemble. (n.d.). The Living Ticket. www.fluxtheatre.org/living-ticket.

Foster + Partners. (n.d.). Millennium Bridge. www.fosterandpartners.com/projects/millennium-bridge.

Fourcade, Marion. (2011). Cents and Sensibility: Economic Valuation and the Nature of "Nature". *American Journal of Sociology*, 116(6): 1721–1777.

Fourcade, Marion, Ollion, Étienne and Algan, Yann. (2015). The Superiority of Economists. *Journal of Economic Perspectives*, 29(1): 89–114.

Fraiberger, Samuel P., Sinatra, Roberta, Resch, Magnus, Riedl, Christoph and Barabási, Albert-László. (2018). Quantifying Reputation and Success in Art. *Science*, 362(6416): 825–829.

Franz, Douglas, Vogel, Carol and Blumenthal, Ralph. (2000, October 8). Private Files Fuel an Art Auction Inquiry. *New York Times*. www.nytimes.com/2000/10/08/us/secret-partners-unraveling-conspiracy-private-files-fuel-art-auction-inquiry.html.

Fraser, Andrea. (2011, September). Le 1% C'est Moi. *Texte zur Kunst* 83: 114–127. Available via Whitney Museum of American Art: https://whitneymedia.org/assets/generic_file/805/_22L_1__C_est_Moi_22.pdf.

Fraser, Andrea. (2018). Artist Writes No. 2 toward a Reflexive Resistance. *X-Tra*, 20(2), www.x-traonline.org/article/artist-writes-no-2-toward-a-reflexive-resistance.

Freeman, Nate. (2016, October 27). Sotheby's Acquires Mei Moses Art Indices, an Analytic Tool That Evaluates Market Strength on Basis of Repeat Sales. *ARTnews*. www.artnews.com/art-news/market/sothebys-acquires-mei-moses-art-indices-an-analytic-tool-that-evaluates-market-strength-on-basis-of-repeat-sales-7208.

Freeman, Nate. (2017, November 15). Leonardo da Vinci's "Salvator Mundi" Sells for $450.3 M at Christie's in New York, Shattering Market Records. *ARTnews*. www.artnews.com/art-news/news/leonardo-da-vincis-salvator-mundi-sells-450-3-m-christies-new-york-9334.

Freeman, Nate. (2018, August 24). How Damien Hirst's $200 Million Auction Became a Symbol of Pre-Recession Decadence. *Artsy*. www.artsy.net/article/artsy-editorial-damien-hirsts-200-million-auction-symbol-pre-recession-decadence.

Frey, Bruno S. and Eichenberger, Reiner. (1995a). On the Rate of Return in the Art Market: Survey and Evaluation. *European Economic Review*, 39 (3–4): 528–537.

Frey, Bruno S. and Eichenberger, Reiner. (1995b). On the Return of Art Investment Return Analyses. *Journal of Cultural Economics* 19(3): 207–220.

Frey, Bruno S. and Pommerehne, Werner W. (1989). *Muses and Markets: Explorations in the Economics of the Arts*. Oxford, UK: Blackwells.

Frey, Bruno S. and Steiner, Lasse. (2012). Pay As You Go: A New Proposal for Museum Pricing. *Museum Management and Curatorship*, 27(3): 223–235.

Frye, Brian. (2017). Equitable Resale Royalties. *Journal of Intellectual Property Law*, 24(2): 237–276.

Gagosian Gallery. (2012). *Damien Hirst: The Complete Spot Paintings 1986–2011*. https://gagosian.com/exhibitions/2012/damien-hirst-the-complete-spot-paintings-1986-2011.

Garrels, Gary. (2000). A Conversation with Sol LeWitt. *Open: Member's Magazine of the San Francisco Museum of Modern Art*.

Gates, Theaster. (n.d.). Rebuild Foundation. www.theastergates.com/project-items/rebuild-foundation.

Gay, Roxane. (2020, March 13). If You Are Broke . . .. https://twitter.com/rgay/status/1238682576669118464?s=20.

Gerber, Alison (2017). *The Work of Art: Value in Creative Careers*, Stanford, CA: Stanford University Press.

Gilbert, Laura. (2018, October 10). Richard Prince Defends Reuse of Others' Photographs. *The Art Newspaper*. www.theartnewspaper.com/news/richard-prince-defends-re-use-of-others-photographs.

Ginsburgh, Victor A. (2007). The Economic Consequences of Droit de Suite in the European Union. In Ruth. Towse, ed., *Recent Developments in Cultural Economics*. Cheltenham, UK: Edward Elgar, pp. 384–393.

Ginsburgh, Victor A. and Throsby, David (Eds.) (2006). *Handbook of the Economics of Art and Culture*. Vol. 1. Boston, MA: North Holland (Elsevier).

Ginsburgh, Victor A. and Throsby, David (Eds.) (2013). *Handbook of the Economics of Art and Culture*. Vol. 2. Boston, MA: North Holland (Elsevier).

Ginsburgh, Victor and Weber, Schlomo. (2020). The Economics of Language. *Journal of Economic Literature*, 58(2): 348–404.

Ginsburgh, Victor A. and Zang, Israel. (2007a). Sharing the Income of a Museum Pass Program. *Museum Management and Curatorship*, 19(4): 371–383.

Ginsburgh, Victor A. and Zang, Israel. (2007b). Bundling by Competitors and the Sharing of Profits. *Economics Bulletin*, 12(16): 1–9.

Gleadell, Colin. (2017, July 28). Artist Pension Trust Faces Yet Another Crisis As Artists Fume over New Storage Fees. *Artnet News*. https://news.artnet.com/market/artist-pension-trust-storage-fee-1035569.

Gleeson-White, Jane. (2012). *Double Entry: How the Merchants of Venice Created Modern Finance*. New York: W.W. Norton.

Glimcher, Marc. (2018, December 5). *The Art of Blockchains: Tech and the Art Market*. Panel with Emmanuel Aidoo, Credit Suisse, Head Distributed Ledger Strategy Nanne Dekking, TEFAF, Chairman of the Board; Artory, Founder & CEO Marc Glimcher, Pace Gallery, President & CEO Dan Long, ARTBLX, Co-Founder & CEO Andy Milenius, MakerDAO, Chief Technology Officer Moderated by Arthur Falls, DFINITY, Director of Communications, Faena Forum, Miami, Florida. www.youtube.com/watch?v=eeha-9JzkJ8.

Glueck, Grace. (1985, February 3). What Part Should the Public Play in Choosing Public Art? *New York Times*. www.nytimes.com/1985/02/03/arts/what-part-should-the-public-play-in-choosing-public-art.html.

Glueck, Grace. (1989, May 10). Castelli Donates Major Work to the Modern, *New York Times*. www.nytimes.com/1989/05/10/arts/castelli-gives-major-work-to-the-modern.html.

Goetzmann, William N. (1993). Accounting for Taste: Art and the Financial Markets over Three Centuries. *American Economic Review*, 83(5): 1370–1376.

Goetzmann, William N. (1996). How Costly Is the Fall from Fashion? Survivorship Bias in the Painting Market. In Victor A. Ginsburgh and Pierre-Michel Menger, eds., *Economics of the Arts: Selected Essays*. Elsevier, Amsterdam.

Goetzmann, William N. and Ibbotson, Roger G. (1994). Do Winners Repeat? *Journal of Portfolio Management*, 20(2): 9–18.

Goetzmann, Zoe. (2017). *Artists on Instagram: The Art World of Instagram.* Thesis in completion of the MA in Art Business, Sotheby's Institute of Art, London.

Gold, Mark S. and Jandl, Stefanie S. (2020, May 18). Why the Association of Art Museum Directors's Move on Deaccessioning Matters so Much. *The Art Newspaper.* www.theartnewspaper.com/comment/why-the-aamd-s-move-on-deaccessioning-matters-so-much.

Goldberg, Emma. (2020, July 8). Ava DuVernay's Fight for Change Onscreen and Off. *New York Times.* www.nytimes.com/2020/07/08/movies/director-ava-duvernay-movies-police-protests.html.

Goodwin, Craufurd. (2006). Art and Culture in the History of Economic Thought. In Victor A. Ginsburgh and David Throsby, eds., *Handbook of the Economics of Art and Culture,* vol. 1. Amsterdam: Elsevier North Holland, pp. 25–68.

Gopnik, Blake. (2020). *Warhol.* New York: HarperCollins.

Graeber, David. (2011, August 23). *David Graeber: The Barter Myth and the Origin of Money.* Bookspan [video]. www.youtube.com/watch?v=CZIINXhGDcs.

Grampp, William D. (1989). *Pricing the Priceless.* New York: Basic Books.

Gramsci, Antonio. (1971). *Prison Notebooks.* London: Lawrence and Wishart.

Granovetter, Mark. (1985). Economic Actions and Social Structure: The Problem of Embeddedness. *American Journal of Sociology,* 91 (3): 481–510.

Greenberger, Alex. (2018, October 19). Signal Gallery, Hotbed for Vanguard Art in Brooklyn, Will Close. *ARTnews.* www.artnews.com/art-news/market/signal-gallery-hotbed-vanguard-art-brooklyn-will-close-11202.

Greffe, Xavier. (2002). *Art and Artists from an Economic Perspective* (trans. Latika Saghal). Paris: UNESCO.

Greffe, Xavier. (2011). The Economic Impact of the Louvre. *Journal of Arts Management, Law, and Society,* 41(2): 121–137.

Griffin, Nora. (2007–8, December–January). Werner Kramarsky and the Art of Collecting. *Brooklyn Rail.* www.brooklynrail.org/2007/12/art/werner.

Groenewegen, Peter. *A Soaring Eagle: Alfred Marshall 1942–1924.* Hants, UK: Edward Elgar.

The Guardian. (2017, September 1). The Parthenon of Books, Kassel, Germany – in Pictures. www.theguardian.com/travel/gallery/2017/sep/01/the-parthenon-of-books-kassel-germany-art-installation-nazi-book-burning-in-pictures.

Guggenheim, Peggy. (2005 [1979]). *Out of This Century: Confessions of an Art Addict.* London: Andre Deutsch.

Haakonssen, Knud. (2006). *The Cambridge Companion to Adam Smith.* Cambridge, UK: Cambridge University Press.

Haigney, Sophie. (2020, February 7). *The Scream* Is Fading: New Research Reveals Why. *New York Times*. www.nytimes.com/2020/02/07/arts/design/the-scream-edvard-munch-science.html.

Halperin, Julia. (2017, December 22). How the High Museum in Atlanta Tripled Its Nonwhite Audience in Two Years. *Artnet News*. https://news.artnet.com/art-world/high-museum-atlanta-tripled-nonwhite-audience-two-years-1187954.

Halperin, Julia and Kinsella, Eileen. (2017, July 21). Cady Noland Sues Three Galleries for Copyright Infringement over Disavowed Log Cabin Structure. *Artnet News*. https://news.artnet.com/art-world/cady-noland-copyright-infringement-log-cabin-1030649.

Hansmann, Henry and Kraakman, Reinier. (2002). Property, Contract, and Verification: The Numerus Clausus Problem and the Divisibility of Rights. *Journal of Legal Studies*, 31(S2): 373–420.

Hardin, Garrett. (1968, December 13). The Tragedy of the Commons. *Science*, 162 (3859): 1243–1248.

Harrison, Nate. (2020, March 8). Presentation on the panel Artists Modeling Legal Futures (Lauren van Haaften-Schick, Nate Harrison, Kenneth Pietrobono, Amy Whitaker) Roundtable. Law, Culture, and the Humanities Conference, Quinnapiac University, Hamden, CT.

Haskell, John. (2015, July 8). Caroline Woolard by John Haskell. *BOMB*. https://bombmagazine.org/articles/caroline-woolard.

Hassani Design BV. (n.d.). About the Founders. http://ha55ani.com/about.

Hauser & Wirth. (n.d.). Publishers. www.hauserwirth.com/publishers.

Hayes, Rob. (2018, January 22). LA's Notoriously Stealthy Freeway Sign. *ABC7*. https://abc7.com/society/las-stealthy-freeway-sign-artist-still-up-to-his-old-tricks/2978744.

Heath, Christian. (2012). *The Dynamics of Auctions: Social Interaction and the Sale*. Cambridge, UK: Cambridge University Press.

Heidegger, Martin. (1993 [1947]). The Origin of the Work of Art. In David Farrell Krell, ed., *Basic Writings*. New York: Harper Perennial, pp. 143–206.

Heilbrun, James and Gray, Charles M. (2001). *The Economics of Art and Culture*. 2nd ed. Cambridge, UK: Cambridge University Press.

Henriques, Diana B. (1995, August 31). Fischer Black, 57, Wall Street Theorist, Dies. *New York Times*, p. B15.

Herbert, Martin. (2016). *Tell Them I Said No*. Berlin, Germany: Sternberg Press.

Hickley, Catherine. (2017, September 12). documenta Faces Yawning Euro 7m Deficit, Seeks Financial Help. *The Art Newspaper*. www.theartnewspaper.com/news/documenta-faces-yawning-euro7m-deficit-seeks-financial-help.

Higgins, Charlotte. (2017, June 22). How Nicholas Serota's Tate Changed Britain. *The Guardian.* www.theguardian.com/artanddesign/2017/jun/22/how-nicholas-serota-tate-changed-britain.

Hillel Italie and Associated Press. (2009, February 4). AP Alleges Copyright Infringement of Obama Image. *San Diego Union Tribune.* www.sandiegouniontribune.com/sdut-obama-poster-020409-2009feb04-story.html.

Hirsch, Fred. (1976). *Social Limits to Growth.* Cambridge, MA: Harvard University Press.

Hoey, Chuck. (2018). Museum Opening in Shanghai. *Table Tennis History Journal.* www.ittf.com/wp-content/uploads/2018/04/MuseumOpeningSpecialEdition.pdf.

Honoré, Tony. (1987). *Making Law Bind: Essays Legal and Philosophical.* Oxford, UK: Oxford University Press.

Horowitz, Noah. (2014). *Art of the Deal: Contemporary Art in a Global Financial Market.* Princeton, NJ: Princeton University Press.

Howarth, Sophie. (2000). Piero Manzoni: *Artist's Shit* 1961, Summary. *Tate.* www.tate.org.uk/art/artworks/manzoni-artists-shit-t07667.

Hudson, Māui, Farrar, Dickie and McLean, Lesley. (2016). Tribal Data Sovereignty: Whakatōhea Rights and Interests. In Tahu Kukutai and John Taylor, eds., *Indigenous Data Sovereignty: Toward an Agenda.* Canberra: Australian National University Press, pp. 157–178.

Human Rights Watch. (2001, October). *Human Rights Watch Backgrounder: Landmine Use in Afghanistan.* www.hrw.org/legacy/backgrounder/arms/landmines-bck1011.pdf.

Hultén, K. G. Pontus. (1968). *The Machine, As Seen at the End of the Mechanical Age.* New York: Museum of Modern Art. Available via the MoMA website: https://assets.moma.org/documents/moma_catalogue_2776_300292931.pdf?_ga=2.45998050.793891684.1593464817-528654.1593362002.

Hutter, Michael. (1996). The Impact of Cultural Economics on Economic Theory. *Journal of Cultural Economics,* 20(4): 263–268.

Hutter, Michael and Throsby, David (Eds). (2008). *Beyond Price: Value in Culture, Economics, and the Arts.* Cambridge, UK: Cambridge University Press.

Hybenova, Katarina. (2012, June 26). Three Bushwick Galleries Came to Their End. *Bushwick Daily.* https://bushwickdaily.com/bushwick/categories/arts-and-culture/581-3-bushwick-galleries-closed.

Hyde, Lewis. (1983). *The Gift: Imagination and the Erotic Life of Property.* New York: Vintage.

Ibbotson, Roger G. and Goetzmann, William N. (2005). History and the Equity Risk Premium. Yale ICF Working Paper No. 05–04. https://ssrn.com/abstract=702341.

Ibbotson, Roger G. and Sinquefield, Rex A. (1989). *Stocks, Bonds, Bills, and Inflation: Historical Returns*. New York: Richard D. Irwin.

International Council of Museums (ICOM). (n.d.). Guidelines on Deaccessioning of the International Council of Museums. https://icom.museum/wp-content/uploads/2019/08/20170503_ICOM_standards_deaccessioning_final_EN-v2.pdf.

International Table Tennis Federation (ITTF). (2018, April 1). ITTF Museum Officially Launched in Shanghai, China. www.ittf.com/2018/03/31/ittf-museum-officially-launched-shanghai-china.

ITTF Museum/CTT Museum. (n.d.). Visitor Guide.

Jackson, Brian Keith. (2019, April 14). Kehinde Wiley's Art Annex. *New York*. www.thecut.com/2019/04/tour-kehinde-wiley-art-annex-in-dakar-senegal.html.

Jacobs, Luis (Ed.). (2011). *Commerce by Artists*. Toronto, ON: Art Metropole.

Jandl, Stefanie. (2019). OMG We Won! The New Museum Union. In Dawn E. Salerno, Mark S. Gold, and Kristina L. Durocher, eds., *For Love or Money: Confronting the State of Museum Salaries*. Edinburgh: MuseumsEtc, pp. 306–325.

Jevons, W. Stanley. (1965 [1871]). Preface to the First Edition. In *The Theory of Political Economy*, 5th ed. New York: Augustus M. Kelly.

Jevons, W. Stanley. (1965 [1879]). Preface to the Second Edition. In *The Theory of Political Economy*, 5th ed. New York: Augustus M. Kelly.

Johnson, Peter and Thomas, Barry. (1998). The Economics of Museums: A Research Perspective. *Journal of Cultural Economics*, 22(2–3): 75–85.

Johnson, Randal. (1993). Introduction. In Randal Johnson, ed., *The Field of Cultural Production*. New York: Polity, pp. 1–28.

Johnston, Bob and Johnston, Nadine. (2012). *White Persian [Cat] in Pansy Patch*. https://fineartamerica.com/featured/white-persian-in-pansy-patch-original-forsale-bob-and-nadine-johnston.html.

Jones, Jonathan. (2012, November 30). Sorry MoMA, Video Games Are Not Art. *The Guardian*. www.theguardian.com/artanddesign/jonathanjonesblog/2012/nov/30/moma-video-games-art.

Kamps, Toby. (2015). *Takis: The Fourth Dimension*. [exhibition], The Menil Collection, Houston, TX, January 24_July 26, 2015. www.menil.org/exhibitions/37-takis-the-fourth-dimension.

Karpik, Lucien. (2010). *Valuing the Unique: The Economics of Singularities*. Princeton, NJ: Princeton University Press.

Katchadourian, Nina. (2020, March 16). Welcome to Stickies's Art School for Kids. www.facebook.com/nina.katchadourian/posts/10156917541462091.

Katchadourian, Nina. (2020, March 19). Aaaannnnddddd …. .Stickies Has FEEDBACK for You …. www.facebook.com/nina.katchadourian/posts/10156928658422091.

Kaufman, Jason Edward. (2008). Why the Guggenheim Won't Open a Branch in Guadalajara. *The Art Newspaper*, 17(June):27.

Kee, Joan. (2019). *Models of Integrity: Art and Law in Post-Sixties America*. Oakland, CA: University of California Press.

Keefe, Patrick Radden. (2012, June 15). Cocaine Incorporated. *New York Times Magazine*. www.nytimes.com/2012/06/17/magazine/how-a-mexican-drug-cartel-makes-its-billions.html.

Kendi, Ibram X. (2019). *How to Be an Antiracist*. New York: Random House.

Kennedy, John F., Jr. (1961, January 20). *Ask Not What Your Country Can Do for You* …. 1961 Presidential Inaugural Address. www.jfklibrary.org/learn/about-jfk/historic-speeches/inaugural-address.

Kennedy, Randy. (2010, January 28). Artists Rights Act Applies in Dispute, Court Rules. *New York Times*. www.nytimes.com/2010/01/29/arts/design/29artist.html.

Kettle's Yard. (n.d.). Timeline. www.kettlesyard.co.uk/collection/recollection/timeline.

Keynes, John Maynard. (2007 [1936]). *The General Theory of Employment, Interest, and Money*. New York: Palgrave Macmillan.

Khaire, Mukti. (2017). *Culture and Commerce: The Value of Entrepreneurship in Creative Industries*. Stanford, CA: Stanford University Press.

Kharchenkova, Svetlana and Velthuis, Olav. (2017). How to Become a Judgment Device: Valuation Practices and the Role of Auctions in the Emerging Chinese Art Market. *Socio-Economic Review*, 16(3): 459–477.

Kim, Kibum and Degen, Natasha. (2017, July 2). The Kitsch Gazes Back: Jeff Koons and Damien Hirst Return. *Los Angeles Review of Books*. https://lareviewofbooks.org/article/the-kitsch-gazes-back-jeff-koons-and-damien-hirst-return.

Kinsella, Eileen. (2015, June 25). Cady Noland Disowns $1.4 Million "Log Cabin" Artwork Sparking Collector Lawsuit. *Artnet News*. https://news.artnet.com/market/cady-noland-log-cabin-lawsuit-311283.

Kinsella, Eileen. (2016, January 11). Sotheby's Acquires Amy Cappellazzo's Art Agency Partners for $50 Million. *Artnet News*. https://news.artnet.com/market/sothebys-pays-50m-art-agency-partners-404951.

Kinsella, Eileen. (2020, February 19). The $450 Marron Collection Is the Art Market's Ultimate Prize. Now, Three of the World's Top Rival Galleries Are Joining Forces to Sell It. *Artnet News*. https://news.artnet.com/market/donald-marron-collection-pace-acquavella-gagosian-1781181.

Kinsella, Eileen and Genocchio, Benjamin. (2015, March 23). Will Sotheby's Again Fall Victim to Corporate Hubris with Dan Loeb, Tad Smith Takeover? *Artnet*

News. https://news.artnet.com/art-world/sothebys-takeover-dan-loeb-tad-smith-278897.

Klamer, Arjo. (2009). The Lives of Cultural Goods. In Jack Amariglio and Joseph W. Childers, eds., *Sublime Economy: On the Intersection of Art and Economics*. London: Routledge.

Klemperer, Paul. (2004). *Auctions: Theory and Practice*. Princeton, NJ: Princeton University Press.

Kline, Katy. (2002). *Pointed Pairings: The Valuing of Art*. Brunswick, ME: Bowdoin College Museum of Art. https://digitalcommons.bowdoin.edu/art-museum-exhibition-catalogs/77.

Knight, Sam. (2016, February 8 and 15). The Bouvier Affair. *The New Yorker*, pp. 62–71.

Korteweg, Arthur, Kräussl, Roman and Verwijmeren, Patrick. (2016). Does It Pay to Invest in Art? A Selection-Corrected Returns Perspective. *Review of Financial Studies*, 29(4): 1007–1038.

Kreuger, Alan B. (2001). An Interview with William J. Baumol. *Journal Economic Perspectives*, 15(3): 211–231.

Krugman, Paul, Wells, Robin and Graddy, Kathryn. (2013). *Essentials of Economics*, 3rd ed. New York: Worth.

Kulenkampff, Annette, Szymczyk, Adam, et al. (2017, December 1). Open Letter Defending Exhibition. *Artforum.* www.artforum.com/news/documenta-14-artists-pen-second-open-letter-defending-exhibition-72702.

Kuzui, Fran. (2018, September 15). Japan's teamLab Transcends Borders of Art and Business. *Nikkei Asian Review.* https://asia.nikkei.com/Life-Arts/Arts/Japan-s-teamLab-transcends-borders-of-art-and-business.

La Berge, Leigh Claire. (2019). *Wages against Artwork: Decommodified Labor and the Claims of Socially Engaged Art*. Durham, NC: Duke University Press.

Lamont, Michele. (2012.) Toward a Comparative Sociology of Valuation and Evaluation. *Annual Review of Sociology*, 38(1): 201–221.

Landmine and Cluster Munitions Monitor. (2019, September 23). Afghanistan: Mine Action. www.the-monitor.org/en-gb/reports/2019/afghanistan/mine-action.aspx.

Langworth, Richard (Ed.). (2008). *Churchill by Himself: The Definitive Collection of Quotations*. New York: Public Affairs.

Laurinavičius, Rokas. (2018). Artist Uses 100,000 Banned Books to Build a Full-Size Parthenon at Historic Nazi Book Burning Site. *Bored Panda.* www.boredpanda.com/parthenon-books-marta-minujin-germany/?utm_source=google&utm_medium=organic&utm_campaign=organic.

Lena, Jennifer C. (2019). *Entitled: Discriminating Tastes and the Expansion of the Arts*. Princeton, NJ: Princeton University Press.

Leo Castelli Gallery. Records, circa 1880–2000, bulk 1957–99. Archives of American Art, Smithsonian Institution.

Leval, Pierre N. (1990). Toward a Fair Use Standard. *Harvard Law Review*, 103(5): 1105–1136.

Leyrer, Jonas. (2017, December 26). The Brannock Device: A 90-Year Monopoly. *JML Blog*. www.jonasleyrer.com/2017/12/26/the-brannock-device-a-90-year-monopoly.

Lippard, Lucy. (1970, November). The Art Workers' Coalition: Not a History. *Studio International*. http://artsandlabor.org/wp-content/uploads/2011/12/Lippard_AWC.pdf.

Lippard, Lucy. (2016). Never Done: Women's Work by Mierle Laderman Ukeles. In Patricia C. Phillips, ed., *Mierle Laderman Ukeles: Maintenance Art*. New York: Prestel; New York: Queens Museum, pp. 14–20.

Lobel, Michael. (2012). *Andy Warhol Flowers*. New York: Eykyn Maclean.

Louden, Sharon (Ed.). (2013). *Living and Sustaining a Creative Life: Essays by 40 Living Artists*. Bristol, UK: Intellect Books.

Lovo, Stefano and Spaenjers, Christophe. (2018). A Model of Trading in the Art Market. *American Economic Review*, 108(3): 744–774.

Lowry, Alexis and Morgan, Jessica (Ed). (2019). *Charlotte Posenenske: Work in Progress*. Cologne, Germany: Walther König.

Luciano-Adams, Beige. (2020, January 31). The Art of Organizing. *The American Prospect*. https://prospect.org/labor/the-art-of-organizing.

Ma, Yo-Yo. (2020, March 13). In These Days of Anxiety . . .. https://twitter.com/YoYo_Ma/status/1238572657278431234.

Mabuchi, Jun. (2019). *Decentralizing the Whiteness in the Museum: Sustainable Framework of DEI*. Thesis in completion of the MA in Visual Arts Administration, New York University.

MacKenzie, Donald. (2008, September 25). What's in a Number? *London Review of Books*, 30(18). www.lrb.co.uk/the-paper/v30/n18/donald-mackenzie/what-s-in-a-number.

Mandiberg, Michael. (2016). *FDIC Insured by Michael Mandiberg*. http://fdic.mandiberg.com/#/about.

Mandiberg, Michael. (2018). Postmodern Times. www.mandiberg.com/postmodern-times.

Maneker, Marion. (2020, May 4). Should We Be Worried about Sotheby's Ability to Meet Its Obligations? *Art Market Monitor*. www.artmarketmonitor.com/2020/05/04/should-we-be-worried-about-sothebys-ability-to-meet-its-obligations.

Marber, Sinclaire D. (2019). Will the Art Market Really Soar? Revisiting Resale Rights after BREXIT. *Art, Antiquity and Law*, 24(2): 137–150.

Markowitz, Harry M. (1952). Portfolio Selection. *Journal of Finance*, 7(1): 77–91.

Marshall, Alfred. (1920 [1890]). *Principles of Economics*, 8th ed. London: MacMillan.

Martin, Charlotte, Maldonado, Sarah and Song, Anthea. (2019). A Case for Salary Transparency in Job Postings. In Dawn E. Salerno, Mark S. Gold, and Kristina L. Durocher, eds., *For Love or Money: Confronting the State of Museum Salaries*. Edinburgh: MuseumsEtc. pp. 306–325.

Maslow, Abraham. (1943). A Theory of Human Motivation. *Psychological Review*, 50(4): 370–396.

Mason, Christopher. (2004). *The Art of the Steal: Inside the Sotheby's–Christie's Auction House Scandal*. New York: Berkley Books.

Massachusetts Museum of Contemporary Art Foundation, Inc. (Mass MoCA). (2005). Form 990 Return of Organization Exempt from Income Tax, 2005. Accessed from Propublica. https://projects.propublica.org/nonprofits/organiza tions/43113688.

Massachusetts Museum of Contemporary Art Foundation, Inc. (Mass MoCA). (2006). Form 990 Return of Organization Exempt from Income Tax, 2006. Accessed from Propublica. https://projects.propublica.org/nonprofits/organizations/43113688.

Massachusetts Museum of Contemporary Art Foundation v. Büchel, No. 08–2199 (1st Cir. Jan. 27, 2010).

McAndrew, Clare. (2007). *The Art Economy*. Dublin, Ireland: Liffey Press.

McAndrew, Clare. (2010). An Introduction to Art and Finance. In Clare McAndrew, ed., *Fine Art and High Finance: Expert Advice on the Economics of Ownership*. New York: Bloomsbury, pp. 1–30.

McAndrew, Clare. (2017). *The Art Market 2017*. Basel, Switzerland: Art Basel and UBS. https://d33ipftjqrd91.cloudfront.net/asset/cms/Art_Basel_and_UBS_The_Art_Market_2017.pdf.

McAndrew, Clare. (2018). *The Art Market 2018*. Basel, Switzerland: Art Basel and UBS. https://d2u3kfwd92fzu7.cloudfront.net/Art%20Basel%20and%20UBS_The%20Art%20Market_2018-1.pdf.

McAndrew, Clare. (2019). *The Art Market 2019*. Basel, Switzerland: Art Basel and UBS. https://d2u3kfwd92fzu7.cloudfront.net/The_Art_Market_2019-5.pdf.

McAndrew, Clare. (2020). *The Art Market 2020*. Basel, Switzerland: Art Basel and UBS. www.artbasel.com/about/initiatives/the-art-market.

McConnell, Campbell, Brue, Stanley and Flynn, Sean. (2018). *Economics,* 21st ed. New York: McGraw-Hill.

McKinsey & Co. (2001). Tate Study, presentation 080501LNZXW293CJDK-P1, p. 39. Tate Gallery Archives, TG 12/1/3/5.

McKinsey & Co. (2001, May 10). Assessing the Economic Impact of Tate Modern. Tate Gallery Archives, TG 12/1/3/11.

McNulty, Tom. (2013). *Art Market Research: A Guide to Methods and Sources.* Jefferson, NC: McFarland and Company.

Meade, James E. (1952). External Economies and Diseconomies in a Competitive Situation. *Economic Journal,* 62(245): 54–67.

Mei, Jianping and Moses, Michael. (2002). Art As an Investment and the Underperformance of Masterpieces. *American Economic Review,* 92(5): 1656–1668.

Mei, Jianping and Moses, Michael. (2005). Vested Interest and Biased Price Estimates: Evidence from an Auction Market. *Journal of Finance,* 60(5): 2409–2435.

Menger, Pierre-Michel. (2014). *The Economics of Creativity: Art and Achievement under Uncertainty.* Cambridge, MA: Harvard University Press.

Merryman, John Henry. (1985). Thinking about the Elgin Marbles. *Michigan Law Review,* 83(8): 1880–1923. http://blogs.bu.edu/aberlin/files/2011/09/Merryman-1985.pdf.

Metropolitan Opera. (2020, March 21). Met Launches "Nightly Met Opera Streams." www.metopera.org/about/press-releases/met-launches-nightly-met-opera-streams-a-free-series-of-encore-live-in-hd-presentations-streamed-on-the-company-website-during-the-coronavirus-closure.

Mill, John Stuart. (2005 [1871]). *The Principles of Political Economy,* 7th ed., edited by Jonathan Riley. Oxford, UK: Oxford University Press.

Montias, John Michael. (1989). *Vermeer and His Milieu: A Web of Social History.* Princeton, NJ: Princeton University Press.

Morningstar. (2015, July 2). Morningstar Acquires Remaining Ownership Interest in Ibbotson Associates Japan Inc. https://newsroom.morningstar.com/news room/news-archive/press-release-details/2015/Morningstar-Acquires-Remaining-Ownership-Interest-in-Ibbotson-Associates-Japan-Inc/default.aspx.

Motz, Lloyd and Duveen, Anneta. (1966). *Essentials of Astronomy.* Belmont, CA: Wadsworth.

Moureau, Nathalie. (2000). *Analyse économique de la valeur des biens d'art: La peinture contemporaine.* Paris: Economica.

Muir, Gregor and Massey, Anne. (2014). *Institute of Contemporary Arts: 1946–1968.* Amsterdam: Roma Publications; London: ICA.

Mullis, Darrell and Orloff, Judith. (2008). *The Accounting Game: Basic Accounting Fresh from the Lemonade Stand*. Naperville, IL: Sourcebooks.

Munger, Michael. (2008, May 5). Orange Blossom Special: Externalities and the Coase Theorem. *The Library of Economics and Liberty*. www.econlib.org/library/Columns/y2008/Mungerbees.html.

Munro, Cait. (2015, May 27). Who Are the Suicide Girls? Inside the Nude Pin-Up Community That Trolled Richard Prince. *Artnet News*. www.news.artnet.com/art-world/suicide-girls-inside-pin-community-challenged-richard-prince-302760.

Musée d'Orsay. (n.d.). Vincent Van Gogh: Dr. Paul Gachet. *Musee-Orsay.fr*. www.musee-orsay.fr/en/collections/works-in-focus/search/commentaire/commentaire_id/dr-paul-gachet-2988.html.

Musée du Louvre. (n.d.1). Free admission to the Musée du Louvre. www.louvre.fr/en/free-admission-musee-du-louvre.

Musée du Louvre. (n.d.2). Hours, Admissions & Directions. www.louvre.fr/en/hours-admission-directions/admission#tabs.

Musée du Louvre. (n.d.3). Membership: Become a Friend of the Louvre! www.louvre.fr/en/membership-become-friend-louvre.

Musée du Louvre. (n.d.4). Patron's Circle. www.louvre.fr/en/patrons-circle.

Museum of Modern Art. (n.d.). UNIQLO Free Friday Nights. *MoMA.org*. www.moma.org/calendar/events/5601.

Museum of Modern Art. (1962). Takis: Tele-Sculpture, Paris 1960 (Cork Added 1962). www.moma.org/collection/works/81217.

Museum of Modern Art. (2011). Massoud Hassani: Mind Kafon Wind-Powered Deminer. www.moma.org/collection/works/160434.

Musumeci, Natalie (2019, December 10). Tampa Police Spoof Art Basel $120k Banana with $200k "Sgt. Donut." *New York Post*. https://nypost.com/2019/12/10/tampa-police-spoof-art-basel-120k-banana-with-200k-sgt-donut.

National Endowment for the Arts. (n.d.). Art and Artifacts Indemnity Program: International Indemnity. www.arts.gov/artistic-fields/museums/arts-and-artifacts-indemnity-program-international-indemnity.

National Endowment for the Arts (1976, April). *Employment and Unemployment of Artists 1970–1975, 1976. Research Division Report #1*. https://credo.library.umass.edu/view/full/mums686-b002-i028.

National Endowment for the Arts. (1978, January). *Minorities and Women in the Arts: 1970. Research Division Report #7*. https://credo.library.umass.edu/cgi-bin/pdf.cgi?id=scua:mums686-b002-i030.

Neuendorf, Henri. (2018, October 12). Christie's Will Become the First Major Auction House to Use Blockchain in a Sale. *Artnet News*. https://news.artnet.com/market/christies-artory-blockchain-pilot-1370788.

Nichols, Camila. (2019). *Immaterial and Ephemeral Art in the Commercial Gallery: An Artist–Dealer Relationship Analysis.* Thesis in completion of the MA in Visual Arts Administration, New York University.

Nickson, Jack W., Jr. and Colonna, Carl M. (1977). The Economic Exploitation of the Visual Artist. *Journal of Cultural Economics*, 1(1): 75–79.

Nie, Taryn R. (2019). Far Too Female: Museums on the Edge of a Pink Collar Profession. In Dawn E. Salerno, Mark S. Gold, and Kristina L. Durocher, eds., *For Love or Money: Confronting the State of Museum Salaries.* Edinburgh: MuseumsEtc, pp. 120–163.

Nkontchou, Bimpe. (2020). Philanthropy in African Art. In Anders Petterson, ed., *Art Patronage in the 21st Century: The TEFAF Art Market Report*, pp. 87–89.

Noh, Megan E. (2020). US Law's Artificial Cabining of Moral Rights: The Copyrightability Prerequisite and Cady Noland's Log Cabin. *Columbia Journal of Law and the Arts*, 43(3): 353–365.

Noonan, Douglas S. (2003). Contingent Valuation and Cultural Resources: A Meta-Analytic Review of the Literature. *Journal of Cultural Economics*, 27 (3–4): 159–176.

Norte Maar. (n.d.). Norte Maar for Collaborative Projects in the Arts. www .nortemaar.org/history.

O'Brien, D. (2010). *Measuring the Value of Culture: A Report to the Department for Culture Media and Sport.* London, UK: Department for Culture, Media and Sport. www.gov.uk/government/uploads/system/uploads/attachment_data/ file/77933/measuring-the-value-culture-report.pdf.

Odell, Jenny. (2019). *How to Do Nothing: Resisting the Attention Economy.* New York: Melville House.

Oi, Walter Y. (1971). A Disneyland Dilemma: Two-Part Tariffs for a Mickey Mouse Monopoly. *Quarterly Journal of Economics*, 85(1): 77–96.

Organization of the Petroleum Exporting Countries (OPEC). (n.d.). Brief History. www.opec.org/opec_web/en/about_us/24.htm.

Oster, Sharon M. (1999). *Modern Competitive Analysis*, 3rd ed. New York: Oxford University Press.

Oster, Sharon M. (1995). *Strategic Management for Nonprofit Organizations.* New York: Oxford University Press.

Ostrom, Elinor. (1990). *Governing the Commons: The Evolution of Institutions for Collective Action.* Cambridge, UK: Cambridge University Press.

Pagano, Ugo (1999). Is Power an Economic Good? Notes on Social Scarcity and the Economics of Positional Goods. In Samuel Bowles, Maurizio Franzini and Ugo Pagano, eds., *The Politics and the Economics of Power*. London: Routledge, pp. 116–145.

Pearce, David, Atkinson, Giles and Mourato, Susana. (2006). *Cost–Benefit Analysis and the Environment: Recent Developments*. Paris: OECD.

Peers, Alexandra. (1996, July 5). British Pension Fund's Bet on Art Pays Off Respectably. *Wall Street Journal*. www.wsj.com/articles/SB836529720395795000.

Perrotin. (n.d.). Maurizio Cattelan: Biography. www.perrotin.com/artists/Maurizio_Cattelan/2#biography.

Pes, Javier. (2018, June 15). Artist Olafur Eliasson's Little Sun Is Teaming up with Ikea on a New Line of Solar Powered Products. *Artnet News*. https://news.artnet.com/art-world/olafur-eliasson-ikea-collaboration-1303436.

Pettit, Clare. (2007). A Dark Exhibition: The Crystal Palace, Bleak House, and Intellectual Property. In Jim Buzard, Joseph Childers, and Eileen Gillooly, eds., *Victorian Prism: Refractions of the Crystal Palace*. Charlottesville, VA: University of Virginia, pp. 250–269.

Petty, M. Elizabeth. (2014). Rauschenberg, Royalties, and Artists' Rights: Potential Droit de Suite Legislation in the United States. *William and Mary Bill of Rights Journal*, 22(3): 977–1009.

Phillips, Patricia C. (2016). Making Necessity Art: Collisions of Maintenance and Freedom. In Patricia C. Phillips, ed., *Mierle Laderman Ukeles: Maintenance Art*. New York: Prestel; New York: Queens Museum, pp. 23–193.

Pigou, Arthur Cecil. (2017 [1920]). *The Economics of Welfare*. London: Routledge.

Pikkety, Thomas. (2013). *Capital in the Twenty-First Century* (trans. Arthur Goldhammer). Cambridge, MA: Belknap Press.

Pink, Daniel H. (2009). *Drive: The Surprising Truth about What Motivates Us*. New York: Riverhead Books.

Pink, Daniel H. and RSA Animate. (2010). Drive: The Surprising Truth about What Motivates Us. www.youtube.com/watch?v=u6XAPnuFjJc.

Plaza, Beatriz, González-Casimiro, Pilar, Moral-Zuaco, Paz and Waldron, Courtney. (2015). Culture-Led City Brands As Economic Engines: Theory and Empirics. *Annals of Regional Science*, 54(1):179–196.

Pogrebin, Robin. (2016, January 11). Sotheby's, in a Gamble, Acquires Boutique Art Advisory Firm. *New York Times*. www.nytimes.com/2016/01/12/arts/sothebys-in-a-gamble-acquires-boutique-art-advisory-firm.html.

Porter, Michael E. (2008). The Five Competitive Forces That Shape Strategy. *Harvard Business Review*. https://hbr.org/2008/01/the-five-competitive-forces-that-shape-strategy.

Potts, Jason. (2015, August 3). The Economics of the Politics of the Arts. *The Conversation*. https://theconversation.com/the-economics-of-the-politics-of-the-arts-40555.

Potts, Maff. (2019, November 27). The Power of Friends and Purpose. Meaning Conference, Brighton, England. www.youtube.com/watch?v=_72KGzeP204.

Pownall, Rachel A. J. (2017). TEFAF Art Market Report 2017. Maastricht, the Netherlands: European Fine Art Foundation. http://1uyxqn3lzdsa2ytyz j1asxmmmpt.wpengine.netdna-cdn.com/wp-content/uploads/2017/03/TEFAF-Art-Market-Report-20173.pdf.

Press, Clayton. (2017, October 24). Artful Art Investment: "The Skin of the Bear." Forbes. www.forbes.com/sites/claytonpress/2017/10/24/artful-art-investment -the-skin-of-the-bear/#55e2935d6988.

Price, Sally. (2020, January 6). Has the Sarr–Savoy Report Had Any Effect Since It Was First Published? Apollo Magazine. www.apollo-magazine.com/sarr-savoy-report-sally-price-dan-hicks.

Project Row Houses. (n.d.). Mission and History. https://projectrowhouses.org/ab out/mission-history.

Prowda, Judith B. (2013). Visual Arts and the Law: A Handbook for Professionals. London: Lund Humphries.

Puglise, Nicole. (2016, August 24). Artist Peter Doig Victorious As Court Agrees "$10m" Painting Is Not His Work. The Guardian. www.theguardian.com/art anddesign/2016/aug/24/artist-peter-doig-landscape-painting-lawsuit.

Pung, Caroline, Clarke, Ann and Patten, Laurie. (2004). Measuring the Economic Impact of the British Library. New Review of Academic Librarianship, 10(1): 79–102.

Queens Museum of Art. (2016). Mierle Laderman Ukeles: Maintenance Art, September 18, 2016–February 19, 2017 [exhibition brochure]. https://queensmu seum.org/wp-content/uploads/2016/12/Mierle%20Laderman%20Ukeles_Mai ntenance%20Art_Brochure.pdf.

Rachleff, Melissa. (2017). Inventing Downtown: Artist-Run Galleries in New York City, 1952–1965. New York: Grey Art Gallery, New York University; New York: DelMonico Books.

Rand, John. (1841). Improvement in the Construction of Vessels or Apparatus for Preserving Paint, US Patent 2252. https://patents.google.com/patent/US2252A/ en.

Regnault, Jules. (1863). Calcul des chances et philosophie de la bourse. Paris: Mallet-Bachelier et Castel.

Reinhardt, Mark. (2017). Vision's Unseen: On Sovereignty, Race, and the Optical Unconscious. In Shawn Michelle Smith and Sharon Sliwinski, eds., Photography and the Optical Unconscious. Durham, NC: Duke University Press, pp. 174–222.

Reitlinger, Gerald. (1961–70). The Economics of Taste. 3 vols. London: Barrie and Rockliffe.

Renneboog, Luc and Spaenjers, Christophe. (2013). Buying Beauty: On Prices and Returns in the Art Market. *Management Science*, 59: 36–53.

Resch, Magnus. (2016). *Management of Art Galleries*, 2nd ed. London: Phaidon Press.

Reyburn, Scott. (2018, October 6). Banksy Painting Self-Destructs after Fetching $1.4 Million at Sotheby's. *New York Times*. www.nytimes.com/2018/10/06/arts/design/uk-banksy-painting-sothebys.html.

Reyburn, Scott. (2019, May 15). Jeff Koons "Rabbit" Sets Auction Record for Most Expensive Work by Living Artist. *New York Times*. www.nytimes.com/2019/05/15/arts/jeff-koons-rabbit-auction.html.

Rijksmuseum. (n.d.). Timeline of Dutch History: 1940 Invasion. www.rijksmuseum.nl/en/rijksstudio/timeline-dutch-history/1940-invasion.

Rivetti, Ermanno. (2016, December 6). Sotheby's Buys Orion Analytical Lab in Fight against Art Fraud. *The Art Newspaper*. www.theartnewspaper.com/news/sotheby-s-buys-orion-analytical-lab-in-fight-against-art-fraud.

Roberts, Sam. (2019, August 25). Werner Kramarsky, Rights Official and Arts Patron, Dies at 93. *New York Times*. www.nytimes.com/2019/08/23/nyregion/werner-kramarsky-dies.html.

Roberts, Veronica (2014). *Converging Lines: Eva Hesse and Sol LeWitt*. New Haven, CT: Blanton Museum of Art in association with Yale University Press.

Roberts, Veronica. (2017). Seat Assignment, Art in Airplane Mode. In Veronica Roberts, ed., *Nina Katchadourian: Curiouser*. Austin, TX: University of Texas Press.

Robertson, Iain. (2016). *Understanding Art Markets: Inside the World of Art and Business*. London: Routledge.

Rosen, Sherwin. (1981). The Economics of Superstars. *American Economic Review*, 71(5): 845–858.

Rosenbaum, Debbie and Del Riego, Alissa (Eds.). (2010, February 2). Massachusetts Museum of Contemporary Art v. Büchel: First Circuit Holds That Artists Have Moral Rights in Unfinished Works. *JOLT (Harvard Journal of Law & Technology) Digest*. http://jolt.law.harvard.edu/digest/massachusetts-museum-of-contemporary-art-foundation-v-buchel.

Rozell, Mary. (2020). *The Art Collector's Handbook: A Guide to Collection Management and Care*, 2nd ed. London: Lund Humphries.

Rub, Guy A. (2014). The Unconvincing Case for Resale Royalties. *Yale Law Journal Forum*. www.yalelawjournal.org/forum/the-unconvincing-case-for-resale-royalties.

Rushton, Michael. (2017). Should Public and Nonprofit Museums Have Free Admission? A Defense of the Membership Model. *Museum Management and Curatorship*, 32(3): 200–209.

Russeth, Andrew. (2019, July 9). The Ringmaster: Is Charles Venable Democratizing a Great Art Museum in Indianapolis – or Destroying It? *ARTnews*. www.artnews.com/art-news/news/charles-venable-newfields-indianapolis-museum-12938.

Russeth, Andrew. (2019, August 23). Wynn Kramarsky, Venturesome Drawings Collector and Arts Patron, Is Dead at 93. *ARTnews*. www.artnews.com/art-news/news/wynn-kramarsky-dead-13143.

Sabbagh, Karl. (2001). *Power into Art: The Making of Tate Modern*. London: Penguin.

Salisbury, Josh. (2018, October 1). Southbank Single Mum Has Tate Modern Building Named after Her in Recognition of Good Deeds. *Southwark News*. www .southwarknews.co.uk/news/southbank-tate-modern-coin-street-natalie-bell.

Salmon, Felix. (2019, November 5). What Is Art Really Worth?, with Julia Halperin. *Slate Money*, at 3:20. https://slate.com/podcasts/slate-money/2019/11/julia-halperin-artnet-art-good-investment.

Salmon, Frances E. (1945, March 20). Letter to Mr. Harold Ede from American Red Cross. Kettle's Yard Archive.

Sarmiento, Sergio Muñoz and van Haaften-Schick, Lauren. (2014). *Cariou v. Prince: Toward a Theory of Aesthetic-Judicial Judgments*. *Texas A&M Law Review*, 1 (4): 941–958.

Sarr, Felwine and Savoy, Bénédicte. (2018). *The Restitution of African Cultural Heritage: Toward a New Relational Ethics* (trans. Drue S. Burk). www.about-africa.de/images/sonstiges/2018/sarr_savoy_en.pdf.

Savino, David M. (2016). Frederick Winslow Taylor and His Lasting Legacy of Functional Leadership Competence. *Journal of Leadership, Accountability and Ethics*, 13(1): 70–76.

Schneider, Michael. (2007). The Nature, History and Significance of the Concept of Positional Goods. *History of Economics Review*, 45(1): 60–81.

Schneider, Tim. (2018, September 12). A Decade After Damien Hirst's Historic "Beautiful Inside My Head Forever" Auction, Resale Prices Are Looking Ugly. *Artnet News*. https://news.artnet.com/market/damien-hirst-beautiful-resales-1346528.

Seaman, Bruce A. (2011). Economic Impact of the Arts. In Ruth Towse, ed., *A Handbook of Cultural Economics*, 2nd ed. Cheltenham, UK: Edward Elgar.

Senie, Harriet. (1989). Richard Serra's *Tilted Arc*: Art and Non-Art Issues. *Art Journal*, 48(4): 298–302.

Serota, Nicholas. (1987). Grasping the Nettle. Tate Gallery Archives.

Shah, Palak. (2019, May 15). Palak Shah. In Paola Antonelli, curator, *MoMA R&D Salon #31: Workspheres*. http://momarnd.moma.org/salons/salon-31-workspheres-1.

Sharpe, William, F. (1964, September). Capital Asset Prices: A Theory of Market Equilibrium under Conditions of Risk. *Journal of Finance*, 19(3): 425–442.

Shaw, Anny and Hanson, Sarah P. (2017, April 30). Did the Art Market Grow or Shrink in 2016? Depends Who You Ask. *The Art Newspaper*. www .theartnewspaper.com/news/did-the-art-market-grow-or-shrink-in-2016-depends-who-you-ask.

Shipley, David E. (2017). Droit de Suite, Copyright's First Sale Doctrine and Preemption of State Law. *Hastings Communications and Entertainment Law Journal*, 39(1): 1–42.

Shnayerson, Michael. (2019). *Boom: Mad Money, Mega Dealers, and the Rise of Contemporary Art*. New York: PublicAffairs.

Shorto, Russell. (2019, February 27). Rembrandt in the Blood: An Obsessive Aristocrat, Rediscovered Paintings, and an Art-World Feud. *New York Times Magazine*. www.nytimes.com/2019/02/27/magazine/rembrandt-jan-six.html.

Shughart, William F., II. (n.d.) Public Choice. *The Library of Economics and Liberty*. www.econlib.org/library/Enc/PublicChoice.html.

Sidgwick, Henry. (1883). *The Principles of Political Economy*. New York: MacMillan and Company.

Siegel, Laurence. (2019, July 25). History of Ibbotson Associates. *American Business History Center*. https://americanbusinesshistory.org/history-of-ibbotson-associates.

Siegelaub, Seth and Projansky, Robert. (1971). *The Artist's Reserved Rights Transfer and Sale Agreement*. New York: School of Visual Arts. https://primaryinformation .org/product/siegelaub-the-artists-reserved-rights-transfer-and-sale-agreement.

Smith, Adam. (1999 [1776]). *An Inquiry into the Nature and Causes of the Wealth of Nations*, books I–III, edited by Andrew Skinner. London: Penguin Classics.

Smith, Adam. (2002 [1759]). *The Theory of Moral Sentiments*. In Knud Haakonssen, ed., *Adam Smith: The Theory of Moral Sentiments*. Cambridge, UK: Cambridge University Press.

Smith, Roberta. (2007, September 16). Is It Art Yet? And Who Decides? *New York Times*. www.nytimes.com/2007/09/16/arts/design/16robe.html.

Smith, Roberta. (2010, October 18). At Tate Modern, Seeds of Discontent by the Ton. *New York Times*. www.nytimes.com/2010/10/19/arts/design/19sun flower.html.

Soskolne, Lise. (2015, February 22). On Merit. *The Artist As Debtor: The Work of Artists in the Age of Speculative Capitalism*. https://artanddebt.org/artist-as-debtor.

Sotheby's Inc. (2008, September 15–16). Beautiful Inside My Head Forever. www.sothebys.com/en/search-results.html?query=Damien%20Hirst%20beautiful%20inside%20my%20head%20forever.

Sotheby's Inc. (2016). Form 10-K: 2015. www.sec.gov/Archives/edgar/data/823094/000082309416000080/bid1231201510k_xbrl2015.htm.

Spaenjers, Christophe, Goetzmann, William. N. and Mamonova, Elena. (2015). The Economics of Aesthetics and Record Prices for Art since 1701. *Explorations in Economic History*, 57: 79–94.

Sprigman, Chris and Rub, Guy A. (2018, August 8). Resale Royalties Would Hurt Emerging Artists. *Artsy*. www.artsy.net/article/artsy-editorial-resale-royalties-hurt-emerging-artists.

Staple, Polly. (2016). Preface. In Chisenhale Gallery, *Maria Eichhorn: 5 Weeks, 25 Days, 175 Hours*. London: Chisenhale, pp. 3–7. https://chisenhale.org.uk/wp-content/uploads/Maria-Eichhorn_5-weeks-25-days-175-hours_Chisenhale-Gallery_2016.pdf.

Stein, Judith E. (2016). *Eye of the Sixties: Richard Bellamy and the Transformation of Modern Art*. New York: Farrar, Straus and Giroux.

Steinhauer, Jillian. (2017, February 10). How Mierle Laderman Ukeles Turned Maintenance Work into Art. *Hyperallergic*. www.hyperallergic.com/355255/how-mierle-laderman-ukeles-turned-maintenance-work-into-art.

Stephenson, Andrew. (2018). A Failed Charm Offensive: Tate and the Peggy Guggenheim Collection. In Alex J. Taylor, ed., *Modern American Art at Tate 1945–1980*. www.tate.org.uk/research/publications/modern-american-art-at-tate/essays/tate-peggy-guggenheim.

Sterngold, Arthur H. (2004). Do Economic Impact Studies Misrepresent the Benefits of Arts and Cultural Organizations? *Journal of Arts Management, Law, and Society*, 34(3): 166–187.

Stevens, Harry. (2020, March 14). Why Outbreaks Like Coronavirus Spread Exponentially and How to "Flatten the Curve." *The Washington Post*. www.washingtonpost.com/graphics/2020/world/corona-simulator.

Stewart, James B. (2001, October 15). Bidding War. *The New Yorker*, pp. 158–175.

Stigler, George J. (1989). Two Notes on the Coase Theorem. *Yale Law Journal*, 99(3): 631–633.

Stim, Richard. (2016). Copyright Basics FAQ, Stanford University Libraries. https://fairuse.stanford.edu/overview/faqs/copyright-basics.

Stim, Richard. (2019). *Getting Permission: How to License and Clear Copyrighted Materials Online and Off*, 7th ed. Berkeley, CA: Nolo.

Strategic National Arts Alumni Project (SNAAP). (2018). *2015, 2016 & 2017 Aggregate Frequency Report*. http://snaap.indiana.edu/pdf/2017/SNAAP15_16_17_Aggregate_Report.pdf

Stuckey, John and White, David. (1993). When and When Not to Vertically Integrate. *Sloan Management Review*, 34(3): 71–83.

Swinkels, Ingrid. (2009). Interview with Massoud Hassani. *DAE (Design Academy Eindhoven) Magazine*. http://massoudhassani-aboutme.blogspot.com/2009/12/where-are-you-from-i-am-originally-from.html.

Sunday, Elisabeth. (In press). *The Collector's Circle*.

Tan, Boon Hui. (2016). No Limits: Zao Wou-Ki. Asia Society website, https://asiasociety.org/new-york/exhibitions/no-limits-zao-wou-ki.

Tate. (n.d.1). Biography: Panayiotis Vassilakis. www.tate.org.uk/art/artists/takis-2019.

Tate. (n.d.2). Wall label for *Magnetic Fields*, 1969.

Tate. (n.d.3). Young British Artists. www.tate.org.uk/art/art-terms/y/young-british-artists-ybas.

Tate. (n.d.4). Takis: 3 July–27 October 2019 [Large Print Guide]. www.tate.org.uk/whats-on/tate-modern/exhibition/takis/exhibition-guide.

Tate. (1991). *The Tate Gallery Biennial Report 1988–1990*. London: Tate Gallery Publications.

Tate. (1999, October 6). New Millennium Sees Major Expansion of Tate Gallery. www.tate.org.uk/press/press-releases/new-millennium-sees-major-expansion-tate-gallery.

Tate. (2019). Kara Walker's *Fons Americanus*. www.tate.org.uk/art/artists/kara-walker-2674/kara-walkers-fons-americanus.

Taylor, Frederick Winslow (1911). *The Principles of Scientific Management*. New York: Harper.

TBR Creative and Cultural Team. (2018, December 14). *Livelihoods of Visual Artists: 2016 Data Report*. London: Arts Council England. www.artscouncil.org.uk/sites/default/files/download-file/Livelihoods%20of%20Visual%20Artists%202016%20Data%20Report.pdf.

TEFAF. (n.d.). Stringent and Transparent Vetting Standards and Procedures. www.tefaf.com/about/vetting.

Thompson, Don. (2008). *The $12 Million Stuffed Shark: The Curious Economics of Contemporary Art*. New York: St. Martin's Griffin.

Thompson, Don. (2017). *The Orange Balloon Dog*. Madeira Mark, BC: Douglas and McIntyre.

Throsby, David. (1994). The Production and Consumption of the Arts: A View of Cultural Economics. *Journal of Economic Literature*, 32(March): 1–29.

Throsby, David. (1999). Cultural Capital. *Journal of Cultural Economics*, 23 (1): 3–12.

Throsby, David. (2001). *Economics and Culture*. Cambridge, UK: Cambridge University Press.

Thurow, Lester C. (1978). Psychic Income: Useful or Useless? *American Economic Review*, 68(2): 142–145.

Tomkins, Calvin. (2012, July 2). The Modern Man. *The New Yorker*. www .newyorker.com/magazine/2012/07/02/the-modern-man.

Towse, Ruth (Ed.). (2020). *Handbook of Cultural Economics*, 3rd ed. Cheltenham, UK: Edward Elgar.

Trepasso, Erica. (2013, August 19). Johannes Vermeer: The 36th Painting. *Artnet News*. https://news.artnet.com/market/johannes-vermeer-the-36th-painting -30525.

UCCA (Ullens Center for Contemporary Art). (n.d.). History. https://ucca.org.cn/ en/about/#:about_1.

Ukeles, Mierle Laderman. (1969). Manifesto! For Maintenance Art. Proposal for an Exhibition "Care." https://queensmuseum.org/wp-content/uploads/2016/04/ Ukeles-Manifesto-for-Maintenance-Art-1969.pdf.

Ukeles, Mierle Laderman. (2019, May 15). Mierle Laderman Ukeles. In Paola Antonelli, curator, *MoMA R&D Salon #31: Workspheres*. http://momarnd .moma.org/salons/salon-31-workspheres-1.

Uniqlo. (n.d.). New York Museum of Modern Art (MoMA) Partnership (US) UNIQLO. www.uniqlo.com/en/sustainability/culture/artmuseum.

Urstadt, Bryant. (2010, May 6). Uniqlones. *New York*. https://nymag.com/fashion/ features/65898.

United Kingdom Competition Act. 1998. Competition Act § 36.

USA Table Tennis. (n.d.) Hall of Fame Profiles: Chuck Hoey. www.teamusa.org/ USA-Table-Tennis/History/Hall-of-Fame/Profiles/Chuck-Hoey.

US 17. US Code § 106 and 107.

US Constitution. Article I, §8, cl. 8.

US Copyright Office (2011). Duration of Copyright, Circular 15a. www .copyright.gov/circs/circ15a.pdf.

US Copyright Office. (2012). Works Made for Hire, Circular 9. www.copyright.gov /circs/circ09.pdf.

US Copyright Office. (2013). *Resale Royalties: An Updated Analysis*. www .copyright.gov/docs/resaleroyalty/usco-resaleroyalty.pdf.

US Copyright Office. (2021). International Copyright Relations of the US Copyright Office, Circular 38A (revised February 2021). www.copyright.gov/circs/circ38a .pdf.

US Department of Health and Human Services. (2017). Poverty Guidelines. https://aspe.hhs.gov/2017-poverty-guidelines#threshholds.

Valentine, Victoria L. (2015, September 20). Mark Bradford's Art + Practice Is on a Mission to Change Lives. *Culture Type*. www.culturetype.com/2015/09/20/mark-bradfords-art-practice-is-on-a-mission-to-change-lives.

Valenzuela, Cristóbal. (2018, May 28). Machine Learning en Plein Air: Building Accessible Tools for Artists. *Medium*. https://medium.com/runwayml/machine-learning-en-plein-air-building-accessible-tools-for-artists-87bfc7f99f6b.

van Gogh, Theo. (1890, January 31). Letter to Vincent van Gogh, Paris. www.vangoghletters.org/vg/letters/let847/letter.html.

Van Gogh Museum. (n.d.1). #27/125: Was Van Gogh Poor? www.vangoghmuseum.nl/en/art-and-stories/vincent-van-gogh-faq/was-van-gogh-poor.

Van Gogh Museum. (n.d.2). Vincent van Gogh: *Almond Blossom*, February 1890. www.vangoghmuseum.nl/en/collection/s0176V1962.

van Haaften-Schick, Lauren. (2018). Conceptualizing Artists' Rights: Circulations of the Siegelaub-Projansky Agreement through Art and Law. *Oxford Handbooks Online*. https://doi.org/10.1093/oxfordhb/9780199935352.013.27.

Veblen, Thorstein. (1953 [1899]). *The Theory of the Leisure Class: An Economic Study of Institutions*. New York: New America Library.

Velthuis, Olav. (2005). *Talking Prices: Symbolic Meanings of Prices on the Market for Contemporary Art*. Princeton, NJ: Princeton University Press.

Velthuis, Olav. (2011). The Venice Effect. *The Art Newspaper*, 20(225): 21–24.

Vermeylen, Filip. (2003). *Painting for the Market: Commercialization of Art in Antwerp's Golden Age*. Turnhout, Belgium: Brepols.

Vickrey, William. (1961). Counterspeculation, Auctions, and Competitive Sealed Tenders. *Journal of Finance*, 16(1): 8–37.

Village Voice. (n.d.). About the Village Voice. www.villagevoice.com/about.

Vohra, Rakesh and Krishmamurthi, Lakshman. (2012). *Principles of Pricing: An Analytic Approach*. Cambridge, UK: Cambridge University Press.

W.A.G.E. (n.d.). About. https://wageforwork.com/about#top.

Wagenknecht, Addie. (2019, December 22). Something Weird about the Art World . . .. @wheresaddie. https://twitter.com/wheresaddie/status/1208677391683469312?s=20.

Wagley, Catherine. (2019, November 25). Museum Workers across the Country Are Unionizing. Here's What's Driving a Movement That's Been Years in the Making. *Artnet News*.

Wagley, Catherine. (2020, March 2). Museum Unions Aren't Just Demanding Higher Pay. They're Also Fundamentally Questioning the Way Their Institutions Work. *Artnet News*.

Wall, Joseph Frazier. (1970). *Andrew Carnegie*. Pittsburgh, PA: University of Pittsburgh Press.

Walls, W. David and McKenzie, Jordi. (2020). Black Swan Models for the Entertainment Industry with an Application to the Movie Business. *Empirical Economics*, 59(6): 3019–3032.

Walt, Melissa J., Weitz, Ankeney and Yun, Michelle. (2016). *Zao Wou-Ki: No Limits*. New York: Asia Society Museum; Waterville, ME: Colby College Museum of Art.

Watson, Peter. (1992). *From Manet to Manhattan: The Rise of the Modern Art Market* New York: Random House.

Weiner, Andrew Stefan. (2017, August 14). The Art of the Possible: With and against documenta 14. Biennial Foundation. www.biennialfoundation.org/2017/08/art-possible-documenta-14.

WeRateDogs. (2020, May 29). Our Account Usually Acts …. https://twitter.com/artdecider/status/1266584418006847488?s=11.

Werner H. Kramarsky Papers [VII.1-2]. Museum of Modern Art Archives, New York. www.moma.org/research-and-learning/archives/finding-aids/Kramarskyb.html.

West Bund. (n.d.). West Bund History. www.westbund.com/en/index/ABOUT-WEST-BUND/History/West-Bund-History.html.

Whitaker, Amy. (2009). *Museum Legs: Fatigue and Hope in the Face of Art*. Tuczon, AZ: Hol Art Books.

Whitaker, Amy. (2014). Ownership for Artists. In Pablo Helguera, Michael Mandiberg, William Powhida, Amy Whitaker, and Caroline Woolard, eds., *The Social Life of Artistic Property*. Hudson: Publication Studio, pp. 70–84.

Whitaker, Amy. (2016a). *Art Thinking*. New York: Harper Business.

Whitaker, Amy. (2016b). *Business Structures and Planning: Performance Practice, Curriculum for Choreographers and Movement Artists*. New York: Lower Manhattan Cultural Council and the Actors Fund.

Whitaker, Amy. (2018). Artist As Owner Not Guarantor: The Art Market from the Artist's Point of View. *Visual Resources*, 34(1–2): 48–64.

Whitaker, Amy. (2019a). Shared Value over Fair Use: Technology, Added Value, and the Reinvention of Copyright. *Cardozo Art and Entertainment Law Journal*, 37 (3): 635–657.

Whitaker, Amy. (2019b). Economic Provenance: The Financial Analysis of Art Historical Records. *Journal of Contemporary Archival Studies*, 6(27): 1–17. https://elischolar.library.yale.edu/jcas/vol6/iss1/27.

Whitaker, Amy. (2019c). Barter: What I Learned about Generosity and Reciprocity. In Caroline Woolard, ed., *Trade School: 2009–2019*. New York: Caroline Woolard, pp. 72–75.

Whitaker, Amy. (2019d). Art and Blockchain: A Primer, History, and Taxonomy of Blockchain Use Cases in the Arts. *Artivate: A Journal of Entrepreneurship in the Arts*, 8(2): 21–46.

Whitaker, Amy and Grannemann, Hannah. (2019). Artists' Royalties and Performers' Equity: A Ground-Up Approach to Social Impact Investment in Creative Fields. *Cultural Management*, 3(2): 33–51.

Whitaker, Amy and Kräussl, Roman. (2020). Fractional Equity, Blockchain, and the Future of Creative Work. *Management Science*, 66(10): 4594–4611.

Whitaker, Amy, Bracegirdle, Anne, De Menil, Susan, Gitlitz, Michelle Ann and Saltos, Lena. (2020). Art, Antiquities, and Blockchain: New Approaches to the Restitution of Cultural Heritage. *International Journal of Cultural Policy*. DOI: 10.1080/10286632.2020.1765163.

White, Harrison C. and White, Cynthia A. (1993 [1965]). *Canvases and Careers: Institutional Change in the French Painting World*. Chicago, IL: University of Chicago Press.

Whitechapel Gallery. (n.d.). Exhibitions: 1950–Present. www.whitechapelgallery.org/about/history/exhibitions-1950-present.

Whitehead, A. N. and Johnson W. E. (1908). Dr. A. N. Whitehead's and Mr. W. E. Johnson's Reports on Mr. Keynes's Dissertation, 1908: The Principles of Probability, pp. 2–4. John Maynard Keynes Papers, King's College Archives, Cambridge University.

Williamson, Oliver E. (1971). The Vertical Integration of Production. *American Economic Review: Papers and Proceedings of the Eighty-Third Annual Meeting of the American Economic Association*, 61(2): 112–123.

Williamson, Oliver E. (1985). *The Economic Institutions of Capitalism: Firms, Markets, Relational Contracting*. New York: Free Press.

Williamson, Oliver E. (1987). *Antitrust Economics: Mergers, Contracting, and Strategic Behavior*. Oxford, UK: Basil Blackwell.

Winkleman, Edward. (2015). *Selling Contemporary Art: How to Navigate the Evolving Market*. New York: Allworth Press.

Winkleman, Edward and Hindle, Patton. (2018). *How to Start and Run a Commercial Gallery*, 2nd ed. New York: Allworth.

World Intellectual Property Organization (n.d.1). What Is WIPO? www.wipo.int/about-wipo/en.

World Intellectual Property Organization. (n.d.2). Summary of the Berne Convention for the Protection of Literary and Artistic Works (1886). www.wipo.int/treaties/en/ip/berne/summary_berne.html.

World Intellectual Property Organization. (1967, July 14). Convention Establishing the World Intellectual Property Organization. www.wipo.int/treaties/en/text .jsp?file_id=283854.

World Intellectual Property Organization. (2021, March). Beijing Treaty. www .wipo.int/beijing_treaty/en.

Woronkowicz, Joanna, Joynes, D. Carroll and Bradburn, Norman. (2014). *Building Better Arts Facilities: Lessons from a US National Study*. London: Routledge.

Wrathall, Claire. (2018, July 12). Touria El Glaoui: Putting Contemporary African Art on the Map. *Christie's Inc*. www.christies.com/features/Touria-El-Glaoui-on-Africas-new-wave-9311-1.aspx.

Wu, Kejia. (2019). Executive Summary TEFAF Art Market Report 2019. www .amr.tefaf.com/chapter/introduction?printMode=true.

Wyma, Chloe. (2014). 1% Museum: The Guggenheim Goes Global. *Dissent* (summer), pp. 5–10.

Youngs, Ian. (2011, December 1). Museums Enjoy 10 Years of Freedom. *BBC*. www .bbc.com/news/entertainment-arts-15927593.

Zaretsky, Donn. (2019, July 5). Cady Noland's Lawsuit Was Dismissed in March. *The Art Law Blog*. http://theartlawblog.blogspot.com/2019/07/cady-nolands-lawsuit-was-dismised-in.html

Zarobell, John. (2017). *Art and the Global Economy*. Oakland: University of California Press.

Zelizer, Viviana. (2001). How and Why Do We Care about Circuits? *Accounts Newsletter of the Economic Sociology Section of the American Sociological Association*, 1(2000): 3–5.

Zhang, Amy Y. (2019). Placing Arts Districts within Markets: A Case Study of 798 Arts District in Beijing. *International Journal of Urban and Regional Research*, 43(6): 1028–1045.

Zittrain, Jonathan L. (2005). *Technological Complements to Copyright*. St. Paul, MN: Foundation Press.

Index

Page numbers in *italics* indicate tables and figures. Titles of written and visual works will be found at the author's/artist's name. Numbers are alphabetized as if spelled out.